Quicken® 4 Made Easy

Quicken® 4

Made Easy

David Campbell
and Mary Campbell

Osborne **McGraw-Hill**

Berkeley New York St. Louis San Francisco
Auckland Bogotá Hamburg London Madrid
Mexico City Milan Montreal New Delhi Panama City
Paris São Paulo Singapore Sydney
Tokyo Toronto

Osborne **McGraw-Hill**
2600 Tenth Street
Berkeley, California 94710
U.S.A.

Osborne **McGraw-Hill** offers software for sale. For information on software, translations, or book distributors outside of the U.S.A., please write to Osborne **McGraw-Hill** at the above address.

Screens produced with InSet, from InSet Systems, Inc.

This book is printed on recycled paper.

Quicken® 4 Made Easy

1234567890 DOC 99876543210

ISBN 0-07-881694-7

We would like to dedicate this book to our sons David and Keith.

CONTENTS
AT A GLANCE

CONTENTS

ACKNOWLEDGMENTS

We wish to thank the many individuals at Osborne/McGraw-Hill and InSet for their help with this project. Special thanks are due to acquisitions editor Roger Stewart, project editor Laura Sackerman, and associate editor Jill Pisoni for helping us meet an impossible time schedule. Special thanks also go to Chris Ruffo for checking all the keystrokes in the exercises.

INTRODUCTION

Whether you are trying to manage your personal finances or those of your business, Quicken can end your financial hassles. The package contains all the features necessary to organize your finances, yet because they're jargon-free you can focus on your financial needs without becoming an accountant or a financial planner.

If you use the package for your personal finances you will find that you can easily determine your financial worth or create a report with the information you need for your tax forms. You can also create budget reports or a list of all your cash, check, or credit card transactions. Everything you do will be with the benefit of menus and easy-to-use quick-key combinations. You will soon wonder how you managed your finances without Quicken.

If you are trying to manage a small business *and* deal with all the financial issues, Quicken can make the task seem manageable. Whether your business is a part-time venture or employs several people, Quicken provides all the capabilities you need to look at your profit and loss picture, analyze your cash flows, or put together a budget. Quicken's ability to handle the recording of payroll information makes it easy to monitor what you owe for federal and state income tax withholding, FICA, and other payroll related costs such as worker's compensation and federal and state unemployment taxes. Although it is not quite the same as having an accountant on your payroll, Quicken can make an otherwise unmanageable task possible.

ABOUT THIS BOOK

This book is designed to help you master Quicken's features so you can apply them to your financial situation. Even if you are a complete novice with the computer, you will find that you can learn from the step-by-step exercises in each chapter. As you work through the exercises you will feel as though you have a seasoned computer pro guiding you each step of the way.

This book offers more than just instruction for using Quicken's features. The exercises throughout the book are based on the authors' personal and business transactions. Although names of the banks, suppliers, and employees as well as dollar amounts have all been changed, all of what you read is based on factual illustrations much like the ones you will need to record your own transactions.

Throughout the book we have included financial tips. When we started our business ten years ago, we had to invest a considerable amount of time in finding answers to even the simplest questions such as federal and state agency filing requirements. We have tried to include some of this information to simplify what you are facing if your business is new.

How This Book Is Organized

This book is divided into three parts to make it easy for you to focus on Quicken basics, personal applications, or business applications. Part I, Quick Start, includes the first five chapters. This section covers all the basic skills needed to use the package. You will find that the exercises within these chapters make you productive with Quicken in a short period of time.

Chapter 1 provides an overview of Quicken's features. You will see examples of reports and screens that you can use for your own applications. Chapter 2 introduces the Quicken account register, in which all Quicken information is recorded. In this chapter you will learn the skills needed to record your basic financial transactions. Chapter 3 teaches you how to print several Quicken reports. You are shown how to select the correct printer settings to print all the reports you will be preparing in the book. Chapter 4 illustrates how easy it is to balance your checkbook (the account register) with Quicken. The exercise actually takes you through the reconciliation steps. Chapter 5 concludes Part I of the book. It teaches you how to create Quicken checks. With one set of entries on a check you can print the check and update your records.

Part II focuses on personal financial applications of Quicken. It shows you how to create accounts for checking, savings, and investments. You will learn how to determine your net worth and to find the information you need to complete your tax returns in this section. Chapter 6 shows you how to set up accounts and categories for personal finances. You will learn how to enter individual transactions as well as how to memorize them and automate their entry through transaction groups. Chapter 7 introduces the concept of budgeting with Quicken. You will learn how to enter your estimates by category and how to monitor actual amounts against budgeted amounts. Chapter 8 illustrates how Quicken can be used to help complete your personal tax return. The example used demonstrates how to record your tax-related financial transactions and how Quicken can be used to summarize your tax-related transactions for the entire year. Chapter 9 shows you how to determine what you are worth financially. You will learn how to keep records on stocks and other investments as well as how to revalue these holdings to market values. Chapter 10 is the final chapter in Part II. It provides a look at additional Quicken reports and the customizing options that you can add.

Part III covers business applications of Quicken. You will learn how to use the package to manage the finances of your business, including record keeping for payroll. Chapter 11 shows you how to create a chart of accounts for your business. You will also look at entering transactions for basic business expenses and revenues. Chapter 12 teaches you about payroll entries with Quicken. It not only prints your employees' paychecks, but can handle all your other payroll-related record keeping. Chapter 13 teaches you how to prepare a business budget with Quicken. You can enter the same value for each month or budget a different amount for each month. The budget reports that Quicken produces can provide an early warning of potential budget trouble spots. Chapter 14 discusses the forms you will need to file for business taxes. It also includes coverage of the income statement (the profit and loss statement) that tells you whether or not your business is profitable. Chapter 15 continues with coverage of other important financial reports. You will have an opportunity to prepare a balance sheet that shows your assets, liabilities, and your equity (or investment) in the business. The chapter also provides an opportunity to record information on payables and receivables. Chapter 16 discusses job or project costing. These features are useful when you must bill hours and material to a particular job.

CONVENTIONS USED

There are step-by-step examples for you to follow throughout the book. Every entry that you need to type is shown in boldface to make these exercises easy to follow. In addition, the names of menus, windows, and reports are shown with the same capitalization followed by Quicken.

The names of keys such as (F2), (ENTER), and (TAB) are shown in keycaps. In situations where two keys must be pressed at the same time, the keycaps are joined with a hyphen as in (CTRL)-(ENTER).

In cases where there are two ways to perform the same task, we have shown you the most efficient approach. As you learn more about the package you can feel free to use whichever approach you prefer.

WHY THIS BOOK IS FOR YOU

If you want to maintain accurate financial records, yet invest a minimum of time, Quicken can provide the answer. You can maintain as much or as little detail as you choose when it comes to recording financial events. With the sample reports shown, you will be able to make the most of your financial assets whether they are large or small.

If you are the owner of a small business, you already have more things to do than there is time. Although you realize that the financial aspects of your business are vital to its success, you never seem to find sufficient time to organize them. With this book, you will learn how Quicken can provide you with this time. With no more time expended than it takes to maintain disorganized manual records, you can have an organized base of information. The reports you need are as simple as menu selections.

You can use Quicken for your financial record keeping. You will want to be sure that you parallel this conversion by keeping manual records for several months. By ensuring that both methods provide the same results before making the switch, you can be certain that you are making decisions with information that is completely accurate.

QUICK START

An Overview of Quicken and Your Computer Components
Making Register Entries
Quicken Reports
Reconciling Your Quicken Register
Writing and Printing Checks

In any package, there are a few features that form the basis for most of the work you do. Quicken is no exception. This section will illustrate the essential Quicken features, so you can get started quickly. Once you finish these chapters you can focus on more advanced applications for home or business.

AN OVERVIEW OF QUICKEN AND YOUR COMPUTER COMPONENTS

Quicken is a powerful single-entry accounting system that allows both individuals and small businesses to track their financial resources. It is an integrated system in that it accumulates the information you enter and then provides a variety of methods to group and present that information.

Quicken is as easy to use as your current manual recording methods—but it is much faster. You will be surprised at how automatic using the package can become. It can memorize and record your regular transactions or write a check for your signature. It also organizes your information for you.

This chapter's overview will show you the components of the package and examples of screens used to enter data and the output that is produced. You do not need to sit at your computer to read and understand this chapter. Later chapters, however, give step-by-step directions for using Quicken's features, and you will want to follow along.

This chapter also introduces the various components of your computer system and their relationship to Quicken. You will learn how Quicken uses your computer system, disk space, memory, and the keyboard. Some of the important keys will be introduced through a series of visual examples. In later chapters you will use these keys to enter and review Quicken data.

QUICKEN OVERVIEW

Quicken can handle all aspects of your financial management. Everything from initial recording and maintenance of information through organizing and reporting is handled by the package. Quicken provides features for recording your financial transactions easily. You can have a direct entry made to a register that is an accounts journal or have Quicken write a check and record the information automatically. Once your information has been recorded, you can have it presented in a variety of standard and customized reports.

Recording Financial Transactions

If you are tired of entering financial transactions in a handwritten journal, you will appreciate the recording abilities of Quicken. Entries are always neat—even if you have corrected several errors in the recording process—and there is no need to worry about math errors, since the package does arithmetic for you.

Accounts are the major organizational units in Quicken. Each piece of information you record will affect the balance in a Quicken account. You can establish checking and savings accounts for both personal and business purposes. In addition you can establish credit card accounts and asset accounts (stocks and real estate) and liability accounts (mortgage and other payable loans). You can also transfer funds among these accounts with the Transfer feature—for example, moving funds from savings to a checking account.

Quicken 4 supports specialized investment accounts to allow you to track a collection of investments. You can enter information for stocks, bonds, mutual funds, and other investments. You can use features like the one shown in Figure 1-1 for updating the market price of your investments and determining your gain or loss.

Quicken can record the details of your financial transactions, both money you earn (income) and what you spend it on (expenses). Quicken can differentiate income from a number of sources, such as salary and dividend income. It also supports entry of all types of expenses, from mortgage payments to clothing purchases. If you use Quicken to record business finances, you can keep track of freight charges, payroll costs, and so on. You can also customize the package to handle additional sources of income or expenses.

The information recorded on a financial event is called a *transaction*. Purchasing an asset such as a car, or making payment for services or goods such as groceries is considered a transaction. In Quicken you must record your transactions in order to have the correct balance in your accounts. This is accomplished by using a *register,* which is similar to a notebook or journal for record keeping. This serves the same purpose as your checkbook register, but with the power of the Quicken system you can generate powerful reports

---

```
F1-Help    F2-Acct/Print    F3-Edit    F4-Quick Entry  F5-Reports   F6-Activities
              Update Prices and Market Value as of:   7/ 6/91
```

SECURITY NAME	TYPE	MKT PRICE		AVG COST	%GAIN	SHARES	MKT VALUE
Pacific Corp Bond	Bond	120	↑	101 1/8	10.7	20	2,400
1st U.S. Bank CD	CD	1,000	*	1,000	0.0	1	1,000
European Fund	Mutual	10.250	↑	9.750	5.1	100	1,025
Global Fund	Mutual	9.750	↓	10	-2.5	100	975
ABC Company	Stock	25 1/2	↑	22 1/2	13.3	50	1,275
▶ Banff Corp	Stock	56	↑	54	3.7	150	8,400
Total Market Value					6.0		15,075

```
Investments               * Estimated Prices              +/- Adjust Price
Esc-Register                F9-All Accounts           Ctrl↵ Record Prices
```

FIGURE 1-1. Updating the market price for your investments

that will help you manage your finances. Thus, one of the major components of the system is the register that you will establish for each of your accounts (checking, savings, and other assets and liabilities). Figure 1-2 provides an example of entries in the Quicken register for a checking account.

With any checking account, reconciling the balance is tedious. Quicken reduces the time needed to reconcile the difference between the bank's balance and yours. Through the reconciliation process you can accurately maintain the balance in your checking account and avoid the embarrassment of overdrawing your account. Quicken adjusts your register for service charges and interest earned on your checking account.

Check writing and printing is another interesting Quicken feature. Quicken is capable of automating all your check writing activities. Figure 1-3 shows a check entry form on the screen. You can acquire checking supplies from Intuit (the company that developed and markets Quicken) that will allow you to write checks directly from the register and print them on your printer. While this option is particularly attractive for business activities, it can be useful for your personal checking account as well. But even if you write your checks by hand, you can still benefit from maintaining your transactions in Quicken.

```
F1-Help   F2-Acct/Print   F3-Edit   F4-Quick Entry   F5-Reports   F6-Activities
```

DATE	NUM	PAYEE · MEMO · CATEGORY	PAYMENT	C	DEPOSIT	BALANCE
1/ 5 1991	101 Memo: Cat:	Small City Times Paper bill Misc	16 50			1,116 00
1/ 7 1991		Deposit-Salary Monthly pay Salary			700 00	1,816 00
1/ 7 1991	102	Small City Market Food Groceries	22 32			1,793 68
1/ 7 1991	103	Small City Apartments Rent Housing	150 00			1,643 68
1/19 1991	104	Small City Market Food Groceries	43 00			1,600 68
1/25 1991	105	Small City Phone Company Phone bill Telephone	19 75			1,580 93

```
1st U.S. Bank
Esc-Main Menu     Ctrl◄─┘ Record                    Ending Balance: $1,605.93
```

FIGURE 1-2. The Quicken register window

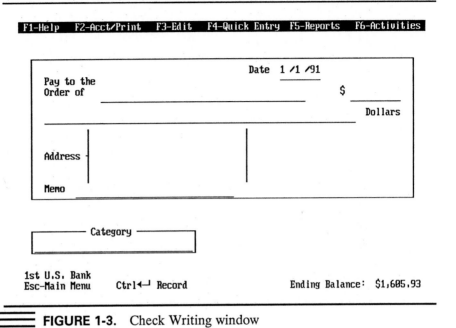

FIGURE 1-3. Check Writing window

Reports Provided by Quicken

The value of any accounting system lies in its ability to generate useful and informative reports that assist you in making financial decisions. With Quicken, you can prepare personal, business, and investment reports, and preview them on the screen before printing. Figure 1-4 shows an onscreen personal Cash Flow report.

PERSONAL REPORTS Besides providing you with a printout of your check register, Quicken generates other reports tailored for personal financial management. They will become valuable as the year progresses, showing how you have spent your money, as well as how much you have. Following are the standard personal reports provided by the package.

- *Cash Flow* This summarizes your cash inflows and outflows for specific periods of time.
- *Monthly Budgets* Quicken allows you to prepare budgets for both your personal and business finances and provides reports to assist you in monitoring your receipts and expenditures.

```
                          CASH FLOW REPORT

                       1/ 1/91 Through 1/31/91
            1st U.S. Bank
            7/ 6/91
                                          1/ 1/91-
                Category Description      1/31/91

            INFLOWS
              Salary Income               700.00

            TOTAL INFLOWS                 700.00

            OUTFLOWS
              Groceries                    65.32
              Housing                     150.00
              Miscellaneous                16.50
              Telephone Expense            19.75
              Water, Gas, Electric         67.50

            TOTAL OUTFLOWS                319.07
                                                            ↓
   1st U.S. Bank
   Esc-Create report          F1-Help      Ctrl M-Memorize    F8-Print
```

FIGURE 1-4. Cash Flow Report screen display

- *Tax Summaries* Quicken can summarize tax-related activities such as charitable contributions and mortgage interest.

- *Net Worth* This gives an overall measure of how well you are managing your finances. The periodic generation of this report allows you to determine whether you are meeting your financial goals.

BUSINESS REPORTS Quicken handles accounting transactions for businesses as well as individuals. Because a small business has reporting needs that are different from an individual's, the package provides a separate list of standard business reports. It also allows you to create customized reports for either home or business use. The following list shows the standard business reports for the package.

- *Profit and Loss (P&L)* This report allows you to look at your profit and losses.

- *Cash Flow* The business Cash Flow report is similar to the personal Cash Flow report in that its focus is cash inflows and outflows. Unlike the personal report, however, the business Cash Flow report does not show transfers between accounts.

- *Balance Sheet* This report uses Quicken's ability to classify accounts by group, and summarizes the account balances in a chosen group.

- *Payroll* This report displays transactions in the payroll category.

- *Accounts Payable* Quicken allows you to record expenses without writing checks. This report provides a monthly summary of your accounts payable, showing both checks written and unprinted checks by month.

- *Accounts Receivable* You can use this report to provide a detailed accounting of your receivables.

- *Job/Project* Quicken allows you to establish classes and assign them to individual transactions. This feature allows you to report on the income and expenses for a particular project.

INVESTMENT REPORTS With Quicken's new investment accounts, you can record and track all of your investments. The five standard investment reports listed here can be obtained with a few keystrokes.

- *Portfolio Value* This report allows you to look at the value of your investments on a specified date and assess the unrealized gain/loss based on current market values.

- *Investment Performance* This report provides the average annual return on your investments.

- *Capital Gains* This report shows short and long term capital gains and is useful for completing Schedule D for tax purposes.

- *Investment Income* This report shows both taxable and nontaxable dividend and interest income as well as capital gains distributions.

- *Investment Transactions* This is a detailed report that shows the effects of individual transactions on market value or the cost basis of investments.

Customizing Options

Quicken provides features for customizing the package to meet your needs. This means you can make changes to fit your exact reporting requirements. It also means you can customize Quicken to work properly with the computer equipment you have selected. Figure 1-5 shows a menu of custom settings for Quicken.

Quicken's Help Features

Onscreen help is only a keystroke away with Quicken. All you ever need to do is press (F1) (Help). Quicken assesses the type of help you need and displays a superimposed help screen. Quicken's assessment of your situation is called *context-sensitive help*. Figure 1-6 shows the help screen that Quicken displays if you press (F1) from the Main Menu. If you are in another area of Quicken, the help presented might be very different. With the register on the screen, for example, Quicken assumes you need help with completing entries and so provides that information. If you need a different type of help than that displayed, press (F1) again for access to the Help Index. You can also press (CTRL)-(F1) for direct access to the Help Index without invoking context-sensitive help first.

QUICKEN AND YOUR COMPUTER SYSTEM

You may have had your computer long enough to feel like a pro operating it, but if Quicken is your first computer package, read the rest of the chapter

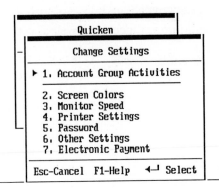

FIGURE 1-5. Change Settings menu

```
┌─────────────────────────────────────────────────┐
│                  The Main Menu                    │
│                                                   │
│   The Main Menu lists Quicken's main activities.  │
│   To select an activity from the menu, type its   │
│   number.                                         │
│                                                   │
│   1. Write/Print Checks                           │
│      Select Write/Print Checks to write and print │
│      checks or to write and transmit electronic   │
│      payments.                                    │
│                                                   │
│   2. Register                                     │
│      Select Register to see the transactions in   │
│      your account. You can also enter and change  │
│      transactions in the Register; usually these  │
│      will be transactions not involving printed   │
│      checks, such as handwritten checks, deposits,│
│      bank fees, electronic transfers, credit card │
│      charges, investment transactions, and so     │
├─────────────────────────────────────────────────┤
│ Esc-Cancel        F1-Help Index      ↓,PgDn-More  │
└─────────────────────────────────────────────────┘
   1st U.S. Bank
```

FIGURE 1-6.   Help screen for the Main Menu

carefully. It will eliminate much of the confusion experienced by new users in attempting to figure out what is in memory, what is on disk, and exactly how their computer makes it possible for a package like Quicken to do so much work so quickly. If you are already knowledgeable about your system, you may want to skim the rest of the chapter quickly, just to see how Quicken works with the computer. It is assumed you are using an IBM PC or compatible running the DOS operating system.

Memory

There are two kinds of memory in your computer: *RAM* and *ROM*. ROM is Read Only Memory—you cannot affect its contents so it's little concern. RAM is Random Access Memory—temporary storage inside your computer. RAM contains the program you are running (for example Quicken, 1-2-3, or dBASE) and the data that you are currently working with in the program.

If you lose the power to your machine, you lose the contents of RAM. This is why permanent storage media such as disks are an essential component of your computer system. If your data is saved to disk, you can always load it into memory again if it is lost in a power failure.

The amount of RAM in your system is determined by the computer you have purchased and any additional memory you may have added to the system. Memory is measured in kilobytes (K) or megabytes (MB) with 1K representing the space required to store approximately a thousand characters of information and 1MB representing the space required to store approximately one million characters. Some systems have as little as 256K of memory, while others may have 1MB or even 6MB of memory capacity. Quicken requires a system with at least 320K in order to run the program. The amount of memory you have will determine the number of transactions you can have in a Quicken account and the complexity of the reports you can generate. Figure 1-7 shows how memory might be allocated in a machine with 640K. The amount of memory occupied by DOS is an average since the actual amount will depend on which version of the operating system you use. Quicken supports all DOS versions from 2.0 to the current version.

You can see in the figure that Quicken actually only needs 225K RAM for the program itself but when the program runs, transactions are created to record your financial information. Each transaction requires approximately 16 *bytes*, or positions, in memory. If your system has 640K and your version of DOS requires 60K, you will have 355K left for transactions—allowing you to have over 22,000 transactions in Quicken. Since the average home user will probably not need more than 500 transactions per account, and the

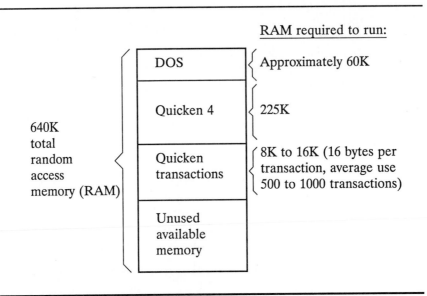

FIGURE 1-7. RAM allocation

average small business is unlikely to have more than a few thousand transactions per account in a year, 640K is more than enough memory. If you have less than that, you should be careful not to load too many "terminate and stay resident" programs (TSRs). TSRs are programs that are loaded and remain in RAM even when they are not in use.

Disk Storage

Disk storage on your system may consist of one or more hard disks or floppy disks in either 5 1/4-inch or 3 1/2-inch sizes. Quicken requires either a hard disk or one 3 1/2-inch or two 5 1/4-inch floppy disk drives. All three media supply space for the permanent storage of both program files and data, but their capacities vary greatly. Like RAM, disk space is measured in either K or MB.

Most hard disks provide from 10 to 60MB of storage capacity. This means you will have room for Quicken as well as other software packages such as dBASE, WordPerfect, or 1-2-3. The 3 1/2-inch disks have capacities from 800K to 1.44MB, depending on whether your system uses double- or high-density 3 1/2-inch disks. The 5 1/4-inch disks have less capacity than the 3 1/2-inch disks. Depending on the size and type of your disk drives, you can store anywhere from 360K to 1.2MB on these disks. Your system will use single-, double-, or high-density disks.

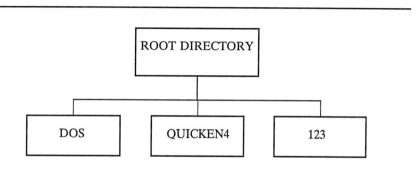

FIGURE 1-8.   Hard disk configuration

A letter is used to represent each drive. Typically, hard disks are called drive C. Floppy disk drives are usually designated drive A and drive B.

If you are using a hard disk, all the files you need for Quicken can be stored on this disk. Figure 1-8 shows a possible configuration of the directories on a hard disk. In this figure, the root directory (main directory) would be used to contain batch files (files containing DOS instructions) on the hard disk. Separate directories are maintained for DOS and any other program. When you install Quicken on your hard disk, it creates its own directory and a batch file called Q.BAT. Table 1-1 shows the type of data contained in each Quicken file placed in your Quicken directory.

File	Contents
Q.EXE	The Quicken program
Q.BAT	Batch file for starting Quicken
Q.HLP	Help information
BILLMIND.EXE	Program that automatically looks for checks that are due
QCHECKS.DOC	Order form for checks
PRINTERS.DAT	Predefined print settings
Q.CFG	Configuration file
Q3.DIR	Account group descriptions and due dates for checks
QDATA.QDT	Data for the first account group
QDATA.QNX	Index file for the first account group
QDATA.QMT	List of memorized transactions for the first account file
QDATA.QDI	Dictionary file for the first account group
Q.OVL	Quicken overlay file to minimize memory requirements

TABLE 1-1. Quicken Files

The Keyboard and the Screen Display

The keyboard and the screen serve as the central communication points between you and Quicken. Everything you want to tell the package must be entered through the keyboard. You will already be familiar with many of the keys; they are used to enter data regardless of the type of program you are using. Function keys and key combinations have special meanings in Quicken; they are used to issue the commands. Even if you have used these keys in other programs, you will find that they provide different options in each program and thus are assigned to different tasks in Quicken.

Quicken uses the screen to communicate information to you. Quicken supports both monochrome monitors (one color) and monitors that can display many colors. Explanation of the screen is also covered here since it often provides information about which keys to use for various features and commands.

KEYBOARD STYLES All keyboards are not alike, although virtually all of them will provide every key you need to use Quicken. However, you may have to look around to find the keys you need, especially if you are getting used to a new keyboard. Figures 1-9 and 1-10 show the two most popular keyboards in use today. The keyboard in Figure 1-9 is found on all the older model PCs and compatibles. The arrow keys move the cursor or highlighting

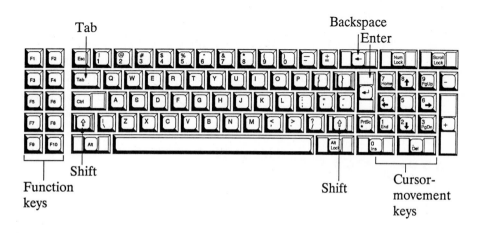

FIGURE 1-9.   IBM PC keyboard

Function keys

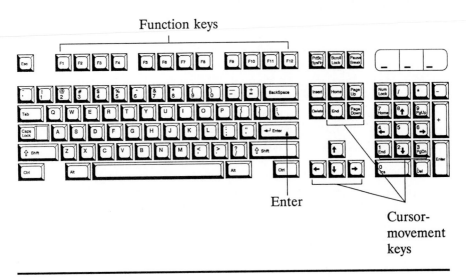

Enter

Cursor-
movement
keys

═══════ **FIGURE 1-10.** Enhanced IBM keyboard

around on your screen. These keys are located on the *numeric keypad,* at the far right side of the keyboard. They are also used to enter numbers when the ⟨NUM LOCK⟩ key is depressed to activate them. With ⟨NUM LOCK⟩ off, the arrow keys move the cursor in the direction indicated on the key top. If these keys are not set properly for your use, just press ⟨NUM LOCK⟩ and they will assume their other function.

The newer model keyboard in Figure 1-10 is called the IBM "enhanced keyboard." It is found on most IBM ATs and all the newer model PS/2 machines. Many compatibles sold in recent years also have this style of keyboard. This keyboard has separate arrow keys to the left of the numeric keypad that move the cursor. This allows you to leave the number lock feature on for numeric data entry and use these arrow keys to move around on the screen.

MENU SELECTIONS

Quicken provides menus to simplify your feature and command selections. Quicken's Main Menu, shown in Figure 1-11, leads to all the major tasks or activities the program performs. You can select any activity from this menu by using the ⟨UP ARROW⟩ and ⟨DOWN ARROW⟩ keys, on the right side of your

```
          ┌──────────────────────────────────┐
          │████████████████████████████       │
          │           Quicken                │
          │           Main Menu              │
          │                                  │
          │  ► 1. Write/Print Checks         │
          │    2. Register                   │
          │    3. Reports                    │
          │    4. Select Account             │
          │    5. Change Settings            │
          │    E. Exit                       │
          │                                  │
          └──────────────────────────────────┘


                        Copyright 1989 Intuit
   1st U.S. Bank              F1-Help                    ← ┘ Select
```

FIGURE 1-11.   Quicken Main Menu

keyboard, to move your cursor to the desired activity, and then pressing the
ENTER key. (The keys on your keyboard will display arrow symbols rather
than words.) You can also type the number or letter to the left of the desired
menu activity. Remember that if you have the older style keyboard, the
arrows are on the numeric keypad, so NUM LOCK has to be off in order to
move the cursor.

When you make a selection from the Main Menu, Quicken sometimes
superimposes another menu on top of it. You make a selection from this
submenu to refine the task you want to complete. Again, you can either use
the arrow keys or type a character to make your selection.

In addition to the Main Menu selections, Quicken also provides pull-down
menus on many of the screens. The name of each menu is shown at the top
of the screen. The menus are activated by pressing one of the keys labeled
F1 through F10 — the *function keys*. These keys are located either at the
top or at the left side of your keyboard, depending on the model. The menus
they open are called pull-down menus since they come down from the top of
the screen, as shown in Figure 1-12. You can make selections from these
menus with the same methods described for the Main Menu. You can also
make selections with the Quick keys, described in the next section, without
pulling down the menu. To close a menu without making a selection, press
the ESC key.

Some selections result in the appearance of a *window* on the screen.
Windows differ from menus in that there are a number of pieces of information for you to complete. If you want to use the option already chosen (the
default), there is no need to make a change. You can simply press ENTER

```
 F1-Help  F2-Acct/Print  F3-Edit  F4-Quick Entry  F5-Reports  F6-Activities
        ► 1. Select/Set Up Account  Ctrl-A
                                              7/ 6/91
          2. Print Checks           Ctrl-P
 Pay t    3. Change Printer Settings          $
 Order
          4. Back Up All Accounts                    Dollars

          5. Export
          6. Import
 Address

 Memo
```

```
        ── Category ──
```

```
1st U.S. Bank                          Ending Balance:  $1,605.93
Esc-Cancel
```

FIGURE 1-12. Pull-down menu

to accept that choice and move to the next *field,* where you will supply information. If you do not understand what is expected in a field, you can press ⟨F1⟩ (Help) for an explanation. Figure 1-13 shows one of the Quicken windows. This one is for entering printer settings when you are customizing printer support.

Quick Keys

Quick keys provide access to commands. They can be used throughout Quicken to speed up transaction entry in the register, check writing, and report printing. All Quick key commands are initiated by pressing the ⟨CTRL⟩ key in combination with another key. When you pull down a menu, you will see "Ctrl-" and a letter next to menu items that can be activated with a Quick key combination. The Quick key combinations will work while the menu is pulled down, but they also work without pulling the menu down. The more you use the Quick keys, the easier it will be to remember the combination needed for each activity.

As you work with them, you will find that a few of the combinations are assigned different tasks depending on the activity you are performing. For example, ⟨CTRL⟩-⟨B⟩ searches backward when you are using Find in the

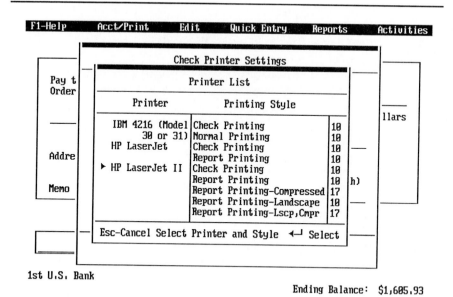

FIGURE 1-13. A Quicken window

register, but it creates a backup of your files when you are at the Main Menu.

As you become familiar with Quicken you will find these keys help you reduce time spent on financial record keeping. The Quick keys are listed on the command card at the end of this book.

SPECIAL KEYS

If you have used your computer with other programs, you will find that many of the special keys work the same in Quicken as in other programs. For example, the (ESC) key is used to cancel your most recent selection. It can be used to close any menu except the Main Menu and also closes most windows, returning you to the previous screen. The (SPACEBAR), at the bottom of the keyboard, is used when making entries to add blank spaces. The (BACKSPACE) key deletes the last character you typed, the character to the left of the cursor. (DEL) deletes the character above the cursor.

The (SHIFT) key is used to enter capital letters and the special symbols at the top of non-letter keys. It also provides access to the numbers on the numeric keypad when (NUM LOCK) is off. (CAPS LOCK) enters all letters in capitals if you press it once, but does not affect the entry of special symbols, which always require the (SHIFT) key. To enter lowercase letters with (CAPS LOCK) on, hold down the (SHIFT) key. To turn (CAPS LOCK) off, just press it a second time.

The (TAB) key will usually move you from field to field. Pressing (SHIFT) and (TAB) together moves the cursor backward through the fields on the screen. (CTRL)-(END) will move the cursor to the bottom of the display; (CTRL)-(HOME) will move you to the top of the display.

The (PGUP) and (PGDN) keys move you up and down screens and menus.

Quicken uses the ⊕ and ⊖ keys on the numeric keypad to quickly increase and decrease numbers such as date and check number. When they are pressed once, the number will increase or decrease by one. However, since the keys all repeat when held down, holding down either of these keys can rapidly effect a major change. The ⊕ and ⊖ keys perform their functions in appropriate fields whether (NUM LOCK) is on or off.

The command card at the end of the book provides a concise reference to each of these keys.

F1-Help	Acct/Print	Edit	Quick Entry	Reports	Activities

Calculator	0 · CATEGORY	PAYMENT	C	DEPOSIT	BALANCE
˄˄˄˄˄˄˄			X	1,200 00	1,200 00
	[1st U.S. Bank]				
77.00	& Light	67 50			1,132 50
* 9.00	→Utilities				
= 693.00	s	16 50			1,116 00
	Misc				
				700 00	1,816 00
	Salary				
7 8 9 * /	et	22 32			1,793 68
4 5 6 - %	Groceries				
1 2 3 + C	tments	150 00			1,643 68
0 . ↵					

Esc-Cancel	F9-Paste

Ending Balance: $1,605.93

FIGURE 1-14. The Quicken calculator

THE CALCULATOR

Quicken has its own calculator, which allows you to perform basic computations on the screen. You can perform computations using the mathematical operators such as + for addition, − for subtraction, * for multiplication, and / for division. Simple calculation involving two numbers or more complex formulas are possible. The calculator displays its results on screen. However, once the numbers leave the screen, you cannot bring them back into view. As a caution, this could make error detection difficult for lengthy calculations.

A significant feature of Quicken's calculator is its ability to compute a payment amount or other figure needed in the *current* transaction entry (the one in use) and then place, or *paste*, the result onto the screen. Figure 1-14 shows the calculator being used to compute the total of nine invoices for $77.00 each. In this manner one check could be written to cover all nine invoices. You can also compute discounts or interest on a loan. Once Quicken computes the amount, you can use the Paste feature to place the amount in the payment field.

You activate the calculator through the menu bar at the top of the Check Register, Write Checks, or Reconciliation screen by pressing F6. You can also activate it using the Quick key CTRL-O. When the calculator is activated, Quicken automatically turns on the numeric keypad so you can use it in making your calculations.

MAKING REGISTER ENTRIES

If you maintain a checking account or monitor a savings account, you are already familiar with the concept of the Quicken register. The register is the backbone of the Quicken system. It allows you to maintain information on checking accounts, cash accounts, and other assets and expenses. With the register, you maintain current status information for an account, so you know the precise balance. You also keep a history of all the transactions affecting the balance. The capabilities of the Quicken register extend beyond the entries normally made in a checkbook register, since they allow you to easily categorize entries as you make them. This extra capability extends the usefulness of the recorded information and facilitates report creation.

In this chapter you will learn to create and maintain a single account. This account will represent a checking account balance, and the transactions will simulate transactions similar to the ones you might have in a personal account. The techniques you learn will be used repeatedly as you work with the Quicken package.

MAINTAINING A REGISTER

Quicken's register works much like the manual checking account register shown in Figure 2-1. Starting with the account balance at the beginning of the period, each check written is recorded as a separate entry, including the date, amount, payee, and check number. Additional information can be added to document the reason for the check. This information can be useful in the preparation of taxes or to verify that an invoice has been paid. As each check is entered, a new balance is computed. Other bank charges such as check printing, overdraft charges, and service fees must also be subtracted from the account balance. Deposits are recorded in a similar fashion. Since interest earned on the account is often automatically credited to the account, it should be entered as it appears on the monthly bank statement. (Quicken cannot compute the interest earned on your account since there is no way for the package to know the dates checks clear at your bank and this information is needed to compute the interest earned.)

Although it is easy to record entries in a manual check register, most individuals at least occasionally make a mistake in computing the new balance. Recording transactions in Quicken's register eliminates this problem. It also provides many other advantages such as categories for classifying each entry, automatic totaling of similar transactions within a category, easily created reports, and a search feature for quickly locating specific entries.

Before entering any transactions in Quicken's register, you will need to set up an account. This means assigning a name to the account and establishing a balance. You will also want to learn a little about Quicken's built-in categories, which allow you to categorize every transaction. You may already do this with some transactions in your check register, marking those you will need to refer back to, for instance. This activity is optional in Quicken, but using the categories will increase the usefulness of the reports you can create.

ESTABLISHING YOUR FIRST ACCOUNT

Establishing your first account is easy. Quicken automatically takes you to the correct screen for entering a new account when you select Register from

RECORD ALL CHARGES OR CREDITS THAT AFFECT YOUR ACCOUNT									
NUMBER	DATE	DESCRIPTION OF TRANSACTION	PAYMENT/DEBIT (−)		√ T	FEE IF ANY (−)	DEPOSIT/CREDIT (+)		BALANCE $
	1/1 1991	Opening Balance for U.S. Bank					1,200	00	1,200 00 / 1,200 00
100	1/4 1991	Small City Gas & Light Gas & Electric	67	50					67 50 / 1,132 50
101	1/5 1991	Small City Times Paper Bill	16	50					16 50 / 1,116 00
	1/7 1991	Deposit — Salary Monthly Pay					700	00	700 00 / 1,816 00
102	1/7 1991	Small City Market Food	22	32					22 32 / 1,793 68
103	1/7 1991	Small City Apartments Rent	150	00					150 00 / 1,643 68
104	1/19 1991	Small City Market Food	43	00					43 00 / 1,600 68
105	1/25 1991	Small City Phone Company Phone Bill	19	75					19 75 / 1,580 93
	2/10 1991	Dividend Check Dividend from ABC Co.					25	00	25 00 / 1,605 93

FIGURE 2-1.   Manual register entries in a checking account register

the Main Menu. It remembers this account when you end your Quicken session and will return you to this account the next time. If you have already made entries in the Quicken package, you should establish a new account and record the sample transactions there to avoid affecting your existing data. You can use this account to enter all the examples in the chapter without jeopardizing other Quicken entries you have created. Start Quicken; then follow these steps from the Main Menu to create the new account. If you like, you can then skip ahead to the beginning of the next section, which discusses Quicken categories.

1. Select item 4, Select Account from the Main Menu. Quicken opens the Select Account to Use window.

2. Move the cursor to <New Account> and press (ENTER). The Set Up New Account window appears.

3. Press (ENTER) to select option 1, Bank Account.

4. Type **1st U.S. Bank** and press (ENTER).

5. Type **1200** and press (ENTER) to supply the balance.

6. Type **1/1/91** and press (ENTER).

7. Type **Checking—Personal** and press (ENTER).

8. Press (ESC) to return to the Main Menu.

To set up the sample Quicken account for combined personal and business expenses, follow these steps:

1. Turn on your computer, boot the operating system, and respond to the date and time prompts. (If you are not familiar with the details of this procedure, you will find detailed instructions in Appendix A.)

If you are working with a 5 1/4-inch floppy disk system, prepare for the next step by placing the Quicken disk in drive A and the Help/Data disk in drive B. With a 3 1/2-inch disk, you do not use a separate Help/Data disk; place the program disk in drive A. If you have a hard disk and have followed the installation instructions in Appendix A, no further preparation is necessary.

2. Start the Quicken package by typing **Q** and pressing (ENTER).

3. Type **1** for a color monitor or **2** for a monochrome monitor if Quicken asks about your monitor's capabilities. This question only occurs the first time Quicken is started.

4. If Quicken prompts you for the date, enter it in the format 10/15/90 and press (ENTER). (This is also a one-time request that sets a beginning date for Quicken. If your system has a clock card you will not be prompted for the date.)

Now that you have finished with the preliminaries, Quicken displays the Main Menu. The next time you use Quicken, only steps 1 and 2 will be required.

5. Type **2** to open the Register window.

Quicken supports two alternatives for every menu item. You can type the number to the left of the desired item or you can use ⌷UP ARROW⌷ and ⌷DOWN ARROW⌷ to highlight the desired selection and then press ⌷ENTER⌷. Remember that moving the cursor alone is not sufficient; Quicken does not process your selection until you press ⌷ENTER⌷. Throughout this book, the number is typed in to select the desired item, but you can use either method.

Selecting Categories

Quicken provides categories for classifying your entries. This allows you to group similar income or expenses together. For example, you might have a water bill, a gas bill, and an electric bill that you pay every month. All three bills are generally considered part of your utilities expense. With Quicken you can categorize each of these payments under Utilities, which will allow you to obtain a quick total of your utility expenses for the month, quarter, or year.

When you set up your first account, Quicken provides the screen in Figure 2-2 to allow you to select from Home, Business, Both, or Neither. A complete list of categories for Home, Business, and Both is shown in Appendix

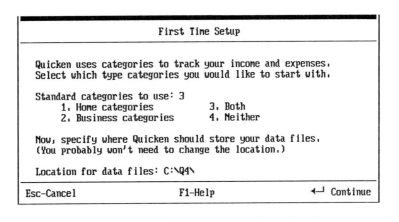

Copyright 1989–1990 Intuit

══════ **FIGURE 2-2.**   Selecting the category types

D. Later, you will learn how to create customized categories, but for now you will choose Both. To make this selection, follow these steps:

1. Type **3** to select Both.
2. Press (ENTER) to finalize your selection and continue with the entries for the first account.

Figure 2-3 provides a sample of some of the categories that will be available to you with this selection.

Selecting a Storage Location for Your Data

If you do not have a hard disk, your data will be stored on a disk in either drive A or B. With a hard disk, you may elect to store your data on the hard disk or you may prefer to keep it on a floppy disk. Quicken needs to know where to put it before storing any data in its files. If you want to use the displayed default location, press (ENTER). Otherwise, type a different drive letter and press (ENTER). In either case, the next window displayed will be the Set Up New Account window, which matches Figure 2-4. This window allows you to enter account information.

```
┌─────────────────────────────────────────────────────────────┐
│              Category and Transfer List                       │
│                                                               │
│      Category      Type       Description          Tax        │
│  ─────────────────────────────────────────────────────────   │
│    Old Age Pension Inc   Old Age Pension            ◆         │
│    Other Inc       Inc   Other Income               ◆         │
│    Rent Income     Inc   Rent Income                ◆         │
│    Salary          Inc   Salary Income              ◆         │
│  ▶ Ads             Expns Advertising                          │
│    Auto Fuel       Expns Automobile Fuel                      │
│    Auto Loan       Expns Auto Loan Payment                    │
│    Auto Serv       Expns Automobile Service                   │
│    Bank Chrg       Expns Bank Charge                          │
│    Car             Expns Car & Truck                ◆         │
│    Charity         Expns Charitable Donations       ◆         │
│    Childcare       Expns Childcare Expense                    │
│    Christmas       Expns Christmas Expenses                   │
│  ─────────────────────────────────────────────────────────   │
│       Ctrl-D Delete   Ctrl-E Edit   Ctrl-P Print              │
│    Esc-Cancel               F1-Help              ↵ Use        │
└─────────────────────────────────────────────────────────────┘
```

FIGURE 2-3. Sample Quicken categories

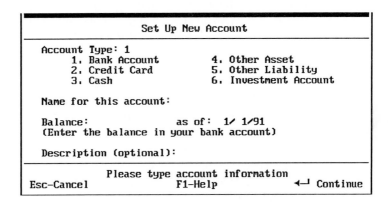

```
┌──────────────────────────────────────────────────────────┐
│                    Set Up New Account                     │
├──────────────────────────────────────────────────────────┤
│  Account Type: 1                                          │
│         1. Bank Account         4. Other Asset            │
│         2. Credit Card          5. Other Liability        │
│         3. Cash                 6. Investment Account      │
│                                                          │
│  Name for this account:                                  │
│                                                          │
│  Balance:                 as of:  1/ 1/91                │
│  (Enter the balance in your bank account)                │
│                                                          │
│  Description (optional):                                  │
├──────────────────────────────────────────────────────────┤
│              Please type account information             │
│  Esc-Cancel               F1-Help          ◄┘ Continue   │
└──────────────────────────────────────────────────────────┘
```

FIGURE 2-4.   Setting up a Quicken account

Entering Beginning Information

Quicken needs to know the name of the account you want to create and what type of transactions it will record. The New Account screen permits the entry of an account balance and an opening date, which can differ from the current date. After you complete the new account entries, Quicken will create four files on disk for this account; then, you can begin to record transactions. The entries you complete for this first account will be the same entries used when creating subsequent accounts in later chapters. Follow these steps to complete the Set Up New Account window:

1. Press (ENTER) to select option 1, Bank Account, as the account type.

The bank account option was chosen for your first account; other account types will be discussed in later chapters.

2. Type **1st U.S. Bank** and press (ENTER).

Quicken allows up to 15 characters for the account name. Spaces, letters, numbers, and many other symbols are allowed; however, you cannot use [ ], /, or : (brackets, slashes, or colons).

3. Type **1200** and press (ENTER) to set the beginning balance.

Quicken automatically adds a comma to separate thousands and a decimal point if there are zeros in the cents positions. You must enter the decimal point if the cents are other than zeros, but you should never enter the comma.

4. Type **1/1/91** for the date and press ⟨ENTER⟩.

In actual use, you may want to use the current date as the opening date when establishing an account. If so, you will only need to press ⟨ENTER⟩. Quicken allows the date change option to let you synchronize the opening date for an account with the date of your last bank statement or another record. For now, enter the dates as shown to ensure that the reporting process and other examples work correctly.

5. Type **Checking—Personal** and press ⟨ENTER⟩.

Quicken allows you to enter as many as 21 characters in the optional account description. When you press ⟨ENTER⟩ after completing the entry in the description field, the Register window you requested earlier is displayed. In subsequent sessions, choosing Register from the Main Menu will bring the Register window to the screen immediately, since the setup options are only required the first time you use the system.

THE QUICKEN REGISTER

Figure 2-5 shows the top of the initial Register window. Although you have not yet recorded any transactions, Quicken has already entered the account

F1-Help	F2-Acct/Print	F3-Edit	F4-Quick Entry	F5-Reports	F6-Activities			
DATE	NUM	PAYEE · MEMO · CATEGORY	PAYMENT	C	DEPOSIT		BALANCE	
		═══ BEGINNING ═══						
1/ 1 1991		Opening Balance [1st U.S. Bank]		X	1,200	00	1,200	00
7/ 6 1991	Memo: Cat:							

FIGURE 2-5. New account register window

name, the opening balance, and the opening date. Quicken has also automatically entered X in the C (cleared) field of the register, indicating that the balance has been reconciled and is correct. This field will be used in Chapter 4, when you reconcile your entire account.

The highlighted area below the opening balance entry is where the first transaction will be entered. Remember, a transaction is just a record of a financial activity such as a deposit or withdrawal (credit or debit). The fields used are the same for all transactions (see Figure 2-5). Table 2-1 provides a detailed description of each of these fields.

As you make the entries for the first transaction you will notice that Quicken moves through the fields in a specific order. After entering data in a field, you press (ENTER) and the cursor automatically moves to the next field in which you can enter data. Some fields, such as Date and Payee, must have an entry in all transactions, and either the Payment or Deposit field requires an entry. Other fields are optional and will only be used when needed. If you do not need an entry in an optional field, you just press (ENTER) and the cursor will move to the next field. For example, the check number (Num) field is only used when writing checks and so would be optional.

Recording Your Transactions in the Register

The highlighting is already positioned for your first transaction entry when you open the Register window. If you have used the (UP ARROW) key to move to the opening balance entry, you will need to press (CTRL)-(END) to reposition the highlight properly. In the next sections you will enter eight sample transactions representing typical personal expenses and deposits. Don't worry if you make a mistake in recording your first transaction. Just leave the mistake in the entry and focus on the steps involved. In the second transaction you will correct your errors. Follow these steps to complete the entries for the first transaction:

1. Type **1/4/91** and press (ENTER).

Notice that "1/4" is displayed on the first line of the Date field and that the cursor automatically moves to the second line of the column the second time you press the $\square$ key. Also note that even though you only entered 91, Quicken displays the full year 1991.

At this point you can see how Quicken dates are changed. Move the cursor to the Date field using (LEFT ARROW), and press $\oplus$ or $\ominus$ to increase or decrease the current date. A light touch to the key will alter the date by one day. Holding down these keys will cause a rapid date change. If you use

Field	Contents
Date	Transaction date. You can accept the current date entry or type a new date.
Num (number)	Check number for check transactions. Field is left blank by pressing (ENTER) for noncheck transactions.
Payee	Payee's name for check transactions. For ATM transactions, deposits, service fees, and so on, a description is entered in this field.
Payment	Payment or withdrawal amount. For deposit transactions, this field is left blank. Quicken supports entries as large as $9,999,999.99.
C (cleared)	Press (ENTER) to skip this field when entering transactions. It is used in Chapter 4 for reconciling accounts and noting checks that have cleared the bank.
Deposit	Deposit amounts. For a payment transaction, this field is left blank. The same rules as for Payment apply.
Balance	A running total or the sum of all prior transactions. It is computed by Quicken after completing each transaction.
Memo	Optional descriptive information documenting the transaction.
Category	Optional entry used to assign a transaction to one of Quicken's categories. Categories are used to organize similar transactions and can facilitate reporting.

TABLE 2-1. Fields in Register Window

the ⊕or ⊖option to change the date, (ENTER) or (TAB) is still required to move to the next field. This feature can be used at any point in Quicken when you wish to change a date on the screen. (If you test this feature now, be sure to reenter the 1/4/1991 date before proceeding.)

2. Type **100** and press (ENTER) to place the check number in the Num field.

3. Type **Small City Gas & Light** and press (ENTER) to complete the entry for Payee for this check.

There is a limit of 31 characters on the Payee line for each transaction. Notice that the cursor moves to the Payment field, where Quicken expects the next entry.

4. Type **67.50** and press (**ENTER**).

Since this is a check transaction, the amount should be placed in the Payment field. Notice that when you type the decimal, Quicken automatically moves to the cents column of the Payment field. Then the cursor moves to the C (cleared) field.

5. Press (**ENTER**) to leave the field blank and move to the Deposit field. Press (**ENTER**) again to move to the Memo field.

6. Type **Gas and Electric** and press (**ENTER**).

You are also limited to 31 characters on the Memo line.

7. Type **Utilities** in the Cat (category) field (your screen should look like Figure 2-6).

If you are going to use a category, you must enter a valid Quicken option to stay within the standard category structure. To see other valid entries, look at Appendix D to check the categories available when Quicken's Both option is selected.

8. Press (**ENTER**) to complete the transaction data entry. Quicken displays the OK to Record Transaction? window to see if you are ready to record the transaction.

```
 F1-Help   F2-Acct/Print   F3-Edit   F4-Quick Entry   F5-Reports   F6-Activities
┌─────┬─────┬────────────────────────────────┬─────────┬─┬─────────┬─────────┐
│DATE │ NUM │ PAYEE  ·  MEMO  ·  CATEGORY     │ PAYMENT │C│ DEPOSIT │ BALANCE │
├─────┼─────┼────────────────────────────────┼─────────┼─┼─────────┼─────────┤
│     │     │                                │         │ │         │         │
│     │     │ ══════ BEGINNING ══════        │         │ │         │         │
│1/ 1 │     │ Opening Balance                │         │X│ 1,200 00│ 1,200 00│
│1991 │     │            [1st U.S. Bank]     │         │ │         │         │
├─────┼─────┼────────────────────────────────┼─────────┼─┼─────────┼─────────┤
│1/ 4 │ 100 │ Small City Gas & Light         │   67 50 │ │         │         │
│1991 │Memo:│ Gas and Electric               │         │ │         │         │
│     │Cat: │ Utilities                      │         │ │         │         │
└─────┴─────┴────────────────────────────────┴─────────┴─┴─────────┴─────────┘
```

FIGURE 2-6.   Screen before completing first sample transaction entry

9. Type **1** to confirm the recording of the transaction. Your screen displays a balance of 1,132.50.

You have now completed your first transaction successfully. Since everyone makes mistakes in entries, you will want to learn how to correct those errors. This is easily done with Quicken.

MAKING REVISIONS TO THE CURRENT TRANSACTION

One of the advantages Quicken has over manual entries is that changes can be made easily and neatly. An incorrect amount or other error can be altered as soon as you notice the mistake or later on. The procedure you use depends on whether you have already recorded the transaction.

Correcting Your Example

In this section you will learn how to correct mistakes in the current transaction. You can employ the techniques covered briefly in Chapter 1. First, make the following transaction entries:

1. Type **1/5/91** and press ⌷ENTER⌷.

Notice that Quicken automatically enters the 1/4/91 date for you. It always records the current date in the field when recording transactions. Here, you must enter the date since you are entering several days' transactions in one session. If you enter transactions every day, you will not need to change the date between transactions since each of your entries will be for the current day.

2. Type **110** and press ⌷ENTER⌷.

Notice that the previous check number was 100. This check number should have been recorded as 101.

3. Press (**LEFT ARROW**) five times to move the cursor to the second 1 in the entry.

4. Type **01** to change 110 to 101 and then press (**ENTER**) to finalize.

This correction method employs Quicken's character replacement feature; new characters type over the old entries.

5. Type **Smalll City Times.**

This entry contains an extra *l*. Use (**CTRL**)-(**LEFT ARROW**) twice to move to the *C* in "City." Then press the (**LEFT ARROW**) key twice to move your cursor to the third *l* and press (**DEL**) to delete the character at the cursor.

6. Press (**ENTER**) to finalize the Payee entry.

7. Type **6.50** for the payment amount.

Note that if you had intended to enter 16.50, moving to the 6 and typing a 1 would change the entry to 1.50, not the 16.50 you need.

8. Move the cursor one position to the left of the 6 by pressing (**LEFT ARROW**) five times. Type **1** and Quicken will place the 1 in front of the 6.

9. Press (**ENTER**) three times to move to the Memo field.

10. Type **Magazine subscription** and press (**ENTER**).

If you had intended this entry to be the newspaper bill, you would need to make a change. Use (**UP ARROW**) to reactivate the Memo field.

11. Press (**CTRL**)-(**BACKSPACE**), which will delete the entire entry. Then, type **Paper bill** and press (**ENTER**).

12. Type **Mic** for the category.

This entry should have read "Misc." To insert the *s,* move the cursor to the *c* with (**LEFT ARROW**), press (**INS**), type **s**, and then press (**INS**) again.

F1-Help	F2-Acct/Print	F3-Edit	F4-Quick Entry	F5-Reports	F6-Activities

DATE	NUM	PAYEE · MEMO · CATEGORY	PAYMENT	C	DEPOSIT	BALANCE
		▬▬▬ BEGINNING ▬▬▬				
1/ 1 1991		Opening Balance [1st U.S. Bank]		X	1,200 00	1,200 00
1/ 4 1991	100	Small City Gas & Light Gas and Electri→Utilities	67 50			1,132 50
1/ 5 1991	101	Small City Times Paper bill Misc	16 50			1,116 00

FIGURE 2-7. Register screen after second sample transaction

Before completing the transaction, look back at your other entries. Any of them can be changed by moving to its field and making the correction. You can even use a quick approach by pressing (CTRL)-(RIGHT ARROW) or (CTRL)-(LEFT ARROW) to move a word at a time in the specified direction.

13. Press (ENTER) to complete your second transaction.

14. Type **1** or press (ENTER) to confirm the update. Your register should look like Figure 2-7.

Although a number of mistakes were included in this transaction, you can see how easy it is to make corrections with Quicken.

ADDITIONAL TRANSACTION ENTRIES

You are now somewhat familiar with recording transactions in the Quicken register. In order to test your knowledge and expand your transaction base for later, enter the following additional transactions in your register, using the same procedure as in the previous transaction entries. Remember to leave a blank space in all the C fields and in the Num field of deposits.

Date: 1/7/91
Payee: Deposit—Salary
Deposit: $700.00
Memo: Monthly pay
Category: Salary

Date: 1/7/91
Num: 102
Payee: Small City Market
Payment: 22.32
Memo: Food
Category: Groceries

Date: 1/7/91
Num: 103
Payee: Small City Apartments
Payment: 150.00
Memo: Rent
Category: Housing

Date: 1/19/91
Num: 104
Payee: Small City Market
Payment: 43.00
Memo: Food
Category: Groceries

Date: 1/25/91
Num: 105
Payee: Small City Phone Company
Payment: 19.75
Memo: Phone bill
Category: Telephone

Date: 2/10/91
Payee: Dividend check
Deposit: 25.00
Memo: Dividends check from ABC Co.
Category: Div Income

After typing and recording the entries for the last transaction, your screen should resemble Figure 2-8. Remember to press (CTRL)-(ENTER) to record the last transaction.

ENDING A QUICKEN SESSION AND BEGINNING A NEW ONE

You do not need to finish all your work with Quicken in one session. You can end a Quicken session after entering one transaction or continue and enter transactions representing up to several months of financial activity, but you should always use the orderly approach provided here and never turn your system off without first exiting from Quicken.

Ending a Quicken session requires that you go to the Main Menu. You can use (ESC) when the register is active to return to the Main Menu. You then have two options. You can either use (DOWN ARROW) to move the cursor

F1-Help	F2-Acct/Print	F3-Edit	F4-Quick Entry	F5-Reports	F6-Activities

DATE	NUM	PAYEE · MEMO · CATEGORY	PAYMENT	C	DEPOSIT	BALANCE
1/ 7 1991		Deposit-Salary Monthly pay Salary			700 00	1,816 00
1/ 7 1991	102	Small City Market Food Groceries	22 32			1,793 68
1/ 7 1991	103	Small City Apartments Rent Housing	150 00			1,643 68
1/19 1991	104	Small City Market Food Groceries	43 00			1,600 68
1/25 1991	105	Small City Phone Company Phone bill Telephone	19 75			1,580 93
2/10 1991		Dividend check Memo: Dividends check from ABC Co. Cat: Div Income			25 00	

1st U.S. Bank
Esc-Main Menu   Ctrl↵ Record   Ending Balance: $1,580.93

FIGURE 2-8.   Register screen after typing entries in last transaction

to the Exit option and then press (ENTER), or you can type **E** to immediately exit Quicken. All of the data in your Quicken files will be saved for subsequent sessions.

To reenter Quicken, use the instructions provided earlier in this chapter to boot your system (if necessary); then, type **Q** and press (ENTER) to access the Quicken package. You will always enter the Main Menu when you first load the package. Typing **R** will take you back to the register to record additional transactions. Quicken always brings the last account you worked with to the screen.

Quicken automatically enters the current date in the Date field for the first transaction in a session.

Remember that for purposes of the examples, you will specify dates that are unlikely to agree with the current date. This approach will allow you to create reports identical to the ones that will be presented later. Each time you enter the Quicken package in this tutorial, you can use ⊕ and ⊖ to change the date Quicken has entered to the date used in the tutorial. If you are now reentering Quicken, use 2/10/91 as the date.

REVIEWING REGISTER ENTRIES

Reviewing transaction entries in the Quicken register is as easy and more versatile than flipping through the pages of a manual register. You can scroll through the register to see all the recorded transactions or use the Find feature to search for a specific transaction. You can also focus on transactions for a specific time period with the Go to Date feature.

Scrolling Through the Register

You can put some of the keys introduced in Chapter 1 to work in the Quicken register. You can probably guess the effects some of the keys will have from their names. The (UP ARROW) and (DOWN ARROW) keys move the highlighting up or down a transaction. Quicken scrolls information off the screen to show additional transactions not formerly in view. Once a transaction is highlighted, the (RIGHT ARROW) and (LEFT ARROW) keys move across the current transaction. The (PGUP) and (PGDN) keys move up and down one screen at a time.

The functions of some keys vary between releases of Quicken; some key functions are not as obvious as those just discussed. The following examples show how the keys work in Quicken 4.

The (HOME) key moves the cursor to the beginning of the current field in a transaction. When (HOME) is pressed twice, the cursor moves to the beginning of the current transaction. If you press (CTRL)-(HOME), Quicken moves the cursor to the top of the register.

The (END) key moves the cursor to the end of the current field. If you press (END) twice, Quicken moves the cursor to the last field in the current transaction. If you press (CTRL)-(END), Quicken moves the cursor to the bottom of the register.

Pressing (CTRL)-(PGUP) moves the highlight to the beginning of the previous month. Pressing (CTRL)-(PGDN) moves the highlight to the first transaction in the next month.

Try these entries to view some of the effects:

1. Press (CTRL)-(HOME) to move to the top of the register.

2. Press (CTRL)-(END) to move to the last transaction in the register, highlighting the blank transaction for 2/10.

3. Press (UP ARROW) until you move to the Small City Phone transaction, and then press (HOME) twice to move to the first field.

4. Press (END) twice to move to the last field (the Category field) in this transaction.

5. Press (HOME) to move to the beginning of this field.

6. Press (DOWN ARROW) to move to the Dividend transaction.

7. Press (PGUP) to move to check 101.

8. Press (CTRL)-(PGDN) to move to the beginning of the next month in the register.

As you enter more transactions, the value of knowing quick ways to move between transactions will become more apparent.

Using the Find Feature

Quicken's Find feature allows you to locate a specific transaction easily. You can find a transaction by entering a minimal amount of information from the transaction on a special Find window. Activate the Find window with the Quick key CTRL-F or by pressing F3 to activate the Edit menu, and then selecting 4 for Find. The Edit menu displays all the Quick key sequences such as CTRL-F for Find.

Quicken can look for an exact match entry in any field with a forward or backward search. You can also use Quicken's wild-card feature to locate a transaction with only part of the information from a field. After looking at the examples in the next two sections, you can refer to the rules for finding entries in Table 2-2, Locating Transactions.

EXACT MATCH ENTRIES To look for a transaction that exactly matches data, all you need to do is fill in some data in the window. Quicken will search for entries in the Num, Payee, Memo, Category, Payment, C, or Deposit field. You do not need to worry about capitalization of your data entry since Quicken is not case sensitive. When you enter the data for your first Find operation, the fields will be blank. For subsequent Find operations you can edit the data in the window, type over what's there, or clear the entire window by pressing CTRL-D and begin again with blank fields. For example, to locate a specific check number in the 1st U.S. Bank register developed earlier, complete the following steps.

Entry	Quicken Finds
electric	electric, Electric, ELECTRIC
electric..	electric power, Electric Company, electric
..electric	Consumer Power Electric, new electric
~electric	groceries, gas—anything but electric
e..c	electric, eccentric
s?n	sun, sin, son—any single letter between an *s* and an *n*
..	ice, fire, and anything else except blanks
~..	all transactions with a blank in that field

TABLE 2-2. Locating Transactions

1. Press CTRL-HOME.

This will ensure that you start at the beginning of the register so you can conduct a complete forward search through the data. (Quicken also supports a backward search to allow you to locate entries above the currently highlighted transaction.)

2. Press F3 to open the Edit menu.

3. Type **5** to select Find.

4. Move the cursor to the Num field by pressing the LEFT ARROW key five times. Type **103**, as shown here:

Transaction to Find						
NUM	PAYEE · MEMO · CATEGORY			PAYMENT	C	DEPOSIT
103 Memo: Cat:						

Esc-Cancel   Ctrl-B/N Find Backward/Next   Ctrl-D Clear ↵ Continue

5. Press CTRL-N to find the next matching transaction. Quicken will close the Find window and highlight the transaction.

Quicken started the search with the current transaction and proceeded toward the bottom of the register attempting to find matching transactions, in this case the one with 103 in the Num field. You could have entered data in other fields in the Find window if you wanted to specify multiple criteria for locating transactions. You might make entries for the Date, Payee, and Memo fields all in one Find window. Quicken only finds transactions that match all of your entries.

The more transactions in the register, the more useful Quicken's Find capability becomes. For instance, you might want to find all the transactions involving a specific payee or all the transactions on a certain date. Visually scanning through hundreds of transactions could take a long time and you would still miss a matching transaction. Quicken makes no mistakes and finds the matching transactions quickly.

You can also speed up the search process by bypassing the Edit menu and using the Quick keys for your Find selections. Let's perform a second Find operation, one that begins the search with the current transaction and searches back toward the first entry in the register. To use the Quick keys to do this, follow these steps:

1. Press ⌈CTRL⌋-⌈F⌋ to open the Find window. (This approach replaces opening the Edit menu and selecting item 5, Find.)

2. Type **100**, and then press ⌈DEL⌋ until the digits from the previous Num entry have been removed.

3. Press ⌈CTRL⌋-⌈B⌋ to search backward through the entries and highlight the transaction for check number 100.

If you were performing a search in which several transactions might match your entry, you could continue to search with repeated presses of ⌈CTRL⌋-⌈N⌋ (forward) or ⌈CTRL⌋-⌈B⌋ (backward) after completing the entries in the Find window.

KEY WORD SEARCH   You can enter a less than exact match and still locate the desired transactions if you search the Payee, Category, or Memo field. Quicken uses the character .. (two consecutive periods) either before or after text to indicate that other characters may precede or follow an entry. You can think of this character as a wild card; it will match anything. Thus, "..Leather, Inc." in the Payee field of the Find window causes Quicken to search this field for an entry that ends with "Leather, Inc.," regardless of the characters that begin the entry. "Blue Leather, Inc." would match as well as "Cheap Leather, Inc." and many other potential names.

Likewise, if you use the .. at the end of the entry, any number of characters may follow. An entry of "Blue.." would match "Blue Leather," "Blue Heather," and many other entries. If you know the middle characters in a field, but not the beginning or end of the entry, you can use the .. character both before and after your entry. Try this for a quick look at the Key Word Search feature:

1. Press ⌈CTRL⌋-⌈F⌋ to open the Find window.

2. Press ⌈CTRL⌋-⌈D⌋ to clear all the entries from this window.

3. Type **Small..** in the Payee field.

4. Press CTRL-N to search from the current location toward the end of the document. Quicken highlights the next entry for "Small City Times."

If you continue to press CTRL-N, Quicken will move through the transaction list highlighting each entry containing "Small." After you have found all matching transactions, pressing CTRL-N again will cause Quicken to display a message indicating there are no matching transactions.

SEARCHING FOR MULTIPLE ENTRIES You can use multiple key word search entries in a Find window or combine the Key Word Search feature with exact match entries. As an example, follow these steps to look for transactions with "Market" at the end of the Payee field, a payment of 22.32, and "Groceries" for the category entry:

1. Press CTRL-HOME to move to the beginning of the register.
2. Press CTRL-F to open the Find window.
3. Press CTRL-BACKSPACE to clear the Num field.
4. Type **..Market** in the Payee field and press ENTER.
5. Type **22.32** in the Payment field and press ENTER four times.
6. Type **Groceries** in the Category field. Your Find entries should look like this:

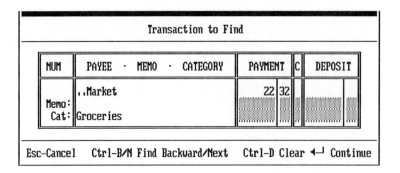

7. Press CTRL-N.

Your transaction for Small City Market should be highlighted. Press CTRL-N again to repeat the forward search. Quicken will display the message indicating that there are no further matches.

8. Press ENTER to end the search.

Using the Go to Date Feature

You may sometimes want to find one or more transactions for a given date. The Go to Date feature allows you to locate the first transaction entry for a specified date. You can use either the Edit menu or (CTRL)-(G) to begin a date search. If you use (F3) to open the Edit menu, you will then select item 8 to open the Go to Date window.

When the window opens, fill in the date that you are searching for. A date search works a little differently than Find since you do not have to be concerned with whether the date is before or after the current transaction. The following steps illustrate a date search:

1. Press (CTRL)-(HOME). Then press (CTRL)-(G) to open the Go to Date window.

2. Type **1/7/91**, as shown here:

```
┌─────────────────────────────────────┐
│ ▬▬▬▬▬▬▬▬▬▬▬▬▬▬▬▬▬▬▬▬▬▬▬▬▬▬▬▬▬▬▬▬▬▬▬  │
│              Go to Date              │
│─────────────────────────────────────│
│                                      │
│    Date to find: 1 /7 /91            │
│                                      │
│─────────────────────────────────────│
│  Esc-Cancel  F1-Help  ←┘ Continue    │
└─────────────────────────────────────┘
```

and press (ENTER). Quicken goes to the first transaction for the date you entered.

You could now examine all the remaining transactions for the date by pressing (DOWN ARROW).

REVISING TRANSACTIONS

You have already learned how to make revisions to transactions in the check register as you are recording a transaction, but sometimes you may need to make changes to previously recorded transactions. It is important to note that although Quicken allows you to modify previously recorded transactions, you cannot change the balance amount without entering another transaction.

This protects you from unauthorized changes in the register account balances. By forcing you to enter another transaction, Quicken is able to maintain a log of any change to an account balance.

You may also find it necessary to void a previously written check, deposit, or any other adjustment to an account. Voiding removes the effect of the original transaction from the account balance, although it maintains the history of the original transaction and shows it as voided. To remove all trace of the original transaction you must use Quicken's Delete Transaction command. You can use either Quick keys or selections from Quicken's Edit menu to void and delete transactions. To reinstate voided transactions, you delete the word "VOID" and the X in the column (which was entered automatically) and press (CTRL)-(ENTER) to finalize the change.

Changing a Previous Transaction

The following steps must be used when changing a previously recorded transaction:

1. Move the highlighting to the desired transaction using (UP ARROW) or (DOWN ARROW).

2. Then use the same techniques discussed in the "Making Revisions to the Current Transaction" section of this chapter.

Quicken does not allow you to change the balance amount directly. You would need to enter another transaction to make an adjustment. Another option is to void the original transaction and enter a new transaction.

Voiding a Transaction

When you void a transaction, you undo the financial effect of the transaction. Using the Void operation creates an automatic audit trail (or record) of all transactions against an account, including those that have already been voided. Let's try the Void option with check number 100; follow these steps:

1. Move the highlighting to check number 100 with (DOWN ARROW) or (UP ARROW).

2. Press **CTRL**-**V** to void the current transaction.

Another option is pressing **F3** and typing **4** to select the Void Transaction item from the Edit menu. With either approach the word "VOID" is now entered in front of the payee name, as shown in Figure 2-9.

3. Press **ESC** to return to the Main Menu. Quicken displays the Leaving Transaction window.
4. Press **ENTER** to select item 1, Record changes, and leave.

If after voiding a transaction you want to continue to work in the check register, you can move to the category field by using **TAB**, **ENTER**, or the arrow keys. Press **ENTER** one more time to select item 1, Record transaction, from the OK to Record Transaction? window. If you change your mind and do not want to void the transaction, you can highlight item 2, Do not record, before pressing **ENTER**.

Deleting a Transaction

You can delete a transaction with **CTRL**-**D** or by opening the Edit menu with **F3** and selecting item 2, Delete transaction. Try this now by deleting the voided transaction for check number 100.

1. If you are at the Main Menu, open the Register window again by moving the cursor to item 2, Register, and pressing **ENTER**.

| F1-Help | F2-Acct/Print | F3-Edit | F4-Quick Entry | F5-Reports | F6-Activities |

DATE	NUM	PAYEE · MEMO · CATEGORY	PAYMENT	C	DEPOSIT	BALANCE
		BEGINNING				
1/ 1 1991		Opening Balance [1st U.S. Bank]		X	1,200 00	1,200 00
1/ 4 1991	100	VOID Small City Gas & Light Memo: Gas and Electric Cat: Utilities		X		1,132 50

FIGURE 2-9. Voided transaction

2. Press ⌈**DOWN ARROW**⌋ to move the highlighting to the voided transaction for check number 100.

3. Press ⌈**CTRL**⌋-⌈**D**⌋ to delete the transaction. Quicken displays the OK to Delete Transaction? window.

4. Press ⌈**ENTER**⌋ to confirm the deletion.

Reinstating a Transaction

There is no "undo" key to eliminate the effect of a delete; you must reenter the transaction. For practice, reinstate the transaction for check number 100 with these steps:

1. Press the ⌈**CTRL**⌋-⌈**END**⌋ key to move to the end of the register.

2. Type **1/4/91** and press ⌈**ENTER**⌋.

3. Type **100** and press ⌈**ENTER**⌋ to supply the check number in the Num field.

4. Type **Small City Gas & Light** and press ⌈**ENTER**⌋ to complete the entry for the payee for this check.

5. Type **67.50** and press ⌈**ENTER**⌋.

6. Press ⌈**ENTER**⌋ to leave the field blank and move to the Deposit field. Press ⌈**ENTER**⌋ again to move to the Memo field.

7. Type **Gas and Electric** and press ⌈**ENTER**⌋.

8. Type **Utilities** and press ⌈**ENTER**⌋ to complete the transaction.

9. Press ⌈**ENTER**⌋ when the OK to Record Transaction? window displays. The transaction is reentered into the register.

You can see from this example that you expended a considerable amount of effort to rerecord this transaction. Avoid unnecessary work by confirming the void or deletion before you complete it.

QUICKEN REPORTS

In Chapter 2 you discovered how easy it is to enter transactions in the Quicken system. In this chapter you will find out about another major benefit—the ability to generate reports. These reports present your data in an organized format that allows you to analyze the data. You can use Quicken to produce a quick printout of the register or create reports that analyze and summarize data. Some of these reports, such as the Cash Flow report and the Itemized Category report, would require a significant amount of work if they were compiled manually. This chapter will focus on these three basic types of reports and some customizing options. More complex report types are covered in later chapters.

Before looking at the various reports, let's look first at how Quicken works with printers. Although Quicken supports most popular printers without any special effort on your part, you should know a few of the essentials of printers. This chapter will teach you how to change the basic print settings if

Quicken does not create acceptable output with the current configuration. You can define three different printers or predefine three different options for one printer.

DEFAULT PRINTER SETTINGS

Quicken is preset to interface with most of the popular printers including IBM Compatibles; Hewlett-Packard LaserJet I and II, DeskJet, and ThinkJet; IBM ProPrinter and 4216; Epson; NEC 3530 and 8023A; and Okidata 83, 92, 182, 192, 292, and 320. Default parameters set the pitch to 10 characters per inch and the parallel printer port to 1 (LPT1), the standard port on your machine for connecting the first printer. If you have one of the printers listed here or own a model that mimics one of them, you will be able to print your Quicken reports without making any changes. If you are using a serial printer, a laser printer producing less than acceptable results, or a printer with a pitch other than 10, consult "Changing the Printer Settings" at the end of this chapter. If not, Quicken will probably interface with your printer and you will not need to make any changes to the Quicken printer settings.

PRINTING THE CHECK REGISTER

Although it is convenient to enter transactions on the screen, a printout of your entries is often easier to review and much more portable than a computer screen. Try printing the register first without changing the print settings. If your output is very different from the sample shown in this chapter, try customizing your print settings and then print the register again. You will find instructions for making these changes at the end of this chapter. To print your register you should:

1. Type **2** to select Register from Quicken's Main Menu.

Your latest register transactions should appear on the screen.

2. Press (**F2**) to open the Acct/Print menu as shown in Figure 3-1.

3. Type **2** to select the Print Register.

DATE	NU	► 1. Select/Set Up Account Ctrl-A	MENT	C	DEPOSIT	BALANCE
1/ 7 1991	102	2. Print Register Ctrl-P 3. Change Printer Settings	22 32			1,793 68
1/ 7 1991	103	4. Back Up All Accounts	50 00			1,643 68
1/19 1991	104	5. Export 6. Import	43 00			1,600 68
1/25 1991	105	Small City Phone Company Phone bill Telephone	19 75			1,580 93
2/10 1991		Dividend check Dividends check→Div Income			25 00	1,605 93
7/ 7 1991		Memo: Cat:				

F1-Help   F2-Acct/Print   F3-Edit   F4-Quick Entry   F5-Reports   F6-Activities

1st U.S. Bank
Esc-Cancel   Ending Balance: $1,605.93

━━━ **FIGURE 3-1.**   Acct/Print menu

Alternatively, pressing (CTRL)-(P) opens the Print Register window directly, without first going through the Acct/Print menu. Your screen will be similar to the one in Figure 3-2, but option 3 under "Print to:" will be "Check printer." Option 3 has been customized for an HP LaserJet II printer in the figure.

4. Type **1/1/91** and press (ENTER).

This entry selects the first transaction to be printed by date.

5. Type **1/31/91** and press (ENTER).

This entry establishes the last transaction to be printed. The dates supplied in steps 4 and 5 are inclusive; that is, Quicken will print all register transactions with dates from 1/1/91 through 1/31/91.

6. Type **1** and press (ENTER) to tell Quicken where to print the output from the print operation.

```
 F1-Help      Acct/Print      Edit      Quick Entry      Reports     Activities
┌────────┬─┬──────────────────────────────────────────────────────┬─────────┐
│ DATE   │N│                    Print Register                     │BALANCE  │
│ 1/ 7   │10│                                                      │1,793 68 │
│ 1991   │  │  Print transactions from:  1/ 1/91 to:  2/10/91      │         │
│ 1/ 7   │10│  Print to: 1                                         │1,643 68 │
│ 1991   │  │      1. Report Printer      3. HP LJetII-Checks       │         │
│ 1/19   │10│      2. Alt Report Printer  4. Disk                  │1,600 68 │
│ 1991   │  │                                                      │         │
│ 1/25   │10│  Title (optional):                                   │1,580 93 │
│ 1991   │  │  Print one transaction per line (Y/N): N             │         │
│ 2/10   │  │  Print transaction splits (Y/N): N                   │1,605 93 │
│ 1991   │  │  Sort by check number (Y/N): N                       │         │
│ ?/ ?   │Me│─────────────────────────────────────────────────────│         │
│ 1991   │C │      Position paper in printer                       │         │
│        │  │  Esc-Cancel        F1-Help          Ctrl↵ Print      │         │
└────────┴─┴──────────────────────────────────────────────────────┴─────────┘
 1st U.S. Bank                                    Ending Balance:  $1,605.93
```

FIGURE 3-2. Print Register window items and options

This is the default option—the selection Quicken will make unless you designate another option. You have the ability to print to three different printers: (1) a report printer, (2) an alternate report printer (second printer or a different print option for the first printer, such as landscape or compressed), or (3) a check printer. Quicken allows you to select different print options for different types of output. Thus, for a quick draft of a report you might select the alternate printer, a high-speed device of marginal quality, and later choose a report printer to print the final copy on a laser printer. You will learn later in the chapter how to select these printing options.

Selecting option 4, Disk, creates an ASCII text file for exporting Quicken data to other computer programs. You would use the Disk option if you wanted to use the data from the register in your word processor or some other program that can read ASCII text files.

7. Type **January Transactions** and press ⟨ENTER⟩.

This customizes the title of the check register. If you do not make an entry in this field, Quicken uses the default option "Check Register" for the report heading. You can use up to 36 characters to customize your heading.

8. Press ⟨ENTER⟩.

This selects Quicken's default option to allow three lines for each transaction Quicken prints. If you want to have more transactions printed on each page, type **Y** and press ⟨ENTER⟩. This option prints the document using only one line per transaction by abbreviating the information printed.

9. Press ⟨ENTER⟩.

You can ignore the prompt about transaction splits. This type of transaction will be introduced in Chapter 6. For now, leave the default setting as N. This is another default option. Quicken prints the register in order by date and then by check number. If you wanted to first sort by check number and then by date you would type **Y** and press ⟨ENTER⟩. If you are writing checks from two different checkbooks, changing this option can affect the order in which transactions are listed.

10. Press ⟨CTRL⟩-⟨ENTER⟩.

Once you have completed the Print Register window, Quicken is ready to print the check register for the period you defined. Make sure your printer is turned on and ready to print before completing this entry.

Your printed register should look like the first few sample transactions shown in Figure 3-3. Notice that the date at the top-left corner of your

```
                              January Transactions
      1st U.S. Bank                                                    Page  1
      7/ 7/91

      Date  Num           Transaction              Payment  C  Deposit    Balance
      ----- -----  ------------------------------- ---------- - ---------- ----------

      1/ 1         Opening Balance                            X  1,200.00   1,200.00
      1991 memo:
           cat:  [1st U.S. Bank]

      1/ 4 100     Small City Gas & Light            67.50                  1,132.50
      1991 memo:  Gas and Electric
           cat:  Utilities

      1/ 5 101     Small City Times                  16.50                  1,116.00
      1991 memo:  Paper bill
           cat:  Misc
```

FIGURE 3-3. 1st U.S. Bank checking account register printout

report is the current date, regardless of the month for which you are printing transactions.

PRINTING THE CASH FLOW REPORT

The Cash Flow report generated by Quicken compares the money you have received during a specified time period with the money you have spent. Quicken provides this information for each category used in the register. In addition, the Cash Flow report will combine transactions from your Bank, Cash, and Credit Card accounts. (Cash and Credit Card accounts will be discussed in Chapter 6.) Preparing the Cash Flow report for the transactions you recorded in the 1st U.S. Bank account in Chapter 2 involves the following steps from the Main Menu:

1. Type **3** to open the Reports menu.

You can also access the Reports menu directly from the register by pressing (F5). You will see a pull-down menu offering options for standard personal, business, and investments reports as well as custom reports.

2. Type **1** to open the Personal Reports menu from the Reports menu.

Quicken then allows you to define the type of report you want from the pull-down menu added to the screen.

3. Type **1** to select the Cash Flow report. You will see the Cash Flow Report window, as shown here:

```
┌─────────────────────────────────────────────────────────┐
│▬▬▬▬▬▬▬▬▬▬▬▬▬▬▬▬▬▬▬▬▬▬▬▬▬▬▬▬▬▬▬▬▬▬▬▬▬▬▬▬▬▬▬▬▬▬▬▬▬▬▬│
│                    Cash Flow Report                       │
│─────────────────────────────────────────────────────────│
│                                                           │
│  Report title (optional):                                 │
│                                                           │
│  Report on months from:  1/91 through:  7/91              │
│                                                           │
│─────────────────────────────────────────────────────────│
│  Esc-Cancel   F1-Help   Ctrl M-Memorize   F8-Customize ◄┘ Continue │
└─────────────────────────────────────────────────────────┘
```

4. Type **Cash Flow Report** - and your name, and then press (ENTER).

If you press ⟨ENTER⟩ without making an entry, Quicken will use the default title for the report. With this report the default title is "Cash Flow Report." If you choose to personalize the report, you can use up to 39 characters for a report title.

5. Press ⊕ or ⊖ to change your beginning report date to 1/91, and press ⟨ENTER⟩.

Quicken automatically places the beginning of the current year's date in this space. You will need to decide whether to press ⊕ or ⊖ depending on the current date in your system.

6. Press either ⊕ or ⊖ to change your report ending date to 1/91.

It is important to note that Quicken is designed to generate reports for an entire month. In this example Quicken will prepare the Cash Flow report for transactions recorded for the month of January 1991. If you want to prepare a report for less than a full month, you need to modify the Quicken settings in order to override the default period of one month. You will learn how to make this modification in Chapter 6.

7. Press ⟨ENTER⟩ and the Cash Flow report will appear on your screen.

Notice that the entire report does not appear on your screen.

8. Press ⟨DOWN ARROW⟩ to bring the rest of the report to the screen.

Notice that the Cash Flow report has the inflows and outflows listed by category.

9. Press ⟨F8⟩ to open the Print Report window.

This brings the Print Report window to your screen. You need to select the type of printer you are using. The default option is the standard report printer.

10. Press ⟨ENTER⟩ to select the Report Printer default option. The report shown in Figure 3-4 is printed.

You have the option of having Quicken send the Cash Flow report to (1) the report printer, (2) an alternate report printer, (3) a check printer, (4) a disk,

```
                    Cash Flow Report - Mary Campbell
                       1/ 1/91 Through 1/31/91
    1st U.S. Bank                                            Page 1
    7/ 7/91
                                          1/ 1/91-
                     Category Description   1/31/91
                    ------------------------  -----------
                    INFLOWS
                      Salary Income          700.00
                                           -----------
                    TOTAL INFLOWS           700.00

                    OUTFLOWS
                      Groceries              65.32
                      Housing               150.00
                      Miscellaneous          16.50
                      Telephone Expense      19.75
                      Water, Gas, Electric   67.50
                                           -----------
                    TOTAL OUTFLOWS          319.07


                                           -----------
                    OVERALL TOTAL           380.93
                                           ===========
```

FIGURE 3-4. Standard Cash Flow report

as an ASCII file, or (5) a disk, as a 1-2-3 file. If you need to customize any of
the printer settings, press (F9) before accepting any of the options. This
allows you to specify a custom report printer or alternate report printer and
then select this new option from the menu. You can use (DOWN ARROW) or
(UP ARROW) to select the printer options listed after step 10.

11. To leave the report, press (ESC) until you have backed out to the Main
    Menu.

PRINTING THE ITEMIZED CATEGORY REPORT

The Itemized Category report lists and summarizes all the transactions for
each category used in the register during a specific time period. Although
here you will be using this report to work only with the information in the 1st

U.S. Bank checking account, it is much more sophisticated than it may appear. This report summarizes information from your Bank, Cash, and Credit Card accounts and, unlike the Cash Flow report, also incorporates category information from Other Asset and Other Liability accounts, which you will establish in Chapter 6.

You can print your Itemized Category report by following these steps (starting from the Main Menu):

1. Type **3** to open the Reports menu.

2. Type **1** to open the Personal Reports menu.

3. Type **3** to open the Itemized Category Report window.

4. If the title field of the Itemized Category Report window is blank, press ⟨**ENTER**⟩. If not, press ⟨**DEL**⟩ until the existing title is erased, and then press ⟨**ENTER**⟩.

This action selects the Quicken default title of "Itemized Category Report." You could also personalize the report title by typing **Itemized Category Report-** and your name and pressing ⟨**ENTER**⟩.

5. Type **1/91** and press ⟨**ENTER**⟩.

Quicken automatically places in this window either the current year's beginning date or the date of the last report you created. You could also change the date by pressing ⊕ or ⊖ until the 1/91 date appears.

6. Type **1/91.**

This tells Quicken to create a report of itemized categories through the end of January.

7. Press ⟨**ENTER**⟩.

This brings the Itemized Category report to the screen. You can scroll down the report by using ⟨**DOWN ARROW**⟩. Also notice that the report on your screen is in half-screen format. You can see the full-screen report by pressing ⟨**F9**⟩. This expands the report and means that you have to move around in the document to examine the contents. This feature is discussed more fully later in this chapter.

8. Press ⟨**F8**⟩.

This opens the Print Report window on your screen.

9. Press ⁅**ENTER**⁆ to print the Itemized Category report.

You have the same options here that you had with the Cash Flow report. By pressing ⁅**ENTER**⁆ you select the Report printer option. Once again you could have selected printing to an alternate report printer or a check printer, or creating an ASCII file or 1-2-3 file. This will print the Itemized Category report. Note that the report is two pages long. If your printer has the compressed print capacity, you may want to print your reports in that mode to capture more of the report on each page. The top of page 1 of the Itemized Category report is shown in Figure 3-5.

10. To leave the report, press ⁅**ESC**⁆ until you are in the Main Menu.

```
                           ITEMIZED CATEGORY REPORT
                            1/ 1/91 Through 1/31/91
     1st U.S. Bank                                              Page  1
     7/ 7/91

       Date   Num     Description       Memo         Category    Clr Amount
       -----  ------  -----------------  --------------  ------------------- - ---------

              INCOME/EXPENSE
                INCOME
                  Salary Income
                  -------------
        1/ 7        Deposit - Salary   Monthly pay   Salary            700.00
                                                                      ---------
                    Total Salary Income                                700.00
                                                                      ---------
                TOTAL INCOME                                           700.00

                EXPENSES
                  Groceries
                  ---------
        1/ 7 102    Small City Market  Food          Groceries        -22.32
        1/19 104    Small City Market  Food          Groceries        -43.00
                                                                      ---------
                    Total Groceries                                    -65.32
```

FIGURE 3-5. Itemized Category report

FORMAT OPTIONS WITH THE CASH FLOW AND ITEMIZED CATEGORY REPORTS

When printing both the Cash Flow and Itemized Category reports you have several customization options. These are not like the custom reports discussed in later chapters, since you can make only limited modifications. In most situations these options will meet your needs, but remember that you can access help on each of the options once you open the Customizing window. Just as in other areas of Quicken, you get help by pressing (F1).

Although the customizing options for the reports require a little time to learn, the end result can be a dramatic difference in the appearance and content of the reports. Since the customization options for the Cash Flow and Itemized Category reports are similar, the important options will be covered together. You can use them to change the labeling information on the report as well as the basic organization of the entries.

Changing the Column Headings

Quicken allows you to change the column headings on both the Itemized Category and Cash Flow reports. You can print a report for the standard monthly time period or change it to one week, two weeks, half a month, one month, a quarter, half a year, or one year. You make this change from the Create Summary Report window, shown in Figure 3-6. Figure 3-7 shows a report created with "Week of" used as the column headings. The report will span two pages unless it is printed with compressed print.

Follow these steps to create a Cash Flow report showing weekly time periods (starting from the Main Menu):

1. Type **3** to open the Reports menu.

2. Type **1** to open the Personal Reports menu.

3. Type **1** to open the Cash Flow Report window.

4. Type **Cash Flow -** and your name and press (ENTER).

5. Type **1/91** and press (ENTER).

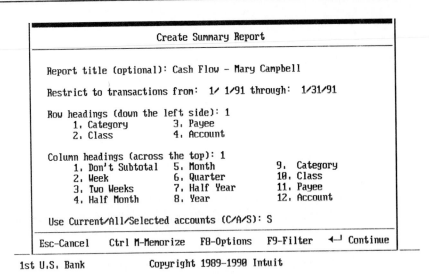

```
                    Create Summary Report
────────────────────────────────────────────────────────────────
Report title (optional): Cash Flow - Mary Campbell

Restrict to transactions from:  1/ 1/91 through:  1/31/91

Row headings (down the left side): 1
       1, Category         3, Payee
       2, Class            4, Account

Column headings (across the top): 1
       1, Don't Subtotal   5, Month        9,  Category
       2, Week             6, Quarter      10, Class
       3, Two Weeks        7, Half Year    11, Payee
       4, Half Month       8, Year         12, Account

Use Current/All/Selected accounts (C/A/S): S
────────────────────────────────────────────────────────────────
Esc-Cancel   Ctrl M-Memorize   F8-Options   F9-Filter   ↵ Continue

1st U,S, Bank          Copyright 1989-1990 Intuit
```

FIGURE 3-6. Create Summary Report window to customize a Cash
Flow report

You can just press (ENTER) if you used this same time period for your last
report.

6. Type **1/91** again.

Pressing (ENTER) will create the report without customizing.

7. Press (F8) to open the Create Summary Report window.

Quicken will respond to your request by displaying the Create Summary
Report window shown in Figure 3-6. Notice that the heading and the dates
from the previous screen are still displayed. You can make further changes if
needed or press (ENTER) four times to move to the Column Headings field.

8. Type **2** and press (ENTER) to select Week.

In addition to the time period you can include either Payee or Category if
you wish (but not both).

9. Type **A** to select All accounts.

10. Press (**ENTER**) to continue.

Quicken displays the completed report on the screen. Figure 3-7 shows the result of the preceding steps.

Changing the Row Headings

The Create Summary Report window shown in Figure 3-6 also allows you to change the row headings shown in a Cash Flow or Itemized Category report. Instead of categories as row headings, as in Figure 3-7, one of your options is to change the screen to show the payee in this location. Figure 3-8 shows the report created after changing the Row Headings field to option 3, Payee, and the column heading back to the default, 1. If you used (**ESC**) to leave the report you just created, you can use (**TAB**) to move from field to field in this window.

```
                          Cash Flow - Mary Campbell
                          1/ 1/91 Through 1/31/91
     1st U.S. Bank                                                    Page  1
     7/ 7/91
                          Week of   Week of   Week of   Week of   Week of   OVERALL
        Category Description  1/ 1     1/ 6     1/13      1/20      1/27      TOTAL
     -----------------------  --------- --------- --------- --------- --------- ---------

     INFLOWS
        Salary Income          0.00    700.00     0.00      0.00      0.00    700.00
                             --------- --------- --------- --------- --------- ---------
        TOTAL INFLOWS          0.00    700.00     0.00      0.00      0.00    700.00

     OUTFLOWS
        Groceries              0.00     22.32    43.00      0.00      0.00     65.32
        Housing                0.00    150.00     0.00      0.00      0.00    150.00
        Miscellaneous         16.50      0.00     0.00      0.00      0.00     16.50
        Telephone Expense      0.00      0.00     0.00     19.75      0.00     19.75
        Water, Gas, Electric  67.50      0.00     0.00      0.00      0.00     67.50
                             --------- --------- --------- --------- --------- ---------
        TOTAL OUTFLOWS        84.00    172.32    43.00     19.75      0.00    319.07


                             --------- --------- --------- --------- --------- ---------
        OVERALL TOTAL        -84.00    527.68   -43.00    -19.75      0.00    380.93
                             ========= ========= ========= ========= ========= =========
```

═══ **FIGURE 3-7.** Weekly report for cash flow

```
                        Cash Flow - Mary Campbell
                          1/ 1/91 Through 1/31/91
     1st U.S. Bank                                              Page   1
     7/ 7/91
                                                    1/ 1/91-
                              Payee                  1/31/91
                     -------------------------  -----------
                     Deposit - Salary               700.00
                     Small City Apartments         -150.00
                     Small City Gas & Light         -67.50
                     Small City Market              -65.32
                     Small City Phone Company       -19.75
                     Small City Times               -16.50
                                                -----------
                     OVERALL TOTAL                  380.93
                                                ===========
```

FIGURE 3-8.   Using payee names as row headings

Changing the Report Options

You can also access a second set of options from the Create Summary Report window by pressing (F8), Options, to display the Report Options window for the Cash Flow report. The options allow you to select report organization and determine how transfers are handled. The Report Options window for the Itemized Category report has a few more items at the bottom compared to the Cash Flow report, as shown in Figure 3-9.

The Report Organization field allows you to change from the default organization of separate totals for income and expenses to one that shows the cash flow basis.

The Transfers field allows you to define how you want your reports to handle transfers between accounts. For example, when Quicken transfers cash from your check register to your savings register, do you want them included or excluded from the individual reports? These will be covered in more detail in Chapter 10.

The extra items at the bottom of the Report Options window for the Itemized Category report allow you to specify that any combination of totals, memos, and categories, or any one of these alone, are shown on the report. Notice that you have the option of showing "cents," subcategories, and subclasses in the report form. The default setting for both options is "Y."

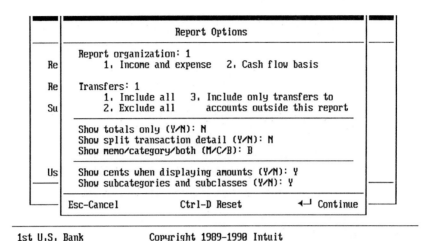

FIGURE 3-9. Report Options for Itemized Category report

Filtering Reports

Filters allow you to select the data to be shown on a report. You can choose to show a specific payee, memo field matches, or category matches. This allows you to create a report for all entries relating to utilities or groceries, for example. You can use a standard report form to display a report for a specific payee, such as Small City Times, or you can use the matching capability shown in Chapter 2 to look for any field that starts with "Small" (by entering **Small..**) or that ends in "Market" (by entering **..Market**). The Filter Report menus are opened from the customization menu report by pressing (**F9**).

The Filter Report option for the Itemized Category Report window is shown in Figure 3-10. The window currently shows "Small.." in the Payee field. Processing this request will create a report of all the records with a Payee entry beginning with "Small." This item allows you to modify the printed report further by limiting the report to transactions meeting the following criteria: payee, memo, category, and class matches. Remember that the matches you designate must be exact to be included in the report.

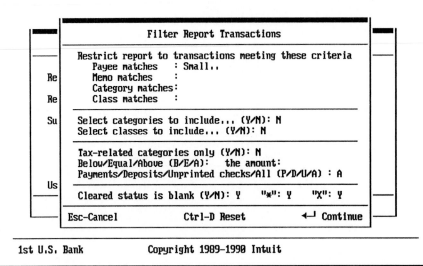

```
                    Filter Report Transactions

     Restrict report to transactions meeting these criteria
          Payee matches    : Small..
Re        Memo matches     :
          Category matches:
Re        Class matches    :

Su   Select categories to include... (Y/N): N
     Select classes to include... (Y/N): N

     Tax-related categories only (Y/N): N
     Below/Equal/Above (B/E/A):   the amount:
     Payments/Deposits/Unprinted checks/All (P/D/U/A) : A
Us
     Cleared status is blank (Y/N): Y      "*": Y      "X": Y

     Esc-Cancel          Ctrl-D Reset          ←┘ Continue
```

1st U.S. Bank   Copyright 1989-1990 Intuit

FIGURE 3-10.   Filter Report Transactions window for Itemized
Category report

The Filter Report window provides many additional options. You can designate whether to include transactions below, equal to, or above a designated amount. To do this, move to the item "Below/Equal/Above" by pressing (ENTER) or (TAB), typing **B**, **E**, or **A**, and pressing (ENTER) again. Next, you would enter the amount to be used in the comparison and press (ENTER).

The next field on the Filter Report window allows you to limit printing to payments, deposits, unprinted checks, or all if you enter a **P**, a **D**, a **U**, or an **A** in this field.

Try Quicken's Filter feature now to create a Cash Flow report for all the transactions that begin with Small in the Payee field. From the Main Menu, complete the following steps:

1. Type **3** to open the Reports menu.

2. Type **1** to open the Personal Reports menu.

3. Type **1** to open the Cash Flow Report window.

4. Type a new title and press (ENTER) or press (ENTER) without an entry to accept the current title.

5. Check the From and Through dates and type **1/91** if either date does not contain this entry.

6. Press (F9) to activate the Filter window.

7. Type **Small..** and press (CTRL)-(ENTER) to return to the Cash Flow Report window.

8. Press (ENTER) to create the report.

Since it shows categories for the row headings, you cannot tell if the correct information is displayed, but you can make a customization to have Quicken list the payee names.

9. Press (ESC) to remove the report from your screen.

10. Press (F8) and then press (ENTER) three times to move to the Row headings item.

11. Type **3** to select Payee and press (ENTER) twice.

12. Type **A** for All accounts and then press (ENTER) to create the report with the payee as the left row heading.

13. Press (ESC) four times to back out to the Main Menu.

Working with Category Totals

You can create an Itemized Category report that only shows the totals. To create a total report for January transactions, follow these steps (starting from the Main Menu):

1. Type **3** to open the Reports menu.

2. Type **1** to open the Personal Reports menu.

3. Type **3** to open the Itemized Category Report window.

4. Press ⌈**ENTER**⌋ to accept the default title.

5. Type **1/91** and press ⌈**ENTER**⌋ for the date if the field does not already contain 1/91. Type **1/91** for the Through date, if it contains a different entry.

6. Press ⌈**F8**⌋ to open the Create Transaction Report window.

7. Press ⌈**F8**⌋ to open the Report Options window.

8. Press ⌈**ENTER**⌋ or ⌈**TAB**⌋ to move to Show totals only and type **Y**.

9. Press ⌈**CTRL**⌋-⌈**ENTER**⌋ to return to the Create Transaction window.

10. Press ⌈**CTRL**⌋-⌈**ENTER**⌋ again to create the report.

WIDE REPORTS

Some of the Quicken reports contain too much information to fit across one screen. You encountered a wide screen report in this chapter when you prepared the Itemized Category report. Although you cannot see the entire report on the screen at once, you can use the arrow keys to navigate around the screen and change the portion of the report that you are viewing.

Quicken automatically prints wide reports on multiple pages. You can tape the sheets together, or if your printer permits, you can use special features such as landscape printing (with the paper turned sideways) on a laser printer, or compressed characters on laser or dot matrix printers. You will learn how to make these changes to the print settings later in this chapter. For now, all you need to know is how Quicken handles a report that is too wide for the screen and how you will navigate to look at the different parts of the screen.

You can tell when you are viewing a wide report by the border framing that Quicken uses. When a complete report is shown, all the edges are framed. When only a partial report is displayed, the edges where there is additional information do not have a frame. When you initially view a wide report, there is no frame on the right edge. You will notice the arrows displayed in the lower-right corner of the screen, indicating the report extension.

Moving Around the Screen

You can move around the report by using the arrow keys. In addition, you may want to move quickly around the report by using several other Quicken keystrokes.

- Press `TAB` or `CTRL`-`RIGHT ARROW` to move one full screen to the right.

- Press `SHIFT`-`TAB` or `CTRL`-`LEFT ARROW` to move one full screen to the left.

- Press `PGUP` to move up one screen.

- Press `PGDN` to move down one screen

- Press `HOME` to move to the upper-left corner of the report.

- Press `END` to move to the lower-right corner of the report.

Full- and Half-Column Options

The Itemized Category report allows you to view the Payee, Memo, and Category fields at full or half width. Figure 3-11 shows the report at the default half-column width setting. This allows the report to print across 80 columns and to display on the screen. To expand the columns to full width press `F9`. Once the columns are shown at full width, pressing `F9` again returns the columns to half width. This kind of key is called a *toggle*.

```
                        ITEMIZED CATEGORY REPORT
                          1/ 1/91 Through 1/31/91
1st U.S. Bank
7/ 7/91

Date   Num      Description        Memo          Category      Clr Amount


       INCOME/EXPENSE
         INCOME
           Salary Income

1/ 7        Deposit-Salary      Monthly pay    Salary              700.00

            Total Salary Income                                    700.00

         TOTAL INCOME                                              700.00


       EXPENSES                                                          ↓

1st U.S. Bank
Esc-Create report   Ctrl M-Memorize   F1-Help   F8-Print  F9-Full column width
```

FIGURE 3-11. Using the default half-column width display for the Itemized Category report

Printing Wide Reports

Quicken normally prints wide reports by printing in vertical strips, which you can then tape together. You do not have to modify your printing instructions in order to print wide reports.

If your printer supports compressed or landscape printing, you can capture more of a report on a page by using one of these features. Landscape mode will print 104 characters across an 11-by-8 1/2-inch page and compressed print will print 132 characters on an 8 1/2-by-11-inch page (at 10 characters per inch). You can use the Change Settings option in the Main Menu, or, when the report is displayed on the screen, go to the Print Report window (F8) and choose Set up printer (F9) to change the settings before printing.

CHANGING THE PRINTER SETTINGS

Unless you want to use a special feature or the current settings are not working properly, you can skip this section. If you choose to go through this section, be sure to have your printer manual handy to check the specific features offered by your printer.

Quicken allows you to set printer parameters for up to three printers or to set up one printer to interface with Quicken in three different modes: the report printer, an alternate report printer, and a check writing printer. The procedure is identical for modifying any of these options once you choose the one you want to change.

As discussed earlier, Quicken is preset to interface with most popular printers. The preset parameters are for a pitch of 10 characters per inch and use of the parallel printer port 1 (LPT1).

You can change the printer settings by selecting option 5, Change Settings, from Quicken's Main Menu and then selecting option 4 to alter the print settings. Another way to accomplish the same task is to press (F8) to open the Print Report window when a Quicken report is displayed on your screen, and then choose Set Up Printer ((F9)). The menus and screens presented will be identical either way. The following example was developed by changing the settings once the report was displayed on the screen.

Once you have a Quicken report displayed, follow these steps to change the print settings:

1. Press (F8) to open the Print Report window.

Quicken displays the Print Report window shown here:

```
┌────────────────────────────────────────────────────────────┐
│ ▬▬▬▬▬▬▬▬▬▬▬▬▬▬▬▬▬▬▬▬▬▬▬▬▬▬▬▬▬▬▬▬▬▬▬▬▬▬▬▬▬▬                  │
│                     Print Report                             │
│ ─────────────────────────────────────────────────────────── │
│                                                              │
│   Print to: 1                                                │
│         1. Report Printer       4. Disk (ASCII file)         │
│         2. Alt Report Printer   5. Disk (1-2-3 file)         │
│         3. Check Printer                                     │
│                                                              │
│   ────────────────────────────────────────────────────────  │
│                  Position paper in printer                   │
│    Esc-Cancel        F9-Set Up Printer         ◄┘ Print      │
└────────────────────────────────────────────────────────────┘
```

If you want to print with one of the default settings, choose option 1 or 2.

2. Press (F9) to select Set Up Printer.

From this step on you will not be able to make the same entries shown in the example. Since each printer is different, you will want to configure Quicken to work with your printer rather than the printer used here. Quicken displays a list of the three printer settings that can be changed: Check Printer Settings, Report Printer Settings, and Alternate Report Settings.

3. Type **1** to choose Check Printer Settings.

Quicken will display a list of printers and their options, like the ones in Figure 3-12. You can move in this list with the arrow keys to locate the printer type that you have. Notice that the list for the HP LaserJet II also contains a Report Printing option. This option corresponds to standard 10-pitch printing, which is the default. Other options include Compressed, Landscape, and a combined Landscape and Compressed. If you select Compressed or Landscape modes (or both), Quicken alters the report display to correspond to your selection.

4. Move the cursor to the desired option and press (**ENTER**). Quicken displays a screen like the one in Figure 3-13. The default is to print to LPT1, which is the standard port on your machine for connecting the first printer. If you are setting up a second printer, you need to know whether it is attached to LPT2 or some other port. Other settings let you set the

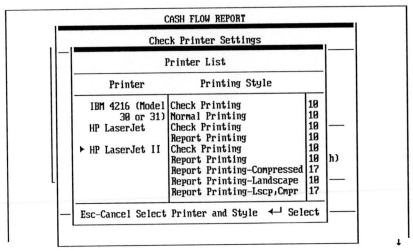

FIGURE 3-12. Selecting a printer and style

```
┌──────────────────────────────────────────────────────────┐
│                     CASH FLOW REPORT                       │
│  ┌──────────────────────────────────────────────────┐     │
│  │              Check Printer Settings               │     │
│  │                                                    │     │
│  │  Name of printer (optional): HP LJetII-Checks      │     │
│  │  Print to: 2                                       │     │
│  │        1. PRN:      4. LPT3:      7. COM2:         │     │
│  │        2. LPT1:     5. AUX:                        │     │
│  │        3. LPT2:     6. COM1:                       │     │
│  │  Indent: 0                                         │     │
│  │  ────────────────────────────────────────────     │     │
│  │           Settings for this printing style        │     │
│  │  Lines per page: 63          Print pitch: 10       │     │
│  │  Characters per line: 80     (characters per inch) │     │
│  │  Pause between pages (Y/N): N                      │     │
│  │  ────────────────────────────────────────────     │     │
│  │  Page-oriented (e.g. laser) printer (Y/N): Y       │     │
│  │  Supports IBM graphics characters (Y/N): N         │     │
│  │  ────────────────────────────────────────────     │     │
│  │  F8-Edit Control Codes   F9-Select Printer From List│    │
│  │  Esc-Cancel                          ◄─┘ Continue  │     │
│  └──────────────────────────────────────────────────┘     │
│  1st U.S. Bank                                             │
└──────────────────────────────────────────────────────────┘
```

FIGURE 3-13.   Choosing specific print settings

lines per page, characters per line, print pitch, and a pause between pages. Table 3-1 lists some hints for altering these settings, although your printer manual will be your specific reference source.

Problem	Solution
Output too wide for a page	Use compressed or landscape mode
No form feed at the end of the report	Change the print control codes
Partial blank page left in printer	Check the page length
Unreadable output	Wrong printer is selected
Strange characters print	Printer cable is loose or incorrect printer type selected
Unable to access font cartridges	Set control codes for desired print options

TABLE 3-1.   Printing Problems and Possible Solutions

5. Press ⟨F8⟩ to display the control codes that are transmitted to your printer every time you print.

Figure 3-14 provides an example of printer control codes generated by Quicken for the HP LaserJet II. You can change these codes to use different fonts, line widths, and so on. Knowing which codes to use is a bit tricky unless you are familiar with your printer manual. Each manufacturer uses different codes to represent the various print features. For now, press ⟨ENTER⟩ to move through them without making changes or press ⟨ESC⟩. Quicken will take you back to the Check Printer Settings window.

6. Press ⟨CTRL⟩-⟨ENTER⟩ to view the Print Report window.

Note that the new selection is now an option in this window.

7. Type the number of the printer you wish to use and press ⟨ENTER⟩.

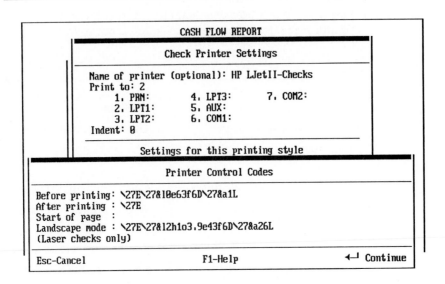

FIGURE 3-14. HP LaserJet II control codes generated by Quicken

chapter 4

RECONCILING YOUR QUICKEN REGISTER

Quicken's Reconciliation Process
Quicken's Reconciliation Reports
Additional Reconciliation Issues and Features

Reconciling your account is the process of comparing your entries with those of the bank. This allows you to determine whether differences between the bank's record of your balance and your record are due to errors or *timing differences*. Timing differences occur because your balance is accurate up to the present date, but the bank records were compiled at an earlier date, before transactions you have recorded cleared the bank. These timing differences must be reconciled to ensure there is no discrepancy caused by an error. If you are serious about monitoring your financial activities, a monthly reconciliation of your checking accounts, both personal and business, should be considered a necessary step in your financial record keeping.

In addition to the timing differences there may be transactions not recorded in your register or errors in the amount entries. With manual check registers there can also be addition and subtraction errors when checks and deposits are recorded. This is one error you do not need to worry about with Quicken, since its calculations are always perfect if you record the amount correctly.

Another cause of differences is transactions the bank has recorded on your bank statement that you haven't entered in your register. For example, you may have automatic monthly withdrawals for house or automobile payments or savings transfers to another bank account or mutual fund. In addition, you may have a bank service charge for maintaining your checking account or printing checks, or you may have earned interest. These differences will be addressed in more detail throughout this chapter.

In this chapter you will look at how reconciliation works and walk through a reconciliation exercise. The last part of the chapter deals with problems that can occur and the methods for getting your account to agree with your bank's records. This part of the chapter does not require entries, since it is designed to show potential problems rather than additional corrections to your entries.

QUICKEN'S RECONCILIATION PROCESS

Quicken reduces the frustration of the monthly reconciliation process by providing a systematic approach to reconciling your checking accounts. Since there are more steps in this process than in the exercises you have completed so far, looking at some overview information first will help you place each of the steps in perspective to the overall objective of the process.

A Few Key Points

There are three points to remember when using the Quicken reconciliation system. First, Quicken will only reconcile one checking account at a time, so you will have to reconcile each of your personal and business accounts separately.

Second, you should make it a habit to reconcile your checking accounts on a monthly basis. You can easily monitor your checking balances once you begin a monthly routine of reconciling your accounts, but attempting to reconcile six months of statements at one sitting is a frustrating experience, even with Quicken.

Third, before beginning the formal Quicken reconciliation process, visually examine your bank statement and look for any unusual entries, such as check numbers that are out of the range of numbers you expected to find on the statement. (If you find checks 501 and 502 clearing, while all the rest of the checks are numbered in the 900s, you might find the bank has charged another customer's checks against your account.) This examination provides an indication of what you will look for during the reconciliation process.

An Overview of the Process

When you begin reconciliation, Quicken asks for information from your current bank statement, such as the opening and ending dollar balances, service charges, and any interest earned on your account. (Quicken also records these transactions in the check register and marks them as cleared since the bank has already processed these items.)

Once you have entered this preparatory information, Quicken presents a summary screen for marking cleared items. All the transactions you recorded in the 1st U.S. Bank account, as well as the service charge and interest-earned transactions, are shown on this screen.

Quicken maintains a running total of your balance as you proceed through the reconciliation process. Each debit or credit is applied to the opening balance total as it is marked cleared. You can determine the difference between the Cleared Balance Amount and the Bank Statement Balance at any time. Your end objective is a difference of zero.

The first step is to check the amounts of your Quicken entries against the bank statement. Where there are discrepancies you can switch to your Quicken register and check the entries. You may find incorrect amounts recorded in the Quicken register or by your bank. You may also find that you forgot to record a check or a deposit. You can create or change register entries from the Register window.

Once you have finished with the entry, you put an asterisk (*) in the C column to mark the transaction as cleared. After resolving any differences between your balance and the bank's you can print the reconciliation reports. The asterisks are used in the cleared column until Quicken confirms an entry. Then Quicken automatically replaces them with an "X," which you will see as this lesson proceeds.

Preparing the Printer for Reconciliation

Before you begin reconciliation you should check your printer settings. This is important because at the end of the reconciliation process you will be given an opportunity to print reconciliation reports. You can't change printer settings after Quicken presents you with the Print Reconciliation Report window; it's too late. If you attempt to make a change by pressing (ESC), you will be returned to the Main Menu and will have to start over. However, you will not need to complete the detailed reconciliation procedure again.

Use the Check Printer Settings window to check your printer settings now. When you return to the Main Menu you will be ready to start the reconciliation example.

A Sample Reconciliation

From reading about the objectives of the reconciliation process you should understand its purpose in concept. Actually doing a reconciliation will fit the pieces together. The following exercise uses a sample bank statement and the entries you made to your register in Chapter 2. These steps assume that you are starting from the Main Menu:

1. Type **2** to enter the register.

You should be in the 1st U.S. Bank register with the entries created in Chapter 2.

2. Press the (F6) key.

Quicken displays the pull-down Activities menu shown here:

```
▶ 1. Write Checks    Ctrl-W

  2. Reconcile
  3. Order Supplies

  4. Calculator      Ctrl-O
  5. Use DOS
```

3. Type **2** again to enter Quicken's reconciliation system.

You will see the Reconcile Register with Bank Statement window, shown in Figure 4-1. Figure 4-2 is a copy of your first bank statement from 1st U.S. Bank; you will use it to respond to Quicken's prompts for information.

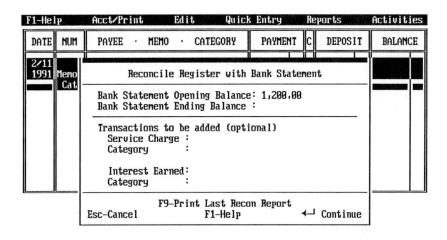

FIGURE 4-1. Reconcile Register with Bank Statement window

4. Press (ENTER) to accept 1,200.00 as the beginning balance in the Bank Statement Opening Balance field. Notice that no dollar sign is required here.

The first time you reconcile an account, Quicken automatically enters the opening balance shown in the register. Since you are reconciling your account with the first monthly bank statement, this should be the balance on your screen.

5. Type **1398.21** and press (ENTER) to complete the Bank Statement Ending Balance field.

6. Type **11.50** and press (ENTER) to complete the Service Charge field.

You must enter all the service and similar charges in a lump sum. In this case the bank has a monthly service charge and a check printing charge that total 11.50 (3.50 + 8.00). Although it is easy enough to add these two simple numbers in your head, if you need to compute a more complex addition, you can always call up the Calculator with (CTRL)-(0). You would type the first number you want to add, press (+), then type the next number, and so on. You can transfer the total into a numeric field on the screen with (F9).

```
1st U.S. Bank                          DATE   2/5/91
P.O. Box 123
Small City, USA                        PAGE  1    OF  1
```

```
John D. Quick
P.O. Box ABC
Small City, USA
```

DATE	DESCRIPTION	AMOUNT	BALANCE
1-2	Deposit	1,200.00	1,200.00
1-6	100 check	77.50-	1,122.50
1-7	Deposit	700.00	1,822.50
1-10	101 check	16.50-	1,806.00
1-11	103 check	150.00-	1,656.00
1-20	102 check	22.32-	1,633.68
2-1	Loan payment deduction	225.00-	1,408.68
2-1	Service Charge	11.50-	1,397.18
2-1	Interest	1.03	1,398.21

Date	Check	No.	Amount
1-6	#	100	77.50-
1-10	#	101	16.50-
1-20	#	102	22.32-
1-11	#	103	150.00-

STATEMENT

FIGURE 4-2.   Bank statement for 1st U.S. Bank account

7. Type **Misc** and press (ENTER).

Entering a category is optional; however, to take full advantage of Quicken's reporting features, you should use a category for all transactions.

8. Type **1.03** and press (ENTER) to complete the Interest Earned field.

9. Type **Int Inc** and press (ENTER).

Figure 4-3 appears on the screen. This is a summary screen where you will mark cleared items. It also shows totals at the bottom. You will find all your register entries and the new service charge and interest transactions in this window. Note that the new transactions are marked as cleared with an asterisk in the C column. Also note that the cleared balance shown is your opening balance of 1,200.00 modified by the two new transactions. Quicken also monitors the difference between this cleared total and the bank statement balance. The date shown for the service charge and interest earned is the current date. Since your date might be before or after the date shown in the example, your transaction could cause a difference in the balance shown.

10. The cursor in the left margin will point to the 1/7/91 deposit. Press (SPACEBAR) after verifying this is the amount shown on your bank statement.

Note that Quicken enters an * in the C column on this screen and also in the C field of your check register.

11. Press (DOWN ARROW) four times and the arrow cursor will point to the entry for check number 100. Since the bank statement entry and the summary entry do not agree, press (F9).

Figure 4-4 will be shown on your screen. The transaction for check number 100 is highlighted in the 1st U.S. Bank register. If you looked at your canceled check for this transaction, you would see that it was for 77.50 and it cleared the bank for that amount. Since the register entry is wrong, you must make a correction.

12. Press (SHIFT)-(TAB), type **77.50**, and press (ENTER).

Because you pressed (F9) in the previous step, your cursor was in the C column. This step lines your cursor up with the beginning of the payment field and allows you to enter the new figure.

```
F1-Help        Acct/Print       Edit      Quick Entry     Reports    Activities
```

NUM	C	AMOUNT	DATE	PAYEE	MEMO
▶		700.00	1/ 7/91	Deposit-Salary	Monthly pay
		25.00	2/10/91	Dividend check	Dividends check from
	*	1.03	7/ 7/91	Interest Earned	
	*	-11.50	7/ 7/91	Service Charge	
100		-67.50	1/ 4/91	Small City Gas & Light	Gas and Electric
101		-16.50	1/ 5/91	Small City Times	Paper bill
102		-22.32	1/ 7/91	Small City Market	Food
103		-150.00	1/ 7/91	Small City Apartments	Rent
104		-43.00	1/19/91	Small City Market	Food
105		-19.75	1/25/91	Small City Phone Compa	Phone bill

```
■ To Mark Cleared Items, press Space Bar   ■ To Add or Change Items, press F9
```

RECONCILIATION SUMMARY
Items You Have Marked Cleared (*)

1	Checks, Debits	-11.50	Cleared (X,*) Balance	1,189.53
1	Deposits, Credits	1.03	Bank Statement Balance	1,398.21
			Difference	-208.68

```
F1-Help          F8-Mark Range        F9-View as Register       Ctrl F10-Done
```

FIGURE 4-3. Screen for marking cleared items

```
F1-Help  F2-Acct/Print   F3-Edit   F4-Quick Entry  F5-Reports   F6-Activities
```

DATE	NUM	PAYEE · MEMO · CATEGORY	PAYMENT	C	DEPOSIT	BALANCE
1/ 4 1991	100	Small City Gas & Light Memo: Gas and Electric Cat: Utilities	67 50			1,132 50
1/ 5 1991	101	Small City Times Paper bill Misc	16 50			1,116 00
1/ 7 1991		Deposit-Salary Monthly pay Salary		*	700 00	1,816 00
1/ 7 1991	102	Small City Market Food Groceries	22 32			1,793 68

RECONCILIATION SUMMARY
Items You Have Marked Cleared (*)

1	Checks, Debits	-11.50	Cleared (X,*) Balance	1,809.53
2	Deposits, Credits	701.03	Bank Statement Balance	1,398.21
			Difference	491.32

```
Esc-Main Menu     F8-Mark Range        F9-View as List           Ctrl F10-Done
```

FIGURE 4-4. Check Register window

13. The cursor is now in the blank C column; type * and press (ENTER).

14. Press (F9) and type 1 when you see the Leaving Transaction window.

Quicken will enter the changes and return to the Uncleared Transaction List window. Notice that you have corrected the amount to 77.50 and that Quicken indicates that the account has been reconciled by the * in the C column.

15. Press (F8) and the Mark Range of Check Numbers as Cleared window will appear.

This Quicken feature allows you to simultaneously mark a series of checks as having cleared the bank during the reconciling period, provided that the checks are consecutive. Before typing the range of checks to be cleared, remember to compare the amounts shown in the uncleared transaction list with the bank statement amounts. Marking a range of check numbers only works when the amounts are the same.

16. Type **101** and press (ENTER).

17. Type **103** and press (ENTER).

Your screen will show that 101 through 103 have had an asterisk added to the cleared column. Notice that your "Difference" amount is 225.00. When you check the bank statement, you might remember that this difference corresponds to the amount of the automatic deduction for an automobile loan you have with 1st U.S. Bank. Since this amount is not shown on your list of uncleared items, the transaction is not yet recorded in your register.

18. Press (F9) to view the register.

19. Press (CTRL)-(END) to move to the end of the register, then press (HOME) twice to move to the first field.

20. Type **2/1/91** in the date column and press (ENTER) twice.

You enter the date 2/1/91 in the date column so the transaction will be recorded on the same date that the bank deducted the amount from your account. You can record the date as the current date if you wish. (ENTER) is pressed twice to move to the Payee field; since this is an automatic deduction, you don't use a check number.

21. Type **Automatic Loan Payment** in the Payee field and press (ENTER).

22. Type **225** in the Payment field and press (ENTER).

23. Type * in the C field and press (ENTER).

24. Press (ENTER) again to move the cursor to the Memo field.

25. Type **Auto payment** and press (ENTER).

26. Press (CTRL)-(C). Press (DOWN ARROW) twice and press (ENTER). This step demonstrates how you can enter a category from Quicken's category list without typing in a category name.

27. Press (CTRL)-(ENTER) to record the transaction.

The transaction will be inserted in the correct date location in the register and the Difference field will indicate that you have balanced your checking account for this month by showing an amount of 0.00. If you move the highlight to the location for the date 2/1, your screen will look like Figure 4-5. You can complete the reconciliation from this screen or press (F9) and return to the List of Uncleared Items screen and end the reconciliation process.

28. Press (CTRL)-(F10) and the Congratulations! Your Account Balances window appears.

```
F1-Help  F2-Acct/Print  F3-Edit  F4-Quick Entry  F5-Reports  F6-Activities

DATE  NUM      PAYEE · MEMO · CATEGORY      PAYMENT  C  DEPOSIT   BALANCE

2/ 1          Automatic Loan Payment          225 00 *|   °       1,345 93
1991 Memo:    Auto payment
     Cat:     Auto Loan
2/10          Dividend check                            25 00     1,370 93
1991          Dividends check→Div Income
2/11          Service Charge                   11 50 *            1,359 43
1991                         Misc
2/11          Interest Earned                        *|   1 03    1,360 46
1991                         Int Inc

                    RECONCILIATION SUMMARY
     Items You Have Marked Cleared (*)
                                      Cleared (X,*) Balance   1,398.21
     6   Checks, Debits    -502.82    Bank Statement Balance  1,398.21
     2   Deposits, Credits  701.03    Difference                  0.00

Esc-Main Menu    F8-Mark Range    F9-View as List    Ctrl F10-Done
```

FIGURE 4-5. Additional entries in the Check Register window

29. Type **Y** and press (**ENTER**); the Print Reconciliation Report window, shown in Figure 4-6, appears. If you have not turned your printer on, you should do so now.

You must complete this window to print the reconciliation reports. As explained in the section preceding step 1, it is too late to change your printer settings at this point.

30. Press (**ENTER**) if Quicken displays the desired printer.

31. Type **2/11/91** and press (**ENTER**).

This changes the reconciliation date to conform to the example date.

32. Press (**ENTER**) to accept the default heading for the report.

33. Type **F** and press (**ENTER**) to select Full report.

You have now completed your reconciliation process, and Quicken is printing your reconciliation reports.

34. When printing stops, press (**ESC**) to close the Print Reconciliation window.

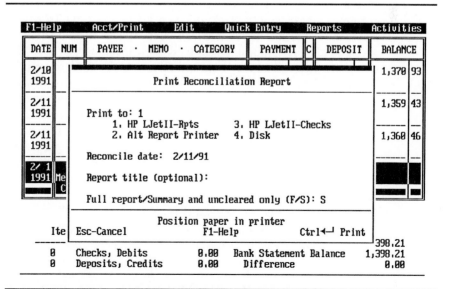

FIGURE 4-6.   Print Reconciliation Report window

After 1990, interest expense for consumer items is not a tax deductible expense. If the automobile is used for business, the interest is tax deductible beyond 1990. Later in the book you will be shown how to modify the category to provide for this.

QUICKEN'S RECONCILIATION REPORTS

Since you selected Quicken's Full Report option, you have received four reconciliation reports entitled Reconciliation Summary, Cleared Transaction Detail, Uncleared Transaction Detail Up to 2/11/91, and Uncleared Transaction Detail After 2/11/91. Some of these reports are shown in Figures 4-7 through 4-9. (Note that spacing in these figures may differ from what appears on your screen because adjustments had to be made to fit all of the on-screen material onto these pages.)

The Reconciliation Summary, shown in Figure 4-7, shows the beginning balance of 1,200.00 and summarizes the activity the bank reported for your account during the reconciliation period in the section labeled "BANK STATEMENT − CLEARED TRANSACTIONS:." The first part of the section headed "YOUR RECORDS − UNCLEARED TRANSACTIONS:." summarizes the difference between your register balance at the date of the reconciliation, 2/11/91, and the bank's balance. In this case there are two checks that have been written and one deposit made to your account that were not shown on the bank statement. The final part of this section shows any checks and deposits recorded since the reconciliation date. In your sample reconciliation, no transactions were entered after 2/11/91, so the register balance at that date is also the register ending balance.

The Cleared Transaction Detail report, shown in Figure 4-8, provides a detailed list with sections called "Cleared Checks and Payments" and "Cleared Deposits and Other Credits"; the items they contain were part of the reconciliation process. Notice that this report provides detail for the Cleared Transaction section of the Reconciliation Summary report.

The Uncleared Transaction Detail Up to 2/11/91 report, shown in Figure 4-9, in sections headed "Uncleared Checks and Payments" and "Uncleared Deposits and Other Credits," provides the details of uncleared transactions included in your register up to the date of the reconciliation. This report provides detail for the Uncleared Transactions section of the Reconciliation Summary report.

```
                              Reconciliation Report
      1st U.S. Bank                                                    Page 1
      2/11/91
                              RECONCILIATION SUMMARY

          BANK STATEMENT -- CLEARED TRANSACTIONS:

             Previous Balance:                                    1,200.00
                                                                 --------------
                 Checks and Payments:        6 Items               -502.82
                 Deposits and Other Credits: 2 Items                701.03
                                                                 --------------
             Ending Balance of Bank Statement:                   1,398.21

          YOUR RECORDS -- UNCLEARED TRANSACTIONS:

             Cleared Balance:                                     1,398.21
                                                                 --------------
                 Checks and Payments:        2 Items               -62.75
                 Deposits and Other Credits: 1 Item                 25.00
                                                                 --------------
             Register Balance as of  2/11/91:                    1,360.46
                                                                 --------------
                 Checks and Payments:        0 Items                 0.00
                 Deposits and Other Credits: 0 Items                 0.00
                                                                 --------------
             Register Ending Balance:                            1,360.46
```

FIGURE 4-7. Reconciliation Summary report

The Uncleared Transaction Detail After 2/11/91 report (not shown) provides detail for those transactions that are recorded in the check register after the date of the reconciliation report. In this illustration there were no transactions recorded; this is shown in the final section of the Reconciliation Summary report.

These four reports are all printed automatically when you select Quicken's Full Report option. If you had selected Quicken's Summary option, which is the default option, you would have received only the Reconciliation Summary report and the Uncleared Transaction Detail Up to 2/11/91 report.

ADDITIONAL RECONCILIATION ISSUES AND FEATURES

The reconciliation procedures shown earlier provide a foundation for using Quicken to reconcile your accounts. However, there are some additional issues covered in this section that may prove useful in balancing your accounts in the future.

```
                              Reconciliation Report
        1st U.S. Bank                                              Page 2
        2/11/91              CLEARED TRANSACTION DETAIL


          Date    Num       Payee          Memo        Category     Clr    Amount
        --------  ------  ----------------  ----------------  ----------------  ---  ------------

        Cleared Checks and Payments

        1/ 4/91  100    Small City Gas &  Gas and Electri  Utilities     X     -77.50
        1/ 5/91  101    Small City Times  Paper bill       Misc          X     -16.50
        1/ 7/91  102    Small City Marke  Food             Groceries     X     -22.32
        1/ 7/91  103    Small City Apart  Rent             Housing       X    -150.00
        2/ 1/91         Automatic Loan P  Auto payment     Auto Loan     X    -225.00
        2/11/91         Service Charge                     Misc          X     -11.50
                                                                             ------------
        Total Cleared Checks and Payments                 6 Items          -502.82

        Cleared Deposits and Other Credits
        1/ 7/91         Deposit-Salary Monthly pay        Salary        X     700.00
        2/11/91         Interest Earned                   Int Inc       X       1.03
                                                                             ------------
        Total Cleared Deposits and Other Credits          2 Items           701.03
                                                                             ============
        Total Cleared Transactions                        8 Items           198.21
```

FIGURE 4-8. Cleared Transaction Detail report

```
                              Reconciliation Report
        1st U.S. Bank                                              Page 3
        2/11/91
                    UNCLEARED TRANSACTION DETAIL UP TO 2/11/91

          Date    Num       Payee          Memo        Category     Clr    Amount
        --------  -----   ----------------  ----------------  --------------  ---  -----------

        Uncleared Checks and Payments
        1/19/91  104    Small City Marke  Food             Groceries          -43.00
        1/25/91  105    Small City Phone  Phone bill       Telephone          -19.75
                                                                            ----------
        Total Uncleared Checks and Payments               2 Items           -62.75

        Uncleared Deposits and Other Credits
        2/10/91         Dividend check    Dividends check  Div Income          25.00
                                                                            ----------
        Total Uncleared Deposits and Other Credits        1 Item             25.00

                                                                            ==========
        Total Uncleared Transactions                      3 Items           -37.75
```

FIGURE 4-9. Uncleared Transaction Detail Up to 2/11/91 report

Updating Your Opening Balance

The importance of maintaining a regular reconciliation schedule has already been noted and you should balance your checking account before you begin to use Quicken to record your transactions. However, there may be times when the opening balance Quicken enters in the Reconcile Register with Bank Statement window differs from the opening balance shown in the check register.

This can happen in three different situations. First, when you reconcile in Quicken the first time, there may be a discrepancy due to timing differences. Second, there may be a difference if you start Quicken at a point other than the beginning of the year and then try to add transactions from earlier in the year. Third, balances may differ if you use the reconciliation feature *after* recording Quicken transactions for several periods.

FIRST TIME RECONCILIATIONS   If you open a new account and begin to use Quicken immediately, there will not be a discrepancy, but a discrepancy will occur if you do not enter the first transaction or two in Quicken. For example, suppose you opened an account on 12/31/90 for 1,300.00 and immediately wrote a check for a 1990 expenditure of 100.00. Then you decided to start your Quicken register on 1/1/91, when the balance in your manual register was 1,200.00. The bank statement would show the opening balance at 1,300.00. In order to correctly reconcile the difference between the bank statement and the Quicken Register balance on 1/1/91, you can do one of two things.

The first alternative is to open the check register by using (F9) while in the reconciliation procedures. Enter the 100.00 check, correct the opening balance to reflect the beginning bank balance of 1,300.00, and proceed with the reconciliation process.

A second option is to have Quicken enter an adjustment in the reconciliation to correct for the difference between the check register's and the bank statement's beginning balances. When Quicken enters the opening balance as 1,200.00 and you change it to agree with the bank statement's 1,300.00, Quicken will display an Opening Balance Does Not Match Bank window, shown in Figure 4-10, which provides a written description of the nature of the problem and lists steps you might take to correct it. When you press (ENTER) to continue, the lower section of the screen now has an Opening Bal Difference field of −100.00, as shown in Figure 4-11.

At this point, you will have a −100.00 balance in the Opening Bal Difference field. Note that your Difference field in Figure 4-11 is −208.68 at this point. You would proceed through the reconciliation process described in the "A Sample Reconciliation" section of this chapter and have a difference balance of 0.00. To correct the Opening Bal Difference field of

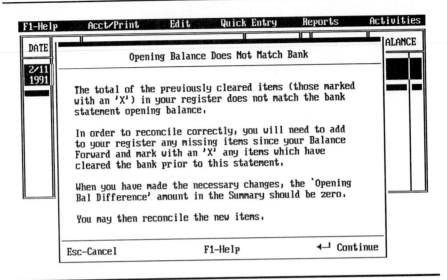

FIGURE 4-10. Opening Balance Does Not Match Bank warning

DATE	NUM	PAYEE · MEMO · CATEGORY	PAYMENT	C	DEPOSIT	BALANCE
2/11 1991	Memo: Cat:	Service Charge / Misc	11 50	*		1,594 43
2/11 1991		Interest Earned / Int Inc		*	1 03	1,595 46
2/11 1991		END				

RECONCILIATION SUMMARY

Items You Have Marked Cleared (*)				
1	Checks, Debits	-11.50	Opening Bal Difference	-100.00
1	Deposits, Credits	1.03	Cleared (X,*) Balance	1,189.53
			Bank Statement Balance	1,398.21
			Difference	-208.68

Esc-Main Menu   F8-Mark Range   F9-View as List   Ctrl F10-Done

FIGURE 4-11. Opening balance difference illustration

−100.00, follow these steps:

1. Press CTRL-END.

Quicken will display a Create Opening Balance Adjustment window and ask whether you want an adjustment made for the difference between the opening bank statement and check register balances: "Add adjustment for $100.00 (Y/N) ?."

2. Type **Y** and press ENTER.

Quicken will then reconcile the balances by making an adjustment to the check register for the 100.00 transaction.

3. Press ENTER and the Problem: Check Register does not balance with Bank Statement window will appear.

4. Press ENTER and the Adding Balance Adjustment Entry window appears.

5. Type **Y** and press ENTER twice; the Register Adjusted to Agree with Statement window will appear.

Note that if you select *N* in any of these windows, you will be returned to the reconciliation process.

6. Type **Y** and press ENTER. Quicken will bring the Print Reconciliation Report window to the screen.

You can now complete the reconciliation report printing process. Your other option is to respond to the prompt by typing **N** and exit the reconciliation process without printing a report.

ADDING PREVIOUS TRANSACTIONS TO QUICKEN You most likely purchased Quicken at a point other than the beginning of your personal or business financial reporting year. In this case you probably started recording your transactions when you purchased Quicken and entered your checking account balance at that time as your opening balance. This discussion assumes that you have been preparing reconciliations using Quicken and now want to go back and record all your previous transactions for the current year in Quicken. Obviously, your bank balance and Quicken balance will not agree after the transactions have been added.

Follow these steps:

1. Since you are going to be adding to your Quicken register, you should be sure to have the latest printout of your Quicken register. If not, print your check register now, before you enter any additional transactions. This gives you a record of your transactions to date, which is important should you later need to reconstruct them.

2. Go to your Quicken Register window and change the date and balance columns to correspond to the bank statement that you used at the beginning of the year.

The importance of saving your earlier bank statements is apparent. Old statements are not only important for the reconstruction of your Quicken system, but also in the event you are audited by the Internal Revenue Service. It only takes one IRS audit to realize the importance of maintaining a complete and accurate history of your financial transactions.

3. Using your manual records and the past bank statements, enter the previous transactions in your Quicken register. Remember to enter bank service charges and automatic payment deductions if you have not been doing so prior to using Quicken.

4. When you have completed the updating process, compare your ending check register balance with the printed copy you made in step 1. This is important because if they do not balance you have made an error in entering your transactions. If this is the case, determine whether the difference is an opening account balance difference or an error. (Your options for fixing any discrepancies between opening balances were described in the preceding section, "First Time Reconciliation.")

5. The next time you reconcile your Quicken account (assuming you have reconciled the account before), type the opening balance on the latest bank statement over that provided by Quicken in the Reconcile Register with Bank Statement window.

6. Before completing the new reconciliation, go to the check register and type **X** to indicate the cleared transactions in the C column for all transactions that have cleared in previous months.

7. Reconcile the current month's transaction. (Go to the section "A Sample Reconciliation" if you need help.)

FIRST TIME RECONCILIATION FOR EXISTING USERS Although you may have been using Quicken for some time, you may not have used the reconciliation feature before. The recommended process is as follows:

1. Begin with the first bank statement, and start reconciling each of the past bank statements as if you were reconciling your account upon receipt of each of the statements, as described in this chapter.

2. Follow this process for each subsequent statement until you have caught up to the current bank statement.

Correcting Errors

Hopefully, there will not be many times when you need Quicken to correct errors during the reconciliation process. However, there may be times when you can't find the amount displayed beside "Difference" on your reconciliation screen, and rather than searching further for your error you want to have Quicken make an adjustment to balance your register with your bank statement.

This situation could have occurred in the 1st U.S. Bank reconciling process described in the section "Quicken's Reconciliation Process." Recall that you made an adjustment of 10.00 to check number 100 in order to correct for your recording error, but if you had been careless in the reconciliation process you might have missed the error when comparing your bank statement with your check register. In this case your Uncleared Transaction List window would show a $10.00 difference after clearing all items. If you search for the difference and still can't find the amount, you can follow these steps to have Quicken make the adjustment.

This process could have a serious impact on your future reports and check register; don't take this approach to the reconciliation difference lightly.

1. Press CTRL-F10 and the Problem: Check Register does not balance with Bank Statement window will appear. This time Quicken informs you that there's a $10.00 difference.

At this point you can still return to the register and check for the difference by pressing the ESC key.

2. Press ENTER and the Adding Balance Adjustment Entry window will appear.

3. Type Y and press ENTER.

You have told Quicken that you do not want to search any longer for the difference and you want an adjustment to be made. The adjustment will be dated the current date and will be recorded as "Balance Adjustment." If you had typed N, Quicken would have returned you to the reconciliation screen and you would have continued to search for the difference.

4. Press ENTER again and the Register Adjusted to Agree With Statement window shown in Figure 4-12 appears.

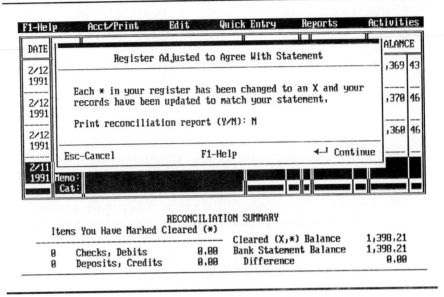

FIGURE 4-12. Register adjustment completed

This indicates that Quicken has made a check register entry for the difference and that you are going to accept the "Balance Adjustment" description in the Payee row of the register (you can always make a correction later if you find the error). Otherwise, you could have used another description such as misc. or expense/income.

5. Type **Y** and press (**ENTER**); a Print Reconciliation Report window, like the one displayed in Figure 4-6, appears. Now you can complete the window as described in the "Sample Reconciliation" section.

WRITING AND PRINTING CHECKS

In addition to recording the checks you write in Quicken's register, you can also enter check writing information on your screen and have Quicken print the check. Although this requires you to order special preprinted checks that conform to Quicken's check layout, it means that you can enter a transaction once — on the check writing screen — and Quicken will print your check and record the register entry.

You can order Quicken checks in five different styles (three traditional and two laser) to meet varying needs. Regardless of the style, there is no problem with acceptance by banks, credit unions, or savings and loans, since they have the required account numbers and check numbers preprinted on the checks.

You can create standard 8 1/2-by-3 1/2-inch checks, a voucher-style check that has a 3 1/2-inch tear-off stub, and wallet-style checks in the 2 5/6-by-6-inch size with a tear-off stub added. You can order all these for traditional printers or order the regular or voucher checks for laser printers directly from Intuit.

You can generate an order form from Quicken's check writing screen. If you want to print out the order form you can choose item 1, Write/Print Checks, from the Main Menu. Then press (F6) to open the Activities menu and select item 3, Order Supplies. If you select a printer number and press (ENTER) the order form will print and you can return to the Main Menu by pressing (ESC) when the printing completes. You will see from the form that Quicken also sells window envelopes to fit the checks and can add a company logo to your checks.

Even if you are not certain whether you want to order check stock, you can still try the exercises in this chapter. You may be so pleased with the ease of entry and the professional-looking appearance of the checks that you will decide to order checks to start entering your own transactions. You will definitely not want to print your own checks without the special check stock since banks will not cancel payments on checks without a preprinted account number.

You can also enter transactions in Quicken for transmission to the Check-Free payment processing service via a modem. Your Quicken register entries will be updated after transmission and the CheckFree Processing Center will handle the payment for you. This chapter will provide some information on this service since you might want to consider it as a next step in the total automation of your financial transactions.

WRITING CHECKS

Writing checks in Quicken is as easy as writing a check in your regular checkbook. Although there are a few more fields on a Quicken check, most of these are optional and are designed to provide better recordkeeping for your expense transactions. All you really need to do is fill in the blanks on a Quicken check form.

Entering the Basic Information

To activate the check writing features you can select item 1, Write/Print Checks, from the Main Menu. The exercise presented here is designed to be entered after the reconciliation example in Chapter 4, but can actually be entered at any time. If you are already in the register there is no need to return to the Main Menu first; all you need to do is press (**F6**) and select item 1, Write Checks, from the pull-down menu, or press (**CTRL**)-(**W**).

Figure 5-1 shows a blank Quicken check form on the screen. The only field that has been completed is the Date field; by default the current date is placed on the first check. On checks after the first, the date will match the last check written. For this exercise you will change the dates on all the checks written to match the dates on the sample transactions.

You should already be familiar with most of the fields on the check writing form from the entries you made in Quicken's register. However, the Address field was not part of the register entries. It is added to the check for use with window envelopes; when the checks are printed, all you have to do is insert them in envelopes and mail them.

As many as three monetary amounts may appear in the bottom-right corner of the screen. The Checks to Print field holds the total dollar amount of all the checks written but not yet printed. This will not show until you fill in the first check and record the transaction.

Current Balance is a field that only changes from 0.00 if you write checks with dates after the current date, called *postdated* checks. Postdated checks do not affect the current balance but alter the ending balance. They are written to record future payments. If you are reading this chapter before

```
 F1-Help   F2-Acct/Print   F3-Edit   F4-Quick Entry  F5-Reports   F6-Activities
```

```
                                      Date    2/13/91
              Pay to the            _____
              Order of                                       $        _____
                       _____
                                                                       Dollars

              Address ┤

              Memo    ────────────────────────────
```

```
        ┌──── Category ────┐
        │                  │
        └──────────────────┘
```

```
    1st U.S. Bank
    Esc-Main Menu      Ctrl↵ Record              Ending Balance:  $1,360.46
```

FIGURE 5-1.   Blank check writing window

February 1991, all of your transactions will be "postdated," since the dates on the checks are in that month. Ending Balance is the balance in the account after all of the checks written have been deducted.

You can use (TAB) or (ENTER) to move from field to field on the check form. If you want to move back to a previous field, you can use (SHIFT)-(TAB). When you are finished entering the check information and are ready to record it, you can press (CTRL)-(ENTER) to automatically record the transaction. Another possibility is to press (ENTER) with the cursor at the end of the last field category. With the latter approach Quicken will prompt you to confirm that you want to record the transaction. If you use this approach, type **1** and press (ENTER); the check will be recorded for later printing.

Follow these instructions to enter the information for your first check:

1. Type **2/13/91** and press (ENTER).

You can also use (+) or (−) to change the date.

2. Type **South Haven Print Supply** and press (ENTER).

3. Type **58.75** and press (ENTER).

Amounts as large as $9,999,999.99 are supported by the package. Notice that when you complete the amount entry, Quicken spells out the amount on the next line and positions you in the Address field. Although this entire field is optional, if you are mailing the check, entering the address here will allow you to use a window envelope.

4. Type a quotation mark (") to automatically copy the payee name down to this line.

5. Type **919 Superior Avenue** and press (ENTER).

6. Type **South Haven, MI 49090** and press (ENTER) until the cursor is in the Memo field.

7. Type **Printing Brochure - PTA Dinner** and press (ENTER).

This is an optional entry that allows you to provide information to the payee indicating the purpose of the check.

8. Press (CTRL)-(C).

This is a quick way to bring up the category list to select an appropriate category.

9. Move the cursor to "Charity" since you are donating the cost of this printing job by paying the bill for the Parent Teacher Association. Press (ENTER) to add the entry to the Category field.

Another shortcut approach to entering a category is to type a single letter that is the letter you think the desired Quicken category starts with, and press (ENTER). Quicken will ask whether you want to create a category or select one. Choose 2, select a category, and you will be in the category list at the letter you entered. Then scroll to the category you want and press (ENTER). With either approach, your screen looks like Figure 5-2.

10. Press (CTRL)-(ENTER) to complete and record the transaction. (You could also press (ENTER), but you will then need to tell Quicken to record the transaction in a separate step if you take this approach.)

```
 F1-Help   F2-Acct/Print   F3-Edit   F4-Quick Entry  F5-Reports   F6-Activities

                                        Date    2/13/91
        Pay to the
        Order of    South Haven Print Supply                    $ 58.75

        Fifty-Eight and 75/100************************************ Dollars

                     South Haven Print Supply
                     919 Superior Avenue
        Address     South Haven, MI 49090


        Memo  Printing Brochure - PTA Dinner


                  ─── Category ───
        Charity


     1st U.S. Bank
     Esc-Main Menu     Ctrl↵  Record              Ending Balance:  $1,360.46
```

FIGURE 5-2. Entering the first check transaction

```
F1-Help   F2-Acct/Print   F3-Edit   F4-Quick Entry  F5-Reports   F6-Activities
```

```
                              Date   2/13/91
Pay to the
Order of   Holland Lumber                              $ 120.00

One Hundred Twenty and 00/100*********************************** Dollars

           |Holland Lumber
           |2314 E. 8th Street
Address   -|Holland, MI 49094

Memo  Deck repair
```

```
        Category
Home Rpair                                                         ↑↓
```

```
1st U.S. Bank                                Checks to Print: $  178.75
Esc-Main Menu    Ctrl←┘ Record               Ending Balance:  $1,181.71
```

FIGURE 5-3. Entering a check for Holland Lumber

```
F1-Help   F2-Acct/Print   F3-Edit   F4-Quick Entry  F5-Reports   F6-Activities
```

```
                              Date   2/13/91
Pay to the
Order of   Fennville Library                          $ 10.00

Ten and 00/100************************************************** Dollars

           |Fennville Library
           |110 Main Street
Address   -|Fennville, MI 49459

Memo  Building func contribution
```

```
        Category
Charity                                                            ↑
```

```
1st U.S. Bank                                Checks to Print: $  178.75
Esc-Main Menu    Ctrl←┘ Record               Ending Balance:  $1,181.71
```

FIGURE 5-4. Entering a check with errors

You can enter as many checks as you want in one session. Use the preceding procedure to enter another transaction. Check each field before you press ⌐TAB⌐ or ⌐ENTER⌐, but don't worry if you make a mistake or two; you will learn how to make corrections in the next section. Enter this check now:

Date:	2/13/91
Payee:	Holland Lumber
Payment:	120.00
Address:	Holland Lumber
	2314 E. 8th Street
	Holland, MI 49094
Memo:	Deck repair
Category:	Home Rpair

You must use the exact spelling to match Quicken's category. Remember, you could use ⌐CTRL⌐-⌐C⌐ to select Home Rpair from the category list.

Press ⌐CTRL⌐-⌐ENTER⌐ when you are through to record the transaction. Although Quicken moves you to the next check, you can press ⌐PGUP⌐ to see the check, as shown in Figure 5-3.

Reviewing and Making Corrections

Corrections can be made to a check before or after completing the transaction. Although it is easiest to make them before completion, the most important thing is catching the error before printing the check. To prevent problems, you will always want to review your transactions before printing.

Now let's enter one more transaction exactly as shown in Figure 5-4, including the spelling error in the Memo field. Then you will take a look at making the required corrections. Press ⌐PGDN⌐ to move to a new check form if you are still looking at the check for Holland Lumber and make the following entries without recording the transaction. (Do not correct the misspelling.)

Date:	2/13/91
Payee:	Fennville Library
Payment:	10.00
Address:	Fennville Library
	110 Main Street
	Fennville, MI 49459
Memo:	Building func contribution
Category:	Charity

One mistake in the entries in Figure 5-4 is obvious. The word "fund" in the Memo field is spelled wrong. Suppose you were planning to be a little more generous with the contribution; the amount you intended to enter was 100.00. Quicken has already generated the words for the amount entry, but it will change the words if you change the amount. All you need to do is move back to the fields and make corrections, since the transaction has not been recorded yet. Follow these instructions:

1. Press ⌈TAB⌋ three times to move to the Amount field.

Although ⌈TAB⌋ normally takes you to the next field, pressing it at the last field takes you to the first field on the screen. Another approach is to press ⌈SHIFT⌋-⌈TAB⌋. Each time you press it, the cursor will move back one field. This will work, but it will need to be pressed a few more times than ⌈TAB⌋ due to the cursor location and the destination field.

2. Use ⌈RIGHT ARROW⌋ to position the cursor immediately after the "1" in the Amount field.

3. Press ⌈INS⌋ to turn on insert mode, and type another **0**.

The amount now reads "100.00."

4. Press ⌈INS⌋ to turn insert mode off.

5. Press ⌈TAB⌋ six times to move to the Memo field.

6. Press ⌈CTRL⌋-⌈RIGHT ARROW⌋ twice to move to the *c* in "contribution." Type **d** to replace the *c* in "func." The correct check will be for $100.00 with a Memo field entry of "Building fund contribution."

7. Press ⌈CTRL⌋-⌈ENTER⌋ to record the transaction.

You can browse through the other transactions using (PGUP) and (PGDN) to move from check to check. (HOME) takes you to the first check and (END) takes you to the last check, which is a blank check form for the next transaction. Make any changes you want, but record them with (CTRL)-(ENTER) before using (PGUP) or (PGDN) to move to a new check. Quicken will update the balances if you change an Amount field.

To delete an entire transaction you can use (CTRL)-(D) and confirm the delete. Since the checks have not been printed, there is no problem in deleting an incorrect transaction. After printing, you must void the entry in the register rather than deleting the check, since you will need a record of the disposition of each check number.

If you are curious about how these entries look in the register, you can pull down the Activities menu with (F6) as shown here:

```
              F6-Activities

  ▶ 1. Register        Ctrl-R
    ─────────────────────────
    2. Reconcile
    3. Order Supplies
    ─────────────────────────
    4. Calculator      Ctrl-0
    5. Use DOS
```

Press (ENTER) to select the register or just press (CTRL)-(R). You will see the checks you have written in the register with ***** in the Num field. Figure 5-5 shows several entries made from the check writing screen.

Postdating Checks

Postdated checks are written for future payments. The date on a postdated check is after the current one; if you enter a check on September 10 for a December 24 payment, the check is postdated. Postdated entries are allowed to permit you to schedule future expenses and write the check entry while you are thinking of it. It is not necessary to print postdated checks when you print checks.

Depending on when you are entering the February 1991 checks in these examples, Quicken may be classifying the entries as postdated. The only difference is you have the option to print only checks before a certain date when postdated checks are recorded.

```
 F1-Help  F2-Acct/Print  F3-Edit  F4-Quick Entry  F5-Reports  F6-Activities
```

DATE	NUM	PAYEE · MEMO · CATEGORY	PAYMENT	C	DEPOSIT	BALANCE
2/10 1991		Dividend check Dividends check→Div Income			25 00	1,370 93
2/11 1991		Interest Earned Int Inc		X	1 03	1,371 96
2/11 1991		Service Charge Misc	11 50	X		1,360 46
2/13 1991	*****	South Haven Print Supply Printing Brochu→Charity	58 75			1,301 71
2/13 1991	*****	Holland Lumber Deck repair Home Rpair	120 00			1,181 71
2/13 1991	***** Memo: Cat:	Fennville Library Building fund contribution Charity	100 00			1,081 71

1st U.S. Bank
Esc-Main Menu   Ctrl◄─┘ Record   Ending Balance: $1,081.71

FIGURE 5-5. Check transactions in the register with asterisks for check numbers

Complete these entries to write a check for an upcoming birthday by entering the following:

Date:	3/8/91
Payee:	Keith Campbell
Payment:	25.00
Memo:	Birthday gift
Category:	Gifts

Note that the Address field was deliberately left blank, since this is a personal check that will not be mailed. What makes this check different than all the others is that while the current date is supposedly 2/13/91, the check is written for 3/8/91 (later than the current date). Press CTRL-ENTER to finalize.

Now that you have written a few checks, you should try printing a few. You can use plain paper even if you have check stock, since these are just practice examples.

Putting Earlier Tactics to Work

Even though you are working with the check writing screen, many of Quicken's special features that you learned to use in earlier chapters still work. You can use the calculator if you need to total a few invoices or perform another computation for the check amount. All you have to do is move to the Amount field and press CTRL-O to activate the calculator. Once you have completed your computations, use F9 to place the result in the Amount field.

The Find and Go to Date options also work. You can use shortcut keys to invoke these features or the pull-down Edit menu activated with F3 (see Chapter 2).

PRINTING CHECKS

Printing checks is easy. The only difficult part of the process is lining the paper up in your printer, but after the first few times even this will seem easy, as Quicken has built some helps into the system for you.

You can print some or all of your checks immediately after writing them, or you can defer the printing process to a later session. Some users wait until a check is due to print it and others elect to print all their checks immediately after they are written.

Check Stock Options

Quicken checks come in three sizes, regular checks, wallet checks, and voucher checks. Figure 5-6 provides a sample wallet check. The voucher design is shown in Figure 5-7. All styles are personalized and can be printed with a logo. The account number, financial institution number, and check number are printed on each check. Special numbers have been added to the edges of the checks for tractor-feed printers to assist in the alignment process.

FIGURE 5-6. A sample wallet check

FIGURE 5-7. A sample voucher check

Printing a Sample to Line Up Checks

Although you are ready to print the checks you created in the last exercise, if you have never lined up checks in the printer before you will want to walk through the steps required. This will ensure perfect alignment of the pre-printed check forms with the information you plan to print. The procedure is different for tractor-feed printers and laser printers. The laser printer is actually the easier of the two, since all you really need to do is insert the checks into the paper tray.

TRACTOR-FEED PRINTERS   Quicken comes with some sample checks for practicing check printing on a tractor-feed printer. Naturally, you will only be interested in this option if you have a tractor-feed printer.

To print a sample check with a tractor-feed printer, follow these instructions from the Write/Print Checks menu:

1. Insert the sample checks in the tracks as you do with any printer paper.

You can purchase Forms Leader pages from Intuit that assure proper alignment of the checks in the printer. This way you won't waste a check at the beginning of each check-writing session.

2. Turn on your printer and make sure that it is on-line and ready to print.

3. Press **F2** to open the Acct/Print menu shown here

```
F2-Acct/Print

 ▶ 1. Select/Set Up Account  Ctrl-A

   2. Print Checks            Ctrl-P
   3. Change Printer Settings

   4. Back Up All Accounts

   5. Export
   6. Import
```

and type **2** to select Print Checks.

Another option is to press CTRL-P rather than opening the Acct/Print menu. The Print Checks window will appear.

4. Type the number of the printer you will be using and press ENTER.

This is likely to be **3** for the check printer.

5. Press F8 to open the Type of Checks window. Select the check style by typing the number corresponding to the style you want to use, and then press CTRL-ENTER.

6. Press F9; then, after reading Quicken's sample check note, press ENTER.

Quicken will print your sample check. Check the vertical alignment by observing whether the "XXX" for date and amount, the word "Payee" for "Pay to the Order of," and the phrase "This is a void check" for the memo are printed just above the lines on the sample check.

 Do not move the check up or down after printing; Quicken will do this automatically.

7. Press ENTER if the sample check has aligned properly. If not, continue with the remaining steps.

8. (You will use this step only if your sample check did not align properly.) Look at the pointer line printed on your sample check. The arrow at each end points to a number on your tractor-feed sheet; this is your printer *position line number.*

 If your pointer line is not on one continuous line, you must check your printer settings to see that the pitch is 10 and that the indent value is 0. You cannot at this time continue with the following steps to achieve the correct results. Note the correct alignment position and consult Correcting Printer Errors.

Press ESC to leave the print process for now.

9. Type the position line number and press ⌜**ENTER**⌝.

Quicken automatically causes a form feed and prints another sample check. This time your check should be properly aligned; if you need to fine-tune the alignment use the knob on your printer to manually adjust the alignment.

10. Make any horizontal adjustments that may be necessary by moving the paper clamps.

Once you have aligned your checks properly you should examine the location of the checks in you printer; notice where your position numbers line up with a part of your printer, such as the edge of the sprocket cover.

11. Press ⌜**ENTER**⌝ in the Typed Position Number field when your sample check is properly aligned.

You are now ready to print your checks.

LASER PRINTERS   Quicken's laser-printer checks come either one or three to a page and, as mentioned, are the easiest of the checks to print. When using these forms, all you need to do is insert the forms into your printer the same way you insert regular paper (face up, with the top of the paper positioned toward the printer, and so on). If you tear the tractor-feed strips off the sample checks that come with Quicken, you can use them with your laser printer. You can also use regular printer paper.
   The key point to remember with laser printers is to check the printer settings before printing your checks. This can be accomplished from Quicken's Write/Print Checks menu:

1. Press ⌜**F2**⌝ to open the Acct/Print menu.

2. Type **3** to select the Change Printer Settings window.

3. Type **1** to tell Quicken you want to examine the Check Printer Settings window.

4. Use ⌜**UP ARROW**⌝ or ⌜**DOWN ARROW**⌝ to place the arrow next to your type of printer and press ⌜**ENTER**⌝.

5. Press (ENTER) or (TAB) seven times to arrive at "Page-oriented," type **Y**, and press (ENTER) (if the setting is already set for **Y** you can just press (ENTER)).

6. Press (CTRL)-(ENTER) to close the Check Printer Settings window.

7. Press (CTRL)-(P) to open the Print Checks window.

8. Press (F9) to print a sample check.

9. Check the sample to determine whether you need to modify your printer settings to better align the printing. If the sample is correct, you are prepared to print your checks. See Table 5-1, Correcting Printer Errors, if there are still problems, and try the samples again.

Selecting Checks to Print

When you are ready to print checks you need to tell Quicken the printer you want to use, the check style you have selected, the checks to print, and the first check number. The instructions which follow assume that you have already checked the alignment for your check stock and that you are beginning from the Main Menu.

1. Type **1** to select Write/Print Checks.

2. Press (F2) to open the Acct/Print menu and type **2** to select Print Checks.

Another option is to press (CTRL)-(P) rather than opening the Acct/Print menu. The Print Checks window will appear.

3. Type the number of the printer you will be using and press (ENTER).

This will probably be **3** for the check printer.

4. Press (F8) to open the Type of Checks window and select the check style by typing the number that corresponds to the style you wish to use and then press (ENTER).

5. Type **S** to print selected checks. Typing **A** will cause Quicken to print all the checks.

If you have postdated checks, you can enter a date in the next field to print all checks before a certain date, and thus exclude postdated checks.

Print Problem	Correction Suggestion
Print lines are too close	Printer is probably set for eight lines to the inch — change to six.
Print lines wrap and the date and amount are too far to the right	Too large a pitch is selected — change to 10 pitch.
Print does not extend across the check — the date and amount print too far to the left	Too small a pitch size is selected (perhaps compressed print) — change to 10 pitch and turn off compressed print if necessary.
Print does not align with lines on check	Checks not aligned properly in printer — reposition following instructions in this chapter.
Print seems to be the correct size but is too far to the right or left	Reposition checks from right to left.
Printout shows the printer control codes	Printer control codes must be preceded with a backslash (\).
Printer is spewing paper or producing illegible print	The wrong printer has probably been selected — check selection in the printer list.
Printer does not print	Printer is probably either not turned on, not on-line, or not chosen in the printer list, or the cable is loose.
Print looks correct but is indented	Change indent setting to 0 in Print Settings window.

══ **TABLE 5-1.** Correcting Printer Errors

Since you have already printed samples there is no need to print additional ones now. In subsequent sessions you might want to use ⟨**F9**⟩ to print a sample before proceeding.

6. Press ⟨**CTRL**⟩-⟨**ENTER**⟩ and the Select Checks to Print window will appear. This allows you to select specific checks.

```
┌────────────────────────────────────────────────────────────────┐
│ F1-Help      Acct/Print     Edit      Quick Entry     Reports      Activities │
│  ┌──────────────────────────────────────────────────────────┐  │
│  │                   Select Checks to Print                    │  │
│  │   Date        Payee              Memo             Amount     │  │
│  │  ────────────────────────────────────────────────────────  │  │
│  │  2/13/91 South Haven Print Sup Printing Brochure - P  58.75 Print │  │
│  │  2/13/91 Holland Lumber        Deck repair          120.00 Print │  │
│  │▶ 2/13/91 Fennville Library     Building fund contrib 100.00 Print │  │
│  │  3/ 8/91 Keith Campbell        Birthday gift         25.00       │  │
│  │                                                            │  │
│  │                                                            │  │
│  │           Space Bar-Select/Deselect     F9-Select All       │  │
│  │  Esc-Cancel            F1-Help              ↵ Continue      │  │
│  └──────────────────────────────────────────────────────────┘  │
│  1st U.S. Bank                    Checks to Print: $  303.75      │
│                                   Ending Balance:  $1,056.71      │
└────────────────────────────────────────────────────────────────┘
```

FIGURE 5-8.   Selecting the checks to print

7. Press (**SPACEBAR**) to select the first check. The word "Print" appears in the far-right column.

8. Press (**DOWN ARROW**) to move to the second check and press (**SPACEBAR**) again.

9. Press (**DOWN ARROW**) to move to the third check and press (**SPACEBAR**) again. Your screen will look like Figure 5-8. Press (**ENTER**) to continue.

If you select any checks in error, press (**SPACEBAR**) a second time with the cursor pointing at the check to turn off the print command for that check.

10. Type **1001** to enter the beginning check number in the Type Check Number window.

Your entry should match the one shown here.

```
┌─────────────────────────────────────┐
│ ▄▄▄▄▄▄▄▄▄▄▄▄▄▄▄▄▄▄▄▄▄▄▄▄▄▄▄          │
│         Type Check Number            │
│ ─────────────────────────────────── │
│  Type the check number of the check  │
│  which is about to be printed,       │
│                                      │
│  Next check number: 1001             │
│ ─────────────────────────────────── │
│        F9-Print First Check Only     │
│  Esc-Cancel     F1-Help    ↵ Continue│
└─────────────────────────────────────┘
```

You must always make this check number agree with the number of the first check you place in the printer. You should double check this entry since Quicken will use it to complete the register entry for the check transaction. As it prints a check, it replaces the asterisks in the register with the actual check number. You can use ⊕ and ⊖ to change the check number.

11. Press (ENTER) to print your checks.

12. Review the checks printed and check for errors in printing. If you had used preprinted check forms your checks might look something like Figure 5-9.

13. Assuming there are no errors, press (ENTER) to close the check printing windows and to return to the Write Checks screen. Press (CTRL)-(R) to look at the register entries with the check numbers inserted. If there are problems with the checks, follow the directions in the next section.

Correcting Mistakes

Quicken allows you to reprint checks that have been printed incorrectly. Since you are using prenumbered checks, new numbers will have to be assigned to the reprinted checks as Quicken prints them. First, make sure before starting again that you correct any feed problems with the printer.

If you find yourself frequently correcting printer jams and having to reprint checks, you may want to print checks in smaller batches or set your printer to wait after each page.

Complete the following steps to restart and finish your printing batch:

1. Since you did not press (ENTER) when you finished printing checks, Quicken is still waiting for you to supply the number of the first check not printed or printed incorrectly. Type the check number of the first check you want to reprint and press (ENTER).

YOUR NAME
YOUR ADDRESS
CITY, STATE ZIP

YOUR BANK
BRANCH OFFICE
CITY, STATE ZIP
00-6789/0000

1285

2/13/91

PAY TO THE ORDER OF South Haven Print Supply $ ******58.75

Fifty-Eight and 75/100*** DOLLARS

SAMPLE

MEMO Printing Brochure - PTA Dinner

001285 000067894 12345678

YOUR NAME
YOUR ADDRESS
CITY, STATE ZIP

YOUR BANK
BRANCH OFFICE
CITY, STATE ZIP
00-6789/0000

1286

2/13/91

PAY TO THE ORDER OF Holland Lumber $ *****120.00

One Hundred Twenty and 00/100*** DOLLARS

SAMPLE

MEMO Deck repair

001286 000067894 12345678

YOUR NAME
YOUR ADDRESS
CITY, STATE ZIP

YOUR BANK
BRANCH OFFICE
CITY, STATE ZIP
00-6789/0000

1287

2/13/91

PAY TO THE ORDER OF Fennville Library $ *****100.00

One Hundred and 00/100** DOLLARS

SAMPLE

MEMO Building fund contribution

001287 000067894 12345678

FIGURE 5-9. Standard check sample printout

2. The Print Checks window will appear. Press ⌈CTRL⌉-⌈ENTER⌉ to open the Select Checks to Print window.

3. Select the checks to be reprinted using ⌈SPACEBAR⌉ and press ⌈ENTER⌉.

4. Check the next Check Number field against the number of the next check in your printer. Type a change if appropriate. Press ⌈ENTER⌉ to confirm the beginning check number for this batch and begin printing.

5. Press ⌈ENTER⌉ to indicate that all the checks have printed correctly when they stop printing.

USING CHECKFREE

CheckFree eliminates the need for printing checks. After entering data into Quicken 4, you can electronically transmit the information to CheckFree. The CheckFree service will handle the payments for you by printing and mailing a paper check or by initiating a direct electronic transfer.

Although the ability to interface with CheckFree is part of Quicken 4, you must subscribe to the service before using it the first time. To subscribe, complete the CheckFree Service Form included in the Quicken package or contact CheckFree at (614) 899-7500. Currently, CheckFree's monthly charge of $9.00 entitles you to 20 transactions without an additional charge.

Setting Up Quicken to Interface with CheckFree

To use CheckFree with Quicken you must change your settings and set up the bank account specified on the CheckFree Service Form. Then, set up your modem so that you can use Quicken's electronic payment capability. You must also compile an electronic payee list and write electronic checks.

COMPLETING MODEM SETTINGS   To set up your modem in order to establish a link between your computer and your bank via the telephone line, select Change Settings from the Main Menu. Next choose Electronic Payment, followed by Modem Settings. The Electronic Payment Settings window shown in Figure 5-10 is displayed. You can accept the defaults for the modem speed and the computer port to which the modem is attached or change them to conform to your needs.

```
┌─────────────────────────────────────────────────┐
│           Electronic Payment Settings           │
│                                                 │
│  Serial port used by modem: 1                   │
│        1. COM1              3. COM3             │
│        2. COM2              4. COM4             │
│                                                 │
│  Modem speed: 2                                 │
│        1. 300              3. 2400             │
│        2. 1200             4. 9600             │
│                                                 │
│  Tone or Pulse Dialing (T/P): T                 │
│                                                 │
│  Telephone number to dial CheckFree Electronic  │
│  Payment Processing Service:                    │
│  (Press F1 for additional information)          │
│                                                 │
│  Turn on Electronic Payment capability (Y/N): N │
│  ─────────────────────────────────────────────  │
│           F8-Custom Modem Initialization        │
│  Esc-Cancel           F1-Help      ◄┘ Continue  │
└─────────────────────────────────────────────────┘
```

1st U.S. Bank

═══════ **FIGURE 5-10.** Electronic Payment Settings window

You must enter the phone number supplied by CheckFree for transmission. Next, turn on the electronic payment feature by typing a **Y** in the last field on the screen. When entering the phone number, a comma is used if your phone system requires a pause. Rather than return to the Main Menu you can edit the settings for the current account to use it with CheckFree, as discussed next.

COMPLETING ACCOUNT SETTINGS You can change your account settings for any bank account for use with CheckFree provided you supply the bank information to CheckFree on their Service Form. To change an account for use with CheckFree, choose Account Settings from the menu presented after selecting Change Settings and Electronic Payment. Quicken presents a window with your current account listed, like the one shown here.

```
┌─────────────────────────────────────┐
│ Set Up Account for Electronic Payment│
│  ┌──────────────────────────────────┤
│  │ Bank Account    Electronic Pmts   │
│  ├──────────────┬───────────────────┤
│  │ ▶ 1st U.S. Bank│                  │
│  │              │                    │
│  │              │                    │
│  │              │                    │
│  │              │                    │
│  ├──────────────┴───────────────────┤
│  │ Esc-Cancel    F1-Help    ◄┘ Select│
└──┴────────────────────────────────────┘
```

Highlight the name of the account you wish to enable electronic transmissions for and press (ENTER). Respond with a **Y** on the next screen to enable payments, and then complete the form shown in Figure 5-11 for your account. CheckFree will supply you with the number for the last field on this form. After returning to the Main Menu, you will be ready to enter electronic payees or check or register transactions and transmit them.

```
┌──────────────────────────────────────────────────────┐
│         Electronic Payment Account Settings           │
├──────────────────────────────────────────────────────┤
│  Your First Name:        MI:   Last:                  │
│                                                        │
│  Street Address    │                    │             │
│                                                        │
│  City:                   State:   Zip:                │
│                                                        │
│  Home Phone:                                           │
│                                                        │
│  Social Security Number:                               │
│  (Press F1 if you have multiple CheckFree accounts)   │
│                                                        │
│  CheckFree Processing Service Account Number:         │
├──────────────────────────────────────────────────────┤
│  Esc-Cancel            F1-Help          ◄┘ Continue   │
└──────────────────────────────────────────────────────┘
```

1st U.S. Bank

FIGURE 5-11. Electronic Payment Acount Settings form

Adding Electronic Payees

Before CheckFree can process a payment, it must have the address or account number of the payee. You can create an entire electronic payee list before entering any transactions or add new payees as you enter transactions. You can set up a list from the register or the Write Checks screen by pressing (CTRL)-(Y). When you select Setup A New Payee, you can enter a payee, a complete address, and an account number of up to 25 characters.

Writing Electronic Checks

The procedure for writing electronic checks is almost identical to the format for creating checks that you print, covered earlier in this chapter. Your check will display Electronic Payment if you have electronic payments set for the current account, although you can toggle to a paper check with (F9) anytime you need to. Quicken automatically postdates the payment date by five working days to allow for transmission of the payment to the payee. The Pay To field must contain the name of an electronic payee. If your entry does not match an existing payee, Quicken will allow you to add it. Once you are finished with your entries, press (CTRL)-(ENTER).

Quicken will list your electronic checks in the register. The check numbers will consist of a number of > symbols before transmission and E_PMT after transmission. You can enter these electronic payments directly in the register rather than through the Write Checks screen if you prefer.

Transmitting Electronic Payments

Electronic payments are transmitted through the Write Checks screen or the register. Press (CTRL)-(I) or (F2) and select Transmit. You can preview your transmission with (F9) or press (ENTER) to start the transmission process.

part **II**

HOME APPLICATIONS

Expanding the Scope of Financial Entries
Quicken as a Budgeting Tool
Using Quicken to Organize Tax Information
Determining Your Net Worth
Creating Custom Reports

Quicken can provide the help you need to organize your personal finances. The package will enable you to establish accounts for
monitoring checking and savings accounts, credit cards, and investments. In
this section you will learn how to record and organize your financial information with Quicken's easy-to-use features. You will also learn how to prepare
reports for taxes, budgeting, and computing your net worth.

EXPANDING THE
SCOPE OF FINANCIAL
ENTRIES

The purpose of the last five chapters was to quickly get you started using Quicken's features. The basics you learned in those chapters will help you better manage your checking account transactions. For some individuals this will be sufficient. Others will want to increase their knowledge of Quicken to take full advantage of its capabilities. Even if you think you learned all the tasks you need in the first few chapters, read the first two sections in this chapter. These sections will teach you about account groups and setting up an account separate from the one you used for the practice exercises. Then, if you feel you know enough to meet your needs, stop reading at the end of the section titled "Account Groups" and enter some of your own transactions.

Even personal finances can be too complex to be handled with a single account. In one household there may be transactions for both individual and joint checking accounts, credit card accounts, and savings accounts. Quicken allows you to set up these accounts within an *account group,* which enables you to include information from multiple accounts in reports.

Accounts alone are not always enough to organize transactions logically. You may find you need to change the categories to assign to your transactions; you may even want to establish main categories with subcategories beneath them. You used categories earlier to identify transactions as utilities expense or salary income. Using subcategories, you might create several groupings under the utilities expense for electricity, gas, and water.

Classes are another way of organizing your transactions to provide a different perspective from categories. You might think of classes as answering the "who," "what," "when," or "where" of a transaction. For example, you could assign a transaction to the clothing category and then set up and assign it to a class for the family member purchasing the clothing.

In this chapter you will also learn how to assign transactions to more than one account—for example, how to transfer funds between accounts.

All of these features are presented here using the assumption that you are recording transactions for your personal finances. If you are interested in using Quicken to record both personal and business transactions, read the chapters in this section first. When you get to Chapter 11, you will learn how to set up Quicken for your business. You can then select a category structure and create accounts that will allow you to manage both business and personal transactions.

The material in these chapters builds on the procedures you have already mastered. You should feel free to adapt the entries provided to match your actual financial transactions. For example, you may want to change the dollar amount of transactions, the categories to which they are assigned, and the transaction dates shown.

Again, be aware of the dates for the transaction entries in these chapters. As you know, the date of the transaction entry, relative to the current date, determines whether a transaction is postdated. The current date triggers the reminder to process groups of transactions you want to enter on a certain date. Using your current date for transaction entries will cause this not to occur. Also, creating reports that match the examples in this book will be difficult unless you use the dates presented for the transaction. The varied dates used permit the creation of more illustrative reports.

ACCOUNT GROUPS

When you first started working in Chapter 2, Quicken automatically assigned an account group to the account you created for 1st U.S. Bank. Quicken called this account QDATA and created four files on your disk to manage your accounts and the information within them. You worked with only one account in QDATA, but you can use multiple accounts within an account group. You might use one account for a savings account and a different one for checking. You can also have accounts for credit cards, cash, assets, and liabilities, although most individuals do not have financial situations that warrant more than a few accounts.

You could continue to enter the transactions from this chapter in the 1st U.S. Bank account in the QDATA account group, or you could set up a new account in the QDATA account group. However, if you adapted the chapter entries to meet your own financial situation, your new data would be intermingled with the practice transactions from the last few chapters. To avoid this, you will need to establish an account group for the practice transactions. You will learn how to set up new transactions that are stored separately from the existing entries. You will also learn how to create a backup copy of an account group to safeguard the data you enter.

Adding a New Account Group

You already have the QDATA account group for all the transactions entered in the first section of this book. Now you will set up a new account group and create accounts within it. Later, if you wish, you can delete the QDATA group to free the space it occupies on your disk.

The new account group will be called PERSONAL and will initially contain a checking account called Cardinal Bank. This account is similar to the 1st U.S. Bank checking account you created in QDATA. Since it is in a new account group a different name is used. Other appropriate names might have been Business Checking and Joint Checking, depending on the type of account. Naturally, if you had more than one account at Cardinal Bank, they could not all be named Cardinal Bank. Later you will add the account Cardinal Saving to this same account group.

From the Main Menu follow these steps to set up the new account group and to add the first account to it:

1. Type **5** to select Change Settings.

2. Type **1** to select Account Group Activities.

3. Type **1** to select Select/Set Up Account Group.

Quicken will display the window shown in Figure 6-1. Notice the entry for the existing account group QDATA.

4. Move the cursor to <Set Up New Grp> and press (ENTER).

Quicken presents a window for entering the account name and the type of categories you wish to use.

5. Type **PERSONAL** as the name for the account group and press (ENTER).

Quicken creates four files for each account group name by adding four different filename extensions to the name you provide. This means you must provide a valid filename of no more than eight characters. Do not include spaces or special symbols in your entries for account names.

6. Type **1** and press (ENTER). This will restrict your categories to Home categories.

```
┌────────────────────────────────────────────────────┐
│              Select/Set Up Account Group             │
├────────────────────────────────────────────────────┤
│           Current Directory: D:\Q4_6                 │
│                  (2624K free)                        │
│                          Next Check      Next        │
│    Account Group   Date   Size  To Print  Group Due  │
│  ▶ <Set Up New Grp>                                  │
│    QDATA          2/14/91  3K Fri  3/ 8/91           │
│                                                      │
│                                                      │
│                                                      │
├────────────────────────────────────────────────────┤
│        Ctrl-D Delete  Ctrl-E Edit  ↑,↓ Select        │
│  Esc-Cancel    F1-Help    F9-Set Directory   ↵ Use   │
└────────────────────────────────────────────────────┘
```

FIGURE 6-1. Setting up a new account group

7. Check the directory shown on the line "Location for data files" and make changes to reference a valid file or directory if a change is required.

8. Press ⟨**ENTER**⟩ to complete the creation of the new account group.

Quicken displays the window for selecting or creating account groups with the PERSONAL account group added, as shown in Figure 6-2.

9. Move the cursor to "PERSONAL" and press ⟨**ENTER**⟩.

Since this is a new account group, Quicken does not yet have any accounts for it. A window is displayed to allow you to create a new account.

10. Press ⟨**ENTER**⟩ and Quicken will display the Set Up New Account window shown in Figure 6-3.

11. Type **1** to choose bank for the account type and press ⟨**ENTER**⟩.

12. Type **Cardinal Bank** and press ⟨**ENTER**⟩.

13. Type **2500** for the balance and press ⟨**ENTER**⟩.

14. Type **7/13/91** and press ⟨**ENTER**⟩.

15. Type **Personal Checking** and press ⟨**CTRL**⟩-⟨**ENTER**⟩.

```
                        Select/Set Up Account Group

                       Current Directory: D:\FIX\
                             (1794K free)
                                        Next Check      Next
       Account Group    Date    Size    To Print      Group Due

   ▶ <Set Up New Grp>
     PERSONAL         7/13/91    1K
     QDATA            2/14/91    1K




              Ctrl-D Delete   Ctrl-E Edit   ↑,↓ Select
     Esc-Cancel       F1-Help        F9-Set Directory        ↵ Use
```

═══════ **FIGURE 6-2.**   Window showing the new PERSONAL account group

```
┌─────────────────────────────────────────────────┐
│ ███████████████████████████████████████████████ │
│                Set Up New Account               │
│                                                 │
│  Account Type: 1                                │
│        1. Bank Account      4. Other Asset      │
│        2. Credit Card       5. Other Liability  │
│        3. Cash              6. Investment Account│
│                                                 │
│  Name for this account: Cardinal Bank           │
│                                                 │
│  Balance: 2,500.00      as of: 7/13/91          │
│  (Enter the balance in your bank account)       │
│                                                 │
│  Description (optional): Personal Checking      │
│                                                 │
├─────────────────────────────────────────────────┤
│          Please type account information        │
│  Esc-Cancel            F1-Help        ←┘ Continue│
└─────────────────────────────────────────────────┘
```

FIGURE 6-3.   Entering selections for the new account

Quicken returns you to the window for selecting an account.

16. Press (ESC) three times to return to the Main Menu.

Changing the Active Account Group

The result of the last exercise was the creation of a second account group. You can work in either account group at any time and select any account within a group. To change from the current account group, PERSONAL, to QDATA, follow these steps:

1. Type **5** to select Change Settings from the Main Menu.

2. Type **1** to select Account Group Activities.

3. Type **1** to select Select/Set Up Account Group.

4. Move the cursor to QDATA in the list and press (ENTER).

5. Move the cursor to 1st U.S. Bank in the account list and press (ENTER).

6. Press (ESC) to return to the Main Menu.

The QDATA account group is now active. If you went to the register or check writing screen you would find that the 1st U.S. Bank account was active. Change the account group back to PERSONAL and activate the account for Cardinal Bank by following the same steps.

Backing Up an Account Group

You will want to create backup copies of the data managed by the Quicken system on a regular basis. This allows you to recover all your entries in the event of a disk failure since you will be able to use your copy to restore all the entries. You will need a blank formatted disk to record the backup information the first time. Subsequent backups can be made on this disk without reformatting it.

If your system has 512K of RAM you can create a formatted disk without exiting Quicken. With less memory you will need to exit before formatting.

FORMATTING A DISK WITH 512K   To format the disk from within Quicken, if you have sufficient memory (512K), first open the register from the Main Menu, and then follow these steps:

1. Press ⌐F6⌐ and select item 5.

The DOS prompt will display on your screen; you can enter DOS commands as if Quicken was not in memory. If you do not have sufficient memory, exit Quicken, format a disk, and start Quicken again.

2. If you do not have a hard disk, remove your Quicken disk and place the DOS disk in drive A. If you have a hard disk ignore this step.

3. Type **FORMAT A:** and press ⌐ENTER⌐.

The system will ask you to insert a new disk for drive A and press ⌐ENTER⌐ when ready.

4. If you do not have a hard disk, remove the DOS disk from drive A. If you have a hard disk you obviously ignore this step since you never placed the DOS disk in drive A.

5. Place a blank disk in drive A, close the drive, and press ⌐ENTER⌐ in response to the DOS prompt to insert a disk.

The system will format the disk and ask you if you want to format another disk.

6. Type **N** and press (ENTER).

7. Type **EXIT** and press (ENTER) to return to Quicken.

If you are working from a floppy disk system, remove the formatted disk and insert your Quicken disk with the essential DOS files on it. (If you installed Quicken with the instructions in Appendix A, these files will be on your disk.) The disk you just formatted will be used to store a backup copy of the files in the current account group.

FORMATTING A DISK WITH LESS THAN 512K   You must exit Quicken to complete the format operation. Follow these steps:

1. Press (ESC) until the Main Menu is on the screen. Type **E** to select Exit.

The DOS prompt will display on your screen.

2. If you do not have a hard disk, remove your Quicken disk and place the DOS disk in drive A. If you have a hard disk ignore this step.

3. Type **FORMAT A:** and press (ENTER).

The system will ask you to insert a new disk for drive A: and strike (ENTER) when ready.

4. If you do not have a hard disk, remove the DOS disk from drive A. If you have a hard disk you obviously ignore this step since you never placed a DOS disk in drive A.

5. Place a blank disk in drive A, close the drive, and press (ENTER) in response to the DOS prompt to insert a disk.

The system will format the disk and ask you if you want to format another disk.

6. Type **N** and press (ENTER).

7. If you do not have a hard disk, remove the formatted disk and place the Quicken disk in drive A.

8. Type **Q** to start Quicken again.

CREATING BACKUP FILES   Quicken has a Backup and Restore feature that allows you to safeguard the investment you have made in entering your data. You can back up all your account files from the Acct/Print menu on the register screen. To back up selected account groups select the Backup option found in the Account Group Activities item on the Change Settings selections. Follow these steps to back up the current account group:

1. Press ⟨**ESC**⟩ to return to the Main Menu and type **5** for Change Settings.
2. Type **1** to select Account Group Activities.
3. Type **2** to select Backup Account Group.
4. Place your blank, formatted disk in drive A and then press ⟨**ENTER**⟩.
5. Select PERSONAL and press ⟨**ENTER**⟩.
6. Press ⟨**ENTER**⟩ to acknowledge the completion of the backup when Quicken displays the successful backup message.
7. Press ⟨**ESC**⟩ three times to return to the Main Menu.

With backups, if you ever lose your hard disk, you can re-create your data directory and then use the Restore option to copy your backup files to the directory. You can also copy Quicken data files from one floppy drive to another as a quick means of backup if you do not have a hard disk. Type **2** to open the register screen, as shown in Figure 6-4.

CUSTOMIZING CATEGORIES

When you set up the new PERSONAL account group you selected Home categories as the standard categories option. This selection provides access to the more than 40 category choices displayed in Table 6-1. You can see that some categories are listed as expenses and others as income. Any subcategories that you create later would also be shown in this column. The last column in the table shows which categories are tax related.

Editing the Existing Category List

You can change the name of any existing category, change its classification as income, expense, or subcategory, or change its tax-related status. To modify a category, follow these steps:

1. Press **CTRL**-**C** from the register to display the category list.

2. Move the arrow cursor to the category you want to change.

3. Press **CTRL**-**E** to edit the information for the category.

4. Change the entries you wish to alter.

5. Press **CTRL**-**ENTER** to complete the changes.

If you change the name of the category, Quicken will automatically change it in any transactions that have already been assigned to that category.

Adding Categories

You can also add your own categories to provide additional options specific to your needs. For example, if you have just set up housekeeping, buying furniture might be a major budget category. Since you would otherwise have to lump these purchases with others in the Household category, you might want to add "Furniture" as a category option. Typing **Furniture** in the

F1-Help	F2-Acct/Print	F3-Edit	F4-Quick Entry	F5-Reports	F6-Activities

DATE	NUM	PAYEE · MEMO · CATEGORY	PAYMENT	C	DEPOSIT	BALANCE
7/13 1991		═══ BEGINNING ═══ Opening Balance [Cardinal Bank]		X	2,500 00	2,500 00
7/13 1991	Memo: Cat:					

Cardinal Bank
Esc-Main Menu   Ctrl↵ Record   Ending Balance: $2,500.00

FIGURE 6-4. Register for the new account

Category	Type	Tax Related
Bonus	Income	Yes
Canada Pen	Income	Yes
Div Income	Income	Yes
Family Allow	Income	Yes
Gift Received	Income	Yes
Int Inc	Income	Yes
Invest Inc	Income	Yes
Old Age Pension	Income	Yes
Other Inc	Income	Yes
Salary	Income	Yes
Auto Fuel	Expense	No
Auto Loan	Expense	No
Auto Serv	Expense	No
Bank Chrg	Expense	No
Charity	Expense	Yes
Childcare	Expense	Yes/No depending on income bracket
Christmas	Expense	No
Clothing	Expense	No
Dining	Expense	No
Dues	Expense	No
Education	Expense	No
Entertain	Expense	No
Gifts	Expense	No
Groceries	Expense	No
Home Rpair	Expense	No
Household	Expense	No
Housing	Expense	No
Insurance	Expense	No
Int Exp	Expense	Yes
Invest Exp	Expense	Yes
Medical	Expense	Yes
Misc	Expense	No
Mort Int	Expense	Yes
Mort Prin	Expense	No
Other Exp	Expense	Yes
Recreation	Expense	No
RRSP	Expense	No
Subscriptions	Expense	No
Supplies	Expense	Yes
Tax Fed	Expense	Yes
Tax FICA	Expense	Yes
Tax Other	Expense	Yes
Tax Prop	Expense	Yes
Tax State	Expense	Yes
Telephone	Expense	No
UIC (Unemploy Ins)	Expense	Yes
Utilities	Expense	No

TABLE 6-1. Standard Personal Categories

category field when you enter your first furniture transaction automatically makes it a category option. When Quicken does not find the category in the existing list, it displays a window asking if you want to select a category or add the category to the list. You would choose Add the category, just as you did when you added the category for Auto loan in Chapter 4.

However, if you have a number of categories to add, it is simpler to add them before starting to enter data. To use this approach for adding the Furniture category, follow these steps:

1. Press (CTRL)-(C) or press (F4) for Quick Entry, and then select item 3, Categorize/Transfer.

Both actions will open the Category and Transfer List window.

2. Press (HOME) to move to the top of the category list.

<New Category> will be the top entry in the list.

3. Press (ENTER).

Quicken will allow you to enter a new category using the window shown here,

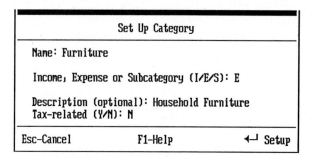

which contains entries for a new Furniture category that you could add to your Category list.

4. Type **Furniture** and press (ENTER).

5. Type **E** and press (ENTER).

6. Type **Household Furniture** and press (ENTER).

7. Type **N** and press ⟨**ENTER**⟩ to complete the entry.

Categories will be added as transactions are entered for the remaining examples in this chapter. You should feel free to customize the categories as you enter them.

 Available RAM will limit the number of categories you can create in each category list. With a 512K system, approximately 1000 categories can be created, whereas 150 is the limit if you only have 320K of memory. You are also limited to 15 characters for each category entry.

Requiring Categories in All Transactions

Another customization option Quicken offers is a reminder to place a category entry in a transaction before it is recorded. If you attempt to record a transaction without a category, Quicken will not complete the transaction until you confirm that you want to enter it without a category.

To require the entry of categories, choose the Change Settings option from the Main Menu and then select Other Settings. Press ⟨**ENTER**⟩ twice to move to the third item in the Other Settings window and type **Y**. Press ⟨**CTRL**⟩-⟨**ENTER**⟩ to finalize the settings change. The next time you attempt to record a transaction without a category, Quicken will stop to confirm your choice before saving.

USING SUBCATEGORIES

Now that you have set up your account group and new account and have customized your categories, you are ready to enter some transactions. Since you are already proficient at basic transaction entry from earlier chapters, you will want to look at some additional ways of modifying accounts as you make entries.

One option is to create categories that are subcategories of an existing category. For instance, rather than continuing to allocate all your utility bills to the Utilities category, you could create more specific subcategories under Utilities that let you allocate expenses to electricity, water, or gas. You could add the subcategories just as you added the new category for furniture, but you can also create them when you are entering transactions and realize that the existing categories do not provide the breakdown you would like.

Entering a New Subcategory

When you enter both a category and a subcategory for a transaction, you type the category name, followed by a colon (:), and then the subcategory name. It is important that the category be specified first and the subcategory second.

You will enter utility bills as the first entries in the new account. Follow these steps to complete the entries for the gas and electric bills, creating a subcategory under Utilities for each:

1. With the next blank transaction in the register highlighted, type **7/25/91** as the date for the first transaction and press ⏎ENTER. Type **101** and press ⏎ENTER.

2. Type **Consumer Power** and press ⏎ENTER. Type **35.45** for the payment amount and press ⏎ENTER. Move the cursor, using ⏎ENTER or ⏎TAB, to the Memo field, type **Electric Bill**, and press ⏎ENTER. Type **Utilities: Electric** and press ⏎ENTER again.

Quicken prompts you with the Category Not Found window and allows you to add the category or select one from the category list. Notice that only the Electric entry is highlighted in the Category field, since Utilities is already in the category list.

3. Type **1** to select Add to Category List. Quicken displays the Set Up Category window for you to define the category.

4. Type **S** to define the entry as a subcategory and then press ⏎ENTER.

5. Type **Electric Utilities** and press ⏎ENTER.

Although this description is optional it is a good idea to enter one so that your reports will be informative. Your screen will look like Figure 6-5.

6. Press ⏎ENTER to select *N* (for No) for Tax-related.

A note is displayed by Quicken prompting you to be sure you understand what you are doing.

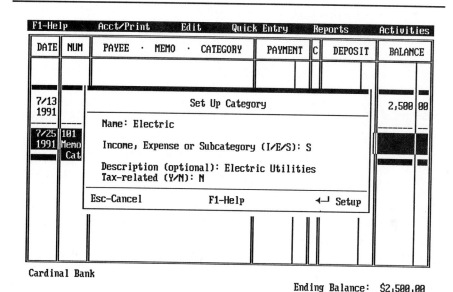

FIGURE 6-5. Setting up the subcategory

7. Press ENTER to close the note box.
8. Press CTRL-ENTER to record the transaction entry.

Completing the Utility Subcategories

To create a subcategory for the gas bill enter the following information in each of the fields shown.

Date:	7/25/91
Num:	102
Payee:	West Michigan Gas
Payment:	17.85
Memo:	Gas Bill
Category:	Utilities:Gas

Then press ⟨**ENTER**⟩ after typing the entry for Category. Again Quicken highlights any category it cannot find and allows you to add it. Use the same entries as in steps 3 through 8 in the preceding section. Use "Gas Utilities" for the optional description in the Set Up Category window. When you complete the steps, there will be two subcategories under Utilities.

You still need to enter the telephone bill, but since Quicken already defines Telephone as a Home category, you cannot consider Telephone as a subcategory of Utilities. However, you could edit the Telephone category and change it from an expense to a subcategory. For now, add it as a separate category, and put the following entries in the transaction fields.

Date:	7/30/91
Num:	103
Payee:	Alltel
Payment:	86.00
Memo:	Telephone Bill
Category:	Telephone

SPLITTING TRANSACTIONS

Split transactions are transactions that affect more than one category. You can decide how the transaction affects each of the categories involved. If you split an expense transaction, you are saying that portions of the transaction should be considered as expenses in two different categories. For example, a check written at a supermarket may cover more than just groceries. You might purchase a $25.00 plant as a gift at the same time you purchase your groceries. Recording the entire amount of the check as groceries would not accurately reflect the purpose of the check. Quicken allows you to record the $25.00 amount as a gift purchase and the remainder for groceries. In fact, after allocating the $25.00 to gifts, it even tells you the remaining balance that needs to be allocated to other categories. You could also enter a transaction in which you cashed a check and use the split transaction capability to account for your spending. As an example, enter the following transaction for check number 100.

Date: 7/20/91
Num: 100
Payee: Cash
Payment: 100.00
Memo: Groceries & Misc

Don't record the transaction. With the cursor in the Category field, follow these steps:

1. Press CTRL-S or open the Edit menu with F3 and select Split transaction.

2. Type **Groceries**, the name of the first category you want to use.

You can also use CTRL-C to display a category list for your selection.

3. Press ENTER and then type **Grocery & Market** and press ENTER again.

4. Type **75** and press ENTER.

5. Type **Misc** as the next category and press ENTER.

6. Type **Drug & Hardware Store** and press ENTER.

Quicken displays 25.00 as the amount for the second category, as shown in Figure 6-6.

7. Press CTRL-ENTER to accept the amount entry.

The first category entered for the split transaction appears in the register as the category. The word "SPLIT" also appears under the check number.

8. Press CTRL-ENTER to record the transaction.

There are many other times when you might elect to use split transactions. Assigning part of a mortgage payment to interest and the balance to principal is a good example. Credit card purchases can also be handled in this fashion if you elect not to set up a special credit card account. Normally, the split transaction approach is a better alternative if you pay your bill in full each month.

```
┌─────────────────────────────────────────────────────────────────────────┐
│ F1-Help      Acct/Print      Edit      Quick Entry    Reports    Activities│
├──────┬────┬─────────────────────────────────┬──────────┬─┬────────┬───────┤
│ DATE │NUM │ PAYEE  ·  MEMO  ·  CATEGORY      │ PAYMENT  │C│ DEPOSIT│BALANCE│
├──────┼────┼─────────────────────────────────┼──────────┼─┼────────┼───────┤
│ 7/20 │100 │ Cash                            │ 100 00   │ │        │       │
│ 1991 │Memo:│Groceries & Misc               │          │ │        │       │
│      │Cat:│                                 │          │ │        │       │
├──────┴────┴─────────────────────────────────┴──────────┴─┴────────┴───────┤
│                          Split Transaction                                 │
│                                                                            │
│           Category              │        Description         │   Amount    │
│      1:Groceries                │ Groceries & Market         │   75.00     │
│      2:Misc                     │ Drug & Hardware Store      │   25.00     │
│      3:                         │                            │             │
│      4:                         │                            │             │
│      5:                         │                            │             │
│      6:                         │                            │             │
│                                                                            │
│           Enter categories, descriptions, and amounts                      │
│  Esc-Cancel     Ctrl-D Delete    F9-Recalc Transaction Total   Ctrl◄─┘ Done│
└────────────────────────────────────────────────────────────────────────────┘
```

FIGURE 6-6. Splitting the cash transaction

Notice that up to where you enter the category, there is no difference between a split transaction entry and any other entry in the register. Complete the following entries to add another split transaction for a credit card payment:

1. Type **8/3/91** as the date and press ⟨ENTER⟩.

2. Type **105** as the check number and press ⟨ENTER⟩.

3. Type **Easy Credit Card** for the Payee entry and press ⟨ENTER⟩.

4. Type **450.00** and press ⟨ENTER⟩ to complete the payment amount entry. Press ⟨ENTER⟩ or ⟨TAB⟩ to move to the Memo field.

5. Type **July 25th Statement** for the Memo field and press ⟨ENTER⟩.

6. Press ⟨F3⟩ and select Split Transaction or press ⟨CTRL⟩-⟨S⟩.

Quicken displays the Split Transaction screen with up to six category fields displayed. You can assign as many as 30 split categories.

7. Press ⟨CTRL⟩-⟨C⟩ with the cursor in the first category field.

8. Select Clothing and press (ENTER) twice.

9. Type **Blue Blouse** in the Description field and press (ENTER).

10. Type **50** and press (ENTER).

Quicken allocates the first $50.00 of credit card expense to Clothing and shows the $400.00 balance below this entry.

11. Complete the remaining entries shown in Figure 6-7 to detail how the credit card expenses were distributed.

When you press (CTRL)-(ENTER) for final processing, you will see the Number field for this transaction contains the word "SPLIT" under the check number, and "Clothing" is displayed in the Category field.

12. Press (CTRL)-(ENTER) to record the transaction.

F1-Help	Acct/Print	Edit	Quick Entry	Reports	Activities

DATE	NUM	PAYEE · MEMO · CATEGORY	PAYMENT	C	DEPOSIT	BALANCE
8/ 3	105	Easy Credit Card ·	450 00			
1991	Memo:	July 25th Statement				
	Cat:					

Split Transaction

Category	Description	Amount
1:Clothing	Blue Blouse	50.00
2:Dining	Dinner at the Boathouse	60.00
3:Auto Fuel	Gasoline - Jeep Wagoneer	23.00
4:Furniture	Green Rocker	217.00
5:Entertain	Play Tickets	50.00
6:Misc		50.00

Enter categories, descriptions, and amounts
Esc-Cancel   Ctrl-D Delete   F9-Recalc Transaction Total   Ctrl◄─┘ Done

FIGURE 6-7. Splitting the credit card transaction

USING MULTIPLE ACCOUNTS

Quicken makes it easy to create multiple accounts. Since here all the accounts will be created in the same account group, you can choose to have separate reports for each account or one report that shows them all. You will have an account register for each account that you create.

Types of Accounts

Savings accounts, investment accounts, cash accounts, and credit card accounts are all possible additional accounts. Savings accounts and investment accounts should definitely be kept separate from your checking account since you will want to monitor both the growth and balance in these accounts.

The need for cash and credit card accounts varies by individual. If you pay the majority of your expenses in cash and need a detailed record of your expenditures, a cash account is a good idea. With credit cards, if your purchases are at a reasonable level and you pay the balance in full each month, the extra time required to maintain a separate account may not be warranted. In the initial example in this chapter neither cash nor credit card accounts are used. If you decide you need them, you can use the same procedures to create them that you used to create the savings account. Near the end of the chapter is a complete section on the detailed entries required to maintain a separate credit card account.

Creating a New Savings Account

If you want to transfer funds from your checking account to a savings account you must have a savings account set up. Follow these steps to create the new account:

1. Press ⌜F2⌝ to open the Acct/Print menu and then type **1** for Select/Set Up Account.

2. Select <New Account> and press ⌜ENTER⌝.

3. Type **1** for Bank Account type and press ⌜ENTER⌝.

4. Type **Cardinal Saving** for the account name and press ⌜ENTER⌝.

5. Type **500.00** for the balance and press ⌈ENTER⌉.

6. Type **7/15/91** as the date and press ⌈ENTER⌉.

7. Type **Savings account** for the description and press ⌈ENTER⌉.

Quicken will open the Select Account to Use window.

8. Select Cardinal Bank and press ⌈ENTER⌉.

Transferring Funds to a Different Account

It is easy to transfer funds from one account to another as long as both accounts are established. You might transfer a fixed amount to savings each month to cover long-range savings plans or to cover large, fixed expenses that are due annually or semi-annually. Follow these steps to make a transfer from the checking account to the savings account:

1. Complete these entries for the transaction fields down to category:

Date:	8/5/1991
Payee:	Cardinal Saving
Payment:	200.00
Memo:	Transfer to savings

2. Press ⌈CTRL⌉-⌈C⌉ with Category highlighted, select Cardinal Saving from the Category and Transfer List and press ⌈ENTER⌉. Your screen will display a Category and Transfer List with Cardinal Saving marked with an arrow, as shown in Figure 6-8, before you press ⌈ENTER⌉.

3. Press ⌈CTRL⌉-⌈ENTER⌉ to confirm the transaction.

You will notice brackets around the account name in the Category field of the register. Although it will not be visible on the screen, Quicken automatically creates the parallel transaction in the other account. It will also delete both transactions as soon as you specify that one is no longer needed.

```
┌─────────────────────────────────────────────────────────┐
│              Category and Transfer List                 │
│  ┌──────────────┬──────┬──────────────────────┬───────┐ │
│  │   Category   │ Type │     Description      │  Tax  │ │
│  ├──────────────┼──────┼──────────────────────┼───────┤ │
│  │ Tax Fed      │Expns │Federal Tax           │   ◆   │ │
│  │ Tax FICA     │Expns │Social Security Tax   │   ◆   │ │
│  │ Tax Other    │Expns │Misc, Taxes           │   ◆   │ │
│  │ Tax Prop     │Expns │Property Tax          │   ◆   │ │
│  │ Tax State    │Expns │State Tax             │   ◆   │ │
│  │ Telephone    │Expns │Telephone Expense     │       │ │
│  │ UIC          │Expns │Unemploy, Ins, Commission│ ◆  │ │
│  │ Utilities    │Expns │Water, Gas, Electric  │       │ │
│  │ Electric     │Sub   │Electric Utilities    │       │ │
│  │ Gas          │Sub   │Gas Utilities         │       │ │
│  │ Cardinal Bank│Bank  │Personal checking     │       │ │
│  │▶Cardinal Saving│Bank│Savings Account       │       │ │
│  └──────────────┴──────┴──────────────────────┴───────┘ │
│                                                         │
│    Ctrl-D Delete  Ctrl-E Edit  Ctrl-P Print             │
│  Esc-Cancel            F1-Help          ↵ Use           │
└─────────────────────────────────────────────────────────┘
```

FIGURE 6-8. List of categories showing Cardinal Saving

MEMORIZED TRANSACTIONS

Many of your financial transactions are likely to repeat. You pay your rent or mortgage payments each month. Likewise, utility bills, credit card payments, and other bills are paid at about the same time each month. Cash inflows in the form of paychecks are also regularly scheduled. Other payments such as groceries also repeat but probably not on the same dates each month.

Quicken can *memorize* transactions that are entered from the register or check writing screen. Once memorized, these transactions can be used to generate similar transactions. Amounts and dates may change, so you can edit these fields without having to reenter the payee, memo, and category information.

Memorizing a Register Entry

Any transaction in the register can be memorized. Memorized transactions can be recalled for later use, printed, changed, and deleted. To try this you will need to add a few more transactions to the account register to complete the entries for August. Add these transactions to your register:

Date:	8/1/91
Payee:	Payroll deposit
Deposit:	1585.99
Memo:	August 1 paycheck
Category:	Salary

Date:	8/2/91
Num:	104
Payee:	Great Lakes Savings & Loan
Payment:	350.00
Memo:	August Payment
Category:	Mort Pay

This is a new category you should add since you do not have the information required to split the transaction between the existing interest and principal categories in the Home category list. Use Entire Mortgage Payment as the description when you add the category.

Date:	8/4/91
Num:	106
Payee:	Maureks
Payment:	60.00
Memo:	Groceries
Category:	Groceries

Date:	8/6/91
Num:	107
Payee:	Orthodontics, Inc.

Payment:	100.00
Memo:	Monthly Orthodontics Payment
Category:	Medical

Date:	8/15/91
Num:	108
Payee:	Meijer
Payment	65.00
Memo:	Groceries
Category:	Groceries

You now have transactions representing an entire month entered in the checking account. You can elect to have Quicken memorize as many as you feel will repeat every month. To memorize the transaction for Consumer Power follow these steps:

1. Highlight the Consumer Power transaction in the register.

2. Press (F4) to open the Quick Entry menu and type 2 to select Memorize Transaction (or press (CTRL)-(M) to select Memorize Transaction without opening the menu).

Quicken will highlight the transaction and prompt you for a response.

3. Press (ENTER) to confirm and memorize the transaction. You can also memorize transactions that have not been recorded in the register, but you will have to press (CTRL)-(ENTER) after memorizing them to update the register.

Using the same procedure memorize all the remaining transactions except the transactions written to Maureks and Meijer.

Quicken will memorize split transactions in the same way as any other transactions. You should carefully review the split transactions for information that changes each month. For example, the entry for the credit card payment is likely to be split across several categories if you are entering the detail in the check register rather than a separate credit card account. You will want to edit both the categories into which the main transaction is split and the amounts.

You can use CTRL-T to display the memorized transactions; your list should match Figure 6-9. If you want to print the list once it is displayed, press CTRL-P, type a number to select your printer, and press ENTER to print. To remove the list from the screen, press ESC.

USING MEMORIZED TRANSACTIONS To recall a memorized transaction and place it in the register, move to the next blank transaction form (unless you want the recalled transaction to replace a transaction already on the screen). Press CTRL-T to recall the Memorized Transactions List window. Use the arrow keys to select the transaction you want to add to the register and then press ENTER. If you type the first few letters of the Payee field before pressing CTRL-T, Quicken will take you to the correct area of the transaction list since transactions are displayed in alphabetical order by payee. The selected transaction appears in the register with the date of the last transaction you entered, not that of the date that was stored when

```
┌───────────────────────────────────────────────────────────────────┐
│                     Memorized Transactions List                      │
├───────────────────────────────────────────────────────────────────┤
│    Description    Split  Memo        Category  Clr  Amount  Type Grp │
├───────────────────────────────────────────────────────────────────┤
│  Alltel                 Telephone B Telephone         86.00 Pmt      │
│▶ Cardinal Saving        Transfer to [Cardinal S      200.00 Pmt      │
│  Consumer Power         Electric Bi Utilities:E       35.45 Pmt      │
│  Easy Credit Card    S  July 25th S Clothing         450.00 Pmt      │
│  Great Lakes Savings    August Paym Mort Pay         350.00 Pmt      │
│  Orthodontics, Inc.     Monthly Ort Medical          100.00 Pmt      │
│  Payroll deposit        August 1 pa Salary         1,585.99 Dep      │
│  West Michigan Gas      Gas Bill    Utilities:G       17.85 Pmt      │
│                                                                       │
│                                                                       │
├───────────────────────────────────────────────────────────────────┤
│         Ctrl-D Delete   Ctrl-P Print   ↑,↓ Select                    │
│   Esc-Cancel                F1-Help                       ↵ Use      │
└───────────────────────────────────────────────────────────────────┘
```

FIGURE 6-9. List of memorized transactions

you memorized the transaction. You can edit the transaction in the register and press (CTRL)-(ENTER) when you are ready to record the entry.

CHANGING AND DELETING MEMORIZED TRANSACTIONS To change a memorized transaction you must recall it from the Memorized Transactions List to a blank transaction in the register. Then make your changes and memorize it again. When you press (CTRL)-(M) to memorize it, Quicken will ask you if you want to replace the transaction memorized earlier or add a new transaction. If you confirm the replacement, Quicken makes the change.

To delete a memorized transaction, you must first activate the transaction list by pressing (CTRL)-(T) or pressing (F4) to open the Quick Entry menu and select Recall Transaction. Select the transaction you want to delete and press (CTRL)-(D). A warning message will appear asking you to confirm the deletion. When you press (ENTER) the transaction is no longer memorized.

Memorizing a Check

The procedure for memorizing transactions while writing checks is identical to the one used for memorizing register transactions, except that you must be in the check writing window. Memorized check and register transactions for the same account will appear in the same Memorized Transactions List and can be edited, deleted, or recalled from either the check writing or register windows.

WORKING WITH TRANSACTION GROUPS

Although recalling a memorized transaction works well for reentering a single transaction, for several transactions that all occur at the same time it is more efficient to define a *transaction group*. When you are ready to pay these transactions you can have Quicken record the entire group for you automatically, after you make any changes in amounts or other information. You can even have Quicken remind you when it is time to record these transactions again.

Defining a Transaction Group

Quicken allows you to set up as many as 12 transaction groups. Defining a group is easy, but it requires several steps after all the transactions that will be placed in the group are recorded. You will need to select a number for the group you want to define. Next you will describe the group. Last, you will need to assign specific memorized transactions to the group. Although expense transactions are frequently used to create groups, you could also include an entry for a direct deposit payroll check that is deposited at the same time each month.

For your first transaction group, which you will title Utilities, you will group the telephone, gas, and electricity transactions that occur near the end of each month. Follow these steps to create the transaction group from the Cardinal Bank account register:

1. Press ⌈F4⌋ to open the Quick Entry menu and type **5** to select Transaction Group.

Quicken displays the window shown in Figure 6-10.

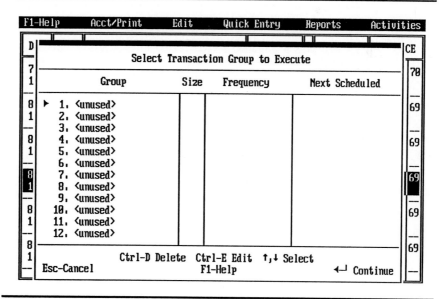

FIGURE 6-10. Setting up a transaction group

2. Highlight 1, since this is the first unused transaction group, and press
   `CTRL`-`ENTER`.

Quicken displays a window to allow you to define the group. Figure 6-11
shows this screen with the entries you will make in the next step.

3. Type **Utilities** as the name for the group and press `ENTER`.

Even though the group is named Utilities, the transaction for the telephone
expense will be included since it is paid at the same time as the utility bills
each month. If you wanted you could use another name such as "Month-End
Bills" and also include the payment to Easy Credit Card. You should look at
your transactions for a month or two to decide how to best define your
transaction groups. You can specify which account to load for this account
group if you are using Quicken 4.

4. Type **6** as the frequency for the reminder and press `ENTER`. When you
   don't want to be reminded you can choose None.

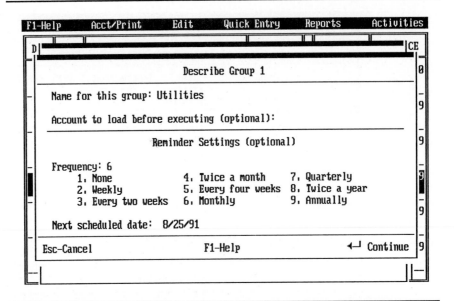

FIGURE 6-11. Defining the memorized transactions in a group

5. Type **8/25/91** as the next scheduled date for the reminder and press
   ⌈ENTER⌋.

Quicken will remind you three days in advance of this date. Later in this
chapter you will learn how to adjust this setting. Next Quicken displays a
window that allows you to assign transactions to Group 1. Only memorized
transactions are present on this list. The transactions are listed in alphabetical order by payee to make it easy to locate the desired transactions.

6. Select Alltel and press ⌈SPACEBAR⌋ to mark the transaction.

Note the 1 in the Group column indicating that the transaction is now a part
of Group 1.

7. Move the cursor to Consumer Power and press ⌈SPACEBAR⌋.
8. Move the cursor to West Michigan Gas and press ⌈SPACEBAR⌋.

Quicken marks this transaction as part of the group.

9. Press ⌈ENTER⌋ to indicate you are finished selecting transactions.

You may want to define other transaction groups to include your payroll
deposit, mortgage payment, and anything else you pay at the beginning of
the month. You do not need to define additional groups to complete the
remaining exercises in this section.
   If you want to create a transaction group that is executable at the Write
Checks screen you will want to include information that will complete a
check form. You can identify these transactions in the Assign Transactions
window with a Chk entry in the Type field instead of entering Pmt, which
indicates an account register transaction.

Changing a Transaction Group

You can add to a transaction group at any time by selecting Set Up Transaction Group after pressing ⌈F4⌋ to open the Quick Entry menu. As you
proceed through the normal definition procedure you can select additional
transactions for inclusion in the group.

To change the description or frequency of the reminder, use the same procedure as before except make the changes on the windows presented.

To delete a transaction group, use (F4) to open the Quick Entry menu and select the Set Up Transaction Group. Select the group you want to delete and press (CTRL)-(D). Quicken eliminates the group but does not delete the memorized transactions that are part of it. It also does not affect any transactions recorded in the register by using the transaction group.

If you want to alter a transaction that is part of the transaction group you will need to alter the recorded, memorized transaction. This means you will have to bring up the recorded transaction on the Write Checks screen or in the register, depending on the type of transaction you have. Then, you will need to rememorize the transaction. Follow the procedures in "Changing and Deleting Memorized Transactions" earlier in this chapter.

Having Quicken Remind You to Record Transactions

Quicken will remind you to enter upcoming transaction groups. This reminder will either occur at the DOS prompt when you boot your system or at the Main Menu when you first load Quicken. Hard disk users who have the default setting for Billminder still set at Yes will see a message at the DOS prompt reminding them to pay postdated checks or record transaction groups. If you do not have a hard disk or if you have turned Billminder off, the prompt will not appear until you start Quicken.

Recording a Transaction Group

Once you have defined a transaction group you do not need to wait for a reminder when you want to record the group in your register or check writing window. Since you can memorize entries for either the register or the check writing window, you must have the appropriate group defined for your current needs. A group type called CHK is created in the check writing window and can be recorded in the account register or the check writing window. Payment (Pmt) groups are recorded in the account register and can only be used to record account register entries. To execute a transaction group from the account register follow these steps:

1. Press ⬚F4⬚ (Quick Entry), then type **5** to select Transaction Groups.

Quicken will display a list of account groups.

2. Select the Utilities group by moving the arrow cursor to it and pressing ⬚ENTER⬚.

Quicken will display the date of the next scheduled entry of the Utilities group, as shown here:

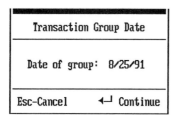

3. Press ⬚ENTER⬚ to confirm that this date is valid and to enter the group of transactions in the account register.

Quicken will indicate when the transactions have been entered to allow you to make modifications if needed. The window displayed is shown here:

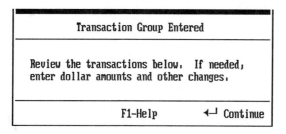

    You will now modify the utilities transaction group entries just recorded and add the last transaction for Meijer to complete the August transactions for your account register. (Press ⬚CTRL⬚-⬚ENTER⬚ to record each transaction after the modifications have been made.)

Num:	109
Payee:	Alltel
Payment:	23.00

Num:	110
Payee:	Consumer Power
Payment:	30.75

Num:	111
Payee:	West Michigan Gas
Payment:	19.25

Record the final transaction for the month of August as follows:

Date:	8/27/91
Num:	112
Payee:	Meijer
Payment:	93.20
Memo:	Food
Category:	Groceries

USING CLASSES

You have used categories as one way of distinguishing transactions entered in Quicken. Since categories are either income, expense, or a subcategory, these groupings generally define the transaction to which they are assigned. Also the status of a category as tax related or not affects the transactions to which it is assigned. Specific category names and descriptions provide more specific information about the transactions to which they are assigned. They explain what kind of income or expense a specific transaction represents. You can tell at a glance which costs are for utilities and which are for entertainment. In summary reports you might see totals of all the transactions contained in a category.

Classes allow you to "slice" the transaction "pie" in a different way. Classes recategorize to show where, to whom, or for what time period the transactions apply. It is important not to think of classes as a replacement for categories; they do not affect category assignments. Classes provide a different view or perspective of your data.

For example, you might use classes if you have both a year-round home and a vacation cottage. One set of utility expenses is for the year-round residence and another is for the vacation cottage utility expenses. If you define and then assign classes to the transactions, they will still have categories representing utility expenses, but you will also have class assignments that let you know how much you have spent for utilities in each of your houses.

Since the expenses for a number of family members can be maintained in one checking account, you might want to use classes for those expenses that you would like to review by family member. You can use this approach for clothing expenses and automobile expenses if your family members drive separate cars. Another method for automobile expenses is to assign classes for each of the vehicles you own. You can then look at what you have spent on a specific vehicle at the end of the year and make an informed decision regarding replacement or continued maintenance.

Quicken does not provide a standard list of classes. As with categories you can set up what you need before you start making entries or you can add the classes you need as you enter transactions. Once you have assigned a class to a transaction you will enter it in the Category field by placing it after your category name (if one exists) and any subcategories. A slash (/) is always typed before entering the class name, as in Utilities: Electric/Cottage.

To create a class before entering a transaction you can use CTRL-L to open the Class List window, as shown in Figure 6-12. You would select <New Class> and press ENTER to create a new entry. Quicken displays the Set Up Class window shown here,

```
┌──────────────────────────────────────────────────┐
│ ▄▄▄▄▄▄▄▄▄▄▄▄▄▄▄▄▄▄▄▄▄▄▄▄▄▄▄▄▄▄▄▄▄▄▄▄▄▄▄▄▄▄▄▄▄▄▄▄▄▄▄ │
│                    Set Up Class                    │
│                                          ─────────  │
│   Name:                                            │
│                                                    │
│   Description (optional):                          │
│                                          ─────────  │
│  Esc-Cancel            F1-Help          ↵ Setup    │
└──────────────────────────────────────────────────┘
```

where you can enter the name and description of a class. Each new class is added to the Class List window. To create a class as you enter a transaction simply type the category and any subcategories, followed by a slash and the class name you want to use and press ENTER. The following is an example

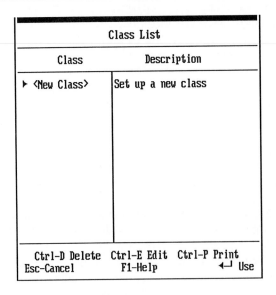

FIGURE 6-12. The Class List window

of a class entry for "Jim" which could be used if you wanted to separately categorize personal expenses for each individual in the household:

If Jim was not an existing class, the Class List would appear for your selection and you could create it. You will find more detailed examples of class entries in later chapters.

USING A SEPARATE CREDIT CARD ACCOUNT

If you charge a large number of your purchases and do not pay your credit card bill in full each month, a separate account for each of your credit cards is the best approach. It will enable you to better monitor your individual payments throughout the year. Also, your reports will show the full detail for all credit card transactions, just as your checking account register shows the details of each check written.

You will need to set up accounts for each card using the procedure followed when you created the account for Cardinal Saving earlier in the chapter. You can enter transactions throughout the month as you charge items to each of your credit card accounts or you can wait until you receive the statements at the end of the month. You should use a reconciliation procedure similar to the one you used for your checking account to verify that the charges are correct. To reconcile your credit card account and pay your bill select Pay Credit Card from the Activities menu of the credit card register.

You can use Quicken's Transfer features to transfer funds between your checking account and credit card. If you have overdraft protection, you can also create a transaction to record the overdraft charges to your credit card and checking accounts.

IMPORTANT CUSTOMIZING OPTIONS AS YOU SET UP YOUR ACCOUNTS

Quicken provides a number of options for customizing the package to meet your needs. These include the addition of passwords for accessing accounts, options already discussed, such as requiring category entries, and other options that affect the display of information on your screen and in reports. Once you know how to access these settings you will find that most are self-explanatory. All of the changes are made by selecting Change Settings from the Main Menu.

Adding Passwords

To add passwords, type **5** to select Password from the Change Settings menu. Quicken presents the menu shown next.

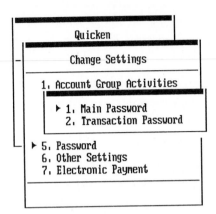

This allows you to decide if you want to password protect an account group by using a main password, or only existing transactions by using a transaction password. Although you can add protection with a password at both levels, you will need to select each individually.

If you select Main Password, Quicken asks you to enter a password. Once you press (**ENTER**) the password will be added to the active account group and anyone wishing to work with that account group must supply it. The transaction password is used to prevent changes to existing transactions prior to a specified date, without the password. If you choose Transaction Password you will be presented with a window that requires you to enter both a password and a date.

If you want to change a password or remove it in a subsequent session, you must be able to provide the existing password. Quicken will then provide a Change Password window for the entry of the old and new passwords, as shown here:

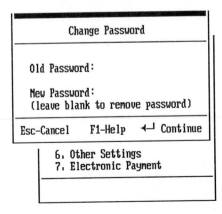

```
┌─────────────────────────────────────────────────────┐
│▄▄▄▄▄▄▄▄▄▄▄▄▄▄▄▄▄▄▄▄▄▄▄▄▄▄▄▄▄▄▄▄▄▄▄▄▄▄▄▄▄▄▄▄▄▄▄▄▄▄▄▄▄│
│                    Other Settings                     │
│                                                       │
│   1.  Beep when recording and memorizing (Y/N): Y     │
│   2.  Request confirmation (for example,              │
│           when changing the Register) (Y/N)  : Y      │
│   3.  Require Category on transactions (Y/N)  : N     │
│   4.  Extra message line on check (printed            │
│           on check but not recorded) (Y/N)   : N      │
│   5.  Days in advance to remind of postdated          │
│           checks and scheduled groups (0-30) : 3      │
│   6.  Change date of checks to today's date           │
│           when printed (Y/N)                 : N      │
│   7.  MM/DD/YY or DD/MM/YY date format (M/D)  : M      │
│   8.  Billminder active (Y/N)                : Y      │
│   9.  Print categories on voucher checks (Y/N): Y     │
│   10. 43 line register/reports (EGA,VGA) (Y/N): N     │
│   11. Show Memo/Category/Both    (M/C/B)     : B      │
│   12. In reports, use category Description/           │
│           Name/Both (D/N/B)                  : D      │
│   13. Warn if a check number is re-used (Y/N) : N     │
│                                                       │
├─────────────────────────────────────────────────────┤
│  Esc-Cancel          F1-Help           ◄─┘ Continue   │
└─────────────────────────────────────────────────────┘
```

════════ **FIGURE 6-13.**   Other Settings options

After completing the entries and pressing (ENTER), the new password will be in effect.

Changing Other Settings

Figure 6-13 shows the screen presented when Other Settings is selected from the Change Settings menu. This screen shows the defaults for each of the options. The first option allows you to turn off the beep you hear when recording and memorizing transactions. The second option controls whether Quicken prompts for confirmation when you make register changes.

Changing option 3 will require category entries on all transactions. Option 4 allows you to print on the checks an extra line that is not recorded. The fifth option allows you to change the days in advance that you will be reminded to pay postdated checks and record transaction groups. You will want to adjust this setting based on how frequently you use Quicken. For example, if you use the package only once a week, a reminder that occurs three days before will often not be sufficient.

Option 6 will change the date printed on checks to the current date instead of the date entered. Option 7 allows you to control the date format. Option 8 allows hard disk users to control whether or not the Billminder prompt will display when DOS is loaded. Other options control the appearance of the screen and reports. If the description on the Other Settings screen is not sufficient, remember you can use ⟨**F1**⟩ (Help) for an expanded description of the option.

Option 9 is useful if you are printing voucher style checks with Quicken. You can change it to *Y* to add the detail of categories to these checks. If you have an EGA or VGA monitor, the high-resolution image your monitor supports allows you to display additional information on the screen. Changing option 10 to *Y* for this type of monitor will display 43 lines from a register or report on the screen.

The information on the second line of a register entry can be changed with option 11. You can use it to display memo information if you change the setting to *M*. Changing option *C* will display category information only. The default setting of *B* will display both types of information. Option 12 allows you to control the use of the Description field on reports. An entry of *D* will use the description if there is one and use the category name when there is not one. Entering *N* will cause the category name to be used instead of the description. Entering *B* for this option will display both. The last option will warn you if a check number is reused. In order to activate this option, you must change the default setting.

QUICKEN AS A
BUDGETING TOOL

Quicken's Budgeting Process
Modifying the Budget Report
Tying the Budget Report to Other Quicken Reports
Budget Report Extension

The popular conception of a budget is that it is a constraint on your spending. But that is not what budgets are designed to be. Instead, a budget is a financial plan that shows your projected income and expenses to allow you to plan your expenses within the limits of your income. Although a budget may sometimes necessitate a temporary denial, this denial will supply the funds for expenses you have given greater priority.

Given the same income, five families would prepare five different budget plans. One family might budget to save enough for a down payment on a new house. Another family might construct its budget to afford a new car. A third family might enjoy eating out and traveling and budget accordingly. Within the constraints of your income the choice is yours.

If a budget is meant to facilitate getting what you want, why do so many people procrastinate in putting together a budget? It may be because budgeting takes time or that it forces decisions, or perhaps it is simply that most people are not sure where to begin. The one thing that is certain is that budgeting is an important component of every successful financial plan. You should create a budget even if you have already successfully built a financial nest-egg. It will allow you to protect your investment and ensure that your spending meets both your short- and long-range goals.

Quicken is ideally suited for maintaining your budget information. The program guides you through the budget development process and requires only simple entries to record budgeted amounts in categories you specify. After an initial modest investment of time, Quicken generates reports for use in monitoring your progress toward your financial goal, and you do not need to wait until the end of the budget period to record your progress. You can enter your expenses daily and check the status of your actual and budgeted amounts whenever you wish.

In this chapter you will prepare budget entries for several months. Transaction groups from Chapter 6 will be used to expedite the entry process while providing a sufficient number of transactions to get a sense of what Quicken can do. After making your entries you will see how Quicken's standard reports can help you keep expenses in line with your budget.

QUICKEN'S BUDGETING PROCESS

Quicken allows you to enter projected income and expense levels for any category. You can enter the same projection for each month of the year or change the amount allocated by month. Quicken matches your planned expenses with the actual expense entries and displays the results in a budget report. There is one entry point for budget information, but Quicken will combine actual entries from all of your bank, cash, and credit card accounts in the current account group. Although Quicken can take much of the work out of entering and managing your budget, it cannot prepare a budget without your projections. If you have never prepared a budget before, you should take a look at a few budget planning considerations, shown in the special Budget Planning section. Once you have put together a plan it is time to record your decisions in Quicken.

You can enter Quicken's budgeting process through the Main Menu (selecting the Reports option) or through the Reports menu entered from the account register or the Write/Print Checks options. The process described in the next section assumes you are in the account register for Cardinal Bank that you prepared in Chapter 6. Quicken's budgeting process will be presented in three stages: entering the Monthly Budget Report menu, specifying budget amounts, and printing the report.

BUDGET PLANNING

T
I
P

The budgeting process must begin before you start making budget entries in Quicken. You must start with an analysis of expected income. If your income flow is irregular, estimate on the low side. Remember to use only the net amount received from each income source. Also, do not include projected salary increases until they are confirmed.

The next step is analyzing projected expenses. The first item considered must be debt repayment and other essentials such as medical insurance premiums. In addition to monthly items such as mortgage and car loan payments, consider irregular expenses that are paid only once or twice a year. Tuition, property tax, insurance premiums, children's and personal allowances, and church pledges are examples. Project expenses such as medical, pharmacy, and dental bills for one year. Compute the required yearly expenses and save toward these major expenses so the entire amount does not need to come from a single month's check.

The next type of expense you should plan into your budget is savings. If you wait until you cover food, entertainment, and all the other day-to-day expenses, it is easy to find that there is nothing left to save. You should plan to write yourself a check for at least five percent of your net pay for savings when you pay your other bills.

The last type of expense you must budget for is the day-to-day expenses such as food, personal care, home repairs, gasoline, car maintenance, furniture, recreation, and gifts.

Naturally, if your totals for expenses exceed income projections, you must reassess the essentials before entering projected amounts in Quicken.

During the first few months of budgeting, err on the side of too much detail. At the end of the month you will need to know exactly how your money was spent. You can make realistic adjustments between expense categories to ensure that your budget stays in balance.

Entering the Monthly Budget Report Menu

You are familiar with entering the Reports window from Quicken's account register since you prepared the Cash Flow and Itemized Category reports in

Chapter 3. The procedure for the Monthly Budget report is similiar, except that Quicken will expect you to enter projected amounts:

1. From the account register press (F5) and the Reports menu will appear on your screen.

2. Type **1** and then **2** to select the Monthly Budget report for a personalized report. Figure 7-1 will appear on your screen.

3. Press (ENTER) to accept Quicken's default report title "Monthly Budget Report."

The title is optional. You could also customize the report title at this point if you wanted to include your name or other information. You are limited to 39 characters if you decide to use a customized report title.

4. Type **8/91** and press (ENTER).

You must identify the month(s) you want to use for the budget beginning and ending dates on your reports. The 8/91 entry matches the first full month of income and expense entries you completed in Chapter 6.

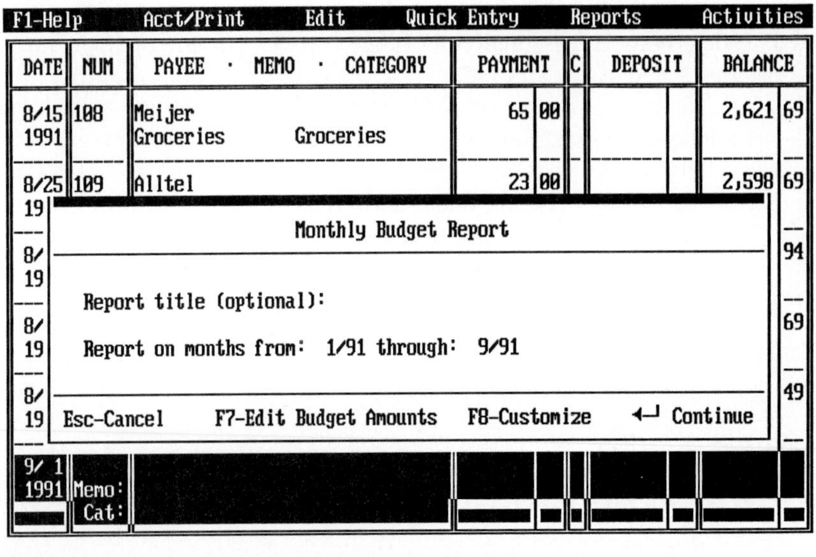

FIGURE 7-1. Monthly Budget Report window

5. Type **8/91** and press ⟨ENTER⟩. Your screen displays a message telling you that Quicken cannot produce a budget report without your entering budget amounts.

Again, the 8/91 entry is appropriate for the data from Chapter 6. Pressing ⟨ENTER⟩ after typing the ending date for the budget caused Quicken to try to produce the budget report that compares actual transactions and budget figures. Since there are no budget entries, the Quicken message tells you that you must supply budgeted amounts for each of the categories in your Cardinal Bank account register from Chapter 6. All the transactions entered in your register with dates between the beginning and end of the month will be included in the actual entries shown in your budget report.

6. Press ⟨ESC⟩ and Quicken will return you to the Monthly Budget Report window.

The next section describes the procedure for entering budget amounts in Quicken categories.

Specifying Budget Amounts

You will enter budget amounts for the transaction categories you entered in the Cardinal Bank account register in this section. Later, when you create your own budget, you will need to expand the budget entries to include all the categories of income and expense you want to monitor.

There are a few points to consider before you complete the budget entries. First, you must enter a budget amount for each category you want included in your budget report. It doesn't matter what period of time you define as the reporting period. (You can also customize the report for other time periods than a monthly reporting basis—for instance, yours could be every quarter or half year.)

Second, all the categories you have available in your category list are shown in the Specify Budget Amounts window, shown in Figure 7-2. This includes Quicken's predefined personal category list as well as any new categories you have added. Any categories you leave blank when completing this window will not be shown on the report. This means that if you want to include a budget item because you will be using it in the future, you must enter 0 (zero) for the category so it will be included in the current report.

```
 F1-Help      Acct/Print     Edit      Quick Entry     Reports      Activities
┌─────────────────────────────────────────────────────────────────────────┐
║                        Specify Budget Amounts                          9  ║
║                                                                           ║
║                                                 Budget       Monthly   9  ║
║        Category      Type       Description     Amount       Detail       ║
║  ┌─────────────────────────────────────────────┬─────────┬─────────┐  9  ║
║  ▶ Bonus            Inc  │Bonus Income          │         │         │     ║
║    Canada Pen       Inc  │Canadian Pension      │         │         │  ─  ║
║    Div Income       Inc  │Dividend Income       │         │         │  4  ║
║    Family Allow     Inc  │Family Allowance      │         │         │     ║
║    Gift Received    Inc  │Gift Received         │         │         │  ─  ║
║    Int Inc          Inc  │Interest Income       │         │         │  9  ║
║    Invest Inc       Inc  │Investment Income     │         │         │     ║
║    Old Age Pension  Inc  │Old Age Pension       │         │         │  ─  ║
║    Other Inc        Inc  │Other Income          │         │         │  9  ║
║    Salary           Inc  │Salary Income         │         │         │     ║
║    Auto Fuel        Expns│Automobile Fuel       │         │         │  ─  ║
║    Auto Loan        Expns│Auto Loan Payment     │         │         │     ║
║  └─────────────────────────────────────────────┴─────────┴─────────┘     ║
║                              ↑,↓ Select                                    ║
║  Esc-Cancel        F1-Help     Ctrl-E Edit Monthly Detail    Ctrl↵ Done ▓ ║
└─────────────────────────────────────────────────────────────────────────┘
```

FIGURE 7-2. Quicken's request for budget amounts

Third, you only set monthly budget amounts once. After that Quicken will assume that the amount established will be used as the budgeted amount for all future months, unless you modify them.

Fourth, you can only assign budget amounts to income and expense categories. You cannot assign budget amounts to subcategories.

To set the budget amounts follow these steps:

1. Press (F7) to select Edit the Budget Amounts.

Since the Monthly Budget Report window is still on the screen, Quicken will interpret your command as a desire to enter budget figures and will open the Specify Budget Amounts window, shown in Figure 7-2. Normally, you would enter realistic amounts that matched your budget plan. In this exercise you will be entering budget amounts that are provided for you.

2. Press the (DOWN ARROW) key until the arrow cursor is next to the Salary category.

3. The regular cursor should be blinking in the Budget Amount column; type **1585.99** and press (ENTER).

4. Using ⟨**DOWN ARROW**⟩ to scroll down the list, move the arrow cursor to the Utilities category. Type **45** and press ⟨**CTRL**⟩-⟨**E**⟩. Quicken will display the Monthly Budget For Category: Utilities window, shown in Figure 7-3.

Notice that Quicken has automatically recorded the dollar value in each of the month cells for you. Quicken assumes this is the amount you want to use for all months during the budget period unless you change the monthly values. Although you entered your utility expenses in subcategories in Chapter 6, you must use the main category for your entries here. Quicken will not accept dollar amounts in any subcategories for budget amount purposes.

5. Move to the entry for October, type **55** to replace the 45.00 value, and press ⟨**ENTER**⟩.

Notice that Quicken changed the dollar amount only for one month. If you want Quicken to change the dollar value for all subsequent months, you would press ⟨**F9**⟩. Try that method now.

6. Press ⟨**UP ARROW**⟩ once to move the arrow cursor to the month you just changed. Press ⟨**F9**⟩.

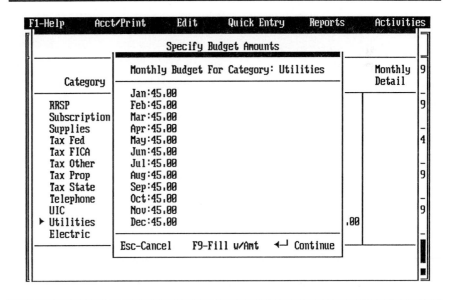

FIGURE 7-3. Automatic acceptance of budget amount for all months

Notice that this time all the values for subsequent months have changed to 55. You might make this type of change because new power rates are expected or because you have installed a number of new outside lights.

7. Press ⌈**CTRL**⌉-⌈**ENTER**⌉ and Figure 7-4 appears on your screen.

Note that Quicken has entered the 45.00 value for the current budget amount and that the Monthly Detail column says "Yes" next to the budgeted amount. This indicates a different value is entered for the remaining months of the budget year for this category.

8. Using the following information, complete the Budget Amount column for the categories. Remember, the process involves using ⌈**UP ARROW**⌉ or ⌈**DOWN ARROW**⌉ to move the arrow cursor to a specific category, typing the budget amount shown in the list, and pressing ⌈**ENTER**⌉. (For the furniture transaction, use the Monthly Budget For Category window to enter 185.00 for the month of October and 250.00 for December. These amounts will match your Chapter 6 entries and supply the budget figures for October and December in this chapter's example.)

```
 F1-Help      Acct/Print      Edit      Quick Entry     Reports      Activities

                          Specify Budget Amounts

                                                       Budget    Monthly    9
        Category      Type       Description           Amount    Detail
                                                                            9
     Subscriptions  Expns Subscriptions
     Supplies       Expns Supplies                                          -
     Tax Fed        Expns Federal Tax                                       4
     Tax FICA       Expns Social Security Tax
     Tax Other      Expns Misc. Taxes                                       -
     Tax Prop       Expns Property Tax                                      9
     Tax State      Expns State Tax
     Telephone      Expns Telephone Expense                                 -
     UIC            Expns Unemploy. Ins. Commission                        9
     Utilities      Expns Water, Gas, Electric         45.00     Yes
   ▶ Electric       Sub   Electric Utilities                                -
     Gas            Sub   Gas Utilities

                              ↑,↓ Select
     Esc-Cancel        F1-Help    Ctrl-E Edit Monthly Detail    Ctrl◄┘ Done
```

═══ **FIGURE 7-4.** A category can contain monthly detail modifications

Category	Budget Amount
Auto Fuel	30
Clothing	70
Dining	55
Entertain	55
Furniture	0
Groceries	200
Medical	120
Misc	75
Mort Pay	350
Telephone	30
Cardinal Saving	200

The zero value was entered in the Furniture category to demonstrate that Quicken will not include categories in the budget report unless a value is entered here during this phase of budget preparation. This means you must enter some value, even zero, for those categories you want to be included in your report or in the future.

In the early stages, it generally takes several months to develop sound estimates for all your expenditure categories. For example, this illustration shows a desired transfer to savings of $200.00 per month. If there are any excess cash inflows at the end of the month you would transfer the excess to savings. On the other hand, if there is an excess of outflow over inflow you would need a transfer from savings. Once you have established your spending patterns and monitored your inflows and outflows, you may find that there are months of excess inflows during parts of the year and excess outflows in others, such as during the holiday season. You can use budgeting to plan for these seasonal needs and anticipate the transfer of funds between savings and checking accounts.

9. Press **CTRL**-**ENTER** after completing the last entry. The Monthly Budget Report window reappears on your screen.

10. Press **CTRL**-**ENTER** and the Monthly Budget report will be displayed.

11. Press **F8** and the Print Report window will open. Select your printer and press **CTRL**-**ENTER**, and the report will be printed as shown in Figure 7-5. If you need to change printer settings, refer to the procedures in Chapter 3.

```
                        MONTHLY BUDGET REPORT
                        8/ 1/91 Through 8/31/91
     PERSONAL-Bank,Cash,CC Accounts                              Page 1
     9/ 1/91
                                    8/ 1/91      -       8/31/91
        Category Description       Actual      Budget       Diff
     ----------------------      -----------------------------------------
     INFLOWS
        Salary Income             1,585.99     1,585.99         0.00
                                  ----------   ----------   ----------
        TOTAL INFLOWS             1,585.99     1,585.99         0.00

     OUTFLOWS
        Automobile Fuel              23.00        30.00        -7.00
        Clothing                     50.00        70.00       -20.00
        Dining Out                   60.00        55.00         5.00
        Entertainment                50.00        55.00        -5.00
        Entire Mortgage Payment     350.00       350.00         0.00
        Groceries                   218.20       200.00        18.20
        Household Furniture         217.00         0.00       217.00
        Medical & Dental            100.00       120.00       -20.00
        Miscellaneous                50.00        75.00       -25.00
        Telephone Expense            23.00        30.00        -7.00
        Water, Gas, Electric         50.00        45.00         5.00
                                  ----------   ----------   ----------
     TOTAL OUTFLOWS               1,191.20     1,030.00       161.20
                                  ----------   ----------   ----------
     OVERALL TOTAL                  394.79       555.99      -161.20
                                  ==========   ==========   ==========
```

FIGURE 7-5.   Monthly Budget report for all accounts

If your printer has compressed print capabilities you may wish to use that setting when printing reports. That way you will capture more of your report on a page. For example, your monthly report will be printed across two pages unless you use the compressed print feature here.

MODIFYING THE BUDGET REPORT

Review your printed copy and notice that the report is dated for the one-month period you defined at the opening budget screen prompt. Also notice that Quicken automatically combines all the bank, cash, and credit card accounts in the actual and budgeted figures of the Monthly Budget report. This means that as you scroll down the report you don't see the $200.00

transfer to Cardinal Saving. Quicken views all of your accounts as a single unit for budget report purposes and considers the transfer to have a net effect of zero since it is within the system. Thus, the $200.00 is not shown on the report. You will see how you can change this a little later since a transfer of $200.00 to savings can be a significant event from a budgeting perspective and, consequently, something that you might want to show on a report.

You can see in Figure 7-5 that you were over your budget for the period by $161.20, represented by a negative value for the overall total difference. When Quicken compares your budgeted versus actual expenditures for each category, if your actual expenditures exceed the budgeted amount a *positive* number is shown in the Diff column of the report. If the actual expenditure is less than the budgeted amount a *negative* number appears in that column. In reading the report you can quickly see whether you met your budget objectives. As noted above, the actual outflows exceed the budgeted outflows (1,191.20 − 1,030.00 = 161.20).

On closer examination you can see there was the unexpected expenditure for furniture during the month that was not budgeted. All your budgeted categories appear with the amount you were over or under budget in each. This category-by-category breakdown is the heart of budget analysis and pinpoints areas for further scrutiny.

You may want to modify the report you just printed to cover only the current account, Cardinal Bank. This change will allow you to see the transfer to the savings account as part of your report for the month. This can be accomplished by following these steps.

1. Go back to the account register and reenter the monthly report generation process by pressing (F5) and typing **1** and then **2**. The Monthly Budget Report window will appear again.

2. Press (F8) in order to customize your report. The Create Budget Report window, shown in Figure 7-6, will open.

3. Press (ENTER) three times, type **5**, and press (ENTER) again. This tells Quicken you want a monthly report prepared.

4. Type **C** and press (ENTER). The modified report will appear on your screen. Notice that only the current account was used in preparing this report.

5. Press (F8) and the Print Report window will open. Select your printer, press (CTRL)-(ENTER), and the report will be printed.

Your new budget report for the account group PERSONAL and the account Cardinal Bank, shown in Figure 7-7, is displayed on the screen and then printed. Notice that the transfer to Cardinal Saving is shown in your report,

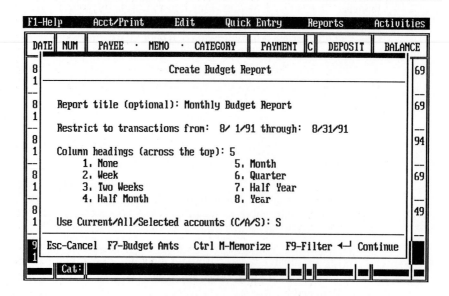

FIGURE 7-6. Modifying Quicken to print the current account

but your results haven't changed. The upper-left corner of your report shows that the report is for the Cardinal Bank account only. Reexamine Figure 7-5 and notice that the report included the bank, cash, and credit card accounts. Unless you have chosen otherwise, Quicken lists these three account types, even though such accounts have not been established.

TYING THE BUDGET REPORT TO OTHER QUICKEN REPORTS

You have now completed the basic steps in preparing your budget report. Now let's see how the report relates to the reports prepared in Chapter 3. Figures 7-8 and 7-9 present a Cash Flow report and a portion of an Item-ized Category report for the budget period for the Cardinal Bank account. Since the example is based on only one month, the Cash Flow report (shown

```
                          Monthly Budget Report
                          8/ 1/91 Through 8/31/91
        PERSONAL-Cardinal Bank                                    Page 1
        9/ 1/91
                                              8/ 1/89    -    8/31/89
                    Category Description      Actual    Budget    Diff
                    --------------------      -----------------------------

                    INFLOWS
                       Salary Income          1,585.99  1,585.99   0.00
                                              ---------  --------  -------
                    TOTAL INFLOWS             1,585.99  1,585.99   0.00

                    OUTFLOWS
                       Automobile Fuel            23.00     30.00   -7.00
                       Clothing                   50.00     70.00  -20.00
                       Dining Out                 60.00     55.00    5.00
                       Entertainment              50.00     55.00   -5.00
                       Entire Mortgage Payment   350.00    350.00    0.00
                       Groceries                 218.20    200.00   18.20
                       Household Furniture       217.00      0.00  217.00
                       Medical & Dental          100.00    120.00  -20.00
                       Miscellaneous              50.00     75.00  -25.00
                       Telephone Expense          23.00     30.00   -7.00
                       Water, Gas, Electric       50.00     45.00    5.00
                       TO Cardinal Saving        200.00    200.00    0.00
                                              --------  -------  -------
                    TOTAL OUTFLOWS            1,391.20  1,230.00  161.20


                                              --------  -------  -------
                    OVERALL TOTAL               194.79    355.99 -161.20
                                              ========  =======  =======
```

FIGURE 7-7.   Monthly Budget report for Cardinal Bank account

in Figure 7-8) and the column labeled "Actual" in the Monthly Budget report (in Figure 7-7) contain the same inflows and outflows. Normally, the budget summary would cover information for a longer period of time (such as a quarter or year) and you would prepare a Cash Flow report for each of the months included in the budget report. You should think through your reporting requirements instead of just printing all the reports.

You may be wondering why the Cash Flow report shows a positive $194.79 net cash inflow, while the budget report indicates that you were over budget by $161.20. This occurs because the Cash Flow report only looks at actual cash inflows and outflows. On the other hand, the budget examines what you want to spend and what you actually spent. Looking at the budget column of Figure 7-7, you can see that there would have been an additional $355.99 to transfer to savings if you had met your budget objectives.

```
                              Cash Flow Report
                            8/ 1/91 Through 8/31/91
       PERSONAL-Cardinal Bank                                    Page 1
       9/ 1/91
                                                    8/ 1/91-
                        Category Description        8/31/91
       ------------------------------  --------------------
       INFLOWS
         Salary Income                              1,585.99
                                                   ----------
       TOTAL INFLOWS                                1,585.99

       OUTFLOWS
         Automobile Fuel                               23.00
         Clothing                                      50.00
         Dining Out                                    60.00
         Entertainment                                 50.00
         Entire Mortgage Payment                      350.00
         Groceries                                    218.20
         Household Furniture                          217.00
         Medical & Dental                             100.00
         Miscellaneous                                 50.00
         Telephone Expense                             23.00
         Water, Gas, Electric:
           Electric Utilities            30.75
           Gas Utilities                 19.25
                                        ----------
         Total Water, Gas, Electric                    50.00
         TO Cardinal Saving                           200.00
                                                   ----------
       TOTAL OUTFLOWS                                1,391.20
                                                   ----------
       OVERALL TOTAL                                  194.79
                                                   ==========
```

═══════ **FIGURE 7-8.** Cash Flow report for budget period

Figure 7-9 provides selected detailed category information for the budget period. Notice that the Easy Credit Card Split Transaction window provides detail for each of the categories used when recording the credit card payment. Also notice that the Groceries category is printed by check number and provides detail for the groceries amount on the Monthly Budget and Cash Flow reports. When looking at extended budget and cash flow reporting, the details provided from the Itemized Category report can provide useful insights into your spending patterns by showing where you spent and the frequency of expenditures by category. This information can help in analyzing the changes you might want to make in your spending patterns. (Please note that some of the lines in Figure 7-9 might look slightly different from what appears on your screen. Some allowances had to be made to fit the material on screen onto the page.)

```
              EXPENSES
                Automobile Fuel
                ---------------
        8/ 3   105  S Easy Credit Card      Gasoline -Jee Auto Fuel        -23.00
                                                                          ---------
                     Total Automobile Fuel                                 -23.00

                Clothing
                --------
        8/ 3   105  S Easy Credit Card      Blue Blouse    Clothing        -50.00
                                                                          ---------
                     Total Clothing                                        -50.00

                Dining Out
                ----------
        8/ 3   105  S Easy Credit Card      Dinner at the Dining           -60.00
                                                                          ---------
                     Total Dining Out                                      -60.00

                Entertainment
                -------------
        8/ 3   105  S Easy Credit Card      Play Tickets   Entertain       -50.00
                                                                          ---------
                     Total Entertainment                                   -50.00

                Entire Mortgage Payment
                -----------------------
        8/ 2   104   Great Lakes Savings   August Payment Mort Pay        -350.00
                                                                          ---------
                     Total Entire Mortgage Payment                        -350.00

                Groceries
                ---------
        8/ 4   106   Maureks               Groceries      Groceries        -60.00
        8/15   108   Meijer                Groceries      Groceries        -65.00
        8/27   112   Meijer                Food           Groceries        -93.20
                                                                          ---------
                     Total Groceries                                      -218.20
```

FIGURE 7-9. Partial Itemized Category report for budget period

BUDGET REPORT EXTENSION

The reports prepared so far in this chapter give you an overview of the budgeting process by looking at expenditures for one month. You would extend your examination over a longer period to tell if the over-budget situation in August was unusual or part of a trend that should be remedied.

To do this you will need to add transactions for other months. Fortunately, the transaction groups discussed in Chapter 6 can be used to make the task easy. As you add more information to the reports you will learn how to create wide reports with Quicken.

Additional Transactions

In order to provide a more realistic budget situation, you will extend the actual budget amounts for several months by creating new register transactions. This will also give you an opportunity to practice techniques such as recalling memorized transactions and making changes to split transactions. Remember, you will be using the transactions recorded in Chapter 6. Figure 7-10 presents the check register entries you will make to expand your database for this chapter. Recording the first transaction in the Cardinal Bank account register would involve these steps:

1. Press ⌐CTRL⌐-⌐T⌐ to display the list of memorized transactions.

You were instructed to memorize most of the transactions in Chapter 6. If you did not, memorize all the transactions from Chapter 6 now, except for the grocery payments to Maureks and Meijer.

2. Move the arrow cursor to the transaction you want to recall, Cardinal Saving, and press ⌐ENTER⌐.

3. Make any changes in the transaction. In this case change the amount to 194.79 and press ⌐CTRL⌐-⌐ENTER⌐.

As explained earlier, excess cash in any month should be transferred to savings. This helps prevent impulsive buying if you are saving for larger outflows in later months of the year. But remember that when you plan an actual budget you can build in varying monthly savings, rather than using the approach of setting a minimum amount and transferring any excess of inflow or outflow at the beginning of each month.

4. Complete the example by entering all the information in your register exactly as shown in Figure 7-10.

In looking at the transactions shown in Figure 7-10, notice that you will primarily be recalling memorized transactions and split transactions throughout the recording process. The only transactions that are not memorized are the grocery checks; for those you will be using regular transaction recording procedures.

You will use the Split Transaction windows to enter the Easy Credit Card transactions for check numbers 114 and 122 respectively. Notice that the Furniture category is not used in check 114 but is part of the credit card transaction for check 122. All the information you need to record these two transactions is included in Figure 7-10.

5. After entering the last transaction in Figure 7-10, press ⌐F5⌐ and the Reports menu will open.

6. Type **1** and then **2** to select Monthly Budget Report.

7. Press ⌐ENTER⌐ to accept Quicken's default report title.

8. Type **8/91** and press ⌐ENTER⌐.

9. Type **10/91,** press ⌐F8⌐, and the Create Budget Report window will appear.

10. Press ⌐ENTER⌐ three times.

11. Type **5** to select month for column headings and press ⌐ENTER⌐.

12. Type **C** and press ⌐ENTER⌐ and the Monthly Budget report appears.

Wide-Screen Reports

The Monthly Budget report you just generated is spread across more than one screen and may be difficult to comprehend until you realize how it is structured. In this section you will explore the wide-screen report and become more familiar with Quicken results.

The steps listed here will help you become familiar with the Monthly Budget report generated from the additional data that you entered.

1. Use ⌐TAB⌐, ⌐SHIFT⌐-⌐TAB⌐, ⌐PGUP⌐, ⌐PGDN⌐, ⌐HOME⌐, and ⌐END⌐ to become familiar with the appearance of the wide report for the budget.

Notice how easy it is to move around the report. Also notice that to open the Print Report window you only have to press ⌐F8⌐, as indicated at the lower-right corner of the screen. ⌐HOME⌐ always returns you to the upper-left

```
                            Check Register
Cardinal Bank                                                     Page 1
9/ 1/91

Date  Num          Transaction         Payment  C  Deposit    Balance
----- -----  ------------------------- ---------- - ---------- ----------

9/ 1         Cardinal Saving             194.79                2,260.70
1991 memo: Transfer to savings
      cat: [Cardinal Saving]

9/ 2         Payroll deposit                        1,585.99   3,846.69
1991 memo: September 1, Paycheck
      cat: Salary

9/ 2 113     Great Lakes Savings & Loan  350.00                3,496.69
1991 memo: September Payment
      cat: Mort Pay

9/ 3 114     Easy Credit Card            233.00                3,263.69
1991 SPLIT August 25th Statement
                 Clothing                 50.00
                    Red Blouse
                 Dining                    60.00
                    Dinner at the Boathouse
                 Auto Fuel                 23.00
                    Gasoline - Jeep Wagoneer
                 Entertain                 50.00
                    Play Tickets
                 Misc                      50.00

9/ 3 115     Maureks                      85.00                3,178.69
1991 memo: Food
      cat: Groceries

9/ 8         Cardinal Saving             200.00                2,978.69
1991 memo: Transfer to savings
      cat: [Cardinal Saving]

9/14 116     Orthodontics, Inc.          170.00                2,808.69
1991 memo: Monthly Orthodontics Payment
      cat: Medical

9/20 117     Maureks                      95.00                2,713.69
1991 memo: Food
      cat: Groceries

9/25 118     Alltel                       29.00                2,684.69
1991 memo: Telephone Bill
      cat: Telephone

9/25 119     Consumer Power               43.56                2,641.13
1991 memo: Electric Bill
      cat: Utilities:Electric
```

FIGURE 7-10. Additional account register entries

```
                            Check Register
Cardinal Bank                                              Page 2
9/ 1/91

  Date   Num          Transaction           Payment  C  Deposit    Balance
 -----  -----  ------------------------------ ---------- - ---------- ---------

 9/25   120    West Michigan Gas                19.29             2,621.84
 1991 memo: Gas Bill
       cat: Utilities:Gas

10/ 1          Cardinal Saving                 166.35            2,455.49
 1991 memo: Transfer to savings
       cat: [Cardinal Saving]

10/ 2          Payroll deposit                          1,585.99 4,041.48
 1991 memo: October 1 paycheck
       cat: Salary

10/ 2   121    Great Lakes Savings & Loan      350.00            3,691.48
 1991 memo: October Payment
       cat: Mort Pay

10/ 4   122    Easy Credit Card                957.00            2,734.48
 1991 SPLIT September 25th Statement
               Clothing                         75.00
                 White Dress
               Dining                           45.00
                 Dinner at the Boathouse
               Auto Fuel                        37.00
                 Gasoline - Jeep Wagoneer
               Furniture                       550.00
                 Table and Chairs
               Entertain                       100.00
                 Play Tickets
               Misc                            150.00

10/ 5   123    Maureks                         115.00            2,619.48
 1991 memo: Food
       cat: Groceries

10/ 5          Cardinal Saving                 200.00            2,419.48
 1991 memo: Transfer to savings
       cat: [Cardinal Saving]

10/ 8   124    Orthodontics, Inc.              100.00            2,319.48
 1991 memo: Monthly Orthodontics Payment
       cat: Medical

10/19   125    Maureks                         135.00            2,184.48
 1991 memo: Food
       cat: Groceries

10/25   126    Alltel                           27.50            2,156.98
 1991 memo: Telephone Bill
       cat: Telephone
```

FIGURE 7-10. Additional account register entries (*continued*)

```
                              Check Register
Cardinal Bank                                                    Page 3
9/ 1/91

  Date  Num           Transaction        Payment  C  Deposit   Balance
  ----- -----  --------------------------- ---------- - ---------- --------

10/25 127    Consumer Power                37.34               2,119.64
1991 memo: Electric Bill
      cat: Utilities:Electric

10/25 128    West Michigan Gas             16.55               2,103.09
1991 memo: Gas Bill
      cat: Utilities:Gas
```

FIGURE 7-10. Additional account register entries (*continued*)

side of the wide-screen report. (END) always takes you to the lower-right side of the report. (TAB) moves you right one screen, and (SHIFT)-(TAB) moves you left one screen. (PGUP) moves you up one screen, while (PGDN) moves you down one screen.

2. If you have the compressed print option, it is recommended that you use that setting to print wide reports. This printer option significantly increases the amount of material you can print on a page.

When you print wide-screen reports Quicken numbers the pages of the report so you can more easily follow on hard copy.

REPORT DISCUSSION Preparing and printing the report will become familiar with a little practice. The real issue is how to use the information. Let's look at the report and discuss some of the findings.

1. Press (END). Quicken takes you to the lower-right side of the quarterly report. This shows that for the quarter you spent $1,030.58 more than you had budgeted.

2. Using (UP ARROW), move up the report one line at a time until the title "OUTFLOWS" is in the upper-left corner of the screen.

You now have the quarterly outflow information on the screen for the three months of data you prepared earlier.

Notice that a part of the explanation for the actual outflows exceeding the inflows is due to $361.14 being transferred to savings. Most of us would not view that as poor results. On the other hand, you can see that you have spent $582.00 more on furniture than you had budgeted. This may be due to the fact that sale prices justified deviating from the budget. But, it could also be compulsive buying that can't be afforded over the long run. If you find yourself over budget, the special section on Dealing with an Over-Budget Situation provides some suggestions for improving the situation.

Figure 7-11 shows the budget summary for the period 8/1/91 through 10/31/91. Remember that the information Quicken uses in the Budget column came from the budgeted amounts you established earlier in this chapter. The information in the Actual column is summarized from the account register entries recorded in your Cardinal Bank checking account. You could also request a Cash Flow report by month for the budget period and examine the monthly outflow patterns. You might want to print out itemized category information for some categories during the period for more detailed analysis of expenditures.

```
                             Monthly Budget Report
                            8/ 1/91 Through 10/31/91
     PERSONAL-Cardinal Bank                                          Page 1
     9/ 1/91
                                       8/ 1/91    -     10/31/91
                  Category Description  Actual    Budget    Diff
                  ----------------------  ------------------------------

     INFLOWS
        Salary Income                  4,757.97  4,757.97      0.00
                                       ----------  ----------  ----------
     TOTAL INFLOWS                     4,757.97  4,757.97      0.00

     OUTFLOWS
        Automobile Fuel                   83.00     90.00     -7.00
        Clothing                         175.00    210.00    -35.00
        Dining Out                       165.00    165.00      0.00
        Entertainment                    200.00    165.00     35.00
        Entire Mortgage Payment        1,050.00  1,050.00      0.00
        Groceries                        648.20    600.00     48.20
        Household Furniture              767.00    185.00    582.00
        Medical & Dental                 370.00    360.00     10.00
        Miscellaneous                    250.00    225.00     25.00
        Telephone Expense                 79.50     90.00    -10.50
        Water, Gas, Electric             166.74    145.00     21.74
        TO Cardinal Saving               961.14    600.00    361.14
                                       ----------  ----------  ----------
     TOTAL OUTFLOWS                     4,915.58  3,885.00  1,030.58

                                       ----------  ----------  ----------
     OVERALL TOTAL                       -157.61    872.97 -1,030.58
                                       ==========  ==========  ==========
```

═════════════ **FIGURE 7-11.**   Three-month budget report

T I P

DEALING WITH AN OVER-BUDGET SITUATION

Expenses cannot continue to outpace income indefinitely. The extent of the budget overage and the availability of financial reserves to cover it will dictate the seriousness of the problem and how quickly and drastically cuts must be made to reverse the situation. Although the causes of an over-budget situation are numerous, the following strategies can help correct the problem:

- If existing debt is the problem, consider a consolidation loan—especially if the interest rate is lower than existing installment interest charges. Then don't use your credit until the consolidated loan is paid in full.

- If day-to-day variable expenses are causing the overrun, begin keeping detailed records of all cash expenditures. Look closely at what you are spending for eating out, entertainment, and impulse purchases of clothing, gifts, and other nonessential items.

- Locate warehouse, discount, thrift, and used clothing stores in your area and shop for items you *need* at these locations. Garage sales, flea markets, and the classified ads can sometimes provide what you need at a fraction of the retail cost.

- Be certain that you are allocating each family member an allowance for discretionary spending and that each is adhering to the total.

- If you cannot find a way to lower expenses any further, consider a free-lance or part-time job until your financial situation improves. Many creative people supplement their regular income with a small-business venture.

- Plan ahead for major expenses by splitting the cost of car insurance, property taxes, and so on over 12 months and transferring each month's portion to savings until it is time to pay the bill. If you have saved for it, you can then transfer the amount saved to the checking account the month of the anticipated expenditure.

chapter **8**

USING QUICKEN TO ORGANIZE TAX INFORMATION

Quicken Tax Overview
Planning to Use Quicken for Taxes
Recording Detailed Tax Information
Printing Quicken's Tax Reports
Tax Summary Report

Quicken's contribution to your financial planning and monitoring goes beyond recording transactions. You have already used Quicken to handle your budget entries and reports. Quicken can also help you with your tax preparation. Although using the package probably won't make tax preparation fun, it can reduce the tax-time crunch by organizing your tax information throughout the year. If you plan your categories and classes correctly and faithfully complete all your entries, the hard part is done. You will be able to use Quicken's summaries to provide the entries for specific lines on tax forms.

In this chapter you will see how Quicken can help you at tax time. After looking at a few ideas for organizing needed tax information, you will modify the account register prepared in Chapters 6 and 7 to better show your tax-related information. You will prepare tax summary information from the Standard Reports option of the package.

 You must remember that Quicken reports will not be considered sufficient documentation of tax-deductible expenses. See the special section on Essential Tax Documentation for a list of some of the forms you might need to substantiate expense claims to the IRS in an audit.

QUICKEN TAX OVERVIEW

This chapter focuses on how Quicken can help you prepare your tax returns. You can use Quicken's categories and classes to categorize data for your taxes. Categories are defined as tax related or not. You can change the tax-related status of any of the existing categories by editing the current category in the category list with CTRL-E. You can also define a tax-related status for any new category as you enter it.

Quicken can be used to collect information for specific line items on tax forms such as the Form 1040, Schedule A (itemized deductions), Schedule B (dividends and interest), and Schedule E (royalties and rents). Figures 8-1 and 8-2 show two of these forms. Defining and using classes for your transactions will allow you to collect additional details from your financial transactions.

In fact, once you become familiar with Quicken you can use the package to accumulate the exact information you need to prepare your taxes. For example, you may decide to tag specific tax information by setting up classes for categories that are tax related and specific to a particular tax form. At the end of the year you can have Quicken print the transactions that you need for a particular line. In your own Quicken system you may want to identify the specific forms associated with these items. For example, "Tax Fed/1040" indicates a class for transactions affecting the Form 1040. Another approach is to create a class that represents a line item on a specific form. For example, "Mort Int/A--9A" is more specific. The class entry "A--9A" indicates Schedule A, line 9A—mortgage interest paid to financial institutions. You could then have Quicken generate the tax-related information by tax form or line item and use these totals to complete your taxes.

T ESSENTIAL TAX
I DOCUMENTATION

P The entries in your Quicken register will not convince the IRS that you incurred expenses at the levels indicated. You need documentation of each expense to substantiate your deductions in the event of an audit. Although you may be able to convince them to accept estimates for some categories based on other evidence, the following are some ideas of the optimal proof that you will want to be able to present:

Expense Claimed	Proof
Dependents other than minor children	Receipts for individuals' support. Records of the individuals' income and support from others
Interest	Creditor statements of interest paid
Investments	Purchase receipts and brokerage firms' confirmation receipts
Medical and dental care	Canceled check with receipt indicating individual treated
Medical insurance	Pay stubs showing deductions or other paid receipts
Moving expenses	Itemized receipts and proof of employment for 12 months in previous job
Pharmacy/drugs	Itemized receipts and canceled checks
Real estate taxes	Receipt for taxes paid. Settlement papers for real estate transactions in the current year
Unreimbursed business expenses	Itemized receipts, canceled checks, and mileage logs

Form **1040**	Department of the Treasury—Internal Revenue Service	1989		OMB No. 1545-0074

U.S. Individual Income Tax Return

For the year Jan.–Dec. 31, 1989, or other tax year beginning , 1989, ending , 19

Label

Use IRS label.
Otherwise,
please print
or type.

Your first name and initial   Last name

If a joint return, spouse's first name and initial   Last name

Home address (number and street). (If a P.O. box, see page 7 of Instructions.)   Apt. no.

City, town or post office, state and ZIP code. (If a foreign address, see page 7.)

Your social security number

Spouse's social security number

For Privacy Act and Paperwork Reduction Act Notice, see Instructions.

Presidential Election Campaign ▶

Do you want $1 to go to this fund? . . . .   Yes   No
If joint return, does your spouse want $1 to go to this fund? .   Yes   No

Note: Checking "Yes" will not change your tax or reduce your refund.

Filing Status

Check only
one box.

1   Single
2   Married filing joint return (even if only one had income)
3   Married filing separate return. Enter spouse's social security no. above and full name here.
4   Head of household (with qualifying person). (See page 7 of Instructions.) If the qualifying person is your child but not your dependent, enter child's name here.
5   Qualifying widow(er) with dependent child (year spouse died ▶ 19). (See page 7 of Instructions.)

Exemptions

(See
Instructions
on page 8.)

If more than 6
dependents, see
Instructions on
page 8.

6a   Yourself   If someone (such as your parent) can claim you as a dependent on his or her tax return, do not check box 6a. But be sure to check the box on line 33b on page 2 . .

b   Spouse . . . .

c   **Dependents:**
(1) Name (first, initial, and last name)

	(2) Check if under age 2	(3) If age 2 or older, dependent's social security number	(4) Relationship	(5) No. of months lived in your home in 1989

d   If your child didn't live with you but is claimed as your dependent under a pre-1985 agreement, check here ▶

e   Total number of exemptions claimed . . . .

No. of boxes checked on 6a and 6b

No. of your children on 6c who:
● lived with you
● didn't live with you due to divorce or separation (see page 9)

No. of other dependents on 6c

Add numbers entered on lines above ▶

Income

Please attach
Copy B of your
Forms W-2, W-2G,
and W-2P here.

If you do not have
a W-2, see
page 6 of
Instructions.

Please
attach check
or money
order here.

7   Wages, salaries, tips, etc. (attach Form(s) W-2) **7**
8a   **Taxable** interest income (also attach Schedule B if over $400) . . .   **8a**
   b   **Tax-exempt** interest income (see page 10). DON'T include on line 8a   **8b**
9   Dividend income (also attach Schedule B if over $400) **9**
10   Taxable refunds of state and local income taxes, if any, from worksheet on page 11 of Instructions .   **10**
11   Alimony received **11**
12   Business income or (loss) (attach Schedule C). **12**
13   Capital gain or (loss) (attach Schedule D) **13**
14   Capital gain distributions not reported on line 13 (see page 11) **14**
15   Other gains or (losses) (attach Form 4797) **15**
16a   Total IRA distributions . .   **16a**   **16b** Taxable amount (see page 11)   **16b**
17a   Total pensions and annuities   **17a**   **17b** Taxable amount (see page 12)   **17b**
18   Rents, royalties, partnerships, estates, trusts, etc. (attach Schedule E) **18**
19   Farm income or (loss) (attach Schedule F) **19**
20   Unemployment compensation (insurance) (see page 13) **20**
21a   Social security benefits. .   **21a**   **21b** Taxable amount (see page 13)   **21b**
22   Other income (list type and amount—see page 13)   **22**
23   Add the amounts shown in the far right column for lines 7 through 22. This is your **total income** ▶   **23**

Adjustments to Income

(See
Instructions
on page 14.)

24   Your IRA deduction, from applicable worksheet on page 14 or 15   **24**
25   Spouse's IRA deduction, from applicable worksheet on page 14 or 15   **25**
26   Self-employed health insurance deduction, from worksheet on page 15   **26**
27   Keogh retirement plan and self-employed SEP deduction . .   **27**
28   Penalty on early withdrawal of savings **28**
29   Alimony paid. **a** Recipient's last name and **b** social security number. . .   **29**
30   Add lines 24 through 29. These are your **total adjustments** . . . . . . ▶   **30**

Adjusted Gross Income

31   Subtract line 30 from line 23. This is your **adjusted gross income.** If this line is less than $19,340 and a child lived with you, see "Earned Income Credit" (line 58) on page 20 of the Instructions. If you want IRS to figure your tax, see page 16 of the Instructions . . . ▶   **31**

═══ **FIGURE 8-1.** Federal Form 1040

SCHEDULES A&B
(Form 1040)
Department of the Treasury
Internal Revenue Service   (0)

Schedule A—Itemized Deductions
(Schedule B is on back)
▶ Attach to Form 1040. ▶ See Instructions for Schedules A and B (Form 1040).

OMB No. 1545-0074

1989
Attachment
Sequence No. 07

Name(s) shown on Form 1040

Your social security number

Medical and Dental Expenses (Do not include expenses reimbursed or paid by others.) (See Instructions on page 23.)	**1a** Prescription medicines and drugs, insulin, doctors, dentists, nurses, hospitals, medical insurance premiums you paid, etc . .	**1a**	
	b Other. (List—include hearing aids, dentures, eyeglasses, transportation and lodging, etc.) ▶		
		1b	
	2 Add the amounts on lines 1a and 1b. Enter the total here . . .	**2**	
	3 Multiply the amount on Form 1040, line 32, by 7.5% (.075) . .	**3**	
	4 Subtract line 3 from line 2. If zero or less, enter -0-. **Total** medical and dental . . ▶	**4**	
Taxes You Paid (See Instructions on page 24.)	**5** State and local income taxes	**5**	
	6 Real estate taxes	**6**	
	7 Other taxes. (List—include personal property taxes.) ▶	**7**	
	8 Add the amounts on lines 5 through 7. Enter the total here. **Total** taxes . . ▶	**8**	
Interest You Paid (See Instructions on page 24.)	**9a** Deductible home mortgage interest (from Form 1098) that you paid to financial institutions. Report deductible points on line 10.	**9a**	
	b Other deductible home mortgage interest. (If paid to an individual, show that person's name and address.) ▶		
		9b	
	10 Deductible points. (See Instructions for special rules.)	**10**	
	11 Deductible investment interest. (See page 25.)	**11**	
	12a Personal interest you paid. (See page 25.) . [12a]		
	b Multiply the amount on line 12a by 20% (.20). Enter the result .	**12b**	
	13 Add the amounts on lines 9a through 11, and 12b. Enter the total here. **Total** interest ▶	**13**	
Gifts to Charity (See Instructions on page 25.)	**14** Contributions by cash or check. (If you gave $3,000 or more to any one organization, show to whom you gave and how much you gave.) ▶	**14**	
	15 Other than cash or check. (You must attach Form 8283 if over $500.)	**15**	
	16 Carryover from prior year	**16**	
	17 Add the amounts on lines 14 through 16. Enter the total here. **Total** contributions . ▶	**17**	
Casualty and Theft Losses	**18** Casualty or theft loss(es) (attach Form 4684). (See page 26 of the Instructions.) . . . . ▶	**18**	
Moving Expenses	**19** Moving expenses (attach Form 3903 or 3903F). (See page 26 of the Instructions.) . . . . ▶	**19**	
Job Expenses and Most Other Miscellaneous Deductions (See page 26 for expenses to deduct here.)	**20** Unreimbursed employee expenses—job travel, union dues, job education, etc. (You MUST attach Form 2106 in some cases. See Instructions.) ▶	**20**	
	21 Other expenses (investment, tax preparation, safe deposit box, etc.). List type and amount ▶	**21**	
	22 Add the amounts on lines 20 and 21. Enter the total.	**22**	
	23 Multiply the amount on Form 1040, line 32, by 2% (.02). Enter the result here	**23**	
	24 Subtract line 23 from line 22. Enter the result. If zero or less, enter -0-. . . . . . ▶	**24**	
Other Miscellaneous Deductions	**25** Other (from list on page 26 of Instructions). List type and amount ▶ .... ▶	**25**	
Total Itemized Deductions	**26** Add the amounts on lines 4, 8, 13, 17, 18, 19, 24, and 25. Enter the total here. Then enter on Form 1040, line 34, the LARGER of this total or your standard deduction from page 17 of the Instructions . . . . ▶	**26**	

For Paperwork Reduction Act Notice, see Form 1040 Instructions.   Schedule A (Form 1040) 1989

FIGURE 8-2. Schedule A for itemized deductions

Establishing classes is just one way of handling tax-related items. Categories might provide all the organization you need. In this chapter tax-related categories for federal income tax withholding and state income tax withholding are created. A category for local income tax withholding will also be established. You will split entries for mortgage payments into mortgage interest and payments against the principal. Also, you will modify some of the transactions from earlier chapters to provide the additional tax information that you'll need here.

In later chapters you will combine Quicken's personal tax-related reports with the business reports. In these you will have a powerful tax-monitoring and planning tool.

PLANNING TO USE QUICKEN FOR TAXES

There is no one correct way to record tax information in Quicken. The best method is to tailor your transaction entries to the information that will be required on your tax forms. This is a good approach even if you have an accountant prepare your return. Remember, if you organize your tax information your accountant will not have to—and you will pay less for tax preparation as a result.

Start the planning process with the forms you filed last year. This may be just the Form 1040 that everyone files or it may include a number of schedules. Although the forms change a little from year to year and your need to file a certain form can be a one-time occurrence, last year's forms make a good starting place. Form 1040, partially shown in Figure 8-1, is the basic tax form used by individuals. Schedule A, shown in Figure 8-2, is used for itemized deductions. If you have unreimbursed business expenses that exceed a certain percentage of your income, you might want to set up a class for Form 2106, which is used exclusively for these expenses. If you own and manage rental properties, you must use Schedule E to monitor income and expenses for these properties. With Quicken you can classify the income and expense transactions for Schedule E.

With Form 2106 expenses, you will not know until the end of the year if you have enough expenses to deduct them, so you would use a class called "2106" for transactions of unreimbursed business expenses and check the total at year-end. Travel and entertainment expenses, meals, and professional association dues and subscriptions would all be assigned this class code to ensure that you collect them all.

Another thing to watch for is the timing of *expense recognition*. Expense recognition determines which tax year expenses at the beginning or end of the year will affect. This is a particular problem for items that are charged since the IRS recognizes an expense as occurring the day you charge it rather than the day you pay for it. Unreimbursed air travel charged in December 1990 and paid by check in January 1991 is counted in 1990 totals since you incur the liability for payment the day you charge the tickets. A separate Quicken account for credit purchases makes these necessary year-end adjustments easier than when you just keep track of credit card payments from your checkbook.

If you decide that categories do not give the information you need, you might decide your class codes should indicate more than the number of the tax form where the information is used. As you look at the forms shown in Figures 8-1 and 8-2, you will find that each of the lines where information can be entered is numbered. For example, line 7 of your 1040 is "Wages, salaries, tips, etc.," which you could probably fill in with the total from the Salary category—if you have only one source of income.

But when you set up Quicken categories for income from several sources, you might want to assign a class called "1040--7" to each income transaction, so you could display a total of all the entries for this class. Likewise, you can set up classes for other line items such as "A--6" for real estate tax or "A--14" for cash contributions. You could also set up "1040--21a" for Social Security benefits and "1040--9" for dividend income, but if you do decide to use classes, there is no need to establish a class for every line on every form—only for those lines that you are likely to use.

 When creating classes you must enter the category, a slash (/), and then the class.

Classes are almost a requirement for rental property management since the same types of expenses and incomes will repeat for each property. You might use the street address or apartment number to distinguish the transactions generated by different properties. You can use the Split Transaction feature if one transaction covers expenses or income for more than one property.

Most of your entries will focus on the current tax year, but there is also longer-term tax-related information that is sometimes needed. When you sell assets such as a house or stock holdings, information must be accumulated over the time you own the asset. Maintaining information on these assets in separate accounts is the best approach to use. Separate accounts can make it much easier to calculate the profit on the sale of the asset. For example, if you purchased a house for $100,000 and sold it five years later for $150,000, it might seem as though the profit is $50,000. However, if you have accurately recorded improvements such as a new deck and a fireplace, these amounts can be added to the cost of the asset since they are items that added value. When the $35,000 cost of these improvements is added to the price of the house, the profit is $15,000 for tax purposes. Take a look at the sample transaction in the next section and the tax reports before making your final decisions about classes and categories for your tax information.

RECORDING DETAILED TAX INFORMATION

In Chapter 7 you recorded detailed transaction information in the account register for your Cardinal Bank checking account. Scroll through those transactions and notice how the monthly paycheck and mortgage payment transactions were treated. For the paycheck you entered the amount of the check, net of deductions for items such as FICA, federal withholding, medical, and state withholding. For the monthly mortgage payment you established a tax-related category called Mort Pay and used that for the entire payment. However, Quicken can provide much better tax-related information in both these areas. The following sections will show you how.

Gross Earnings and Salary Deductions

Highlight the first payroll transaction you recorded in your Cardinal Bank personal account register in Chapter 6. The amount of the net deposit was $1585.99—you didn't record any of the tax-related information for deductions. The entry you made then was adequate for maintaining a correct check register. It is also adequate for budgeting purposes since you only need to match cash inflows and outflows and the net amount of the payroll check represents the inflow for the period. However, for tax purposes more information is needed. By completing the following entry you will be able to monitor the amounts on your pay stub. You will also be able to verify the accuracy of your Form W2 at the end of the year.

To expand the payroll transaction you need additional information. The gross earnings for the pay period were $2000.00. The deductions withheld for FICA taxes were $142.00, medical insurance was $42.01, federal taxes were $140.00, state taxes were $80.00, and local taxes were $10.00.

The steps on the next page illustrate how you can use Quicken's Split-Transaction feature to capture all the information related to the tax aspects of your paycheck and still show the net deposit of $1585.99 to the checking account.

1. With the first payroll entry highlighted, press (CTRL)-(S) and the Split Transaction window appears on your screen.

2. Press (ENTER) to leave Salary as the category.

3. Type **Gross Wages Earned** in the Description field and press (ENTER).

4. Type **2000.00** in the Amount field and press (ENTER).

These modifications set your Salary category as your gross earnings for the period. Each time you record your paycheck this way, Quicken will accumulate your year-to-date gross earnings. After recording this portion of the transaction, you are left with " −414.01" in the Amount field. This is Quicken's way of telling you there is currently a negative difference between the amount of the net deposit and the gross wages recorded. This difference equals the amount of withholding from your paycheck that will be recorded in the remaining steps.

5. Type; **Tax FICA** and press (ENTER).

6. Type **FICA Withholding** and press (ENTER).

7. Type **−142.00** and press (ENTER).

Once again Quicken records the information in the Split Transaction screen and leaves a balance of −272.01 in the Amount field for row 3. This category is predefined as tax related in Quicken, even though FICA withholding is not ordinarily tax deductible on your Form 1040. This is because you should monitor this amount if you change jobs during the year. Since there is a limit on the amount of earnings taxed for FICA, switching jobs can cause you to pay more than you owe since the second employer will not know what was withheld by the first. You can include excess FICA payments on your Form 1040 with other withholding amounts (on line 60). If you earn less than the upper limit, this category will not be used in your tax preparation process.

8. Type **Medical** and press (ENTER).

9. Type **Health Ins** and press (ENTER).

10. Type **−42.01** and press (ENTER).

11. Type **Tax Fed** and press (ENTER).

12. Type **Federal Income Tax** and press (ENTER).

13. Type **−140.00** and press (ENTER) to record the amount.

14. Type **Tax State** and press (ENTER).

15. Type **State Income Tax** and press (ENTER).

16. Type **−80.00** and press (ENTER).

17. Type **Tax Local** and press (ENTER).

Quicken will prompt you by stating that this is not a predefined category. Tell Quicken to enter the category with the following steps:

18. Type **1** in response to the Category Not Found window prompt.

19. Type **E** and press (ENTER).

20. Type **Local Tax Withholding** and press (ENTER).

21. Type **Y** and press (ENTER) to identify this as a tax-related category in response to the Set Up Category window.

22. Press (ENTER) when the Set Up Category window closes.

23. Type **Local Income Tax,** and press (ENTER).

Figure 8-3 is shown on your screen. Notice that there is no balance left to explain in the Split Transaction screen.

24. Press (CTRL)-(ENTER) and Quicken returns you to the Register window.

Since you memorized this transaction in Chapter 6, be sure to rememorize it after this change by pressing (CTRL)-(M).

25. Press (CTRL)-(ENTER) again to tell Quicken to accept the changed transaction.

After you complete this process all the information in the Split Transaction screen is recorded in your accounts. Your reports will show gross earnings for tax purposes at $2,000.00, with tax-related deductions for FICA, medical, and federal, state, and local taxes.

```
┌──────────────────────────────────────────────────────────────────────────┐
│ F1-Help      Acct/Print      Edit      Quick Entry    Reports    Activities│
├────┬────┬──────────────────────────────────┬─────────┬─┬─────────┬────────┤
│DATE│ NUM│  PAYEE  ·  MEMO  ·  CATEGORY      │ PAYMENT │C│ DEPOSIT │BALANCE │
├────┼────┼──────────────────────────────────┼─────────┼─┼─────────┼────────┤
│8/ 1│    │Payroll deposit                   │         │ │1,585 99 │3,846 69│
│1991│SPLIT│August 1 paycheck                │         │ │         │        │
│────│ Cat:│Salary                           │         │ │         │        │
│8/ 2│104 │Great Lakes Savings & Loan        │ 350 00  │ │         │3,496 69│
└────┴────┴──────────────────────────────────┴─────────┴─┴─────────┴────────┘
```

Split Transaction

	Category	Description	Amount
1:	Salary	Gross Wages Earned	2,000.00
2:	Tax FICA	FICA Withholding	-142.00
3:	Medical	Health Ins	-42.01
4:	Tax Fed	Federal Income Tax	-140.00
5:	Tax State	State Income Tax	-80.00
6:	Tax Local	Local Income Tax	-10.00

Enter categories, descriptions, and amounts
Esc-Cancel   Ctrl-D Delete   F9-Recalc Transaction Total   Ctrl⏎ Done

FIGURE 8-3. Split Transaction window after recording withholding and other deductions

Mortgage Principal and Interest

The mortgage payment transaction recorded in Chapter 6 was fine for recording changes to your checking account balance or monitoring budgeted expenses. However, it didn't capture the tax-related aspects of the transaction. While you identified the transaction as tax related, the mortgage principal and interest were not isolated. You would not be able to tell how much to list on your tax return as interest expense. But perhaps your bank will provide you a statement with this information at the end of the year. In some cases the bank even divides your previous month's payment among principal, interest, and escrow on the current month's bill. However, if you purchased from a private individual you will not receive this information and will need to look it up in a loan amortization table at your library or bank, since accurate records are necessary to take the mortage interest expense as a tax deduction. So long as you have the necessary information, Quicken can assist you by organizing it in the recording process.

On your screen, highlight the first Great Lakes Savings & Loan mortgage payment of $350.00 on 8/2/91 that you made in Chapter 6. Using Quicken's Split Transaction feature again, you will modify the record of this transaction to distribute the payment between principal and interest. The steps outlined here assume that you have principal and interest information available for each payment and that you pay your insurance and taxes directly to the insurer and local taxing unit with checks recorded separately in your register. If the financial institution has established an escrow account for these payments you could easily add that amount to this transaction. Quicken has predefined a tax-related category called Escrow.

The following procedures will illustrate how Quicken can be used to track your mortgage principal and interest payments:

1. With the first mortgage payment entry highlighted on the screen press CTRL-S and the Split Transaction window appears on your screen.

2. Type **Mort Prin** and press ENTER.

Notice that Quicken did not prompt you concerning the category since this is predefined on the list.

3. Type **Principal Payment** and press ENTER for the transaction description.

4. Type **49.21** and press ENTER to record the portion of the transaction related to principal.

5. Type **Mort Int** and press ENTER.

6. Type **Interest Portion of Payment** and press ENTER.

7. The amount shown in the last column, "300.79," is correct so just press ENTER. Figure 8-4 is shown on your screen.

8. Press CTRL-ENTER and Quicken returns you to the highlighted transaction for the mortgage payment in your register.

9. Press CTRL-ENTER to record the new split transaction information.

After recording these two transactions, you can see the expanded benefits of the information when it is organized by Quicken. Once again you would want to rememorize this transaction for monthly recording purposes. The next section takes a look at the tax information you have now entered into your Quicken system.

```
 F1-Help        Acct/Print       Edit      Quick Entry     Reports      Activities
┌────┬────┬─────────────────────────────────────┬─────────┬──┬─────────┬─────────┐
│DATE│ NUM│ PAYEE  ·  MEMO  ·  CATEGORY          │ PAYMENT │C │ DEPOSIT │ BALANCE │
├────┼────┼─────────────────────────────────────┼─────────┼──┼─────────┼─────────┤
│8/ 2│104 │Great Lakes Savings & Loan           │ 350│00  │  │         │3,496│69 │
│1991│Memo│August Payment                       │         │  │         │         │
│    │Cat:│Mort Pay                             │         │  │         │         │
│8/ 3│105 │Easy Credit Card                     │ 450│00  │  │         │3,046│69 │
└────┴────┴─────────────────────────────────────┴─────────┴──┴─────────┴─────────┘

                              Split Transaction

              Category                        Description              Amount
     1:Mort Prin                     Principal Payment                  49.21
     2:Mort Int                      Interest Portion of Payment       300.79
     3:
     4:
     5:
     6:

              Enter categories, descriptions, and amounts
     Esc-Cancel    Ctrl-D Delete    F9-Recalc Transaction Total   Ctrl◄┘ Done
```

FIGURE 8-4.   Split Transaction window after distributing principal and interest

PRINTING QUICKEN'S TAX REPORTS

The summary tax information generated by Quicken can be used to provide detailed information for preparing your taxes. In this section you will examine the reports generated using the information from the Cardinal Bank account register for the first month (8/1/91 through 8/31/91). The following steps will generate Quicken's Tax Summary report:

1. From the account register press **F5**, type **1**, then **4**. Quicken's Tax Summary Report window will appear on your screen.

2. Press **ENTER** to accept the default title of "Tax Summary Report."

3. Press **F8** and the Create Transaction Report window appears.

This step is performed so you can have Quicken print the reports for the current account and specified time period only. If you had proceeded

through the previous window, reports would have been automatically prepared for all the accounts in the account group. You will remember this step
from previous chapters.

4. Press (ENTER), type **8/1/91**, and press (ENTER) again.

5. Type **8/31/91** and press (ENTER).

6. Press (ENTER) to accept "Subtotal by Category."

7. Type **C** to select the current account and press (ENTER).

The Tax Summary report will appear on your screen. You can use (F9) to
change from full-width to half-width reports. You can also use the arrow
keys to move through the report (the directions in which the report extends
are shown in the lower-right corner of the screen).

8. Press (F8) and the Print Report window will appear on the screen.

9. Choose your printer option and press (ENTER). Quicken will print the
   tax summary by category as shown in Figure 8-5.

TAX SUMMARY REPORT

Figure 8-5 was printed on a laser printer with compressed print. Notice that
this is the full-width version of the report, with complete information for all
transaction fields. If you had printed the same version of the report without
the wide-print option, it would appear as shown in Figure 8-6. Although the
same information is included on both reports, the full-width version presents

```
                              Tax Summary Report
                            8/ 1/91 Through 8/31/91
        PERSONAL-Cardinal Bank                                    Page 1
        9/ 2/91

        Date  Num     Description          Memo        Category   Clr Amount
        ----- -----  ---------------------  --------------------  -------------- - -------

               INCOME/EXPENSE
                 INCOME
                   Salary Income
                   --------------
        8/ 1       S Payroll deposit      Gross Wages Earned  Salary      2,000.00
                                                                         ----------
                       Total Salary Income                               2,000.00
                                                                         ----------
                   TOTAL INCOME                                          2,000.00

                 EXPENSES
                   Federal Tax
                   -----------
        8/ 1       S Payroll deposit      Federal Income Tax  Tax Fed     -140.00
                                                                         ----------
                       Total Federal Tax                                  -140.00

                   Local Tax Withholding
                   ---------------------
        8/ 1       S Payroll deposit      Local Income Tax   Tax Local     -10.00
                                                                         ----------
                       Total Local Tax Withholding                         -10.00

                   Medical & Dental
                   ----------------
        8/ 1       S Payroll deposit      Health Ins         Medical       -42.01
        8/ 6 107   Orthodontics, Inc.     Monthly Orthodontics
                                          Payment            Medical      -100.00
                                                                         ----------
                       Total Medical & Dental                            -142.01
```

FIGURE 8-5. Tax Summary report for the Cardinal Bank checking
account using full-width printing

the detail with fewer abbreviations. The additional space between fields also
makes it easier to understand. This format would be preferable for presenta-
tion to tax consultants and preparers.

Quicken prints the complete detail for each of the tax-related categories
as the default report. This format allows you to use the totals generated at

```
                              Tax Summary Report
                            8/ 1/91 Through 8/31/91
   PERSONAL-Cardinal Bank                                       Page  1
   9/ 2/91

     Date  Num    Description        Memo        Category  Clr Amount
     ----- -----  -----------------  ---------------  ---------------  - -------
            INCOME/EXPENSE
              INCOME
                Salary Income
                --------------
      8/ 1      S Payroll deposit   Gross Wages Ea  Salary        2,000.00
                                                                  ---------
                Total Salary Income                               2,000.00
                                                                  ---------
              TOTAL INCOME                                        2,000.00

              EXPENSES
                Federal Tax
                -----------
      8/ 1      S Payroll deposit   Federal Income  Tax Fed       -140.00
                                                                  ---------
                Total Federal Tax                                 -140.00

                Local Tax Withholding
                ---------------------
      8/ 1      S Payroll deposit   Local Income T  Tax Local      -10.00
                                                                  ---------
                Total Local Tax Withholding                        -10.00

                Medical & Dental
                ----------------
      8/ 1      S Payroll deposit   Health Ins      Medical        -42.01
      8/ 6 107  Orthodontics, Inc.  Monthly Orthod  Medical       -100.00
                                                                  ---------
                Total Medical & Dental                            -142.01
```

═══ **FIGURE 8-6.** Tax Summary report for the Cardinal Bank checking account without the wide-print option

the end of the tax year for entry on your tax returns. The totals generated in Figure 8-5 would be used on the following lines of your personal income tax form for 1989:

Income/Expense Category	Tax Return Location
Total Salary Income	Form 1040 line 7
Total Federal Tax Withholding	Form 1040 line 56
Total Medical & Dental	Schedule A line 1a
Total Mortgage Interest Exp	Schedule A line 9a
Total State Tax Withholding	Schedule A line 5
Total Local Income Tax	Schedule A line 5

This also provides an excellent summary and could prove useful in the event of an IRS tax audit inquiry.

As you will see in a later chapter, all Quicken reports can be customized in many different report formats (months, quarters, half years, and so on). One variation discussed in the previous chapter compared reports prepared for a separate account, Cardinal Bank, and one prepared for all accounts. The report for all accounts used the bank checking accounts, cash, and credit card accounts from the PERSONAL account group. Here, while Figures 8-5 and 8-6 were prepared for a single account, Cardinal Bank, Figure 8-7 illustrates a Tax Summary report including all accounts in the PERSONAL account group. Note that the second column from the left (Acct) shows the source of the tax-related transaction. In this report all the sources were from the Cardinal Bank account, but in a more complex situation you could see how this would be useful in tracking the source of a tax-related transaction. For year-end tax purposes a report of all accounts provides an overview by category that integrates the various accounts. For your tax-reporting needs you should select the report format that will generate the information best suited to your tax preparation and planning needs.

```
                           Tax Summary Report
                         8/ 1/91 Through 8/31/91
PERSONAL-All Accounts                                              Page 1
9/ 2/91

  Date    Acct    Num     Description       Memo        Category  Clr Amount
 -----  -------  ------  ---------------  ---------------  ------------ - --------
        INCOME/EXPENSE
          INCOME
            Salary Income
            -------------
 8/ 1 Cardinal      S Payroll deposit   Gross wages    Salary       2,000.00
                                                                   ---------
            Total Salary Income                                     2,000.00
                                                                   ---------
          TOTAL INCOME                                              2,000.00

          EXPENSES
            Federal Tax
            ------------
 8/ 1 Cardinal      S Payroll deposit   Federal Inc    Tax Fed      -140.00
                                                                   --------
            Total Federal Tax                                       -140.00

            Local Tax Withholding
            ---------------------
 8/ 1 Cardinal      S Payroll deposit   Local Incom    Tax  Local    -10.00
                                                                   ---------
            Total Local Tax Withholding                              -10.00
```

FIGURE 8-7. Tax Summary report for all accounts in the PERSONAL account group using wide-screen printing

```
                        Tax Summary Report
                       8/ 1/91 Through 8/31/91
PERSONAL-All Accounts                                    Page 1
9/ 2/91

Date   Acct    Num    Description      Memo        Category   Clr Amount
-----  -------  ------  ----------------  -------------  -----------  -  --------
           Medical & Dental
           ----------------
8/ 1 Cardinal      S Payroll deposit  Health Ins   Medical        -42.01
8/ 6 Cardinal          Orthodontics, In Monthly Ort  Medical       -100.00
                                                                ---------
           Total Medical & Dental                               -142.01

           Mortgage Interest Exp
           ---------------------
8/ 2 Cardinal 104 S Great Lakes Savi Interest Po  Mort Int      -300.79
                                                                ---------
           Total Mortgage Interest Exp                          -300.79

           Social Security Tax
           -------------------
8/ 1 Cardinal      S Payroll deposit  FICA Withho  Tax FICA      -142.00
                                                                ---------
           Total Social Security Tax                            -142.00

           State Tax
           ---------
8/ 1 Cardinal      S Payroll deposit  State Incom  Tax State      -80.00
                                                                ---------
           Total State Tax                                       -80.00
                                                                ---------
       TOTAL EXPENSES                                           -814.80

                                                                ---------
    TOTAL INCOME/EXPENSE                                        1,185.20
                                                                =========
```

FIGURE 8-7. Tax Summary report for all accounts in the PERSONAL account group using wide-screen printing (*continued*)

Another example of modifying Quicken's report features is shown in Figure 8-8. In this case Quicken was instructed to print only the Medical category. Although this information was included in the report shown in

```
                              Tax Summary Report
                            8/ 1/91 Through 8/31/91

PERSONAL-All Accounts                                              Page 1
9/ 2/91

    Date    Acct    Num    Description        Memo       Category   Clr Amount
    -----   ------- ------  ----------------  ----------  --------------- - -------

            INCOME/EXPENSE
              EXPENSES
                Medical & Dental
                ----------------
    8/ 1  Cardinal        S Payroll deposit  Health Ins  Medical        -42.01
    8/ 6  Cardinal 107    Orthodontics, In   Monthly Ort Medical       -100.00
                                                                       --------
                Total Medical & Dental                                 -142.01
                                                                       --------
            TOTAL EXPENSES                                             -142.01

                                                                       --------
            TOTAL INCOME/EXPENSE                                       -142.01
                                                                       ========
```

FIGURE 8-8. A sample Tax Summary report filtered for a specific
category

Figure 8-5, you can see the benefits of a filtered report as you increase the
number of transactions recorded by Quicken and want details on particular
items during the year-end tax planning and reporting process. Quicken's
procedures for generating this type of report will be covered in Chapter 10.

The final point to note on all Quicken reports is that the date of report
preparation is displayed in the upper-left corner of the report. When using
Quicken reports, always note the report preparation date so you can be sure
you are using the most recent report when making your financial decisions.

DETERMINING YOUR NET WORTH

I n previous chapters you used Quicken as a tool for financial planning and monitoring. Many of the activities were simply repetitive steps; you applied the same techniques repeatedly to record transactions. These activities were procedural—they did not require analysis before entry and each transaction followed the exact same steps. Although these activities are an important part of managing your finances, they do not provide the total picture.

BASIC CONCEPTS OF FINANCIAL MANAGEMENT

You probably have financial goals you would like to meet, such as buying a new car, purchasing a house, or retiring at age 60. Whatever your goals may be, you will need a certain level of financial resources to meet them. You might attempt to accumulate the necessary resources through savings or the acquisition of investments such as stocks or bonds. In this chapter you will learn to measure how successful you have been in your financial management activities.

One important measure of your financial status is your *net worth*. Net worth measures the difference between your total assets and your total liabilities at a given time. By looking at your net financial position at two points in time you can tell how well you have managed your assets and liabilities. If your net worth has increased, you have increased your financial assets. If your net worth decreased over this time period, your financial resources have declined. The process of preparing a statement of net worth will differ from the procedural activities of earlier chapters. To estimate your net worth you will need to make judgments estimating the worth of items purchased earlier. Some investments, such as stock, have clearly defined market value since they are publicly traded. Other investments, such as land or real estate, require a more subjective evaluation.

You have to look at more than the assets you own to determine your net worth. Although you may live in a $300,000 house, in all likelihood the bank owns more of it than you do. For net worth purposes you have to determine what your remaining financial obligation is on the house. If you still have a mortgage of $270,000, your net worth in the property is $30,000. The following equation might give you a better perspective of your financial condition:

Financial Resources − Financial Obligations = Net Worth

As you can see, net worth describes your financial position after considering all your financial holdings and deducting all your financial obligations. In accounting terms your financial resources are things of value that you hold (*assets*). Your assets may include checking, savings, and money market accounts. These are examples of *liquid* assets—they can be readily converted into cash. Stocks, bonds, real estate holdings, and retirement funds (Individual Retirement Accounts—IRAs—and Keogh plans) are other examples of investments you might hold. These investment assets are not as liquid as the previous group since converting them to cash depends on the market at the time you attempt to sell them. Your residence, vacation property, antiques, and other items of this nature would be classified as *personal* assets. These assets are the least liquid since antique and real estate values can decline, and it may take considerable time to convert these assets to cash.

The other part of the net worth equation is your financial obligations. Financial obligations would include credit card balances and other shorter-term loans such as those for automobiles. In addition, you must consider longer-term loans for the purchase of a residence, vacation property, or land.

Net worth is the measure most people focus on when monitoring the success of their financial planning activities. The key point to remember is that net worth increases when your financial resources increase—through savings, compounding, and appreciation, and when you reduce the amount of your financial obligations. Take a look at the special section on Effects of Compounding Interest to see the effect of compounding on an investment and the rapid rate at which even a small investment can grow. The values shown are the result of investing $100 a month at the rates shown.

T I P — EFFECTS OF COMPOUNDING INTEREST ON $100 INVESTED MONTHLY FOR 20 YEARS

Worth at the end of	6% return	8% return	10% return
1 year	$1,234	$1,245	$1,257
2 years	$2,543	$2,593	$2,645
3 years	$3,934	$4,054	$4,178
4 years	$5,410	$5,635	$5,872
5 years	$6,977	$7,348	$7,744
10 years	$16,388	$18,295	$20,484
15 years	$29,082	$34,604	$41,447
20 years	$46,204	$58,902	$75,937

Remember that financial obligations are not necessarily a sign of poor financial management. If you can borrow money and invest it so that it returns more than you are paying to use it you have *leveraged* your resources. Of course, there is more risk in this avenue of financial planning. Don't take on more risk than you can handle—both financially and emotionally.

After completing this chapter you will be able to begin monitoring your financial condition. In accounting terms you can look at the *bottom line*. The bottom line in personal financial management is your net worth if you value your assets realistically. How you manage your financial assets and related obligations to increase your personal wealth will determine your net worth.

If you set an annual goal of increasing your net worth by a certain percentage you can use Quicken to assist in recording your financial activities and monitoring your success in meeting your goal. For example, if you started using Quicken in January and record your assets and obligations throughout the year, you could contrast your financial condition at the beginning and end of the year and compare the results of your financial management with your goals. As a result of this comparison you might decide to change your strategy in some areas of your financial plan. For instance, you might decide to switch from directly managing your portfolio of stocks to using a mutual fund with its professional managers, or you might decide to shift some assets from real estate to liquid assets that can be converted to cash more quickly.

ESTABLISHING ACCOUNTS FOR THIS CHAPTER

In earlier chapters, you have used bank accounts in an account group called PERSONAL to record all your transactions. In this chapter, you will learn about Quicken's other account types. These accounts are ideally suited for recording information on assets you own, debts you have incurred, and investments. You will establish an account group called INVEST for the examples in this chapter. This will make it easier to obtain the same reporting results shown in this chapter even if you did not complete the examples in earlier chapters. This new account group will be established for illustration purposes only. In fact, for your own financial planning you will probably record all your activities in a single account group. That way, Quicken will have access to all your personal information when preparing your reports and assessing your net worth.

Adding a New Account Group

You have already used the following process in the "Adding a New Account Group" section of Chapter 6. In the new account group, INVEST, you will establish six new accounts to use throughout this chapter. From the Main Menu follow these steps to set up the new account:

1. Type **5** to select Change Settings.

2. Type **1** to select Account Group Activities.

3. Type **1** to select Select/Set Up Account Group.

Your screen will have account groups for QDATA and PERSONAL.

4. Select < Set Up New Grp > and press ⟨**ENTER**⟩.

5. Type **INVEST** as the name of the account group and press ⟨**ENTER**⟩.

Quicken creates four files from each account group name. This means you must provide a valid filename of no more than eight characters. Do not include spaces or special symbols in your entries for account names.

6. Type **1** to restrict your categories to home categories and press ⟨**ENTER**⟩.

7. Check the location for your data files and make changes to reference a valid file or directory if a change is required.

8. Press ⟨**CTRL**⟩-⟨**ENTER**⟩ to create the account setup.

Quicken displays the screen for selecting or creating account groups, but this time it also shows INVEST.

9. Select INVEST and press ⟨**ENTER**⟩.

10. Highlight the INVEST account group and press ⟨**ENTER**⟩.

Setting Up Your New Accounts

The new accounts you will establish in this chapter are used to separately maintain records for different assets and liabilities, and you will be establishing some new types of accounts. A little background on when to use each account type will be helpful in making selections when you start recording your own information. The three new account types and some suggested uses for each follow.

Investment   Investment accounts are a new feature in Quicken 4. These accounts are tailored to investments with fluctuating prices, such as stocks, mutual funds, bonds, or an Individual Retirement Account (IRA). You can establish an Investment account for each of your investment holdings or establish one account to parallel your transactions with a brokerage firm. In addition to special fields such as shares and investment accounts, these accounts can track a cash balance in an account.

Other Asset   Other Asset accounts are appropriate for investments with a stable price, such as a CD or Treasury bill. They are also the most appropriate selection when there is no share price—for example, a real estate holding.

Other Liability   Other Liability accounts are used to record your debts. A mortgage on a property or a car loan are examples of obligations that decrease your net worth and should be recorded in an Other Liability account.

The steps outlined next will guide you through the establishment of an Investment account. After establishing the Investment account, set up the remaining accounts shown in Figure 9-1 using the account types and balances shown.

```
                          Select Account to Use

                 Current Account Group: C:\Q4_9\INVEST
                                                  Num    Ending    Checks
        Account       Type      Description       Trans  Balance   To Prt

   ► <New Account>          Set up a new account
     Great Lakes Chk Bank   Personal Checking       1    4,000.00
     Great Lakes Sve Bank   Personal Savings        1    2,500.00
     Price Money Mkt Bank   Money Market Account    1   15,000.00
     Residence       Oth A  444 Ferndell            1  100,000.00
     Great Lakes Mtg Oth L  Mortgage on Ferndell    1   85,000.00
     Investments     Invst  Personal Investments    0        0.00


           Ctrl-D Delete   Ctrl-E Edit   ↑,↓ Select
     Esc-Cancel              F1-Help                          ↵ Use
```

FIGURE 9-1.   Select Account to Use window for the INVEST account group

1. Select <New Account> in the Account field and press (ENTER). This will display the Set Up New Account window, shown in Figure 9-2.

2. Type **6** and press (ENTER) to establish the account type as an Investment account.

3. Type **Investments** and press (ENTER).

Notice in Figure 9-1 that you will establish some accounts under Other Asset and Other Liability. When you are setting them up you will type **4** or **5** to this prompt and press (ENTER). Because Investment accounts are always established with a zero balance, you will not be asked to supply a beginning balance or date as you are when you create other account types. For all the other accounts you will use the balances shown with a date of 8/1/91.

4. Press (ENTER) to accept *N* for the next entry since the account will be used to record information on multiple investments. When you wish to establish an account for a single mutual fund, you would type a **Y**.

5. Type **Personal Investments** and press (ENTER).

```
┌──────────────────────────────────────────────────────────┐
│                    Set Up New Account                      │
├──────────────────────────────────────────────────────────┤
│ Account Type: 6                                            │
│         1. Bank Account       4. Other Asset               │
│         2. Credit Card        5. Other Liability           │
│         3. Cash               6. Investment Account         │
│                                                            │
│ Name for this account: Investments                         │
│                                                            │
│ Account is a single mutual fund (Y/N): N                   │
│ (Press F1 for more information)                            │
│                                                            │
│ Description (optional): Personal Investments               │
├──────────────────────────────────────────────────────────┤
│              Please type account information               │
│ Esc-Cancel                 F1-Help          ◄┘ Continue    │
└──────────────────────────────────────────────────────────┘
```

FIGURE 9-2.   Sample Set Up New Account window

Figure 9-2 shows the window as it looked before pressing (ENTER). After pressing (ENTER), Quicken displays a warning message to inform you of the advanced nature of Investment accounts. Press (ENTER) to eliminate this warning. Quicken then returns you to the Select Account to Use window. Your first account should conform to the Investments account shown at the bottom of the screen in Figure 9-1.

6. Establish the five remaining accounts as shown in Figure 9-1. Be sure to enter the correct account type and balance. Use 8/1/91 as the date when entering your beginning balance for each account.

Establishing the Initial Balance in Your Investments Account

Investment accounts are always established with an initial balance of zero. To transfer existing holdings to an Investment account you will want to transfer the shares in at cost. You can establish a complete list of securities before beginning, or add the information for each security as you enter the information to establish its cost. To activate the Investments account and record the securities, follow these steps:

1. Press (ESC) to return to the Main Menu, move the arrow cursor to Select Account, and press (ENTER).
2. Move the arrow cursor to Investments and press (ENTER).

Quicken displays a first time setup message telling you to use ShrsIn to establish the cost basis for each security.

3. Press (ENTER) to proceed to the Investment register.

You will notice that the fields are different than the bank account registers you have used previously since they are tailored to investments with a share price.

4. Type **10/10/88** as the purchase date and press (ENTER).

You can type an action from, those listed in Table 9-1 or use (CTRL)-(L) to highlight the action code in Quicken's list.

5. Press (CTRL)-(L).

Action Group	Action	Description
Add/Remove shares	ShrsIn	Used to transfer shares into an investment account
	ShrsOut	Used to transfer shares out of an account
Buy shares	Buy	Used to buy a security with cash in the Investment account
	BuyX	Used to buy a security with cash from another account
Capital gains distr	CGLong	Used to record cash received from long-term capital gains distribution
	CGLongX	Used to transfer cash received from long-term capital gains distribution to another account
	CGShort	Used to record cash received from long-term capital gains distribution
	CGShortX	Used to transfer cash received from short-term capital gains distribution to another account
Dividend	Div	Used to record cash dividends in the Investment account
	DivX	Used to transfer cash dividends to another account
Interest	IntInc	Used to record interest income in the investment account

TABLE 9-1.   Investment Actions

Action Group	Action	Description
	MargInt	Used to pay margin loan from cash account
Other transactions	MiscExp	Used to pay miscellaneous expense from cash
	Reminder	Used with Billminder feature to notify of pending event
	RtrnCap	Used to recognize cash from return of capital
	StkSplit	Used to change number of shares from a stock split
Reinvest	ReinvDiv	Used to reinvest dividends in additional shares
	ReinvLg	Used to reinvest long-term capital gains distribution
	ReinvSh	Used to reinvest short-term capital gains distribution
Sell shares	Sell	Used when you sell a security and leave the proceeds in the Investment account
	SellX	Used to transfer the proceeds of a sale to another account
Transfer cash	XIn	Used to transfer cash into the Investment account
	XOut	Used to transfer cash out of investment account

TABLE 9-1. Investment Actions (*continued*)

The arrow cursor is on Add/Remove shares.

6. Press (ENTER) to select it and display the two action codes shown in Figure 9-3.

7. Press (ENTER) to select ShrsIn and move to the Security field.

8. Type **Haven Publishing** and press (ENTER).

Quicken displays a message informing you that the security is not in the security list.

9. Press (ENTER) to select Add to Security List. A Set Up Security screen appears.

10. Type **HPB** for the symbol and press (ENTER).

11. Press (CTRL)-(L) to select the security type from a list, and then move the arrow cursor to Stock and press (ENTER).

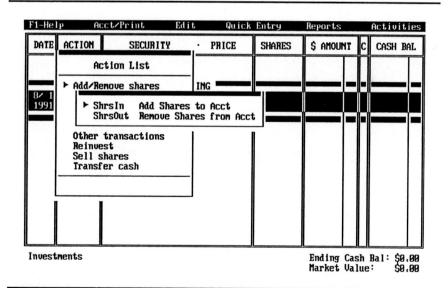

FIGURE 9-3. Action List for Investments

12. Press CTRL-L to select an optional investment goal from a list, and then move the arrow cursor to Growth and press ENTER.

Your screen will look like this:

```
┌─────────────────────────────────────────────────────────┐
│ ▬▬▬▬▬▬▬▬▬▬▬▬▬▬▬▬▬▬▬▬▬▬▬▬▬▬▬▬▬▬▬▬▬▬▬▬▬▬▬▬▬▬▬▬▬▬▬▬ │
│                    Set Up Security                        │
├─────────────────────────────────────────────────────────┤
│  Name: Haven Publishing                                   │
│  Symbol (optional): HPB                                   │
│                                                           │
│  Type: Stock              Goal (optional): Growth         │
├─────────────────────────────────────────────────────────┤
│                  Ctrl L-List Types, Goals                 │
│  Esc-Cancel              F1-Help          ←┘ Continue     │
└─────────────────────────────────────────────────────────┘
```

Alternately, you can use CTRL-Y at any time from the Investments register to update the entire investment list at once.

13. Press ENTER, then type **20** for the per share cost and press ENTER again.

14. Type **500** for the number of shares.

15. Press ENTER to accept the price computation.

16. Type **Initial Cost** in the Memo field and press CTRL-ENTER.

F1-Help	F2-Acct/Print	F3-Edit	F4-Quick Entry	F5-Reports	F6-Activities		
DATE	ACTION	SECURITY · PRICE		SHARES	$ AMOUNT	C	CASH BAL
		▬ BEGINNING ▬					
10/10 1988	ShrsIn	Haven Publishing ·20 Initial Cost		500	10,000 00		0 00
3/ 8 1989	ShrsIn	Ganges Mutual Fund·11.950 Initial Cost		1,000	11,950 00		0 00
8/20 1989	ShrsIn	Glenn Packing ·30 1/2 Memo: Initial Cost		100	3,050 00		0 00

FIGURE 9-4. Initial Investment transactions

Repeat the process for Ganges Mutual Fund and Glenn Packing using the entries shown in Figure 9-4. When required to set up the new securities, repeat steps 10, 11, and 12 with the following information:

	Ganges Mutual Fund	**Glenn Packing**
Symbol	GMF	GPK
Type	Mutual fund	Stock
Goal	Growth	Growth & income

Although you now have your stock holdings entered at cost, you still have an additional step since you want to establish a current market value for your holdings.

Revaluing Your Assets to Market Value

An important point to note when using Quicken is that in order to determine your net worth you must assign values to your investments, liabilities, and other assets. This means that you will need to exercise some judgment in evaluating asset worth. Don't be intimidated; it's not as complex as it might seem. The easiest assets to evaluate are your checking, savings, and money market accounts. In these cases you know what your cash balance is in each of the accounts, so you can easily determine the value at a specific time. After you complete your monthly reconciliation you have the current value of your accounts at a given time. If you own stocks and bonds you can generally determine the valuation at a given time by looking in the financial section of your local newspaper. If you own stock in a closely held corporation you will have to use other sources for valuation—for example, recent sales of similar companies in your industry or area. In the case of land you might ask a realtor familiar with the local area the approximate value of your lot or other property holdings, or once again you might be able to use recent sale prices of similar properties in your area.

Your residence presents similar problems. You know what you paid for the property, and with Quicken you can accumulate the additional cost incurred in improving it. The question is what value to place on the property when you prepare your net worth report. Once again, watch what properties in your area are selling for, and consider how your house compared in price with neighboring properties when you bought it. This would provide a basis for comparison in the future. However, remember that improvements you made to your house may increase the value of your home relative to others in the area. For example, adding a new bath and renovating the kitchen may significantly enhance the value of your home over time, but adding a swimming pool in a cold climate may not help the value at all.

The amount you owe or the associated liability on your home should be easy to track. You receive annual statements from the financial institutions you have borrowed money from for your residence and any home improvements. These statements indicate the remaining financial obligation you have on the house and should be used for net worth valuation purposes.

Remember to use prudent judgment in determining values for some of your assets when preparing your net worth report. A conservative but not very useful approach would be to say that any values you cannot determine from external sources should be valued at what you paid for the asset. Accountants call this *historical cost.* For your own planning and monitoring this is not a realistic approach to determining your net worth. Attempt to determine fair value, or what you think your home could be sold for today, by taking into consideration current national and local economic conditions, and use reasonable values. Those familiar with the local market will certainly have some knowledge of the value of homes in your area. Remember that over-inflating the value of your properties does not help in accurately assessing your net worth.

The following procedure allows you to enter the current value of your stocks:

1. From the Investment register, press (CTRL)-(U) to activate the Update Prices and Market Value window.

Your next step is to establish the date for which you want to make the estimated market values as 7/31/91. You can change the date displayed to the next day with (CTRL)-(RIGHT ARROW), to the previous day with (CTRL)-(LEFT ARROW), to the next month with (CTRL)-(PGUP), and to the previous month with (CTRL)-(PGDN).

2. Press the appropriate combination of keys to make the date at the top of your screen read 7/31/91.

You can enter new market prices for any of the investments or use the ⊕ and ⊖keys to change them by 1/8 in either direction.

3. With the arrow cursor on Ganges Mutual Fund, type **13.210** and press CENTER.

4. With the arrow cursor on Glenn Packing, press the ⊖ key four times to change the market price to 30, and then press CENTER.

5. With the arrow cursor on Haven Publishing, type **22** and press CENTER.

Figure 9-5 shows the updated prices. You will notice that Quicken computes a new market value as well as a percentage gain.

Your First Net Worth Report

In completing the steps in the previous section you have recorded balances in all the accounts in your INVESTMENTS account group. At this point you can determine your net worth. Remember, your net worth is determined by the following formula.

```
 F1-Help   F2-Acct/Print   F3-Edit   F4-Quick Entry  F5-Reports   F6-Activities
                        Update Prices and Market Value
                              As of:  7/31/91
     Security Name       Type    Mkt Price     Avg Cost   %Gain    Shares   Mkt Value

 ▶ Ganges Mutual Fund  Mutual  13.210    ↑ 11.950       10.5     1,000    13,210
   Glenn Packing       Stock   30        ↓ 30 1/2       -1.6       100     3,000
   Haven Publishing    Stock   22        ↑ 20           10.0       500    11,000




   Total Market Value                                    0.0              27,210

 Investments                                               +/- Adjust Price
 Esc-Register                       F9-All Accounts       Ctrl↵ Record Prices
```

FIGURE 9-5. Updated prices in the Investment register

Financial Resources − Financial Obligations = Net Worth

The following procedure will print your first net worth statement:

1. Press (ESC) to return to the Investments account register, press (F5), and then type **1** for Personal followed by **5** for Net Worth.

The Net Worth Report window appears.

2. Press (ENTER).
3. Type **8/1/91** and press (ENTER).

The Net Worth Report appears on your screen.

4. Press (F8) and the Print Report window appears.
5. Complete the window prompts. When you press (ENTER) to leave the window, your printer will print the report shown in Figure 9-6. (Again, spacing may differ because of adjustments made to fit the material onto these pages.)

Notice that the Net Worth Report is presented for a specific date, in this example 8/1/91. The report presents your assets and liabilities at this date and gives you a base point against which to make future comparisons. As you can see your net worth at 8/1/91 is $63,710.00. At the end of this chapter you will prepare another Net Worth Report and compare how your net worth has changed.

IMPACT OF INVESTMENTS AND MORTGAGE PAYMENTS ON NET WORTH

In this section you will record various transactions in the account group to demonstrate the effect of certain types of transactions on your net worth. You will see how Quicken can monitor your mortgage balance as part of your monthly record-keeping in your checking account. You will also see how you can record a transaction only once and trace the financial impact on both checking and investment account registers.

```
                              NET WORTH REPORT
                               As of 8/ 1/91
        INVEST-All Accounts
        9/ 3/91                                              Page 1

                                                          8/ 1/91
                              Acct                         Balance
        --------------------------------------------  ------------
        ASSETS
           Cash and Bank Accounts
              Great Lakes Chk-Personal Checking          4,000.00
              Great Lakes Sve-Personal Savings           2,500.00
              Price Money Mkt-Money Market Account      15,000.00
                                                       ------------
           Total Cash and Bank Accounts                 21,500.00

           Other Assets
              Residence-444 Ferndell                   100,000.00
                                                       ------------
           Total Other Assets                          100,000.00

           Investments
              Investments-Personal Investments          27,210.00
                                                       ------------
           Total Investments                            27,210.00

                                                       ------------
        TOTAL ASSETS                                   148,710.00

        LIABILITIES
           Other Liabilities
              Great Lakes Mtg-Mortgage on Ferndell      85,000.00
                                                       ------------
           Total Other Liabilities                      85,000.00

                                                       ------------
        TOTAL LIABILITIES                               85,000.00

                                                       ------------
        OVERALL TOTAL                                   63,710.00
                                                       ============
```

FIGURE 9-6. Net Worth Report for 8/1/91

Additional Stock Transactions

When you printed your Net Worth Report you were in the Investments account. You will now record the acquisition of some additional stock, dividends, dividends reinvested, and the sale of stock. The following steps demonstrate the ease of recording the transaction with Quicken 4's Investment accounts.

1. You are currently in the Investments account. Press the (ESC) key until you are in Quicken's Main Menu.

2. Select 2 Register and press (CTRL)-(END) to move to the last entry.

3. Type **8/2/91** and press ⌷ENTER⌷.

4. Press ⌷CTRL⌷-⌷L⌷, move the arrow cursor to Buy shares, and press ⌷ENTER⌷.

5. Move the arrow cursor to BuyX to buy securities with money from another account and press ⌷ENTER⌷.

An extra line is added to the register entry to allow for the entry of an account field and the computation of a transfer amount.

6. Type **Douglas Marine** and press ⌷ENTER⌷.

Since this security is not in the security list, it must be added.

7. Press ⌷ENTER⌷ to accept Add to Security List.

8. Type **DGM** and press ⌷ENTER⌷.

9. Press ⌷CTRL⌷-⌷L⌷, move the arrow cursor to Stock, and press ⌷ENTER⌷.

10. Press ⌷CTRL⌷-⌷L⌷, move the arrow cursor to Growth, and press ⌷ENTER⌷.

11. Press ⌷ENTER⌷ to finalize the security list entries.

12. Type **25** and press ⌷ENTER⌷.

13. Type **100** and press ⌷ENTER⌷ twice.

14. Type **Buy 100 Douglas Marine** and press ⌷ENTER⌷.

15. Type **50** for the commission and press ⌷ENTER⌷.

The transfer amount is automatically computed as the price of the stock plus the commission.

16. Press ⌷CTRL⌷-⌷C⌷, move the arrow cursor to Price Money Mkt, and press ⌷ENTER⌷.

17. Press ⌷CTRL⌷-⌷ENTER⌷ to finalize the entry.

The next transactions will record dividends and transfer them to another account or reinvest them in shares of the stock. Rather than transferring funds in and out for each transaction, you can choose to leave a cash balance in your brokerage account. Quicken 4 allows you to mirror almost any investment situation. To record the dividend transaction, follow these steps:

1. Type **8/10/91** and press (ENTER).

2. Press (CTRL)-(L), move the arrow cursor to Dividend, and press (ENTER).

3. Move the arrow cursor to DivX and press (ENTER).

4. Type **Haven Publishing** and press (ENTER).

5. Type **200** for the $ Amount and press (ENTER).

6. Type **Div @ .40 per share** and press (ENTER).

7. Press (CTRL)-(C), move the arrow pointer to Great Lakes Sve, and press (ENTER).

8. Press (CTRL)-(ENTER) to finalize the transaction.

The next transaction also recognizes a dividend distribution. These dividends will be reinvested in shares purchased at the current market price. Follow these steps to record the transaction:

1. Type **8/15/91** and press (ENTER).

2. Press (CTRL)-(L), move the arrow cursor to Reinvest, and press (ENTER).

3. Move the arrow cursor to ReinvDiv and press (ENTER).

4. Type **Ganges Mutual Fund** and press (ENTER).

5. Type **13.2785** and press (ENTER) twice to move to the $ Amount field.

Quicken will supply the number of shares if you enter the price and the amount of the dividend that you are reinvesting.

6. Type **100.00** and press (ENTER).

7. Type **Dividend Reinvestment** and press (CTRL)-(ENTER).

To record the sale of stock with the transfer of proceeds to another account, follow these steps:

1. Type **8/25/91** and press (ENTER).

2. Press (CTRL)-(L), move the arrow cursor to Sell shares, and then press (ENTER).

3. Move the arrow cursor to SellX to sell the stock and transfer the cash to another account, and press (ENTER).

4. Type **Haven Publishing** and press (ENTER).

5. Type **23 1/4** and press ⟨ENTER⟩.

6. Type **100** and press ⟨ENTER⟩ twice.

7. Type **Sell 100 Haven Publishing** and press ⟨ENTER⟩.

8. Type **25** for the commission and press ⟨ENTER⟩.

9. Press ⟨CTRL⟩-⟨C⟩, move the arrow cursor to Price Money Mkt, and press ⟨ENTER⟩.

10. Press ⟨CTRL⟩-⟨ENTER⟩.

Your register entries will look like Figure 9-7.

Mortgage Payment Transaction

You recorded mortgage payments in earlier chapters, but here you will see how you can monitor your principal balance when you make your payment. In this example, you will make your monthly payment from your checking account and monitor the impact of the payment on your principal balance in

F1-Help	F2-Acct/Print	F3-Edit	F4-Quick Entry	F5-Reports	F6-Activities			
DATE	ACTION	SECURITY · PRICE		SHARES	$ AMOUNT	C	CASH BAL	
8/20 1989	ShrsIn	Glenn Packing ·30 1/2 Initial Cost		100	3,050 00		0 00	
8/ 2 1991	BuyX	Douglas Marine ·25 Buy 100 Douglas Marine		100	2,550 00		0 00	
8/10 1991	DivX	Haven Publishing · Div @ .40 per share			200 00		0 00	
8/15 1991	ReinvDiv	Ganges Mutual Fund ·13.2785 Dividend Reinvestment		7.531	100 00		0 00	
8/25 1991	SellX	Haven Publishing ·23 1/4 Sell 100 Haven Publishing		100	2,300 00		0 00	

FIGURE 9-7. Investment account register after August transactions

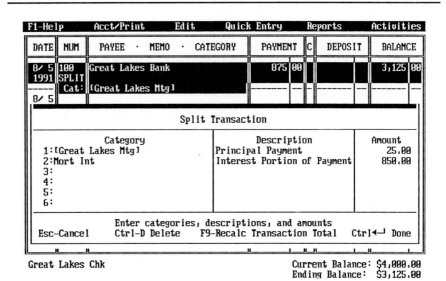

FIGURE 9-8.   Split Transaction window in checking account

the Great Lakes Mtg liability account. The following steps will record this transaction from the Main Menu:

1. Enter the Great Lakes Chk register and move the cursor to the Date field in the highlighted new transaction form. Type **8/5/91** and press (ENTER).

2. Type **100** in the Num field and press (ENTER).

3. Type **Great Lakes Bank** in the Payee field and press (ENTER).

4. Type **875.00** in the Payment field.

5. Press (ENTER) four times; your cursor will be in the Category field.

6. Press (CTRL)-(S) and the Split Transaction window appears on the screen. When you finish completing this window your screen will look like Figure 9-8.

7. Press (CTRL)-(C) and the Category and Transfer List window appears. Use (DOWN ARROW) to highlight the Great Lakes Mtg account and press (ENTER).

8. Press (ENTER), type **Principal Payment**, press (ENTER), type **25.00** in the Amount field, and press (ENTER) again.

You have recorded the first part of the transaction shown in Figure 9-8.

9. Type **Mort Int** and press (ENTER). Type **Interest Portion of Payment** and press (ENTER). Press (CTRL)-(ENTER).

This step returns you to the account register.

10. Press (CTRL)-(ENTER) again and the transaction is recorded in the register.

As you can see, the balance in the account has been reduced by the amount of the payment. At the same time Quicken has recorded the transaction in your Great Lakes Mtg account and reduced the obligation by the $25.00 principal portion of the payment.

How Transactions Affect Your Net Worth

Let's take a look at the effect of the previous transactions on net worth. If you compare Figure 9-9 to the previous Net Worth Report, you'll see that your net worth would have increased by $68.50 compared to the initial net worth shown in Figure 9-6. This difference is the net effect of the transactions you recorded during the month of August in your investment, cash, and bank accounts.

You can see from this that your net worth can grow either by increasing the value of your financial resources or by decreasing the amount of your obligations. In the next section you will see how increases in the value of your investments are recorded and the effect they have on your net worth.

Recording Appreciation in Your Investment Holdings

In this section you will record the increased appreciation in your investments and residence occurring since the Net Worth Report prepared on 8/1/91. Although the amounts may seem high, remember that this is an example. Also, remember that what you make in the stock market and housing market this year could be lost next year.

APPRECIATED INVESTMENTS   Quicken permits you to record increases and decreases in the value of your holdings. As noted in the net worth formula, changes in the value of your holdings have the potential to significantly affect your net worth over a period of years. Remember the effect of compounding on your investments. The following steps illustrate the changes

```
                        NET WORTH REPORT
                         As of 8/31/91
        INVEST-All Accounts                          Page 1
        8/ 1/91
                                                8/31/91
                            Acct                Balance
        -------------------------------------- ------------
        ASSETS
          Cash and Bank Accounts
            Great Lakes Chk-Personal Checking      3,125.00
            Great Lakes Sve-Personal Savings       2,700.00
            Price Money Mkt-Money Market Account  14,750.00
                                                ------------
          Total Cash and Bank Accounts            20,575.00

          Other Assets
            Residence-444 Ferndell               100,000.00
                                                ------------
          Total Other Assets                     100,000.00

          Investments
            Investments-Personal Investments      28,178.50
                                                ------------
          Total Investments                       28,178.50

                                                ------------
        TOTAL ASSETS                             148,753.50

        LIABILITIES
          Other Liabilities
            Great Lakes Mtg-Mortgage on Ferndell  84,975.00
                                                ------------
          Total Other Liabilities                 84,975.00

                                                ------------
        TOTAL LIABILITIES                         84,975.00

                                                ------------
        OVERALL TOTAL                             63,778.50
                                                ============
```

_____
══════   **FIGURE 9-9.**   Net Worth Report after acquiring stock and making mortgage payment

of your investments for the month of August:

1. Choose Select Account from the Main Menu to open the Investments account register from your INVEST account group.

2. Press ⌈**CTRL**⌉-⌈**U**⌉ to access the Update Prices and Market Value screen.

You will notice that the market value for Ganges Mutual Fund is marked with an asterisk and has been updated since your initial adjustments on July 31, 1991. The asterisk indicates that Quicken has estimated the market value. This estimate is based on the value you entered for the dividend reinvestment transaction on 8/15.

3. Press ⌈**CTRL**⌉-⌈**RIGHT ARROW**⌉ or ⌈**CTRL**⌉-⌈**LEFT ARROW**⌉ until the date at the top reads 8/25/91.

Notice the asterisks next to the prices. An asterisk tells you that Quicken is using an estimated value for the investment. For example, Quicken valued the Haven Publishing shares at $22 per share. Since there were no shares of this stock bought or sold during August, Quicken will use the 7/31/91 price shown in Figure 9-5 until you revalue the stock. Notice that the Ganges Mutual Fund is shown at its actual value on 8/15/91 since you recorded the dividend reinvestment transaction in your account on that date. The point to note is that Quicken automatically updates your market valuation each time you provide new price information when preparing account transactions throughout the year.

4. Press ⌈**CTRL**⌉-⌈**RIGHT ARROW**⌉ until the date at the top reads 8/31/91.

5. Enter the new market prices for the stocks, as shown in Figure 9-10.

6. Press ⌈**CTRL**⌉-⌈**ENTER**⌉ to record the changes, then press ⌈**ESC**⌉ to return to the Main Menu.

APPRECIATED RESIDENCE   As your home increases in value you will want to record this change in Quicken since it will affect your net worth. In this example, as a result of recent sales in your neighborhood you feel $105,000 would be a conservative estimate of the market value of your home. Since you only have one asset to adjust, you can use a new Quicken feature

```
 F1-Help   F2-Acct/Print   F3-Edit   F4-Quick Entry  F5-Reports   F6-Activities
┌─────────────────────────────────────────────────────────────────────────────┐
│                     Update Prices and Market Value                            │
│                          As of :  8/31/91                                     │
│      Security Name        Type  Mkt Price     Avg Cost  %Gain   Shares  Mkt Value │
│                                                                               │
│► Ganges Mutual Fund  Mutual 13.400    ↑ 11.960    12.0    1,000    13,501 │
│  Douglas Marine      Stock  25 1/8    ↑ 25 1/2    -1.5     100     2,513 │
│  Glenn Packing       Stock  31        ↑ 30 1/2     1.6     100     3,100 │
│  Haven Publishing    Stock  23 1/2    ↑ 20        17.5     400     9,400 │
│                                                                               │
│                                                                               │
│                                                                               │
│                                                                               │
│                                                                               │
│  Total Market Value                               11.2            28,513 │
└─────────────────────────────────────────────────────────────────────────────┘
   Investments                                    +/- Adjust Price
   Esc-Register                    F9-All Accounts    Ctrl↵ Record Prices
```

FIGURE 9-10. Updated register after recording revaluations

to make the adjustment. The following steps illustrate the procedure for valuing your home at $105,000:

1. From the Select Account to Use window select the Residence account and press (ENTER).

Quicken opens the Register window for this account and places the highlighting in the next blank transaction.

2. Press (F6) and the Activities menu appears.

3. Type **2** and the Update Account Balance window appears.

4. Type **105000** and press (CTRL)-(ENTER). Quicken records the new value in the account for you.

5. Type **8/31** in the Date field of the highlighted new transaction form and press (CTRL)-(ENTER).

Your screen should look like Figure 9-11.

DATE	REF	PAYEE · MEMO · CATEGORY	DECREASE	C	INCREASE	BALANCE
8/ 1 1991		BEGINNING Opening Balance [Residence]			100,000 00	100,000 00
8/31 1991	Memo: Cat:	Balance Adjustment			5,000 00	105,000 00

Menu bar: F1-Help F2-Acct/Print F3-Edit F4-Quick Entry F5-Reports F6-Activities

FIGURE 9-11. Residence register after revaluing adjustment

note If you had typed the date before recording the new value, Quicken would have automatically dated the transaction with the current system date, regardless of your date entry.

ENDING NET WORTH DETERMINATION

Having prepared the adjustments to the various accounts in the INVEST account group, you are now prepared to print your Net Worth Report for the end of the period.

1. From any register press (**F5**), type **1**, and type **5**. The Net Worth Report window appears.
2. Press (**ENTER**), type **8/31/91**, and press (**ENTER**).

The Net Worth Report appears on your screen.

3. Press (**F8**) and the Print Report window appears.
4. Complete the appropriate selections in the window. When you press (**CTRL**)-(**ENTER**) to leave the window your printer will print the report as shown in Figure 9-12.

An examination of Figures 9-6 and 9-12 reveals that your net worth increased by almost $7,000 during the time period. What were the reasons for these changes? For the most part the increased values of your investments and residence explain the greater net worth.

```
                        NET WORTH REPORT
                          As of 8/31/91
     INVEST-All Accounts                          Page 1
     8/ 1/91
                                              8/31/91
                              Acct            Balance
     -------------------------------------- ------------
     ASSETS
       Cash and Bank Accounts
         Great Lakes Chk-Personal Checking      3,125.00
         Great Lakes Sve-Personal Savings       2,500.00
         Price Money Mkt-Money Market Account  14,950.00
                                              ------------
       Total Cash and Bank Accounts            20,575.00

       Other Assets
         Residence-444 Ferndell               105,000.00
                                              ------------
       Total Other Assets                     105,000.00

       Investments
         Investments-Personal Investments      28,513.42
                                              ------------
       Total Investments                       28,513.42

                                              ------------
     TOTAL ASSETS                             154,088.42

     LIABILITIES
       Other Liabilities
         Great Lakes Mtg-Mortgage on Ferndell  84,975.00
                                              ------------
       Total Other Liabilities                 84,975.00

                                              ------------
     TOTAL LIABILITIES                         84,975.00

                                              ------------
     OVERALL TOTAL                             69,113.42
                                              ============
```

FIGURE 9-12. Net Worth Report for 8/31/91 after recording all transactions affecting the INVEST account group

The importance of monitoring your net worth has been stressed through-out this chapter. The focus of this book is the use of Quicken to assist in your financial planning and monitoring activities. Once you have a good picture of your net worth from the Quicken reports you can focus on additional planning. You might want to set your net worth goal for a future point or make plans to protect your existing holdings. If you have not taken any actions regarding estate planning, this is another area that must be addressed. Making a will is a most important part of this process and should not be delayed. Although the complexities of planning for the transfer of your estate are significant, the special The Need for a Will section highlights some problems that can be encountered when estate planning is not combined with financial planning activities. You may also be surprised to learn that a lawyer's fee for a simple will can be as little as $50. Another option is writing a will with one of the new microcomputer software packages specifically designed for that purpose.

QUICKEN 4'S INVESTMENT REPORTS

Quicken 4 provides five investment reports that provide information on your investments from different perspectives. You can look at detailed investment transactions with these reports or assess your gain or loss in investment value over a period of time. The many options available provide different variations on each of the basic reports.

Portfolio Value Report

A Portfolio Value Report values all the investments in your portfolio at a given date based on price information stored in the system. The Portfolio Value Report displays the number of shares, current price, the cost basis of the shares, the gain or loss, and the current value of the shares. Follow these steps to create the report from the Investments account:

1. From the Main Menu, type **3** to activate the Report menu.
2. Type **3** to activate the Investment Reports menu.
3. Type **1** to display the Portfolio Value Report window.
4. Press (**ENTER**) to accept the default report title.
5. Type **8/31/91** for the report date and press (**ENTER**).
6. Press (**ENTER**) twice to accept the default entries of Don't Subtotal and Current.

The report displays on your screen. A copy of the printed report is shown in Figure 9-13.

```
                        PORTFOLIO VALUE REPORT
                          As of 8/31/91
   INVEST-Investments                                        Page 1
   9/ 3/91

           Security      Shares  Curr Price  Cost Basis  Gain/Loss   Balance
   --------------------  --------  ----------  ----------  ----------  -----------
     Douglas Marine       100.00     25 1/8     2,550.00     -37.50    2,512.50
     Ganges Mutual fund  1,007.53    13.400    12,050.00   1,450.92   13,500.92
     Glenn Packing        100.00        31      3,050.00      50.00    3,100.00
     Haven Publishing     400.00     23 1/2     8,000.00   1,400.00    9,400.00
                                                ----------  ----------  -----------
   Total Investments                            25,650.00   2,863.42   28,513.42
                                                ==========  ==========  ===========
```

═══ **FIGURE 9-13.** Portfolio Value Report

Investment Performance Report

The Investment Performance Report allows you to look at the gain or loss achieved between two points in time. The Investment Performance Report indicates your return and projects an average annual return based on the results of the period selected. Follow these steps to create an Investment Performance Report:

1. Press (ESC) until the Investment Report menu displays, then type **2** to select Investment Performance Report.
2. Press (ENTER) to accept the default report title.
3. Type **8/1/91** and press (ENTER); then type **8/31/91** and press (ENTER).
4. Press (ENTER) to accept the default of Don't Subtotal.
5. Type **Y** for Show transaction detail.
6. Press (CTRL)-(ENTER) to accept the Current account default and display the report on the screen.

A printed copy of the report showing an annualized return of 64.5 percent is shown in Figure 9-14.

Capital Gains Report

The Capital Gains Report is useful for tax purposes since it shows the gain or loss on sales of investments. One example of a Capital Gains Report that

```
                        INVESTMENT PERFORMANCE REPORT
                          8/ 1/91 Through 8/31/91
   INVEST-Investments                                              Page 1
   9/ 3/91
                                                              Avg. Annual
      Date Action        Description      Investments  Returns Tot. Return
      ----- ------  ---------------------- ----------- -------- -----------
              8/ 1/91 -  8/31/91
              -------------------
      7/31          Beg Mkt Value           27,210.00
      8/ 2 BuyX     100 Douglas Marine       2,550.00
      8/10 DivX     Haven Publishing                     200.00
      8/25 SellX    100 Haven Publishing               2,300.00
      8/31          End Mkt Value                      28,513.42

              TOTAL  8/ 1/91 -  8/31/91     29,760.00 31,013.42       64.5%
```

FIGURE 9-14. Investment Performance Report

you can create allows you to look at the difference between short- and long-term capital gains. Follow these steps to create the report:

1. Press (ESC) until the Investment Report menu displays.

2. Type **3** to select Capital Gains Report.

3. Press (ENTER) to accept the default.

4. Type **8/1/91** and press (ENTER).

5. Type **8/31/91** and press (ENTER).

6. Press (CTRL)-(ENTER) to display the Capital Gains (Schedule D) report.

Figure 9-15 shows a printout of this report.

Investment Income Report

The Investment Income Report reports on the total income or expense from your investments. Dividends and both realized and unrealized gains and

```
                    CAPITAL GAINS (SCHEDULE D) REPORT
                         8/ 1/91 Through 8/31/91
   INVEST-Investments                                              Page 1
   9/ 3/91

      Security      Shares  Bought    Sold   Sales Price  Cost Basis  Gain/Loss
   -------------   -------- --------  ------- -----------  ----------- -----------
                    LONG TERM

   Haven Publish       100 10/10/88  8/25/91    2,300.00    2,000.00     300.00

                                                -----------  ----------- -----------
                    TOTAL LONG TERM              2,300.00    2,000.00     300.00
                                                ===========  =========== ===========
```

FIGURE 9-15. Capital Gains Report

losses can be shown on this report. Follow these steps to create the report:

1. Press (ESC) until the Investment Report menu displays.
2. Type **4** to select Investment Income Report.
3. Press (ENTER) to accept the default.
4. Type **8/1/91** and press (ENTER).
5. Type **8/31/91** and press (ENTER).
6. Press (CTRL)-(ENTER) to display the report on your screen.

Your report will match the printout shown in Figure 9-16.

Investment Transactions Report

The Investment Transactions Report is the most detailed of the five, and reports on all investment transactions during the selected period. Follow these steps to create the report:

1. Press (ESC) until the Investment Report menu displays.
2. Type **5** to select Investment Transactions Report.
3. Press (ENTER) to accept the default.

```
                    INVESTMENT INCOME REPORT
                     8/ 1/91 Through 8/31/91
      INVEST-Investments                                    Page 1
      8/ 6/91
                                              8/ 1/91-
                     Category Description     8/31/91
                     ----------------------- -----------
                     INCOME/EXPENSE
                       INCOME
                         Dividend               300.00
                         Realized Gain/Loss     300.00
                                              -----------
                       TOTAL INCOME            600.00


                                              -----------
                     TOTAL INCOME/EXPENSE      600.00
                                              ===========
```

══════ **FIGURE 9-16.** Investment Income Report

```
                        INVESTMENT TRANSACTIONS REPORT
                            8/ 1/91 Through 8/31/91
      INVEST-Investments                                            Page 1
      9/ 6/91
                                                            Invest.  Cash +
                                                            Value    Invest.
      Date  Action  Secur       Categ     Price  Shares Commssn  Cash  Value  Invest.
      ----- ------- ----------- --------- ------ ------ ------- ------ ------- -------

            Balance 7/31/91
                                                              0  27,210  27,210

      8/ 2  UnrlzGn Douglas Marin Unrealized Gain/  25             -50     -50

      8/ 2  BuyX    Douglas Marin              25    100    50 -2,550  2,550
                                 [Price Money             2,550
                                                                        2,550

      8/10  DivX    Haven Publish Dividend                     200      200
                                 [Great Lakes               -200     -200

      8/15  UnrlzGn Ganges Mutual Unrealized G 13.2785         69      69

      8/15  ReinvDi Ganges Mutual            13.2785  7.531  -100   100
                                 Dividend                    100
                                                                        100

      8/25  UnrlzGn Haven Publish Unrealized G 23 1/4        300     300

      8/25  SellX   Haven Publish            23 1/4  100    25  2,000 -2,000
                                 [Price Money              -2,300
                                                                       -2,300
                                 Realized Gain/Loss          300
                                                                        300

      8/31  UnrlzGn Haven Publish Unrealized G 23 1/2        100     100
      8/31  UnrlzGn Glenn Packing Unrealized Gain/  31       100     100
      8/31  UnrlzGn Ganges Mutual Unrealized G 13.400        122     122
      8/31  UnrlzGn Douglas Marin Unrealized G 25 1/8         13      13
                                                          ------- ------- -------
            TOTAL  8/ 1/91 - 8/31/91                       0  1,303  1,303

            BALANCE 8/31/91                                0 28,513  28,513
```

══════ **FIGURE 9-17.** Investment Transactions Report including unrealized gains/losses

4. Type **8/1/91** and press ⌷ENTER⌷.

5. Type **8/31/91** and press ⌷ENTER⌷.

6. Press ⌷F8⌷ to activate the report Options.

7. Press ⌷ENTER⌷ twice.

8. Type **Y** to include unrealized gains, and press ⌷ENTER⌷.

9. Type **N** to display only whole dollars in the report, and press ⌷ENTER⌷.

10. Press ⌷CTRL⌷-⌷ENTER⌷ to display the report on your screen.

Your report will match the printout shown in Figure 9-17 except that the zeros are omitted from the printout to conserve space.

T I P

THE NEED FOR A WILL

A will is important to ensure that your heirs benefit from the net worth that you have accumulated and to make sure your wishes control the distribution of your assets at your death. Without a will, the laws of your state and the rulings of a probate court would decide what happens to your assets and award the custody of your minor children. The following may also occur:

- A probate court may appoint an administrator for your estate.

- State laws may distribute your assets differently than you might wish.

- Fees for probate lawyers will consume from 5 to 25 percent of your estate. The smaller your estate, the higher the percentage will be for the probate lawyer.

- If your estate is large enough to be affected by federal estate taxes ($600,000 or more), not focusing on a will and other estate planning tasks can increase the tax obligations on your estate.

chapter 10

CREATING CUSTOM REPORTS

Creating a Custom Net Worth Report
Creating a Custom Transaction Report
Creating a Summary Report
Memorizing Reports

Quicken can prepare both standard and custom reports. Standard reports have a predefined format most Quicken users will find acceptable for their personal, business, and investment reporting needs. However, as you become more familiar with Quicken, you may want to customize your reports to meet your unique needs. Custom reports allow you to alter the report format to meet your specific requirements.

Quicken supports creating five different standard reports for personal use: Cash Flow, Monthly Budget, Itemized Category, Tax Summary, and Net Worth. You can create any one of these reports by selecting Personal Reports from the Reports menu, shown in Figure 10-1. You have seen several examples of standard reports in earlier chapters.

Quicken allows you to customize any of the standard reports by pressing (F8) (Customize) while in a standard report window. Figure 10-1 shows that Quicken 4 has the ability to access reports that you have memorized (more on memorized reports at the end of this chapter).

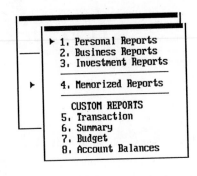

PERSONAL–Cardinal Bank   Copyright 1989–1990 Intuit

FIGURE 10-1. Reports menu

Quicken also provides four custom report types in the Reports menu: Transaction, Summary, Budget, and Account Balances. Selecting any of these items causes a custom Create Report window to be displayed on the screen, which allows you to create many different report frameworks. Although the exact contents of the window depend on the type of report you are creating, each of the custom windows allows you to enter information such as the accounts you want to use, directions for totaling and subtotaling the report, the type of cleared status for included transactions, and specific transactions you wish to include. Some of these options are specified with direct entries in the Report window and others require the use of ⌷F8⌷ for additional report options or ⌷F9⌷ to filter records that will be included.

You have already seen a custom option in Chapter 7, when you selected the current account item in Figure 7-6 to customize the Monthly Budget report for Cardinal Bank, shown in Figure 7-7. In this chapter you will look at additional custom reporting options and report filtering features as you build three new custom reports. After looking at the exercises in this chapter you will be able to create your own custom reports and memorize them for later use. Be sure to look at the special Documenting Your Decisions section to learn how to safeguard your time investment.

T I P DOCUMENTING YOUR DECISIONS

As you work with Quicken's features you will probably try a number of custom report options before you decide on the exact set of reports that meet your needs. If you had an accountant prepare these same reports, there might also be some trial and error the first time before the exact format to use would be determined. Once the decisions were made, the accountant would document them to ensure you received the exact reports you requested on a regular basis. You will benefit by following the same procedure and documenting the custom reports and options you select with Quicken. The following are appropriate steps to take in putting together your documentation:

- Place all your report documentation in one folder.

- Include a copy of each report you want to produce on a regular basis.

- If you are using a Quicken report to obtain information for another form, include a copy of the form and note on it which field in the Quicken report is used to obtain that number.

- Include the selections you used in the custom report windows. If you have a screen capture utility you can capture and print this screen when you create the report the first time.

- Include your entries on the Filter window. You can write them down or use a screen capture utility.

- If you are creating multiple copies of some reports, write down the information on the extra copies and what must be done with the copies.

- Memorize each custom report to make it instantly available when you need it again.

CREATING A CUSTOM NET WORTH REPORT

You can create a Net Worth Report by selecting the Net Worth option from the Personal Reports menu. If you choose the standard report item from the list of Personal Reports and don't make any changes, Quicken will prepare the report for assets and liabilities and show the balance of each of your asset and liability accounts. You used this standard option in Chapter 9 to assess your net worth.

Report Intervals

If you want to look at the effect of financial management activities on your net worth over time, the standard report will not provide what you need since it provides your balances at a specific time. The Create Account Balances Report window, which opens when you select customize for the Net Worth Report, allows you to specify intervals for the report. Figure 10-2 shows the Create Account Balances Report window and the many interval options that can be chosen. You can select report intervals ranging from a week to a year. If you don't specify an interval, the default option is the specific time identified as the last date on the line "Report balances on dates through" (see Figure 10-2). In this example, if you request the report interval of Week, Quicken will prepare a Net Worth Report at the end of each week for the month of August.

Changing the Accounts Used to Prepare the Report

The standard Net Worth Report presents all accounts in the account group when preparing the report. If you are only concerned with some of your balances, you can select those accounts you want to appear in the report. Entering **C** in the fourth field of the Create Account Balances Report window produces a report for the current account

```
┌────────────────────────────────────────────────────────────┐
│ ▁▁▁▁▁▁▁▁▁▁▁▁▁▁▁▁▁▁▁▁▁▁▁▁▁▁▁▁▁▁▁▁▁▁▁▁▁▁▁▁▁▁▁▁▁▁▁▁▁▁▁▁▁▁▁▁▁▁ │
│                 Create Account Balances Report               │
│ ──────────────────────────────────────────────────────────── │
│                                                              │
│  Report title (optional): Net Worth Report                   │
│                                                              │
│  Report balances on dates from:  8/ 1/91 through:  8/31/91   │
│                                                              │
│  Report at intervals of: 1                                   │
│         1. None                    5. Month                  │
│         2. Week                    6. Quarter                │
│         3. Two Weeks               7. Half Year              │
│         4. Half Month              8. Year                   │
│                                                              │
│  Use Current/All/Selected accounts (C/A/S): A                │
│ ──────────────────────────────────────────────────────────── │
│  Esc-Cancel    Ctrl M-Memorize    F8-Options    F9-Filter  ◄┘ Continue │
└────────────────────────────────────────────────────────────┘
```

INVEST-Investments

FIGURE 10-2.   Custom Create Account Balances Report window

only. Entering **S** allows you to select from a list of all the accounts in the account group.

Displaying Detailed Information on the Net Worth Report

When you created the Net Worth Report in Chapter 9, all the detail available on your investments was not displayed. This occurred because Quicken's standard Net Worth Report does not show all the detail. Including detailed information would provide a better picture of your investment holdings. To obtain this information you need to customize the standard report.

To include detailed investment information on the Net Worth Report you need to enter **S** for "Selected accounts" in the last field of the Create Account Balances Report window (Figure 10-2). You will use the Investments account in the INVEST account group, created in Chapter 9. Since the last example used that account group, you may already be there. If not, go to the "Changing Account Groups" section of this chapter for instructions.

Follow these steps from the Main Menu to produce a Net Worth Report with class detail.

1. Type **3** to select Reports.

Quicken will display the Reports menu showing both standard (Personal Reports and Business Reports) and custom report items.

2. Type **1** to select Personal Reports.

3. Type **5** to select Net Worth.

4. Press (**F8**) to customize the report.

Quicken displays the Create Account Balances Report window shown in Figure 10-2.

5. Press (**ENTER**) to use the default report title.

6. Type **8/1/91** and press (**ENTER**).

7. Type **8/31/91** and press (**ENTER**).

8. Press (**ENTER**) to accept None for the Report at intervals of field.

9. Type **S** to use selected accounts in the report and press (**ENTER**). The Select Accounts to Include window, shown in Figure 10-3, appears on your screen.

10. Press (**DOWN ARROW**) until the arrow cursor moves to Investments.

11. Press (**SPACEBAR**) until the word Detail appears in the Include in Report column.

Pressing (**SPACEBAR**) changes the entry in the Include in Report column from "Include" to "Detail" to blank. "Detail" causes the detailed information to be shown in the report if any exists. A blank space means the account will be excluded from the report. "Include" shows information from the account but does not use all the detail. Make sure your screen looks like that shown in Figure 10-3 before proceeding.

12. Press (**ENTER**) and the Net Worth Report appears on your screen.

13. Press (**F8**) to display the Print Report window.

14. Select your printer and press (**ENTER**).

Quicken will produce the report shown in Figure 10-4. Notice that the report looks the same as the one generated in Chapter 9, except that the Investments section shows detailed stock information.

CREATING A CUSTOM TRANSACTION REPORT

You can print all the transactions in any Quicken account register by opening the Print Register window from the Acct/Print menu. This procedure prints a listing of all the transactions in a given time frame. You can use this approach for printing a complete listing of register activity for backup purposes. However, it does not provide much information for decision-making. The custom Transaction Report item provides an alternative. By selecting this feature you can choose to subtotal transaction activity in many different ways, use all or only selected accounts, or show split

```
                    ┌──────────────────────────────────────────────┐
                    │            Select Accounts to Include          │
                ┌───┤                                                │───┐
                │   │                                    Include      │   │
                │   │   Account      Type    Description  in Report   │   │
              Re│   │ Great Lakes Chk Bank  Personal Checking  Include │   │
                │   │ Great Lakes Sve Bank  Personal Savings   Include │   │
              Re│   │ Price Money Mkt Bank  Money Market Account Include│   │
                │   │ Residence      Oth A  444 Ferndell       Include │   │
              Re│   │ Great Lakes Mtg Oth L Mortgage on Ferndell Include│   │
                │   │ ► Investments  Invst  Personal Investments Detail │   │
                │   │                                                │   │
              Us│   │                                                │   │
                │   │           Space Bar-Include/Exclude/Detail     │   │
                │   │ Esc-Cancel    F1-Help    F9-Select All  ↵ Continue│  │
                    └──────────────────────────────────────────────┘
  INVEST-Investments
```

FIGURE 10-3. Select Accounts to Include window

```
                    ACCOUNT BALANCES REPORT
                        As of 8/31/91
INVEST-Selected Accounts
9/17/91                                              8/31/91
                        Acct                         Balance
------------------------------------- ---------------------------

ASSETS
   Cash and Bank Accounts
      Great Lakes Chk-Personal Checking                 3,125.
      Great Lakes Sve-Personal Savings                  2,700.
      Price Money Mkt-Money Market Account             14,750.
                                                    ------------
   Total Cash and Bank Accounts                        20,575.

   Other Assets
      Residence-444 Ferndell                          105,000.
                                                    ------------
   Total Other Assets                                 105,000.

   Investments
      Investments-Personal Investments
         Douglas Marine                 2,512.50
         Ganges Mutual Fund            13,500.92
         Glenn  Packing                 3,100.00
         Haven Publishing               9,400.00
         —Cash—                             0.00
                                       -----------
      Total Investments-Personal Investments          28,513.
                                                    ------------
   Total Investments                                   28,513.

                                                    ------------
TOTAL ASSETS                                          154,088.

LIABILITIES
   Other Liabilities
      Great Lakes Mtg-Mortgage on Ferndell            84,975.
                                                    ------------
   Total Other Liabilities                             84,975.

                                                    ------------
TOTAL LIABILITIES                                      84,975.
                                                    ------------
OVERALL TOTAL                                          69,113.
                                                    ============
```

FIGURE 10-4. Account Balances Report

transaction detail. Thus, you are allowed to select the specific transaction details you need for better decision-making. Let's take a look at some examples.

Changing Account Groups

All the remaining examples generated in this chapter are prepared in the PERSONAL account group. The following sequence of steps demonstrates how to change from one account group to another within Quicken:

1. While in Quicken, press (ESC) until you return to the Main Menu.

2. Type 5 and the Change Settings window appears.

3. Type 1 to select Account Group Activities.

4. Type 1 and the Select/Set Up Account Group window appears.

5. Move the arrow cursor to the PERSONAL account group and press (ENTER). The Select Account to Use window appears.

6. Move the arrow cursor to the Cardinal Bank account, if necessary, and press (ENTER). Quicken takes you to the account register for the Cardinal Bank account.

7. Press (ESC) to go to the Main Menu.

Showing Split Transaction Detail

If a transaction is split among several categories, the word "SPLIT" will appear in the Category field when the account register is printed. Suppose you want to prepare a customized report that captures all of the detail recorded in each split transaction within a selected time frame.

1. Type 3 to select the Reports item.

Quicken will display the Reports menu showing both standard (Personal Reports, Business Reports, and Investment Reports) and custom report items.

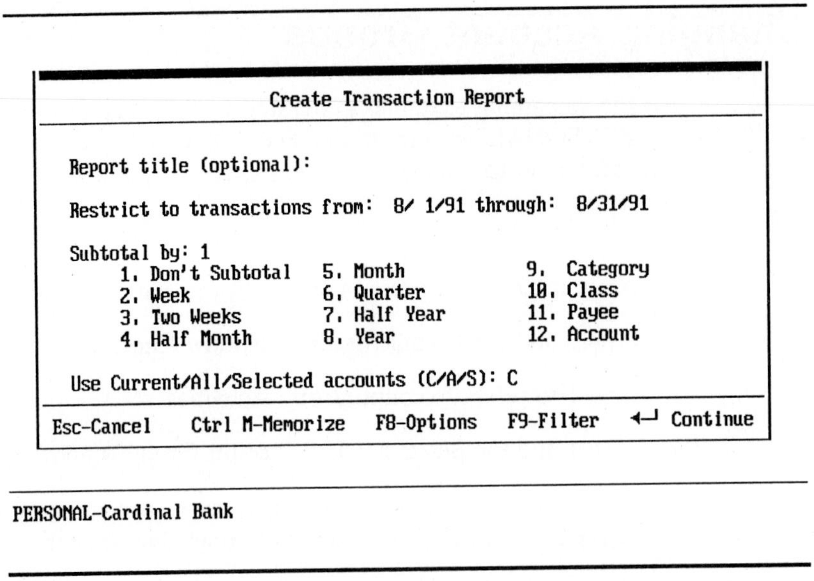

```
┌──────────────────────────────────────────────────────────────┐
│                    Create Transaction Report                   │
│ ──────────────────────────────────────────────────────────── │
│                                                                │
│  Report title (optional):                                      │
│                                                                │
│  Restrict to transactions from:  8/ 1/91 through:  8/31/91     │
│                                                                │
│  Subtotal by: 1                                                │
│        1. Don't Subtotal   5. Month        9. Category         │
│        2. Week             6. Quarter     10. Class            │
│        3. Two Weeks        7. Half Year   11. Payee            │
│        4. Half Month       8. Year        12. Account          │
│                                                                │
│  Use Current/All/Selected accounts (C/A/S): C                  │
│ ──────────────────────────────────────────────────────────── │
│  Esc-Cancel   Ctrl M-Memorize   F8-Options   F9-Filter  ⏎ Continue │
└──────────────────────────────────────────────────────────────┘
```

PERSONAL-Cardinal Bank

FIGURE 10-5.   Create Transaction Report window

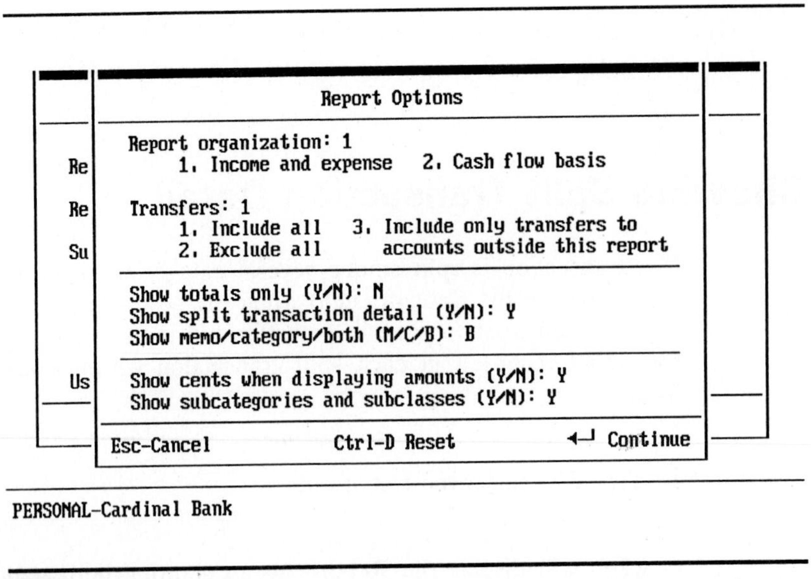

```
┌────┬─────────────────────────────────────────────────┬────┐
│    │                  Report Options                   │    │
│ Re │  Report organization: 1                           │    │
│    │        1. Income and expense   2. Cash flow basis │    │
│ Re │                                                   │    │
│    │  Transfers: 1                                     │    │
│ Su │        1. Include all    3. Include only transfers to │
│    │        2. Exclude all       accounts outside this report │
│    │ ───────────────────────────────────────────────── │    │
│    │  Show totals only (Y/N): N                        │    │
│    │  Show split transaction detail (Y/N): Y           │    │
│    │  Show memo/category/both (M/C/B): B               │    │
│    │ ───────────────────────────────────────────────── │    │
│ Us │  Show cents when displaying amounts (Y/N): Y      │    │
│    │  Show subcategories and subclasses (Y/N): Y       │    │
│    │ ───────────────────────────────────────────────── │    │
│    │  Esc-Cancel          Ctrl-D Reset       ⏎ Continue │    │
└────┴─────────────────────────────────────────────────┴────┘
```

PERSONAL-Cardinal Bank

FIGURE 10-6.   Report Options window for split transaction detail

2. Type **5** to select Transaction from the Custom Reports section of the Reports menu.

Quicken displays the Create Transaction Report window.

3. Press (**ENTER**) to use the default report title.
4. Type **8/1/91** and press (**ENTER**).
5. Type **8/31/91** and press (**ENTER**).
6. Press (**ENTER**) to accept the default option, Don't Subtotal.
7. Type **C** to use the current account in the report.

At this point your screen should match Figure 10-5.

8. Press (**F8**) and the Report Options window appears.
9. Press (**ENTER**) to accept option 1, Income and expense, for the report organization.
10. Press (**ENTER**) to accept option 1, Include all, in the Transfers field.

This will include in the report all transfers between the Investments account and others in the account group.

11. Press (**ENTER**) to accept *N* in the Show totals only field.
12. Type **Y** to indicate you want to show the split transaction detail and press (**ENTER**)

Your screen will match the window shown in Figure 10-6.

13. Press (**ENTER**) to accept *B* in the next field, indicating that both memo and category data will be displayed.

14. Press (**CTRL**)-(**ENTER**) to accept the remaining defaults.

The Create Transaction Report window reappears on your screen.

15. Press (**ENTER**) and the Transaction report appears on the screen.
16. Press (**F8**) to display the Print Report window.
17. Select your printer and press (**ENTER**) to create the report. Figure 10-7 shows the first few transactions in this report.

Notice that the report shows the details of the split transaction on 8/1, 8/2, and 8/3.

```
                            TRANSACTION REPORT
                          8/ 1/91 Through 8/31/91
   PERSONAL-Cardinal Bank                                    Page 1
   9/17/91

   Date  Num    Description       Memo           Category      Clr  Amount
   ----  -----  ---------------   -------------   ------------  -   ----------

        BALANCE  7/31/91                                            2,260.70

   8/ 1     S Payroll deposit    Gross Wages Ea  Salary            2,000.00
                                 FICA Withholdi  Tax FICA           -142.00
                                 Health Ins      Medical             -42.01
                                 Federal Income  Tax Fed            -140.00
                                 State Income T  Tax State           -80.00
                                 Local Income T  Tax Local           -10.00
   8/ 2 104 S Great Lakes Savings Principal Paym Mort Prin           -49.21
                                 Interest Porti  Mort Int           -300.79
   8/ 3 105 S Easy Credit Card   Blue Blouse     Clothing            -50.00
                                 Dinner at the   Dining              -60.00
                                 Gasoline - Jee  Auto Fuel           -23.00
                                 Green Rocker    Furniture          -217.00
                                 Play Tickets    Entertain           -50.00
                                                 Misc.               -50.00
```

═══════ **FIGURE 10-7.** Transaction report with split transaction detail

Adding Subtotals to the Transaction Report

When you produce a Transaction report without subtotals the transactions will simply be listed in order by date. If you change the subtotaling option you can choose from the options Week, Two Weeks, Half Month, Month, Quarter, Half Year, or Year. This will still list the transactions by date but will also provide a subtotal of the transactions each time the selected interval occurs; selecting monthly will result in a subtotal for each month. If you choose one of the options Category, Class, Payee, or Account for the subtotal option, the transactions will be ordered by the field selected, and a subtotal will be printed whenever the value in the selected field changes. For example, a subtotal by Category for 8/1 to 8/31 transactions will cause Quicken to list the transactions alphabetically by category and by date within each category, with a subtotal for each category.

Follow these steps from the Main Menu for the Cardinal Bank account (in the PERSONAL account group) to create a Transaction report subtotaled by category:

1. Type **3** to select the Reports item.

Quicken will display the Reports menu showing both standard (Personal, Investment, and Business Reports) and custom report items.

2. Type **5** to select Transaction and the Create Transaction Report window appears.

3. Press (**ENTER**) to use the default report title.

4. Type **8/1/91** and press (**ENTER**).

5. Type **8/31/91** and press (**ENTER**).

6. Type **9** and press (**ENTER**) to subtotal by category.

7. Type **C** and press (**ENTER**) to use the current account in the report.

The Transaction Report by Category will display on your screen.

8. Press (**F8**) to display the Print Report window.

9. Select your printer and press (**ENTER**).

The bottom of the first page of the report will show three transactions for the Groceries category, as shown in this partial report:

```
              Groceries
              ---------
8/ 4 106      Maureks      Groceries      Groceries      -60.00
8/15 108      Meijer       Groceries      Groceries      -65.00
8/27 112      Meijer       Food           Groceries      -93.20
                                                        ---------
              Total Groceries                            -218.20
```

This report is essentially the same as the Itemized Category report you saw in Chapter 7, unless you choose to make additional customization changes, such as selecting accounts or filtering the information presented.

CREATING A SUMMARY REPORT

Summary reports allow you to create reports based on categories, classes, payees, or accounts. You can use them to analyze spending patterns, prepare tax summaries, review major purchases, or look at the total charge card purchases for a given period.

With a Summary report you have more control over the layout of information than in other reports. You can select from a number of options to determine what information to place in rows and columns of the report. You can combine the summary features with the filtering features to further select the information presented.

Subtotaling a Summary Report by Month

Although you can choose any of the time intervals to control the subtotals for the report, a month is commonly chosen since many users budget expenses by month. This type of report allows you to look at a monthly summary of your financial transactions. Follow these steps from the Main Menu for the Cardinal Bank account (in the PERSONAL account group) to create the Summary Report by Month:

1. Type **3** to select the Reports item.

Quicken will display the Reports menu showing both standard (Personal, Investment, and Business Reports) and custom report items.

2. Type **6** to select Summary and the Create Summary Report window appears.

3. Press (**ENTER**) to use the default report title.

4. Type **8/1/91** and press (**ENTER**).

5. Type **10/31/91** and press (**ENTER**).

6. Press (**ENTER**) to accept the default Row headings item.

7. Type **5** and press (**ENTER**) to select Month for the Column headings field.

8. Type **C**; then press (**F8**). The Report Options window appears.

9. Type **2** and press (**ENTER**).

This step instructs Quicken to prepare the report on a cash flow basis. The report will be organized by cash inflows and outflows. This is the same basis as the monthly budget reports prepared in Chapter 7. It allows you to compare this report with those prepared earlier and provides additional information for assessing your budget results.

10. Type **1** and press CTRL-ENTER. You are returned to the Create Summary Report window.

11. Press ENTER and the Summary Report by Month appears on your screen. Figure 10-8 shows a printout of this report.

```
                        SUMMARY REPORT REPORT BY MONTH
                          8/ 1/91 Through 10/31/91
       PERSONAL-Cardinal Bank                                        Page 1
       9/17/91

            Category Description       8/91         9/91        10/91      OVERALL
       ------------------------------ ------------ ------------- ------------- --------------
          INFLOWS
            Salary Income             2,000.00     2,000.00     2,000.00     6,000.00
                                      ----------   ----------   ----------   ----------
          TOTAL INFLOWS              2,000.00     2,000.00     2,000.00     6,000.00

          OUTFLOWS
            Automobile Fuel              23.00        23.00        37.00        83.00
            Clothing                     50.00        50.00        75.00       175.00
            Dining Out                   60.00        60.00        45.00       165.00
            Entertainment                50.00        50.00       100.00       200.00
            Federal Tax                 140.00       140.00       140.00       420.00
            Groceries                   218.20       180.00       250.00       648.20
            Household Furniture         217.00         0.00       550.00       767.00
            Local Tax Withholding        10.00        10.00        10.00        30.00
            Medical & Dental            142.01       212.01       142.01       496.03
            Miscellaneous                50.00        50.00       150.00       250.00
            Mortgage Interest Exp       300.79       300.29       299.69       900.77
            Mortgage Principal           49.21        49.71        50.31       149.23
            Social Security Tax         142.00       142.00       142.00       426.00
            State Tax                    80.00        80.00        80.00       240.00
            Telephone Expense            23.00        29.00        27.50        79.50
            Water, Gas, Electric:
              Electric Utilities         30.75        43.56        37.34       111.65
              Gas Utilities              19.25        19.29        16.55        55.09
                                       ----------   ----------   ----------   ----------
            Total Water, Gas, Electric   50.00        62.85        53.89       166.74
            TO Cardinal Saving          200.00       394.79       366.35       961.14
                                       ----------   ----------   ----------   ----------
          TOTAL OUTFLOWS             1,805.21     1,833.65     2,518.75     6,157.61

                                       ----------   ----------   ----------   ----------
          OVERALL TOTAL                194.79       166.35      -518.75      -157.61
                                       ==========   ==========   ==========   ==========
```

FIGURE 10-8. Summary Report by Month

Unless you adjusted all of your salary and mortgage payment transactions to agree with the August entries discussed in Chapter 8, some of your entries will look different. You can make your report match Figure 10-8 by extending the August changes to the September and October payroll deposit and mortgage payment entries.

12. Press ⌐F8⌐ to display the Print Report window.

13. Select your printer and press ⌐ENTER⌐.

The report presents a cash inflow and outflow summary by month for the period of August through October. It provides additional cash flow information about the budget reports prepared in Chapter 7. Thus, the Summary Report by Month supplements the previously prepared Monthly Budget reports.

Filtering to See Tax-Related Categories

Filters allow you to selectively present information in a report. In Chapter 3 you used a filter to look for a payee name containing "Small." Other possible selection choices include memo, category, or class matches. You can also choose specific categories or classes for inclusion. Additional options allow you to specify tax-related items or transactions greater or less than a certain amount. You can also choose payments, deposits, unprinted checks, or all transactions. Checking the cleared status is another option; that is, you may wish to prepare a report using only transactions that have cleared the bank as part of your reconciliation process.

In the example that follows you will create a Summary report for tax-related items. Use the Cardinal Bank account in the PERSONAL account group. Starting from the Main Menu, follow these steps:

1. Type **3** to select Reports.

Quicken will display the Reports menu showing both standard (Personal Reports, Business Reports and Investment Reports) and custom report items.

2. Type **6** to select Summary. The Create Summary Report window appears on your screen.

3. Press ⌐ENTER⌐ to use the default report title.

4. Type **8/1/91** and press ⌐ENTER⌐.

5. Type **10/31/91** and press ⌐ENTER⌐.

6. Press (ENTER) to accept Category for the row headings.

7. Type **1** and press (ENTER) to select the default Don't Subtotal option.

8. Type **C** to select the Current account.

9. Press (F9) (Filter) to display the Filter Report Transactions window on your screen.

10. Press (ENTER) six times to move to the Tax-related categories only field. Type **Y** and press (ENTER). The Filter Report Transactions window will look like Figure 10-9.

11. Press (CTRL)-(ENTER) to return to the Create Summary Report window.

12. Press (F8) to open the Report Options window.

13. Type **2** and press (ENTER).

14. Press (CTRL)-(ENTER) to accept the default, option 1, which instructs Quicken to include in the report all transfers between this account and others. You are returned to the Create Summary Report window.

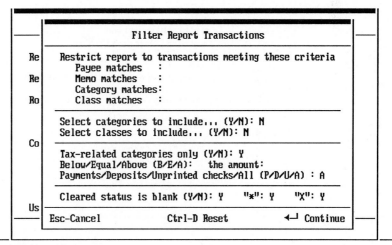

PERSONAL-Cardinal Bank

FIGURE 10-9. Filter Report Transactions window

15. Press (**ENTER**) and the Summary report appears on your screen.

16. Press (**F8**) to display the Print Report window.

17. Select your printer and press (**ENTER**).

Don't clear the report from you screen since you will want to use it in the next section.

Figure 10-10 shows the completed report with the information filtered for tax-related transactions only. (If you made the changes suggested earlier for Figure 10-8, your report will now agree with Figure 10-10, too.) This type of report can be used to monitor your tax-related activities for any part of the tax year or for the year-to-date activity. You can use this information for tax planning as well as tax preparation.

```
                          SUMMARY REPORT
                     8/ 1/91 Through 10/31/91
    PERSONAL-Cardinal Bank                                   Page 1
    8/1/91
                                          8/ 1/91-
                     Category Description  10/31/91
                     -----------------------  -----------
                     INCOME EXPENSE
                       INCOME
                         Salary Income      6,000.00
                                            -----------
                       TOTAL INCOME         6,000.00

                       EXPENSES
                         Federal Tax          420.00
                         Local Tax Withholding 30.00
                         Medical & Dental     496.03
                         Mortgage Interest Exp 900.77
                         Social Security Tax  426.00
                         State Tax            240.00
                                            -----------
                       TOTAL EXPENSES       2,512.80

                                            -----------
                     TOTAL INCOME/EXPENSE   3,487.20
                                            ===========
```

FIGURE 10-10. Filtered Summary report of tax-related transactions

MEMORIZING REPORTS

You have already seen the productivity that you can gain with Quicken's memorized transactions. Quicken 4 also allows you to memorize reports. Memorized reports store your custom report definitions and allow you to produce a new report instantly by recalling the memorized report definition. This means you can enter a title or filter once and use it again if you memorize the report.

To memorize a report, you use the same $\boxed{\text{CTRL}}$-$\boxed{\text{M}}$ sequence used to memorize transactions. The only difference is that you must have a report displayed on the screen. The following box will display to allow you to enter a name for the report:

```
┌─────────────────────────────────────────────────┐
│                Memorizing Report                  │
├─────────────────────────────────────────────────┤
│                                                   │
│    Title:                                         │
│                                                   │
├─────────────────────────────────────────────────┤
│  Esc-Cancel          F1-Help        ↵ Continue    │
└─────────────────────────────────────────────────┘
```

If you were memorizing the definition for the tax summary by month shown in Figure 10-8, you might enter the title as Tax Related Summary By Month. Although you can use the entire line for your name, you will want to ensure that the first 27 characters of your entry uniquely define your report since this is the entry that will display in the list of memorized reports.

To create a report from a memorized report definition, select Memorized Reports from the Report menu. A list of memorized reports will display in a window like the one shown in Figure 10-11, which shows a Tax Related Summary by Mont option. The *h* in Month is truncated from the display since it exceeds the 27-character display limit. After moving the arrow cursor to the desired report and pressing $\boxed{\text{ENTER}}$, the desired report is displayed on the screen. If you press $\boxed{\text{ESC}}$, you can access the report definition and change it before displaying the report again.

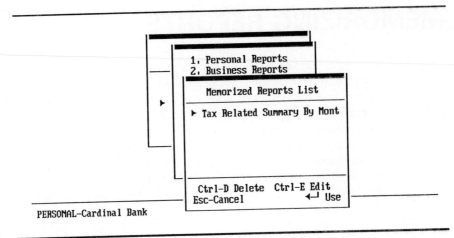

FIGURE 10-11. Memorized Reports List window

Now that you've had a chance to look at both standard and custom report options, you should have some idea of the types of reports you will need. You will want to take full advantage of Quicken's ability to memorize reports in order to save time and produce a consistent set of reports for each time period.

BUSINESS APPLICATIONS

Setting Up Quicken for Your Business
Quicken's Payroll Assistance
Preparing Budget Reports and Cash Flow Statements
Organizing Tax Information and Other Year-End Needs
Monitoring Financial Conditions
Advanced Quicken Features

Managing the financial aspects of your business is an essential activity that is often overlooked. Quicken's easy-to-use features can make the task proceed much quicker than you ever imagined. In this section you will learn how to create a chart of accounts to organize finances for your needs. You will also learn how to prepare the reports you need for payroll accounting, tax reports, income statements, and balance sheets. Soon you will find yourself relying on Quicken reports to improve your business operations.

SETTING UP
QUICKEN FOR
YOUR BUSINESS

Many small businesses will find that the Quicken system of record keeping can improve the quality of financial information used in making business decisions. Quicken can be used to record business transactions in your check register, while maintaining cost and depreciation records for assets in other registers. Quicken can also be used to budget cash flow, track the cost of jobs in progress, monitor and record payroll, and generate summary tax information to assist in tax return preparation. If you are a contractor you can track the cost incurred on various jobs as they progress through construction. If you provide landscaping services you can track the cost incurred for each job and prepare summary reports to determine the profits generated by job. If you are an author you can use Quicken to monitor royalties by publisher and record the costs incurred in your writing activities.

Even though Quicken improves your ability to record and monitor your business's financial transactions, it may not eliminate the need for accounting services. There are important tax issues that affect the business transactions you record. In addition, you may want your accountant to establish the hierarchy of categories you use to record transactions. This hierarchy, used to categorize all transactions, is called a *chart of accounts*. Your accountant should help establish the structure for your chart of accounts, which will ensure the information is organized to reduce the time required for other services, such as year-end tax preparation, that the accountant will continue to supply. This is particularly important if you will be recording business expenses in both your personal and business checking accounts.

The first section of this book introduced you to the basic features of Quicken. If you completed the exercises in Chapters 6 through 10 you built on the basic skills with split transactions, such as mortgage payments allocated between principal and interest, and with memorization of reccurring transactions. In those chapters you also used Quicken to prepare and monitor budgets, collect tax-related transactions, and prepare customized reports. In the remaining chapters you will look at some of these concepts again, from a business perspective. If you plan to use Quicken for home and business use, you may find it beneficial to read through the earlier chapters, if you haven't done so, rather than moving directly to business transactions.

This chapter is longer than the others since there are many decisions you need to make as you begin. There are also a number of basic skills you need to develop to apply Quicken to all aspects of your business. The first step is to consider some alternatives. The next sections provide an overview of two important decisions that must precede all other activities with the package. If you need additional guidance, consult your accountant to be certain your information will be in the format you need for your entire business year.

CASH VERSUS ACCRUAL ACCOUNTING

The first decision you need to make is the timing of recording financial transactions. You can either record a transaction as soon as you know that it will occur, or you can wait until cash changes hands between the parties in the transaction. The former alternative is *accrual basis* accounting, and the latter *cash basis* accounting. There is a third method called *modified cash basis* that will be discussed shortly. If your business is organized as a corporation, the accrual method must be used.

Most small businesses use the cash basis because it corresponds to their tax-reporting needs and the financial reports prepared provide information summarizing the cash-related activities of the business. With cash basis accounting you report income when you receive cash from customers for services you provide. For example, if you are in the plumbing business, you would recognize income when a customer makes payment for services. You might provide the services in December and not receive the customer's check until January. In this case you would record the income in January when you received and deposited the customer's check. Similarly, you recognize your expenses when you write your checks for the costs you incurred. Thus, if you ordered supplies in December, but didn't pay the bill until January, you would deduct the cost in January when you wrote a check to the supplier. Briefly, with a purely cash basis accounting system you recognize the income when you receive cash and recognize expenses when you pay for expenses incurred for business purposes.

With the accrual basis approach you record your revenues and expenses when you provide services to your customer, regardless of when the cash flow occurs. Using the plumbing example from the preceding paragraph, you would recognize the income from the plumbing services in December, when you provided the services to the customer, even though the cash would not be received until the next year. Likewise, if you purchased the supplies in December and paid for them in January, the cost of the supplies would be recorded in December, not in January when they were actually paid for. The same information is recorded under both methods.

The basic difference between the cash and accrual bases of accounting is what accountants call *timing differences*. When a cash basis is used, the receipt of cash determines when the transaction is recorded. When the accrual basis is used, the time the services are provided determines when the revenue and expenses are recorded.

A third method of reporting business revenues and expenses is the modified cash basis approach. This method uses the cash basis as described, but modifies it to report depreciation on certain assets over a number of years. In this case you must spread the cost of trucks, computer equipment, office furniture, and similar assets over the estimated number of years they will be used to generate income for your business. The Internal Revenue Service has rules for determining the life of an asset. In addition, the tax laws also allow you to immediately deduct the first $10,000 of the acquisition cost of certain qualified assets each year without worrying about depreciation. Once again, these are areas where your accountant could be of assistance in setting up your Quicken accounts.

Whether you use the cash, accrual, or modified cash basis in recording your transactions is determined by a number of factors. Some of the considerations are listed for you in the special Cash Versus Accrual Methods section.

Since many small businesses use the modified cash basis of recording revenues and expenses, this method is illustrated in all the examples in Chapters 11 through 15. The accrual method is used in Chapter 16.

ESTABLISHING YOUR CHART OF ACCOUNTS

You can use the basic set of categories that Quicken provides to categorize your business transactions, or you can create a whole new set. Each of the existing categories will have a name similar to the category options used in earlier chapters. For example, there is a category name of "Ads" with the description "Advertising." In Quicken these organizational units are called categories despite the fact that you may have been referring to them as accounts in your manual system.

If you do not have an existing chart of accounts, making a few modifications to Quicken's standard category options is the best approach. The names included in Quicken's categories are suitable for most businesses. Later in this chapter you will learn to add a few accounts of your own.

If you already have an existing set of accounts, you will want to retain this structure for consistency. Many businesses assign a number to each category of income or expense, such as using 4001 as the account number for book sales. They may use the first two digits of the number to group asset, liability, income, and expense accounts together. If you have this structure, you will

T
I
P

CASH VERSUS ACCRUAL METHODS

Tax requirements   You must decide what your tax reporting obligations are and whether those requirements alone will dictate the method you will select for financial reporting. For most small businesses this is the overriding factor to consider. For instance, if inventories are part of your business you must use the accrual method for revenues and purchases. If inventories are not a part of your business you will probably find it best and easiest to use the cash basis of accounting.

Users of the financial reports   The people who use your financial reports can have a significant influence on your reporting decisions. For example, do you have external users such as banks and other creditors? If so, you may find they require special reports and other financial information that will influence how you set up your accounting and reporting system.

Size and type of business activity   The kind of business you have will influence the type of financial reports you need to prepare and the method of accounting you will adopt. Are you in a service, retail, or manufacturing business? Manufacturing concerns will use the accrual method, since they have sales that will be billed and collected over weeks or even months and they carry inventories of goods. Retail stores such as small groceries would also use the accrual method of accounting, at least for sales and purchases, since they have inventories that affect the financial reports they will prepare. On the other hand, a small landscaping business will probably use the cash basis since there are no inventories and the majority of the cost associated with the business is payroll and other costs that are generally paid close to the time the services are performed. In this case the use of business equipment will call for the modified cash basis to record depreciation on the property.

need to invest a little more time initially to establish your chart of accounts. You can delete the entries in the existing list of categories and then add new categories, or you can edit the existing categories one by one. The category names in your category list (chart of accounts) might be numbers, such as "4001" or "5010," and the corresponding descriptions "4001—Book Sales" and "5010—Freight," respectively. When you are finished, each category will contain your account number and each description will contain both the account number and text describing the income or expense recorded in the category. You should work through all the examples in this chapter before setting up your own categories.

A QUICK LOOK AT THE BUSINESS USED IN THE SECTION EXAMPLES

An overview of the business used for the examples in Chapters 11 through 15 will be helpful in understanding some of the selections made in the exercises. The business is run by an individual and is organized as a sole proprietorship. The individual running the business is married and must file a Form 1040 showing both business income and W2 income earned by the spouse. Income categories, in addition to the standard ones provided with Quicken, will be needed for the different types of income generated. Since the company in the example offers services rather than merchandise, the income categories will be appropriate for a service-type business. Quicken can also be used for retail or wholesale businesses that sell goods. You can use Quicken for any organization, including sole proprietorships, partnerships, and small corporate entities. Look at the special Business Organization Options section for a definition of these three types of businesses.

The business is home-based, which necessitates splitting some expenses, such as utilities and mortgage interest, between home and business categories. Other expenses, such as the purchase of office equipment, are business expenses. A number of expenses incurred by the business do not have appropriate entries in the category list provided by Quicken; this will require adding categories.

The example selected is a little more complicated than a business run from outside the home that has no transactions split between business and personal expenses. When you have a clear separation you can simply establish an account group for all of your business accounts and another account group for personal transactions. The example used here has separate checking accounts for business and personal records but places both accounts within one account group. The use of separate accounts should be considered almost mandatory. All business income should be deposited into a separate account and all expenses that are completely business related should be paid from this account. Anyone who has experienced an IRS audit can testify to the necessity of having solid documentation for business transactions. One part of that documentation is the maintenance of a business

T I P BUSINESS ORGANIZATION OPTIONS

Sole Proprietorship   A sole proprietorship provides no separation between the owner and the business. The debts of the business are the personal liabilities of the owner. The profits of the business are included on the owner's tax return since the business does not pay taxes on profits directly. This form of business organization is the simplest.

Partnership   A partnership is a business defined as a relationship between two or more parties. Each person in the partnership is taxed as an individual for his or her share of the profits. A partnership agreement defines the contributions of each member and the distribution of the profits.

Corporation   A corporation is an independent business entity. The owners of the corporation are separate from the corporation and do not personally assume the debt of the corporation. This is referred to as "limited liability." The corporation is taxed on its profits and can distribute the remaining profits to owners as dividends. The owners are taxed on these dividends, resulting in the so-called "double tax" with the corporate structure. Unlike sole proprietorship and partnership businesses, corporations pay salaries to the owners.

S Corporation   A special form of corporation that avoids the double tax problem of a regular corporation. A number of strict rules govern when an S corporation can be set up. Some of the limitations are that only one class of stock is permitted and there is an upper limit of 35 shareholders.

checking account and supporting receipts for your expenses and revenues. If you maintain a separate business account, your bank statement provides the supporting detail for business transactions in a clear and concise manner that supports your documentation of business activities. If your business is so small that it is not feasible to establish and maintain two checking accounts, you will need to be particularly careful when recording entries in your Quicken register.

ACCOUNT GROUPS

When you first use Quicken it automatically creates an account group. Quicken calls this account group QDATA and creates four files on your disk to manage all the accounts and information within them. You could use this account group to record all your transactions if you decide to handle your business and personal financial transactions through a single account.

In the first five chapters, you worked with only one account in QDATA. If you completed Chapters 6 through 10 you learned that it was possible to create additional accounts such as a separate savings account and an investment account. You can also have accounts for credit cards, cash, assets, and liabilities. A new account group, PERSONAL, was created in Chapter 6 to organize all the personal accounts.

You could continue to enter the transactions in this chapter in the QDATA account group or you could set up a new account in the QDATA account group. The new data would then be intermingled with the practice transactions in earlier chapters. However, since you will want to learn how to set up new transactions that are stored separately from existing accounts, you should create a new account group. You will also learn how to create a backup copy of an account group to safeguard your data entry.

Adding a New Account Group

If you completed Chapters 1 through 9, you already have account groups for QDATA, PERSONAL, and INVEST with all of the transactions entered in the first two sections of this book. If you skipped Chapters 6 through 10, you still have only the QDATA account group. In this section you will learn how to create a new account group and create accounts within it. You need to decide if you want to delete the other account groups to free the space on your disk. They can be deleted from the Select/Set Up Account Group window when you are finished creating the new account group.

You will use an account group called BUSINESS and will initially set up a business checking account, a personal checking account, and an asset account. The asset account will be used to record information on equipment. Later you will establish other accounts for this group. From the Main Menu, follow these steps to set up the new account group and add the first three accounts to this group:

1. Type **5** to select Change Settings.

2. Type **1** to select Account Group Activities.

3. Type **1** to select Select/Set Up Account Group.

Quicken will display the window for selecting or setting up an account group. Notice the existing account groups. If you skipped Chapters 6 through 10 you will only have one account group.

4. Move the cursor to < Set Up New Grp > and press (ENTER).

Quicken opens the window for creating a new account group.

5. Type **BUSINESS** as the name for the account group and press (ENTER).

Quicken creates four DOS files from each account group name and adds four different filename extensions to the name that you provide. This means you must provide a valid filename of no more than eight characters. Do not include spaces or special symbols in your entries for account names.

6. Type **3** and press (ENTER) to select Both, which will provide access to both home and business categories.

7. Check the location for your data files and make changes to reference a valid file or directory if a change is required.

If you use the default directory, yours will display as C:\QUICKEN4\.

8. Press (ENTER) to complete the creation of the new account group.

Note that you can see the size of all the account groups you have created here. You can delete them at this time if you need to clear disk space.

Quicken redisplays the window for selecting or creating account groups but shows the BUSINESS account group this time.

9. Move the cursor to BUSINESS and press (ENTER).

Since this is a new account group, Quicken does not have any accounts in the group. The window shown in Figure 11-1 appears to allow you to create a new account. Leave your screen as it is for a few minutes while you explore some new account options.

```
┌─────────────────────────────────────────────────────────────┐
│                    Select Account to Use                      │
│                                                               │
│         Current Account Group: C:\Q4_11\BUSINESS             │
│                                            Num   Ending  Checks│
│         Account      Type      Description Trans Balance To Prt│
│                                                               │
│   ► <New Account>          │ Set up a new account            │
│                            │                                  │
│                            │                                  │
│                            │                                  │
│                            │                                  │
│                            │                                  │
│                            │                                  │
│                            │                                  │
│                            │                                  │
│         Ctrl-D Delete  Ctrl-E Edit  ↑,↓ Select                │
│                        F1-Help                                │
│   Esc-Cancel                                        ←┘ Use    │
└─────────────────────────────────────────────────────────────┘
```

FIGURE 11-1. Creating the first account in the new group

Adding Accounts to the New Account Group

Quicken makes it easy to create multiple accounts. All the accounts here will be created in the same account group, so you will be able to create one report for all of them as well as print reports for individual accounts. There will be an account register for each account that you create.

Savings accounts, investment accounts, cash accounts, asset accounts, liability accounts, and credit card accounts are all possible additions. Savings accounts and investment accounts should definitely be kept separate from your checking account since you will be interested in monitoring both the growth and balance in these accounts separately. As mentioned earlier, separate business and personal checking accounts are another good idea.

Quicken accounts can be set up to conform to the needs of your business. In this section you will add the first few accounts. In later chapters additional accounts will be established to monitor other business activities. If you are not still at the Select Account to Use window, you can return to that screen from the Main Menu by typing **5**, typing **1** twice, moving the arrow cursor to BUSINESS, and pressing (ENTER). Follow these steps to enter the new account:

1. Press (ENTER) and Quicken will display the window shown in Figure 11-2 for setting up a new account.

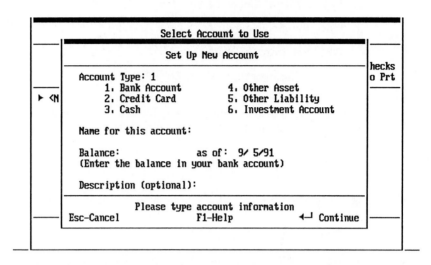

FIGURE 11-2. Entering information for the new account

2. Type **1** to choose Bank Account for the account type and press
    (ENTER).
3. Type **ANB Business** and press (ENTER).

ANB represents the bank name and Business indicates that it is the business
checking account. Although you could use Cardinal Bank again in this new
account group, ANB (for American National Bank) will be used to eliminate
confusion with the earlier examples.

4. Type **4000** for the balance and press (ENTER).
5. Type **1/1/91** and press (ENTER).
6. Type **Business Checking** and press (ENTER).

Quicken returns you to the window for selecting an account.

7. Move the arrow cursor to <New Account> and press (ENTER).
8. Type **1** and press (ENTER).
9. Type **ANB Personal** and press (ENTER).
10. Type **2500** and press (ENTER).
11. Type **1/1/91** and press (ENTER).

12. Type **Personal Checking** and press (ENTER).

13. Move the arrow cursor to <New Account> and press (ENTER).

14. Type **4** and press (ENTER).

15. Type **Equipment** and press (ENTER).

This account type selection is for Other Assets and is used to record financial transactions affecting the equipment you use in your business.

16. Type **0** and press (ENTER).

You will enter the value of these assets later in this chapter.

17. Type **1/1/91** and press (ENTER).

18. Type **Capital Equipment** and press (ENTER).

19. Press (ESC) three times to return to the Main Menu.

You have now created a new account group and three accounts for organizing personal and business transactions.

Changing the Active Account Group

The result of the last exercise was to create another account group. You can work in any account group at any time and can work with any account within a group. To change from the BUSINESS account group to QDATA from the Main Menu, follow these steps:

1. Type **5** to select Change Settings.

2. Type **1** to select Account Group Activities.

3. Type **1** to select Select/Set Up Account Group.

4. Move the cursor to QDATA in the list and press (ENTER).

5. Move the cursor to 1st U.S. Bank in the account list and press (ENTER).

6. Press (ESC) to return to the Main Menu.

The QDATA account group is now active. If you went to the register or
check writing screen you would find that the 1st U.S. Bank account was
active. Change the account group back to BUSINESS and open the account
for ANB Business by following the same procedure.

Backing Up an Account Group

You should create backups of the data managed by the Quicken system on a
regular basis. This will allow you to recover all your entries in the event of a
disk failure since you will be able to use your copy to restore all the entries.
You will need a blank formatted disk to record the backup information the
first time. Subsequent backups can be made on this disk without reformatting it. If you do not have formatted disks available, consult Appendix A for
detailed instructions on formatting a disk.

CREATING BACKUP FILES Quicken provides a Backup and Restore feature that allows you to safeguard the investment of time you have made in
entering your data. You can back up all your account files from the Acct/
Print menu on the register screen. To back up specific account groups select
the backup option found in the Account Group Activities screen, accessed
from the Change Settings menu. Follow these steps to back up the current
account group:

1. Press (ESC) to return to the Main Menu and type **5** for Change Settings.

2. Type **1** to select Account Group Activities.

3. Type **2** to select Backup Account Group.

4. Place your blank, formatted disk in drive A and then press (ENTER).

5. Select BUSINESS and press (ENTER).

6. Press (ENTER) to acknowledge the completion of the backup when
   Quicken displays the successful backup message.

7. Press (ESC) three times to return to the Main Menu.

If you ever lose your hard disk, you can re-create your data directory and
use the Restore option to copy your backup file to the directory. You should
schedule backups on a regular basis to minimize the risk of data loss. You
can also copy the Quicken data files from one floppy drive to another as a
quick means of backup if you do not have a hard disk.

8. Type **2** to open the register screen, as shown in Figure 11-3, and continue to work in the register.

CUSTOMIZING CATEGORIES

When you set up the new BUSINESS account group you were instructed to select Both as the categories option. This selection provides access to the more than 60 category choices shown in Table 11-1. You can see from this table that some categories are listed as expenses and others as income. Later, you will learn how to create more detailed subcategories beneath an existing category entry. Note the column in the table that shows you which categories are tax-related.

Editing the Existing Category List

You can change the name of any existing category, change its classification as income, expense, or a subcategory, or change your assessment of its being tax-related. To make a change to a category follow the steps on page 271.

F1-Help	F2-Acct/Print	F3-Edit	F4-Quick Entry	F5-Reports	F6-Activities

DATE	NUM	PAYEE · MEMO · CATEGORY	PAYMENT	C	DEPOSIT	BALANCE
1/ 1 1991		BEGINNING Opening Balance [ANB Business]		X	4,000 00	4,000 00
8/ 1 1991	Memo: Cat:					

ANB Business
Esc-Main Menu   Ctrl↵ Record   Ending Balance: $4,000.00

FIGURE 11-3. Register for the new account

Category	Description	Tax Rel	Type
Bonus	Bonus Income	*	Inc
Canada Pen	Canadian Pension	*	Inc
Div Income	Dividend Income	*	Inc
Family Allow	Family Allowance	*	Inc
Gift Received	Gift Received	*	Inc
Gr Sales	Gross Sales	*	Inc
Int Inc	Interest Income	*	Inc
Invest Inc	Investment Income	*	Inc
Old Age Pen	Old Age Pension	*	Inc
Other Inc	Other Income	*	Inc
Rent Income	Rent Income	*	Inc
Salary	Salary Income	*	Inc
Ads	Advertising	*	Expns
Auto Fuel	Automobile Fuel		Expns
Auto Loan	Automobile Loan Payment		Expns
Auto Service	Automobile Service		Expns
Bank Chrg	Bank Charge		Expns
Car	Car & Truck	*	Expns
Charity	Charitable Donations	*	Expns
Childcare	Childcare Expenses		Expns
Christmas	Christmas Expenses		Expns
Clothing	Clothing		Expns
Commission	Commissions	*	Expns
Dining	Dining Out		Expns
Dues	Dues		Expns
Education	Education		Expns
Entertain	Entertainment		Expns
Freight	Freight	*	Expns
Gifts	Gift Expenses		Expns
Groceries	Groceries		Expns
Home Rpair	Home Repair & Maint.		Expns
Household	Household Misc. Exp		Expns
Housing	Housing		Expns

TABLE 11-1.   Category List for an Account Group of BOTH

Category	Description	Tax Rel	Type
Insurance	Insurance		Expns
Int Exp	Interest Expense	*	Expns
Int Paid	Interest Paid	*	Expns
Invest Exp	Investment Expense	*	Expns
L&P Fees	Legal & Prof. Fees	*	Expns
Late Fees	Late Payment Fees	*	Expns
Medical	Medical & Dental	*	Expns
Misc	Miscellaneous		Expns
Mort Int	Mortgage Interest Exp.	*	Expns
Mort Prin	Mortgage Principal		Expns
Office	Office Expenses	*	Expns
Other Exp	Other Expenses	*	Expns
Recreation	Recreation Expense		Expns
Rent Paid	Rent Paid	*	Expns
Repairs	Repairs	*	Expns
Returns	Returns & Allowances	*	Expns
RRSP	Reg. Retirement Sav. Plan		Expns
Subscriptions	Subscriptions		Expns
Supplies	Supplies	*	Expns
Tax Fed	Federal Tax Withholding	*	Expns
Tax FICA	Social Security Tax	*	Expns
Tax Other	Misc. Taxes	*	Expns
Tax Prop	Property Tax	*	Expns
Tax State	State Tax Withholding	*	Expns
Taxes	Taxes	*	Expns
Telephone	Telephone Expense		Expns
Travel	Travel Expenses	*	Expns
UIC	Unemployment Ins.	*	Expns
Utilities	Water, Gas, Electric		Expns
Wages	Wages & Job Credits	*	Expns

TABLE 11-1. Category List for an Account Group of BOTH (*continued*)

1. Press ⟨**CTRL**⟩-⟨**C**⟩ from the register to display the category list.

2. Move the arrow cursor to the category you want to change.

3. Press ⟨**CTRL**⟩-⟨**E**⟩ to edit the information for the category.

4. Change the fields you wish to alter.

5. Press ⟨**CTRL**⟩-⟨**ENTER**⟩ to complete the changes.

If you change the name of the category, Quicken will automatically change it in any transactions that have already been assigned to the category.

If you need to totally restructure the categories, you may find it easier to delete the old categories and add new ones with the instructions in the next section. To delete a category follow these steps:

1. Press ⟨**CTRL**⟩-⟨**C**⟩ from the register to display the category list.

2. Move the arrow cursor to the category you want to delete.

3. Press ⟨**CTRL**⟩-⟨**D**⟩ to delete the information in the category.

You should not delete categories that are already assigned to transactions. Otherwise, you will delete that part of the transactions in your register. You should make any changes in which you delete categories before you start recording transactions.

4. Press ⟨**CTRL**⟩-⟨**ENTER**⟩ to complete the changes.

Adding Categories

You can also add categories to provide additional options specific to your needs. Each type of business will probably have some unique categories of income or expenses. For the example in this chapter both income and expense category additions are needed.

The business in this example has three sources of business income: consulting fees, royalties, and income earned for writing articles. It would be inappropriate to use the Inc Sal category since this should be reserved for income earned from a regular employer (reported on Form W2 at year-end). You could use the Gross Sales category to record the various types of income for the business. Another solution would be to create new categories for each income source. The examples in this chapter will use three new income categories.

Many of the existing expense categories are suitable for recording business expenses, but for this example additional expense categories are needed. Equipment maintenance, computer supplies, and overnight mail service categories are needed. Although a category already exists for freight, a more specific postage category is also needed. New categories are not needed to record computer and office equipment and furniture purchases. These will be handled through an "other asset" type account, with the specific purchase listed in the Payee field to the transaction.

You can add a new category by entering it in the Category field when recording a transaction in a register or on a check writing screen. Pressing (ENTER) to record the transaction will cause Quicken to indicate that the category does not exist in the current list. You are then given the choice of selecting another category already in the list or adding the new category to the list. You would choose to add it, just as you did with the category for auto loans in Chapter 4.

If you have a number of categories to add, it is simpler to add them before starting data entry. To use this approach to add the new categories needed for the exercises in this chapter, follow these steps:

1. Press (CTRL)-(C) (or press (F4) for Quick Entry and then type **3**, Categorize/Transfer).

Either one will open the Category and Transfer List.

2. Press (HOME) to move to the top of the category list. <New Category> will be the top entry in the list.

3. Press (ENTER).

Quicken will allow you to enter a new category using the window shown here,

```
┌─────────────────────────────────────────────────────┐
│ ███████████████████████████████████████████████████  │
│                    Set Up Category                    │
├─────────────────────────────────────────────────────┤
│  Name: Inc Roy                                        │
│                                                       │
│  Income, Expense or Subcategory (I/E/S): I            │
│                                                       │
│  Description (optional): Royalty Income               │
│  Tax-related (Y/N): Y                                 │
├─────────────────────────────────────────────────────┤
│  Esc-Cancel          F1-Help          ←┘ Setup        │
└─────────────────────────────────────────────────────┘
```

which contains entries for a new royalty income category called "Inc Roy." Note the use of Inc first in the category name. This allows you to later select all income categories by entering **Inc..** in a report filter window such as the one shown in Figure 3-10 (in Chapter 3).

4. Type **Inc Roy** and press ⌈**ENTER**⌉.

5. Type **I** and press ⌈**ENTER**⌉.

6. Type **Royalty Income** and press ⌈**ENTER**⌉.

7. Type **Y** and press ⌈**ENTER**⌉ to complete the entry.

Quicken will return you to the Category and Transfer List window.

8. Repeat steps 3 through 7 for each of the categories that follow; then press ⌈**ESC**⌉ to return to the Register window.

Name:	Inc Cons
Income:	I
Description:	Consulting Income
Tax Related:	Y

Name:	Inc Art
Income:	I
Description:	Article Income
Tax Related:	Y

Name:	Equip Mnt
Expense:	E
Description:	Equipment Maintenance
Tax Related:	Y

Name:	Supp Comp
Expense:	E
Description:	Computer Supplies
Tax Related:	Y

Name:	Postage
Expense:	E
Description:	Postage Expense
Tax Related:	N

Name:	Del Overngt
Expense:	E
Description:	Overnight Delivery
Tax Related:	Y

Note that the Postage category is shown as not tax related. This will prevent personal postage expenses from appearing on personal tax reports. Business postage expenses will still appear on business tax reports because *all* expenses appear.

You should feel free to customize Quicken by adding any categories you need. However, be aware that available random access memory will limit the number of categories you can create in each category list. With a 512K system, approximately 1000 categories can be created; 150 is the limit if you only have 320K of memory.

Requiring Categories in All Transactions

Another customization option Quicken offers is a reminder that a category should be entered for each transaction before it is recorded. If you attempt to record a transaction without a category, Quicken will not complete the process until you confirm that you want the transaction added without a category.

To require categories in all transactions you choose Change Settings from the Main Menu and then select Other Settings. Press (ENTER) twice to move to the third item in the Other Settings window and type **Y**. Press (CTRL)-(ENTER) to finalize the settings change. The next time you attempt to record a transaction without a category, Quicken will stop to confirm your choice before saving.

USING CLASSES

Classes are another way of organizing transactions. They allow you to define the who, when, or why of a transaction. It is important to understand that

although they, too, allow you to group data, classes are distinct from categories. You will continue to use categories to provide specific information
about the transactions to which they are assigned. Categories tell you what
kind of income or expense a specific transaction represents. You can tell at a
glance which costs are for utilities and which are for entertainment. In
summary reports you might show transactions totaled by category.

Classes allow you to slice the transaction pie in a different way. They
provide a different view or perspective of your data. For example, you can
continue to organize data in categories such as Utilities or Snow Removal,
yet also classify it by the property requiring the service. Classes were not
needed in the earlier chapters of this book since categories provide all the
organization you need for very basic transactions. But if you want to combine
home and business in one account group, classes are essential for differenti-
ating between the two types of transactions. Here, every transaction you
enter will be classified as either personal or business. Business transactions
will have a class entered after the category. By omitting the class entry from
personal transactions you classify them as personal. Class assignments can be
used without category assignments, but in this chapter they will be used in
addition to categories.

Defining Classes

Quicken does not provide a standard list of classes. As with categories, you
can set up what you need before you start making entries, or you can add the
classes you need as you enter transactions. To assign a class while entering a
transaction, you type the class name in the Category field after the category
name (if one is used). A slash (/) must be typed before the class name.

To create a class before entering a transaction, follow these steps from the
account register to add a class for business:

1. Press CTRL-L to open the Class List window.

2. Press ENTER with the arrow cursor on <New Class>. Quicken displays the Set Up Class window, shown here:

```
                       Set Up Class

     Name:

     Description (optional):

     Esc-Cancel              F1-Help              ↵ Setup
```

3. Type **B** and press ⟨ENTER⟩.

You can use a longer entry, such as Business, but you are limited in the number of characters used to display categories, classes, and other organizational groupings, so you should keep it as short as possible.

4. Type **Business** and press ⟨ENTER⟩.

Quicken completes the entry for the first class and adds it to the list in the Class List window. You could create a second class for personal transactions, but it is not really necessary. You can consider any transaction without a class of B to be personal.

5. Press ⟨ESC⟩ to return to the Register window.

Each new class is added to the Class List window.

To create a class as you enter a transaction, simply type the category followed by a slash (/) and the class you want to use, and then press ⟨ENTER⟩.

6. Move the highlight to the opening balance transaction.
7. Tab to the Category field; then press the ⟨END⟩ key.
8. Type **/B.**
9. Press ⟨CTRL⟩-⟨ENTER⟩ to record the changed entry.

Entering Transactions with Classes

You record the business transaction in the same manner as earlier transactions. It is important that you remember to enter the class in the Category field. Follow these instructions:

1. Press ⟨HOME⟩ twice to move the Date field.
2. Type **1/2/91** and press ⟨ENTER⟩ twice.
3. Type **Arlo, Inc.** and press ⟨ENTER⟩ three times.
4. Type **12500** in the Deposit field and press ⟨ENTER⟩.
5. Type **Seminars conducted in Nov. 90** and press ⟨ENTER⟩.

6. Type **Inc Cons/B**.

The first part of this entry categorizes the transaction as consulting income. The slash (/) and the B classify the transaction as business related.

7. Press [CTRL]-[ENTER] to record the transaction. Your screen will look like the one shown here:

F1-Help	F2-Acct/Print	F3-Edit	F4-Quick Entry	F5-Reports	F6-Activities

DATE	NUM	PAYEE · MEMO · CATEGORY	PAYMENT	C	DEPOSIT	BALANCE
		▬▬▬ BEGINNING ▬▬▬				
1/ 1 1991		Opening Balance [ANB Business]→		X	4,000 00	4,000 00
1/ 2 1991		Arlo, Inc. Seminars conduc→Inc Cons/B			12,500 00	16,500 00

You can record an expense transaction in the ANB Business account in a similar fashion. Follow these instructions:

1. Type **1/2/91** and press [ENTER].

2. Type **101** and press [ENTER].

3. Type **Office All** and press [ENTER].

4. Type **65** and press [ENTER] three times.

5. Type **Cartridge for copier** and press [ENTER].

6. Press [CTRL]-[C], move the arrow cursor to Supplies, and then press [ENTER].

This approach allows you to select the category from the list rather than typing it.

7. Type **/B** and press [CTRL]-[ENTER].

The Register window matches Figure 11-4.

```
F1-Help  F2-Acct/Print  F3-Edit  F4-Quick Entry  F5-Reports  F6-Activities
```

DATE	NUM	PAYEE · MEMO · CATEGORY	PAYMENT	C	DEPOSIT	BALANCE
		▬▬▬ BEGINNING ▬▬▬				
1/ 1 1991		Opening Balance [ANB Business]→		X	4,000 00	4,000 00
1/ 2 1991		Arlo, Inc. Seminars conduc→Inc Cons/B			12,500 00	16,500 00
1/ 2 1991	101	Office All Cartridge for c→Supplies/B	65 00			16,435 00

FIGURE 11-4. Recording business transactions in the Register window

The next transaction is for clothing. Since this is a personal expense paid with a personal check, it cannot be added to the current account. You must open the ANB Personal account for your entry. Follow these steps:

1. Press ESC to return to the Main Menu.

2. Type **4** to choose Select Account.

3. Move the arrow cursor to ANB Personal.

4. Press ENTER to open the account.

When you enter the transaction for the clothing, the fact that you are not using a class will indicate that it is a personal expense. Although you could have created another class, called P, for personal entries, the approach used here minimizes typing; only business transactions require the extra entry. Follow these steps to add the transaction:

1. Type **1/3/91** and press ENTER.

2. Type **825** and press ENTER.

This check number is not sequential with the last business check used since it is in your personal account.

3. Type **Discount Coats** and press ⟨ENTER⟩.

4. Type **120** and press ⟨ENTER⟩ three times.

5. Type **New winter coat** and press ⟨ENTER⟩.

6. Type **Clothing**.

Notice that no slash (/) is used since a class is not being added for personal expenses.

7. Press ⟨CTRL⟩-⟨ENTER⟩ to record the transaction. Your entries should match the ones shown here:

F1-Help	F2-Acct/Print	F3-Edit	F4-Quick Entry	F5-Reports	F6-Activities

DATE	NUM	PAYEE · MEMO · CATEGORY	PAYMENT	C	DEPOSIT	BALANCE
		══ BEGINNING ══				
1/ 1 1991		Opening Balance [ANB Personal]		X	2,500 00	2,500 00
1/ 3 1991	825	Discount Coats New winter coat Clothing	120 00			2,380 00

SPLITTING TRANSACTIONS

Split transactions are transactions that affect more than one category or class. You decide how a transaction affects each of the categories or category-class combinations involved. If you split an expense transaction you are saying that a portion of the transaction should be considered as an expense in two different categories or classes. For example, a purchase at an office products store might include school supplies for your children and products for the office. You need to know exactly how much was spent for personal versus business expenses in this transaction. Many expenses can be part business and part personal, especially if you operate a business from your home. Quicken allows you to allocate the amount of any transaction among different categories or classes with a special Split Transaction window. Before using the Split Transaction feature you can define categories more precisely with the Subcategory feature, explained in the next section.

Quicken will display a Split Transaction window for entries in the Category field if you press CTRL-S. You can enter different categories or classes for each part of the transaction with this method. Even though the largest portion of the following expense was for business, it was paid with a personal check and so must be recorded in the ANB Personal account. Follow these steps to complete an entry for the purchase at Campus Stationery, which includes both personal and office supply expenses:

1. Type **1/3/91** and press ENTER.

2. Type **826** and press ENTER.

3. Type **Campus Stationery** and press ENTER.

4. Type **82** and press ENTER three times.

5. Type **New calendar and computer paper** and press ENTER.

6. Press CTRL-S to activate the Split Transaction window.

7. Type **Supp Comp/B** and press ENTER.

8. Type **Paper for laser printer** and press ENTER.

Quicken displays the entire amount of the transaction in the Amount field but will adjust it as you make a new entry.

9. Type **75.76** and press ENTER.

Quicken subtracts this amount from $82.00 and displays the amount remaining on the next line.

10. Type **Misc** and press ENTER.

11. Type **New calendar for kitchen.**

This completes the entries since $6.24 is the cost of the calendar. Your screen should look like Figure 11-5.

12. Press CTRL-ENTER to close the Split Transaction window.

13. Press CTRL-ENTER to record the transaction.

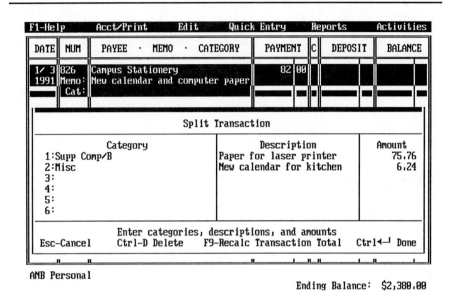

ANB Personal

Ending Balance: $2,380.00

━━━━━ **FIGURE 11-5.**   Split Transaction window for Campus Stationery
transaction

The register entry looks like this:

USING SUBCATEGORIES

Since you are quickly becoming proficient at basic transaction entry, you will
want to see some other options for recording transactions. One new option is
to create subcategories of an existing category. These subcategories further
define a category. Unlike classes, which use a different perspective for organizing transactions, subcategories provide a more detailed breakdown of the
existing category. For instance, you could continue to allocate all your utility

bills to the Utilities category but create subcategories that allow you to allocate expenses to electricity, water, or gas. You will still be able to classify these transactions as either business or personal expenses using the classes you established.

You can add the subcategories by modifying the category list, as when you add new categories, or you can create them as you enter transactions and realize the existing category entries do not provide the breakdown you want.

Entering a New Subcategory

When you enter a subcategory for a transaction, you will type the category name, followed by a colon (:), and then the subcategory name. It is important that the category be specified first and the subcategory second. If a transaction has a class assigned, the class name comes third in the sequence, with a slash (/) as the divider.

The business used in this example is run from the home of the owner, which necessitates the splitting of certain expenses between business and personal. Tax guidelines state that the percentage of the total square footage in the home that is used exclusively for business can be used to determine the portion of common expenses, such as utilities, allocated to the business. The business in these examples occupies 20 percent of the total square footage in the home. You can use Quicken's calculator to perform these computations and use both subcategories and split transactions to record the first transactions.

Enter the utility bills in the new account. Follow these steps to complete the entries for the gas and electric bills, creating a subcategory under Utilities for each, and allocating 20 percent of each utility bill to business by splitting the transactions between classes:

1. With the next blank transaction in the register highlighted, type **1/3/91** as the date for the transaction.

2. Type **827** and press ⟨ENTER⟩.

3. Type **Consumer Power** and press ⟨ENTER⟩.

4. Type **80.00** for the payment amount and press ⟨ENTER⟩.

5. Move the cursor using ⟨ENTER⟩ or ⟨TAB⟩ to the memo field and type **Electric Bill** and then press ⟨ENTER⟩.

The cursor is now in the Category field.

6. Press <u>CTRL</u>-<u>S</u> to open the Split Transaction window.

7. Type **Utilities:Electric/B** and press <u>ENTER</u>.

Quicken prompts you with the Category Not Found window. Notice that only "Electric" is highlighted in the Category field since Quicken already has Utilities in the category list and B in the class list.

8. Type **1** to select Add to Category List. Quicken displays the Set Up Category window for you to define the category.

9. Type **S** to define the entry as a subcategory and then press <u>ENTER</u>.

10. Type **Electric Utilities** and press <u>ENTER</u>.

Although this description is optional, it is a good idea to enter one so that your reports will be informative. The Set Up Category window shown here should match the one on your screen:

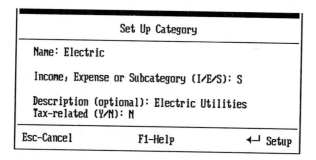

```
┌─────────────────────────────────────────────────────┐
│                                                       │
│                   Set Up Category                     │
│                                                       │
├───────────────────────────────────────────────────── │
│  Name: Electric                                       │
│                                                       │
│  Income, Expense or Subcategory (I/E/S): S            │
│                                                       │
│  Description (optional): Electric Utilities           │
│  Tax-related (Y/N): N                                 │
│                                                       │
├───────────────────────────────────────────────────── │
│  Esc-Cancel            F1-Help              ↵ Setup   │
└─────────────────────────────────────────────────────┘
```

11. Press <u>ENTER</u> to accept *N* for no under Tax-related.

Even though you have specified not tax-related, Quicken will continue to show the expense on business reports. The not tax-related entry will prevent Quicken from displaying electric utility expenses for your home on your personal tax reports.

12. Press <u>ENTER</u> to close the window and move to the Description field in the Split Transaction window.

A note may be displayed by Quicken prompting you to be sure you understand what you are doing since subcategories are considered an advanced technique.

13. Type **Business portion of elect** and press (ENTER).
14. Press (CTRL)-(0) to open the calculator and compute the portion of the expense allocable to business.
15. Type *.20 and press (ENTER) to multiply by .20.

Since the Amount field was highlighted, Quicken placed its value in the calculator. Quicken will display the result on the Calculator window.

16. Press (F9) to paste the result into the Amount field.
17. Press (ENTER) to move to the next line.
18. Type **Utilities:Electric** and press (ENTER).

Note that a class was not added to the entry so Quicken will consider the entry a personal expense.

19. Type **Home portion of electric** and press (ENTER).

The Split Transaction window looks like Figure 11-6; Quicken has computed the difference between $80.00 and $16.00 and displayed it in the Amount field.

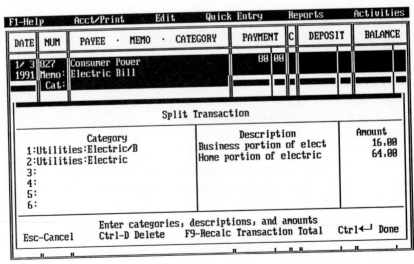

FIGURE 11-6. Split Transaction window for electric utilities

20. Press (CTRL)-(ENTER) to close the Split Transaction window.

21. Press (CTRL)-(ENTER) to record the transaction entry.

The transaction will display in the Register window, as shown here:

Completing the Utility Subcategories

You have one more utility bill to enter. The one for gas utilities will also require a new subcategory. Make these entries to create a subcategory for the gas bill and complete the transaction entry:

1. Enter the following information in each of the fields shown:

    Date: 1/7/91
    Check: 828
    Payee: Western Michigan Gas
    Payment: 40.00
    Memo: Gas Bill

2. After completing the Memo field entry, press (CTRL)-(S) to request the Split Transaction window.

3. Type **Utilities:Gas/B** and press (ENTER).

4. Type **1** to select Add to Category List. Quicken displays the Set Up Category window for you to define the category.

5. Type **S** to define the entry as a subcategory and then press (ENTER).

6. Type **Gas Utilities** and press (ENTER).

7. Press (ENTER) to accept *N* for Tax-related; then press (CTRL)-(S) to open the Split Transaction window.

8. Press (ENTER) to move to the Description field in the Split Transaction window.

9. Type **Business portion gas bill** and press (ENTER).

10. Press (CTRL)-(O) to open the Calculator window.

11. Type ***.20** and press ⟨**ENTER**⟩. Quicken will display the result on the Calculator window.

12. Press ⟨**F9**⟩ to paste the result in the Amount field.

13. Press ⟨**ENTER**⟩ to move to the next line.

14. Type **Utilities:Gas** and press ⟨**ENTER**⟩.

15. Type **Home portion gas bill** and press ⟨**ENTER**⟩.

16. Press ⟨**CTRL**⟩-⟨**ENTER**⟩ to close the Split Transaction window.

17. Press ⟨**CTRL**⟩-⟨**ENTER**⟩ to record the transaction entry.

If you press ⟨**CTRL**⟩-⟨**HOME**⟩ to move to the top of the register, your entries will look like Figure 11-7.

ENTERING THE REMAINING BUSINESS TRANSACTIONS

You have now been introduced to all the skills needed to enter transactions that affect either a business or personal account. You should, however,

```
 F1-Help   F2-Acct/Print   F3-Edit   F4-Quick Entry   F5-Reports   F6-Activities
┌──────┬─────┬─────────────────────────────────┬─────────┬─┬─────────┬─────────┐
│ DATE │ NUM │  PAYEE · MEMO · CATEGORY        │ PAYMENT │C│ DEPOSIT │ BALANCE │
├──────┼─────┼─────────────────────────────────┼─────────┼─┼─────────┼─────────┤
│      │     │         BEGINNING               │         │ │         │         │
│ 1/ 1 │     │Opening Balance                  │         │X│2,500 00 │2,500 00 │
│ 1991 │Memo:│                                 │         │ │         │         │
│      │Cat: │[ANB Personal]                   │         │ │         │         │
│ 1/ 3 │825  │Discount Coats                   │ 120 00  │ │         │2,380 00 │
│ 1991 │     │New winter coat  Clothing        │         │ │         │         │
│ 1/ 3 │826  │Campus Stationery                │  82 00  │ │         │2,298 00 │
│ 1991 │SPLIT│New calendar an→Supp Comp/B      │         │ │         │         │
│ 1/ 3 │827  │Consumer Power                   │  80 00  │ │         │2,218 00 │
│ 1991 │SPLIT│Electric Bill    Utilities:Elec→ │         │ │         │         │
│ 1/ 7 │828  │Western Michigan Gas             │  40 00  │ │         │2,178 00 │
│ 1991 │SPLIT│Gas Bill        Utilities:Gas/B  │         │ │         │         │
└──────┴─────┴─────────────────────────────────┴─────────┴─┴─────────┴─────────┘
 ANB Personal
 Esc-Main Menu      Ctrl↵ Record                        Ending Balance:  $2,061.00
```

FIGURE 11-7.   Register entries in ANB Personal account

complete the remaining transactions for January. Keystrokes for split transactions are shown in detail. The other transactions are shown in summary
form; each field in which you need to enter data is shown with the entry for
that field. Use these steps to complete the remaining entries:

1. Press (ESC) to return to the Main Menu.

2. Type **4** to choose Select Account.

3. Move the arrow cursor to ANB Business and press (ENTER).

4. Type **1/8/91** and press (ENTER).

5. Type **102** and press (ENTER).

6. Type **Computer Outlet** and press (ENTER).

7. Type **300** and press (ENTER) three times.

8. Type **Cartridges, ribbons, disks** and press (ENTER).

9. Press (CTRL)-(S) to open the Split Transaction window.

The same category and class will be used for each transaction entered in this
window. The transaction is split to provide additional documentation for
purchases.

10. Complete the entries in the Split Transaction window as shown in
    Figure 11-8.

11. Press (CTRL)-(ENTER) twice.

The first time you press (CTRL)-(ENTER), Quicken will close the Split
Transaction window. The second time, Quicken will record the transaction.

12. Enter the following transactions by completing the entries in the fields
    shown and pressing (CTRL)-(ENTER) after each transaction:

Date:	1/15/91
Num:	103
Payee:	Quick Delivery
Payment:	215.00
Memo:	Manuscript Delivery
Category:	Del Overngt/B
Date:	1/15/91
Num:	104

Payee:	Safety Airlines
Payment:	905.00
Memo:	February Ticket
Category:	Travel/B

Date:	1/20/91
Num:	105
Payee:	Alltel
Payment:	305.00
Memo:	Telephone Bill
Category:	Telephone/B

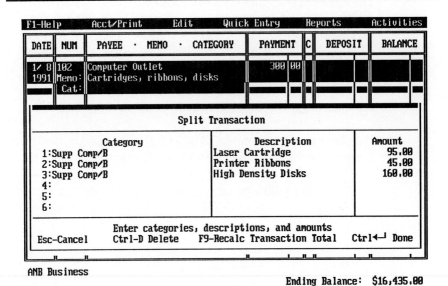

FIGURE11-8. Splitting the cash transaction for office supplies

13. Enter the beginning of this transaction as follows:

Date:	1/20/91
Num:	106
Payee:	Postmaster
Payment:	28.25
Memo:	Postage for Mailing

14. Press (CTRL)-(S) with the cursor in the Category field.

15. Complete the entries shown on the Split Transaction window in Figure 11-9.

16. Press (CTRL)-(ENTER) twice.

If you press (UP ARROW) several times you will see that the entries in your register match the ones in Figure 11-10.

17. Complete this transaction to record a maintenance expense for existing equipment:

Date:	1/22/91
Num:	107
Payee:	Fix-It-All
Payment:	1100.00
Memo:	Equipment Contract
Category:	Equip Mnt/B

18. Press (CTRL)-(ENTER) to record the transaction.

The only remaining transactions relate to equipment. You will need to use the Equipment account you created earlier to handle these transactions.

USING THE OTHER ASSET ACCOUNT

Earlier in the chapter you established an other asset type account called Equipment. You will be able to use this account to track total equipment

```
┌──────────────────────────────────────────────────────────────────────┐
│ F1-Help      Acct/Print     Edit      Quick Entry     Reports    Activities │
├──────┬──────┬──────────────────────────────┬─────────┬──┬─────────┬─────────┤
│ DATE │ NUM  │ PAYEE  ·  MEMO  ·  CATEGORY  │ PAYMENT │C │ DEPOSIT │ BALANCE │
├──────┼──────┼──────────────────────────────┼─────────┼──┼─────────┼─────────┤
│ 1/20 │ 106  │Postmaster                    │  28 25  │  │         │         │
│ 1991 │Memo: │Postage for Mailing           │         │  │         │         │
│      │ Cat: │                              │         │  │         │         │
```

```
┌────────────────────────────────────────────────────────────────────┐
│                         Split Transaction                            │
├──────────────────────────────┬─────────────────────────┬────────────┤
│           Category           │       Description       │   Amount   │
│  1:Postage/B                 │ Mail Teach Yourself dBASE│   28.00    │
│  2:Postage                   │ Mail birthday card       │    0.25    │
│  3:                          │                          │            │
│  4:                          │                          │            │
│  5:                          │                          │            │
│  6:                          │                          │            │
├──────────────────────────────────────────────────────────────────────┤
│           Enter categories, descriptions, and amounts                 │
│  Esc-Cancel     Ctrl-D Delete    F9-Recalc Transaction Total   Ctrl↵ Done │
└──────────────────────────────────────────────────────────────────────┘
```

```
ANB Business
                                    Ending Balance:  $14,710.00
```

FIGURE 11-9.   Splitting the postage transaction

```
┌──────────────────────────────────────────────────────────────────────┐
│ F1-Help  F2-Acct/Print   F3-Edit   F4-Quick Entry  F5-Reports  F6-Activities │
├──────┬──────┬──────────────────────────────┬─────────┬──┬─────────┬─────────┤
│ DATE │ NUM  │ PAYEE  ·  MEMO  ·  CATEGORY  │ PAYMENT │C │ DEPOSIT │ BALANCE │
├──────┼──────┼──────────────────────────────┼─────────┼──┼─────────┼─────────┤
│ 1/ 2 │ 101  │Office All                    │  65 00  │  │         │16,435 00│
│ 1991 │Memo: │Cartridge for copier          │         │  │         │         │
│      │ Cat: │Supplies/B                    │         │  │         │         │
│ 1/ 8 │ 102  │Computer Outlet               │ 300 00  │  │         │16,135 00│
│ 1991 │SPLIT │Cartridges, rib→Supp Comp/B   │         │  │         │         │
│ 1/15 │ 103  │Quick Delivery                │ 215 00  │  │         │15,920 00│
│ 1991 │      │Manuscript Deli→Del Overngt/B │         │  │         │         │
│ 1/15 │ 104  │Safety Airlines               │ 905 00  │  │         │15,015 00│
│ 1991 │      │February Ticket Travel/B      │         │  │         │         │
│ 1/20 │ 105  │Alltel                        │ 305 00  │  │         │14,710 00│
│ 1991 │      │Telephone Bill   Telephone/B  │         │  │         │         │
│ 1/20 │ 106  │Postmaster                    │  28 25  │  │         │14,681 75│
│ 1991 │SPLIT │Postage for Mai→Postage/B     │         │  │         │         │
```

```
ANB Business
Esc-Main Menu      Ctrl↵  Record            Ending Balance:  $14,681.75
```

FIGURE 11-10.   Register entries in ANB Business account

holdings and depreciation expense. Purchase transactions for equipment will be recorded in your business checking account register as a transfer to the Equipment account. Other transactions, such as entering information on equipment purchased before you started using Quicken and a depreciation transaction, will be entered directly in this other asset register. In the next section you will look at recording transactions for existing equipment and a new purchase. In Chapter 14 you will learn how to record depreciation expense as the asset ages and declines in value.

Recording Transactions for Existing Equipment Holdings

The existing equipment cannot be recorded as a purchase since you do not want to affect the balance in the business checking account. You need to make the transaction entry directly in the Equipment account. Note that the fields are somewhat different in this type of account compared to previous account registers, as shown in Figure 11-11. Follow these steps to record the equipment:

1. Press (ESC) to return to the Main Menu.

2. Type 4 to choose Select Account.

F1-Help	F2-Acct/Print	F3-Edit	F4-Quick Entry	F5-Reports		F6-Activities	
DATE	REF	PAYEE · MEMO · CATEGORY	DECREASE	C	INCREASE	BALANCE	
		▬▬▬▬ BEGINNING ▬▬▬▬	▬	▬▬	▬	▬	
1/ 1 1991		Opening Balance [Equipment]				0 00	
1/ 1 1991		High Tech Computer Original cost o→[Equipment]/B			3,000 00	3,000 00	
1/ 1 1991		High Tech Computer Depreciation Ex→[Equipment]/B	600 00			2,400 00	

FIGURE 11-11. Equipment transactions

3. Move the arrow cursor to Equipment and press ⏎ENTER.

4. Type **1/1/91** and press ⏎ENTER twice.

5. Type **High Tech Computer** to enter the name of the asset in the Payee field.

You can record an inventory number as part of this entry if one is assigned.

6. Press ⏎ENTER three times.

7. Type **3000** and press ⏎ENTER to record the original purchase price in the Increase field.

8. Type **Original cost of equipment** and press ⏎ENTER.

9. Type **Equipment/B** and press ⏎CTRL-⏎ENTER.

Quicken will display the category as [Equipment] since the category is an account name and will increase the balance of the account. (The brackets are always added when an account name is added in the Category field.)

To change the book value of the asset, another adjusting transaction is required. This transaction reduces the book value by the amount of the depreciation expense recognized last year. It must be recorded against the Equipment account rather than as a depreciation expense, or the amount of the depreciation for last year will appear in this year's expense reports. You do not want to record the depreciation expense in your checking account register because you are not writing a check for this expense. Follow these steps to complete the second transaction entry:

1. Type **1/1/91** and press ⏎ENTER twice.

2. Type **High Tech Computer** and press ⏎ENTER.

It is important to use the same name in all transactions relating to a given piece of equipment.

3. Type **600** in the Decrease field. Press ⏎ENTER three times.

4. Type **Depreciation Expense** and press ⏎ENTER.

5. Type **Equipment/B** and press ⏎CTRL-⏎ENTER.

The register entries should match Figure 11-11.

Adding a New Equipment Purchase

Purchasing an asset reduces the balance in a checking account. When the asset is equipment there must also be an entry to the Equipment account. If you list the Equipment account as the Category field in the transaction, Quicken will handle the transfer. The other part of this transaction entry that differs is that you use the name of the asset in the Payee field in the check register. You will have to use the Memo field Equipment account to record the payee's name. Follow these steps to record the purchase of a laser printer:

1. Press (ESC) to return to the Main Menu.

2. Type **4** to choose Select Account.

3. Move the arrow cursor to ANB Business and press (ENTER).

4. Type **1/25/91** and press (ENTER).

5. Type **108** and press (ENTER).

6. Type **Laser 1** and press (ENTER).

7. Type **1500** and press (ENTER) three times.

8. Type **Printer from Harry's Computers** and press (ENTER).

9. Type **Equipment/B**.

10. Press (CTRL)-(ENTER) to record the transaction.

Your transaction will look like this:

11. Press (ESC) to return to the Main Menu.

12. Type **4** to choose Select Account, select Equipment, and press (ENTER).

Figure 11-12 shows the transactions in the Equipment account after the transfer transaction is recorded.

F1-Help	F2-Acct/Print	F3-Edit	F4-Quick Entry	F5-Reports	F6-Activities

DATE	REF	PAYEE · MEMO · CATEGORY	DECREASE	C	INCREASE	BALANCE
		▬▬▬ BEGINNING ▬▬▬				
1/ 1 1991		Opening Balance [Equipment]				0 00
1/ 1 1991		High Tech Computer Original cost o→[Equipment]/B			3,000 00	3,000 00
1/ 1 1991		High Tech Computer Depreciation Ex→[Equipment]/B	600 00			2,400 00
1/25 1991		Laser 1 Printer from Ha→[ANB Business]→			1,500 00	3,900 00

FIGURE 11-12.   Register entries in Equipment account after printer purchase

MEMORIZED TRANSACTIONS

Many of your financial transactions are likely to repeat; you pay your utility bills each month, for instance. Likewise, overnight delivery charges, phone bills, payroll, and other bills are paid at about the same time each month. Cash inflows for some businesses are daily, weekly, or monthly. Other payments, such as supply purchases, also repeat, but perhaps not on the same dates each month.

As discussed in Chapter 6, Quicken can memorize transactions entered in the register or check writing screen. Once memorized, these transactions can be used to generate identical transactions. Although amounts and dates may change, you can edit these fields and not have to reenter payee, memo, and category information.

Memorizing a Register Entry

Any transaction in the account register can be memorized. Memorized transactions can be recalled for later use, printed, changed, and even deleted. You can elect to memorize as many transactions as you feel will repeat in the same relative time frame. To memorize the transaction for Consumer Power follow these steps:

1. Press (ESC) to return to the Main Menu.

2. Type **4** to choose Select Account.

3. Move the arrow cursor to ANB Personal and press (ENTER).

4. Highlight the Consumer Power transaction in the register.

5. Press (F4) to open the Quick Entry menu and type **2** to select Memorize Transaction (or press (CTRL)-(M) to select Memorize Transaction without opening the menu).

Quicken will highlight the transaction and prompt you to press (ENTER) to memorize or (ESC) to cancel.

6. Press (ENTER) to confirm and memorize the transaction.

Using the same procedure, memorize the transaction for Western Michigan Gas. Quicken memorizes split transactions in the same way as any other transactions. You will want to carefully review the split transaction screen transactions for amounts that change each month to reduce errors.

7. Press (CTRL)-(T) to display the memorized transactions; your list should match the one shown here.

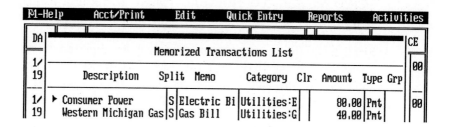

If you want to print the list once it is displayed, press (CTRL)-(P), type a number to select your printer, and press (ENTER) to print.

Now you can open the ANB Business account and memorize some transactions from that account. Follow the steps listed next.

1. Press (ESC) twice to return to the Main Menu.

2. Type **4** to choose Select Account.

3. Move the arrow cursor to ANB Business and press (ENTER).

4. Highlight the Quick Delivery transaction in the register.

5. Press (F4) to open the Quick Entry menu and type **2** to select Memorize Transaction (or press (CTRL)-(M) to select Memorize Transaction without opening the menu).

Quicken will highlight the transaction and prompt you for a response.

6. Press (ENTER) to confirm and memorize the transaction.

7. Press (CTRL)-(T) to display the memorized transactions; your list should include Quick Delivery.

Quicken maintains only one list of memorized transactions for each account group and does not show the account name in the list. Here, each of the memorized transactions has a type of "Pmt" since it was memorized from the register. Transactions memorized from the check writing window will have a type of "Chk."

8. Press (ESC) to return to the account register.

USING MEMORIZED TRANSACTIONS   To recall a memorized transaction and place it in the register, move to the next blank transaction record. If you recall a memorized transaction while a previously recorded transaction is highlighted, the existing transaction will be replaced by the memorized transaction. Press (CTRL)-(T) to recall the Memorized Transactions List window. The next step is to use the arrow keys to select the transaction you want to add to the register and then press (ENTER). If you type the first few letters of the payee name before pressing (CTRL)-(T), Quicken will take you to the correct area of the transaction list since it is in alphabetical order by payee. When it is added, the selected transaction appears with the date of the preceding transaction in the register, not the date with which it was last recorded. You can edit the transaction in the register and press (CTRL)-(ENTER) when you are ready to record the entry.

Follow these steps to record a payment to Quick Delivery for later in the month:

1. Press CTRL-END to move to the end of the register entries.
2. Press CTRL-T.
3. Move the arrow cursor to the Quick Delivery transaction and then press ENTER.

Quicken adds the transaction to the register.

4. Press SHIFT-TAB three times, type **1/30/91** in the Date field, and press ENTER.
5. Type **109** in the Num field and press ENTER twice.
6. Type **55.00** and press CTRL-ENTER to record the transaction.

The transaction looks like this:

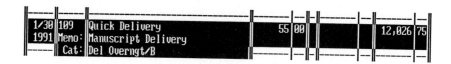

CHANGING AND DELETING MEMORIZED TRANSACTIONS To change a memorized transaction you must first recall it from the memorized transaction list to a blank transaction in the register. Then make your changes and memorize it again. When you press CTRL-M to memorize it again, Quicken will ask you if you want to replace the transaction memorized earlier or add a new transaction. If you confirm the replacement, Quicken makes the change.

To delete a memorized transaction, you must first open the transaction list by pressing CTRL-T or by pressing F4 to open the Quick Entry menu and then selecting Recall Transaction. Select the transaction you want to delete and press CTRL-D. A warning message will appear asking you to confirm the deletion. When you press ENTER the transaction is no longer memorized.

Memorizing a Check

The procedure for memorizing transactions while writing checks is identical to the one used to memorize register transactions. You must be in the check writing window when you begin, but otherwise it is the same. Check and register transactions for the same account will appear in the same memorized transaction list and can be edited, deleted, or recalled from either the check writing or account register window.

WORKING WITH TRANSACTION GROUPS

Although you can recall memorized transactions individually as a way to reenter similar transactions, a better method is to define several memorized transactions that occur at the same time as a transaction group. When you are ready to pay these transactions, you can have Quicken record the entire group for you automatically after you make any changes in amounts or other parts of the transaction entries. You can even have Quicken remind you when it is time to record these transactions again.

Defining a Transaction Group

Quicken allows you to set up as many as 12 transaction groups. Defining a group is easy, but it requires several steps after memorizing all the transactions that will be placed in the group. You will need to select the number of transactions in the group you want to define. Then you will need to describe the group. Finally, you will need to assign specific memorized transactions to the group. Although expense transactions are frequently used to create groups, you can also include an entry for a direct deposit payroll check that is deposited at the same time each month.

For your first transaction group, which you will title Utilities, you will group the gas and electric transactions that occur near the end of each month. Follow these steps to open the ANB Personal account and create the transaction group:

1. Press (ESC) to return to the Main Menu.

2. Type **4**, move the arrow cursor to ANB Personal, and press (ENTER).

3. Press (F4) to open the Quick Entry menu and type **5** to select Transaction Groups.

Quicken displays the window shown in Figure 11-13.

```
┌─────────────────────────────────────────────────────────────────┐
│                    Select Transaction Group to Execute            │
├─────────────────────────────────────────────────────────────────┤
│         Group              Size      Frequency      Next Scheduled │
│ ▶  1. <unused>                                                    │
│    2. <unused>                                                    │
│    3. <unused>                                                    │
│    4. <unused>                                                    │
│    5. <unused>                                                    │
│    6. <unused>                                                    │
│    7. <unused>                                                    │
│    8. <unused>                                                    │
│    9. <unused>                                                    │
│   10. <unused>                                                    │
│   11. <unused>                                                    │
│   12. <unused>                                                    │
├─────────────────────────────────────────────────────────────────┤
│            Ctrl-D Delete   Ctrl-E Edit  ↑,↓ Select               │
│  Esc-Cancel                   F1-Help              ↵ Continue     │
└─────────────────────────────────────────────────────────────────┘
```

FIGURE 11-13.   Execute Transaction Group window

4. Be sure the cursor is pointing at 1, since this is the first unused transaction group, and press ⟨ENTER⟩.

Quicken displays a window to allow you to define the group. Figure 11-14 shows this screen with the entries you will make in the next steps.

5. Type **Utilities** as the name for the group and press ⟨ENTER⟩ twice.

6. Type **6** as the frequency for the reminder and press ⟨ENTER⟩.

When you don't want to be reminded weekly, every two weeks, twice a month, every four weeks, monthly, quarterly, twice a year, or annually, you can choose None.

7. Type **2/3/91** as the next scheduled date for the reminder and press ⟨ENTER⟩.

Quicken will remind you three days in advance of this date. Later in this chapter you will learn how to adjust this setting. Quicken displays a window

```
                        Describe Group 1

   Name for this group: Utilities

   Account to load before executing (optional):
   ─────────────────────────────────────────────────────
                    Reminder Settings (optional)

   Frequency: 6
        1, None          4, Twice a month   7, Quarterly
        2, Weekly        5, Every four weeks 8, Twice a year
        3, Every two weeks 6, Monthly        9, Annually

   Next scheduled date:  2/3 /91
   ─────────────────────────────────────────────────────
   Esc-Cancel                   F1-Help              ←┘ Continue
```

FIGURE 11-14. Setting up a transaction group

listing transactions you can assign to Group 1. Only memorized transactions
are present in this list. They are listed in alphabetical order by payee to
make it easy to locate the desired transactions.

8. Move the arrow cursor to Consumer Power and press ⟨SPACEBAR⟩ to
   mark the transaction.

Note the 1 in the group column, which indicates that the transaction is now a
part of Group 1.

9. Move the arrow cursor to Western Michigan Gas and press ⟨SPACEBAR⟩.

Quicken also marks this transaction as part of Group 1, as shown here:

```
 F1-Help     Acct/Print     Edit     Quick Entry     Reports     Activities
┌─┬──────────────────────────────────────────────────────────────────┬──┐
│D│                                                                    │CE│
├─┤          Assign Transactions to Group 1:Utilities                  ├──┤
│1│──────────────────────────────────────────────────────────────────│88│
│1│  Description   Split  Memo      Category  Clr  Amount  Type Grp    │  │
│ │────────────────────────────────────────────────────────────────  │──│
│1│  Consumer Power    S Electric Bi Utilities:E   80,00 Pmt  1        │88│
│1│  Quick Delivery      Manuscript  Del Overngt  215,00 Pmt           │  │
│─│▶ Western Michigan Gas S Gas Bill Utilities:G   40,00 Pmt  1        │──│
```

10. Press (ENTER) to indicate you are finished selecting transactions.

You may want to define other transaction groups to include payroll, loan payments, and anything else that you might pay at the beginning of the month. You are not required to define additional groups in order to complete the remaining exercises in this section.

You can also create transaction groups that generate checks for you. These groups contain transactions that are memorized from the check writing window. The procedure is the same as that just shown. You can identify these transactions in the Assign Transactions window by the "Chk" entry in the Type field. Remember that "Pmt" in the Type field indicates an account register transaction.

Changing a Transaction Group

You can add to a transaction group at any time by selecting Transaction Groups after pressing (F4) to open the Quick Entry menu. As you proceed through the normal group definition procedure you can select additional transactions for inclusion in the group.

To make a change to the description or frequency of the reminder, use the same procedure and make the necessary changes in the Describe Group window.

To delete a transaction group, open the Quick Entry menu (with (F4)) and select Transaction Groups. Select the group you want to delete and press (CTRL)-(D). Quicken eliminates the group but does not delete the memorized transactions that are part of it. It also does not affect any transactions recorded in the register by earlier executions of the transaction group.

If you want to alter a transaction that is part of the transaction group, you will need to alter the memorized transaction. This means you will have to recall the transaction on the check writing screen or in the account register, depending on the type of transaction you have. Next, you will need to make your changes and memorize the transaction again. Follow the procedures in "Changing and Deleting Memorized Transactions," earlier in this chapter.

Having Quicken Remind You to Record Transactions

Quicken will remind you to enter upcoming transaction groups. The reminder will either occur at the DOS prompt when you boot your system or at the Main Menu when you first load Quicken. Hard disk users who have the default setting for Billminder still set at Yes will see a message at the DOS prompt reminding them to pay postdated checks or to record transaction groups. If you do not have a hard disk or if you have turned Billminder off, the prompt will not appear until you start Quicken.

Recording a Transaction Group

Once you have defined a transaction group you do not need to wait for the reminder to record the group in your register or check writing window. Since you can memorize entries for either the register or the check writing window, make sure you have the group correctly defined for your current needs. A group type of Chk is created in the check writing window and can be recorded in either the account register or the check writing window. Payment (Pmt) groups are recorded in the account register and can only be used to record account register entries.

   To execute a transaction group from the account register, follow these steps:

1. Press ⟨F4⟩ (Quick Entry) then type **5** to select Transaction Groups.

Quicken will display a list of account groups.

2. Select the Utilities group, as shown here:

```
 F1-Help      Acct/Print      Edit      Quick Entry      Reports      Activities
┌──────────────────────────────────────────────────────────────────────────┐
│ D                                                                    │CE
│ ═       Select Transaction Group to Execute                          ═══
│ 1 ─────────────────────────────────────────────────────────────       00
│ 1     Group           Size   Frequency        Next Scheduled
│ ─
│ 1  ►  1. Utilities     │2  │Monthly     │ 2/ 3/91 (Sunday)          00
└──────────────────────────────────────────────────────────────────────────┘
```

3. Press ⟨ENTER⟩.

Quicken will display the date of the next scheduled entry of the Utilities group, as shown here:

```
┌────────────────────────────────────┐
│ ████████████████████████████████   │
│                                    │
│    Transaction Group Date          │
│                                    │
│    Date of group:  2/ 3/91         │
│                                    │
│ ─────────────────────────────────  │
│    Esc-Cancel      ◄─┘ Continue    │
└────────────────────────────────────┘
```

4. Press (**ENTER**) to confirm that this date is valid and to enter the group of transactions in the account register.

Quicken will indicate when the transaction has been entered and recorded and allows you to make modifications if needed. The window displayed is shown here:

```
┌──────────────────────────────────────────┐
│ ████████████████████████████████████     │
│                                          │
│       Transaction Group Entered          │
│ ───────────────────────────────────────  │
│  Review the transactions below.  If needed, │
│  enter dollar amounts and other changes.   │
│ ───────────────────────────────────────  │
│         F1-Help        ◄─┘ Continue      │
└──────────────────────────────────────────┘
```

5. Press (**ENTER**) to continue.

The new transactions are entered with a date of 2/3/91, as shown here:

2/ 3 1991	SPLIT Cat:	Consumer Power Electric Bill Utilities:Electric/B	80 00		2,098 00
2/ 3 1991	SPLIT	Western Michigan Gas Gas Bill Utilities:Gas/B	40 00		2,058 00

The check numbers and amounts will need to be altered for the new utility bills. Here, you will also need to use (**CTRL**)-(**S**) to open the Split Transaction window for each transaction and distribute the new amounts.

6. Highlight the Consumer Power entry for 2/3/91, move the cursor to the Payment field, type **72.00** and press (**ENTER**) four times.

7. Press (**CTRL**)-(**S**) and record **14.40** as the business portion of the expense and **57.60** as the home portion of the bill.

8. Press (**CTRL**)-(**ENTER**) twice.

9. Move the cursor to the Payment field in the Western Michigan Gas entry, type **45.00** and press (**ENTER**) four times.

10. Press (**CTRL**)-(**S**) and record **9.00** as the business portion of the expense and **36.00** as the home portion of the bill.

11. Press (**CTRL**)-(**ENTER**) twice.

IMPORTANT CUSTOMIZING OPTIONS AS YOU SET UP YOUR ACCOUNTS

Quicken provides a number of options for customizing the package to meet your needs. These include the addition of passwords for accessing accounts, options already discussed such as requiring category entries, and other options that affect the display of information on your screen and in reports. Once you know how to access these settings you will find that most are self-explanatory. All of the changes are made by selecting Change Settings from the Main Menu.

Adding Passwords

To add a password, type **5** to select Password from the Change Settings menu. Quicken presents a menu that allows you to decide if you want to protect an account group using Main Password or protect existing transactions with Transaction Password. Although you can add protection with a password at both levels, you will need to select each individually.

If you select Main Password, Quicken will ask you to enter a password. Once you do so and press (**ENTER**), the password will be added to the active account group and anyone wishing to work with the account group must

supply it. Transaction Password is used to prevent changes to existing transactions entered before a specified date without the password. If you choose
Transaction Password, you will be presented with a window that requires you
to enter both a password and a date.

If you want to change or remove a password, you must be able to provide
the existing password. Quicken will then provide a Change Password window
for the entry of the old and new passwords. After completing the entries and
pressing (**ENTER**), the new password will be in effect.

Changing Other Settings

Figure 11-15 shows the window presented when Other Settings is selected
from the Change Settings menu. It shows the default choice for each of the
options. The first option allows you to turn off the beep you hear when
recording and memorizing transactions. The second option controls whether
Quicken prompts for confirmation when you make register changes.

Changing option 3 will require category entries on each transaction.
Option 4 allows you to print on the check an extra line that will not be
recorded. Option 5 allows you to change the number of days in advance that

```
┌─────────────────────────────────────────────────────┐
│                    Other Settings                     │
├─────────────────────────────────────────────────────┤
│   1.  Beep when recording and memorizing (Y/N): Y     │
│   2.  Request confirmation (for example,              │
│           when changing the Register) (Y/N)   : Y     │
│   3.  Require Category on transactions (Y/N)  : N     │
│   4.  Extra message line on check (printed            │
│           on check but not recorded) (Y/N)    : N     │
│   5.  Days in advance to remind of postdated          │
│           checks and scheduled groups (0-30) : 3      │
│   6.  Change date of checks to today's date           │
│           when printed (Y/N)                  : N     │
│   7.  MM/DD/YY or DD/MM/YY date format (M/D)  : M     │
│   8.  Billminder active (Y/N)                 : Y     │
│   9.  Print categories on voucher checks (Y/N): Y     │
│  10.  43 line register/reports (EGA,VGA) (Y/N): N     │
│  11.  Show Memo/Category/Both     (M/C/B)     : B     │
│  12.  In reports, use category Description/           │
│           Name/Both (D/N/B)                   : D     │
│  13.  Warn if a check number is re-used (Y/N) : N     │
├─────────────────────────────────────────────────────┤
│  Esc-Cancel              F1-Help          ↵ Continue  │
└─────────────────────────────────────────────────────┘
```

FIGURE 11-15.   Other Settings options

you will be reminded to pay postdated checks and record transaction groups. You will want to adjust this setting based on how frequently you use Quicken. For example, if you use the package only once a week, a reminder that occurs three days before will often not be sufficient.

Option 6 will change the date printed on checks to the current date instead of the date entered for the check. Option 7 allows you to control the date format. Option 8 allows hard disk users to control whether or not the Billminder prompt will display when DOS is loaded.

Options 9 through 12 control the appearance of the screen and reports. Option 9 is useful if you are printing voucher style checks with Quicken. You can change it to *Y* to add the detail of categories to these checks. If you have an EGA or VGA monitor, the high-resolution image your monitor supports allows you to display additional information on the screen. Changing option 10 to *Y* for this type of monitor will display 43 lines from a register or report on the screen.

The information on the second line of a register entry can be changed with option 11. You can use it to display memo information if you change the setting to *M*. Changing option 11 to *C* will display category information only. The default setting of *B* will display both types of information. Option 12 allows you to control the use of the Description field on reports. An entry of *D* will use the category description when there is one and use the category name if there is no description. Entering *N* will cause the category name to be used instead of the description. Entering *B* for this option will display both. If the description on the screen is not sufficient, remember that you can always use ⟨**F1**⟩ (Help) for an expanded description of the option. The last option (13) will warn you if you have entered a previously used check number when entering a transaction. The default setting will not provide the warning. By resetting the option to *Y* you would be notified if a check number is reused.

chapter 12

QUICKEN'S PAYROLL ASSISTANCE

The Quicken Payroll System
Recording Payroll Activity
Completing the Payroll Entries
Payroll Reports

For a small-business owner under the day-to-day pressure of running a business, preparing the payroll can be a time-consuming and frustrating task. Besides withholding forms and tables to complete, there are annual earnings limits that affect the amount you withhold in Social Security taxes from employees. In addition to these weekly considerations, there are monthly, quarterly, and year-end reports that may need to be filed for either the federal, state, or local governments.

In this chapter you will see how Quicken can help to reduce the effort of preparing your payroll. Although you must still invest some time, you'll find that an early investment will substantially reduce your payroll activities once the system is running. With Quicken you can easily prepare the payroll entry for each employee and maintain information for the Internal Revenue Service (IRS) about federal income tax withholding, Federal Insurance Contribution Act (FICA) withholding, and employer FICA payments. You can also maintain accounts for any state and local withholding taxes or

309

insurance payments that must be periodically deposited. In addition to this information you can accumulate data to be used in the preparation of W-2 forms for your employees at the end of the year. See the special Payroll Forms section for a list of some of the standard payroll-related payment and tax forms that Quicken can assist you in preparing.

T I P

PAYROLL FORMS

If you are thinking of hiring employees, you need to be prepared for your paperwork to increase. You must complete forms at the federal, state, and local level regarding payroll information.

Federal Payroll Forms

The following list provides an overview of the payroll-related tax forms that employers need to file with the Internal Revenue Service. You can obtain copies of the federal forms that you need by calling the IRS toll free number (800) 424-3676. If this number is not valid in your locale, check your telephone directory for the correct number. You will probably need to file these forms:

- *SS-4, Application For Federal Employer Identification Number* The federal employer identification number is used to identify your business on all business-related tax forms.

- *Form 46-190, Federal Tax Deposit Receipt* This is your record of deposits of withholding and payroll taxes made to a Federal Reserve Bank or an authorized commercial bank.

- *Form 940, Employer's Annual Federal Unemployment (FUTA) Tax Return* This is a return filed annually with the IRS summarizing your federal unemployment tax liability and deposits.

- *Form 941, Employer's Quarterly Federal Tax Return* This return summarizes your quarterly FICA taxes and federal income tax withholding liability and the amount of deposits your business has made during the quarter.

- *Form 943, Employer's Annual Tax Return For Agricultural Employees* This is a special form completed annually for FICA taxes and federal income tax withholding liability for agricultural employees.

- *Form 1099-MISC, Statement For Recipients of Miscellaneous Income* This must be filed for all non-employees paid $600.00 or more in income in the current tax year.

- *Form W-2, Wage and Tax Statement* This is a six-part form (an original and five duplicates) summarizing an employee's gross earnings and tax deductions for the year. The form must be prepared annually for each employee by January 31.

- *Form W-3, Transmittal of Income and Tax Statements* This form summarizes your business's annual payroll, related FICA taxes, and federal income tax withheld during the year. Sent with the Social Security Administration's copy of the W-2 by February 28th of the following year.

- *Form W-4, Employee's Withholding Allowance Certificate* This form is completed annually by employees and is used to declare the number of withholding exemptions they claim.

State and Local Government Payroll Information

These forms will vary by state. The following list provides an indication of some of the forms you are likely to need to file.

- Unemployment insurance tax payments

- Workers' compensation tax payments

- State income tax withholding payments

- Local income tax withholding payments

- Form W-2, Wage and Tax Statement (one copy of federal form)

THE QUICKEN PAYROLL SYSTEM

Payroll entries are processed along with your other business-related payments in your Quicken account register. To set up your system to do this you will need to establish some new categories and subcategories specifically related to payroll.

- Payroll:Gross keeps track of the total wages earned by employees.

- Payroll:Co keeps track of the amount of payroll taxes your company pays. These include the employer's FICA contribution, federal and state unemployment tax expense, and payments for workers' compensation.

In addition, you will need to establish several *liability accounts* to maintain records of taxes withheld and other employee-authorized payroll deductions for medical insurance, charitable contributions, and so on. These are liability accounts since you are holding the withheld funds for payment to a third party. Some examples of these are

- Payroll-FICA — FICA Withholding from employees

- Payroll-FICA-Co — FICA liabilities owed by employer

- Payroll-FWH — federal income tax liabilities for employee withholdings

- Payroll-SWH — state income tax liabilities for employee withholdings

Notice that all of these account names begin with "Payroll." This allows Quicken to prepare the payroll report by automatically finding all transactions with a category title beginning with Payroll. All the categories listed in this section start with Payroll and have subcategories added, for example Payroll:Gross. When you prepare the Payroll report in this chapter you will see the relationship between the category designation and the preparation of the report.

Another point to note is that although employees must pay federal, state, and local taxes, the employer is responsible for the actual withholding and payment of these funds to the appropriate agencies. In addition, there are certain payroll taxes that the employer must pay, such as unemployment, workers' compensation, and matching FICA. The amount of these taxes is not withheld from the employee's pay since the responsibility for these payments rests with the employer. With Quicken you can monitor your liability for these payments. This is important since you will be assessed penalties and late fees for failing to file these payments on time. Quicken's ability to memorize payment formats and remind you of dates for periodic payments can be most helpful in this situation.

RECORDING PAYROLL ACTIVITY

You will be using the account group BUSINESS, established in Chapter 11, to record your payroll entries in this chapter. As noted in the previous section you need to expand your category list and accounts in order to accumulate the payroll information. Once you have completed the example for processing payroll you will be able to customize your accounts to handle your own payroll needs. For example, you might withhold medical and life insurance premiums from your employees' checks. These amounts can be recorded in another liability account established just for that purpose. The entry of these payroll deductions will follow the same procedure as for federal income tax or any other withholding amount.

The example used in this chapter assumes your work force consists of salaried workers paid monthly. This means their pay and deductions will be the same month after month. John Smith is paid $2,000.00 a month and Mary McFaul is paid $3,000.00 a month. If your employees are paid hourly, with a varying number of hours in each pay period, you will need to recompute the pay and deductions for each period. Otherwise, the same procedures shown in this chapter will apply. In this example, you draw payroll checks on the last day of the month.

Establishing Payroll Liability Accounts

The first step in recording payroll in the Quicken system is to establish the payroll liability accounts you will use throughout the year. The objective of establishing these accounts is to allow you to accumulate the amounts you withhold from employees so you can make periodic payments when they become due to the various governmental agencies, health insurance companies, and pension plans involved. When the payments are due you can open the liability account to determine the balance in the account. This tells you the amount of the payment due.

Make sure you are in the BUSINESS account group. Then, from the Main Menu follow these steps to establish the payroll liability accounts you will use in this chapter:

1. Type **4** and the Select Account to Use window appears.

2. Move the arrow cursor to <New Account> and press ENTER.

The Set Up New Account window appears on your screen.

3. Type **5** and press ENTER.

4. Type **Payroll-FICA** and press ENTER.

This identifies the new account as a liability in the BUSINESS account group. You will accumulate all employee FICA withholdings in this account.

5. Type **0** and press ENTER.

The opening balance is 0.00 in this example since this is the first pay period for the business illustrated. When you set up your own account, you would enter the amount you owe at the time you begin to use Quicken. Thus, if you were in business the previous year, you will probably have outstanding tax liabilities that would not be paid until January or February. The amount of these liabilities would be entered as the balance for each account.

6. Type **1/1/91** and press ENTER.

7. Type **FICA Withholding** and press ENTER.

Quicken returns you to the Select Account to Use window.
Complete steps 2 through 7 again to establish the additional other liability accounts for the information that follows:

Account name:	Payroll-FWH
Account type:	5
Balance:	0
Date:	1/1/91
Description:	Federal Withholding

This establishes an account that will keep track of all employee federal income tax withholding during the year.

Account name:	Payroll-SWH
Account type:	5
Balance:	0
Date:	1/1/91
Description:	State Withholding

This account will keep track of all employee state income tax withholding during the year.

Account name:	Payroll-FICA-Co
Account type:	5
Balance:	0
Date:	1/1/91
Description:	FICA Matching

This account will keep track of the amount of your FICA matching payment each pay period.

After adding these other liability accounts, your screen will look like Figure 12-1. Press (ESC) to return to the Main Menu. Then type **2** to open the ANB Business account register.

Establishing New Payroll Categories

Several new categories are needed to record the payroll information. Follow these steps to establish Payroll and Gross Earnings as categories with Gross and Co (for company) as subcategories under Payroll:

1. Press (CTRL)-(C) to open the Category and Transfer List window.

2. Press (HOME) to move to < New Category >.

3. Press (ENTER) to open the Set Up Category window.

4. Type **Payroll** and press (ENTER).

```
┌────────────────────────────────────────────────────────────────┐
│                     Select Account to Use                        │
├────────────────────────────────────────────────────────────────┤
│           Current Account Group: C:\Q4_12\BUSINESS               │
│                                              Num    Ending  Checks│
│           Account      Type      Description Trans  Balance To Prt│
├────────────────────────────────────────────────────────────────┤
│  ▶ <New Account>          │Set up a new account                  │
│    ANB Business     Bank  │Business checking   11   12,026.75     │
│    ANB Personal     Bank  │Personal Checking    7    2,061.00     │
│    Equipment        Oth A │Capital Equipment    4    3,900.00     │
│    Payroll-FICA     Oth L │FICA Withholding     1        0.00     │
│    Payroll-FICA-Co  Oth L │FICA Matching        1        0.00     │
│    Payroll-FWH      Oth L │Federal Withholding  1        0.00     │
│    Payroll-SWH      Oth L │State Withholding    1        0.00     │
│                           │                                      │
│                           │                                      │
│                                                                  │
├────────────────────────────────────────────────────────────────┤
│           Ctrl-D Delete   Ctrl-E Edit   ↑,↓ Select               │
│   Esc-Cancel                  F1-Help                     ↵ Use  │
└────────────────────────────────────────────────────────────────┘
BUSINESS-ANB Business
```

FIGURE 12-1. Adding the other liability accounts

5. Type **E** and press ⟨ENTER⟩.

6. Type **Payroll Expense** and press ⟨ENTER⟩.

7. Type **Y** and press ⟨ENTER⟩.

8. Press ⟨ENTER⟩ to select <New Category>.

9. Type **Gross** and press ⟨ENTER⟩.

10. Type **S** and press ⟨ENTER⟩.

11. Type **Gross Earnings** and press ⟨ENTER⟩.

12. Type **Y** and press ⟨ENTER⟩ to complete the Set Up Category window.

13. Press ⟨ENTER⟩ to select <New Category>.

14. Type **Co** and press ⟨ENTER⟩.

15. Type **S** and press ⟨ENTER⟩.

16. Type **Payroll Taxes** and press ⟨ENTER⟩.

17. Type **Y** and press ⟨ENTER⟩ to complete the Set Up Category window.

18. Press ⟨ESC⟩ to return to the Register window.

Monthly Payroll Entries

In this section you will be recording paycheck entries for John Smith and Mary McFaul on January 31. Many steps are required to complete the entire entry for an individual. After recording basic information, such as check number and employee name, amounts must be determined. You establish each of the withholding amounts and subtract the total from the gross pay to compute net pay. For hourly workers, a computation will be needed to determine the gross pay as well. Tax tables are used to determine the correct withholding for federal, state, and local taxes. For figures such as FICA and net pay you can use Quicken's calculator when computing the amount.

Once you have determined withholding amounts and net pay, you need to enter this information. Each of the withholding amounts, such as federal income tax, FICA, and state withholding, is entered on a Split Transaction screen. Follow these steps to record the transactions:

1. Press CTRL-END to highlight the next blank transaction in the ANB Business account register.

2. Type **1/31/91** and press ENTER.

3. Type **110** and press ENTER.

4. Type **John Smith** and press ENTER.

5. Type **1538.00** and press ENTER three times.

This amount is equal to John's gross pay of $2,000.00 less federal income tax, state income tax, and FICA.

6. Type **000-00-0001** and press ENTER.

This identifies the employee's Social Security number. You may find this field useful in filtering payroll reports.

7. Press CTRL-S and the Split Transaction window appears on your screen.

Figure 12-2 shows the entries you will complete in the next series of steps.

8. Type **Payroll:Gross/B** and press ENTER.

9. Type **Gross Earnings** and press ENTER.

10. Type **2000.00** and press ⟨ENTER⟩.

11. Press ⟨CTRL⟩-⟨C⟩ and the Category and Transfer List window appears on your screen. Use ⟨DOWN ARROW⟩ to move the arrow cursor to Payroll-FICA, press ⟨ENTER⟩, and type /B.

Quicken automatically records the brackets around the Payroll-FICA category, as shown in the Split Transaction window in Figure 12-2, when the transaction involves a transfer between two Quicken accounts. Here, Quicken records the other liability account name in the Category field. This indicates that you are keeping track of the amount of your employee withholding in this account until you make your payment to the IRS.

12. Press ⟨ENTER⟩ to move to the Description field.

13. Type **FICA Withholding** and press ⟨ENTER⟩.

14. Type **−153.00** and press ⟨ENTER⟩.

This is the amount of FICA withheld from John's paycheck. The negative amount indicates that this is a deduction from the $2,000.00 gross earnings entered above. For 1990, the rate is .0765 on the first $50,400.00 of earnings

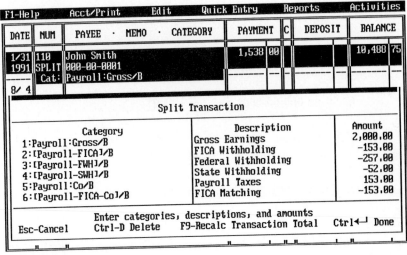

FIGURE 12-2. Split Transaction window for Smith payroll entries

per employee. You can calculate this amount with the Quicken calculator before starting the transaction. Although the $50,400.00 earnings limit does not affect the employees in this example, Quicken can be used to help monitor employees' gross earnings to determine when the limit is reached.

15. Press (CTRL)-(C), move the arrow cursor in the category list to Payroll-FWH, press (ENTER), and type **/B.**

16. Press (ENTER) to move to the Description field.

17. Type **Federal Withholding** and press (ENTER).

18. Type **−257.00** and press (ENTER).

This is the amount of federal income tax withheld from John's paycheck. Remember, you must manually determine the amounts from withholding tables before beginning the payroll transaction entry since you need it to compute net pay.

19. Press (CTRL)-(C), move the arrow cursor to Payroll-SWH, press (ENTER), and type **/B.**

20. Press (ENTER) to move the cursor to the Description field.

21. Type **State Withholding** and press (ENTER).

22. Type **−52.00** and press (ENTER).

Once again you would use the appropriate state withholding tables to determine the amount of the deduction from John's paycheck. If you live in an area where local taxes are also withheld, you would need to add another liability account to accumulate your liability to that governmental agency. At this point you have recorded John Smith's gross and net earnings and the related payroll withholding amounts. The remaining steps record your matching employer FICA expense.

23. Type **Payroll:Co/B** and press (ENTER).

As an employer you have to match your employees' FICA contributions. This is an expense of doing business and must be recorded in your category list.

24. Type **Payroll Taxes** and press (ENTER).

25. Type **153.00** and press (ENTER).

This records the amount of your matching payroll expense. Notice that this is a positive amount because this is a business expense that Quicken will record in the account register.

26. Press (CTRL)-(C), use (DOWN ARROW) to select Payroll-FICA-Co, press (ENTER), and type /B.

27. Press (ENTER) to move the cursor to the Description field.

28. Type **FICA Matching** and press (ENTER).

29. Type **-153.00** and press (CTRL)-(ENTER).

30. Press (CTRL)-(ENTER) to record the transaction in the account register.

You have now completed the payroll entry for John Smith for the month of January. You must now complete the recording process for Mary McFaul. Follow these steps to record the transaction from the ANB Business account register:

1. Type **1/31/91** and press (ENTER).

2. Type **111** and press (ENTER).

3. Type **Mary McFaul** and press (ENTER).

4. Type **2329.50** and press (ENTER) three times.

5. Type **000-00-0002** and press (ENTER).

6. Press (CTRL)-(S) and the Split Transaction window appears on your screen. Figure 12-3 shows how your Split Transaction window will appear after entering Mary's split transaction.

7. Type **Payroll:Gross/B** and press (ENTER).

8. Type **Gross Earnings** and press (ENTER).

9. Type **3000.00** and press (ENTER).

10. Press (CTRL)-(C) and the Category and Transfer list appears on your screen. Use (DOWN ARROW) to move the arrow cursor to Payroll-FICA, press (ENTER), and type /B.

11. Press (ENTER) to move to the Description field.

12. Type **FICA Withholding** and press (ENTER).

13. Type **-229.50** and press (ENTER).

14. Press (CTRL)-(C), move the arrow cursor in the category list to Payroll-FWH, press (ENTER), and type /B.

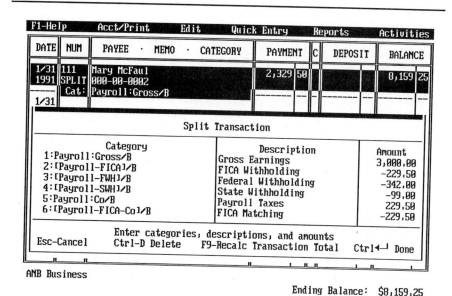

FIGURE 12-3. Split Transaction window for McFaul payroll entries

15. Press (**ENTER**) to move to the Description field.

16. Type **Federal Withholding** and press (**ENTER**).

17. Type **−342.00** and press (**ENTER**).

18. Press (**CTRL**)-(**C**), move the arrow cursor to Payroll-SWH, press (**ENTER**), and type **/B.**

19. Press (**ENTER**) to move the cursor to the Description field.

20. Type **State Withholding** and press (**ENTER**).

21. Type **−99.00** and press (**ENTER**).

22. Type **Payroll:Co/B** and press (**ENTER**).

23. Type **Payroll Taxes** and press (**ENTER**).

24. Type **229.50** and press (**ENTER**).

25. Press (**CTRL**)-(**C**), move the arrow cursor to Payroll-FICA-Co, press (**ENTER**), and type **/B.**

26. Press (**ENTER**) to move the cursor to the Description field.

27. Type **FICA Matching** and press (**ENTER**).

28. Type **−229.50** and press (CTRL)-(ENTER).

29. Press (CTRL)-(ENTER) to record the transaction in the account register.

The paycheck transactions recorded in this section show the basic payroll expenses and liabilities associated with the payment of wages. Your payroll entries will be more complex if you withhold medical insurance, pension contributions, and other amounts such as contributions to charity or deposits to savings accounts from employee checks. The basic format of the split transaction remains the same; the number of categories in the split transaction would simply be expanded and additional liability accounts added to cover your obligation to make payment to the parties involved. Regardless of the number of withholding categories, the procedures performed above can be used to expand your withholding categories and liabilities.

Recording Periodic Deposits for the Internal Revenue Service

You must periodically make deposits to the Internal Revenue Service for the amount of FICA and federal income tax withheld from employees' paychecks, as well as your matching FICA contribution. You make your deposits to authorized banks within the Federal Reserve System. You should check with your bank to be sure they can provide this service; otherwise you must take cash or a bank check, along with the appropriate forms, to an authorized bank and make your deposit. To record the withholding deposit, you will designate the Internal Revenue Service as the payee in your entry.

There are specific guidelines concerning the timing of the payments. At the time of this writing, the fictitious company used in this example would be required to make a withholding deposit for the January paychecks under the IRS's $500.00 rule. The rule states you must make a deposit for Social Security taxes and withheld federal income tax by the fifteenth of the following month if the total taxes you owe at the end of the month are $500.00 or more. (This can be more than one month's worth.) See the special section on IRS Deposit Rules for other conditions that may apply to your situation. In this example your total tax liability for the month is $1,364.00. You should consult your accountant or read the IRS Form 941 for a full explanation of the other deposit rules. Depending on the size of your payroll, you may have to make periodic payments throughout the month in order to comply with the regulations.

The following entry demonstrates how you would record a payment for your business's federal tax liabilities for Social Security taxes and federal withholding taxes. You would record the transaction in the ANB Business account register when you paid the federal government the amount of the liabilities for FICA (both employee withholding and your matching contribution) and federal income tax withholding for the two paycheck entries recorded in the previous section.

From the ANB Business account register record the following transaction for the required deposit:

1. Press CTRL-END to highlight the blank new transaction form and move the cursor to the Date field.

2. Type **2/1/91** and press ENTER.

3. Type **112** and press ENTER.

IRS DEPOSIT RULES

**T
I
P**

The frequency with which you must make deposits of Social Security and federal income taxes is dependent on the amount of your liability. If your payroll is small you may be able to make deposits as infrequently as once per quarter. With a large payroll, deposits may need to be made every pay period. To determine whether you need to make a payment you must look at your liability at the end of each deposit period. These periods end on the 3rd, 7th, 11th, 15th, 19th, 22nd, 25th, and the last day of each month. You can look at these three rules to determine if you are obligated to make a deposit:

The $3,000.00 Rule—If you owe $3,000.00 at the end of a period, you must make a deposit within three banking days. This deposit must cover at least 95 percent of your liability.

The $500.00 Rule—If you owe at least $500.00 at the end of the month, you are obligated to deposit 100 percent of the amount by the 15th of the following month.

The End of Quarter Rule—Outstanding liabilities at the end of a quarter that do not fall under the $3,000.00 or $500.00 rule must be deposited by the end of the following month.

4. Type **Internal Revenue Service** and press ⟨ENTER⟩.

5. Type **1364.00** and press ⟨ENTER⟩ three times.

6. Type **Form 941 Withholding Payment** and press ⟨ENTER⟩.

7. Press ⟨CTRL⟩-⟨S⟩ to open the Split Transaction window. Figure 12-4 shows how your Split Transaction window will appear after completing all the entries but before recording the split.

8. Press ⟨CTRL⟩-⟨C⟩, move the arrow cursor to Payroll-FICA, press ⟨ENTER⟩, and type **/B**. This account is now recorded in the Category field on the Split Transaction window.

9. Press ⟨ENTER⟩ to move the cursor to the Description field.

10. Type **FICA Withholding** and press ⟨ENTER⟩.

11. Type **382.50** and press ⟨ENTER⟩.

12. Press ⟨CTRL⟩-⟨C⟩, move the arrow cursor to Payroll-FICA-Co, press ⟨ENTER⟩, and type **/B**.

13. Press ⟨ENTER⟩ to move the cursor to the Description field.

14. Type **FICA Matching** and press ⟨ENTER⟩.

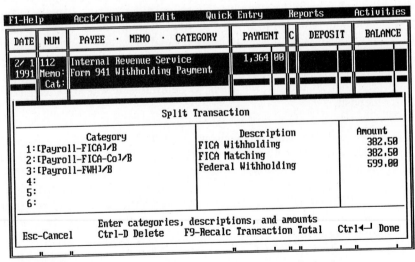

FIGURE 12-4. Split transaction entries for the IRS deposit

15. Type **382.50** and press ⟨**ENTER**⟩.

16. Press ⟨**CTRL**⟩-⟨**C**⟩, move the arrow cursor to Payroll-FWH, press ⟨**ENTER**⟩, and type **/B**.

17. Press ⟨**ENTER**⟩ to move the cursor to the Description field.

18. Type **Federal Withholding** and press ⟨**ENTER**⟩.

19. Press ⟨**CTRL**⟩-⟨**ENTER**⟩. This records the split.

20. Press ⟨**CTRL**⟩-⟨**ENTER**⟩ to record the transaction in the account register.

You will follow these same steps to record the payment of the state withholding tax liability when the required payment date arrives.

Notice that no expense category was charged in the Split Transaction window shown in Figure 12-4. This is because the deposit reduces the liability account balances that were established when payroll checks were written on 1/31/91. Looking at those transactions (Figures 12-3 and 12-4), you can see that the gross earnings were charged to the Payroll:Gross category and your matching FICA contribution as an employer was charged to the Payroll:Co category. Both these categories are classified as expenses and will be shown on your business Profit and Loss statement. On the other hand, the amounts withheld for payroll taxes were charged to liability accounts that will be paid at a future date. Thus, when you pay these liabilities, as you just did, you are meeting your financial obligation to the government, not incurring additional expenses.

Other Liability Accounts

Let's look at the impact of recording the paychecks and the IRS payment on the other liability accounts. Specifically, you will see the effects of these transactions on the Payroll-FWH other liability account. Follow these steps to enter the Payroll-FWH account from the ANB Business account register:

1. Press ⟨**ESC**⟩ to return to the Main Menu.

2. Type **4** and the Select Account to Use window appears.

3. Move the arrow cursor to the Payroll-FWH account and press ⟨**ENTER**⟩. Figure 12-5 appears on your screen.

| F1-Help | F2-Acct/Print | F3-Edit | F4-Quick Entry | F5-Reports | F6-Activities |

DATE	REF	PAYEE · MEMO · CATEGORY	INCREASE	C	DECREASE	BALANCE
		▬▬▬ BEGINNING ▬▬▬				
1/ 1 1991		Opening Balance [Payroll-FWH]				0 00
1/31 1991		John Smith 000-00-0001 [ANB Business]→	257 00			257 00
1/31 1991		Mary McFaul 000-00-0002 [ANB Business]→	342 00			599 00
2/ 1 1991		Internal Revenue Service Form 941 Withho→[ANB Business]→			599 00	0 00

▬▬▬ **FIGURE 12-5.**   Activating the Payroll-FWH account

Notice that the account had accumulated $599.00 as the FWH withholding liability for the January paychecks. Also note that the 2/1/91 entry reduced the balance to zero when you made your deposit. This will occur each month when you record your deposit to the IRS.

4. Press (**ESC**) to return to the Main Menu of the Payroll-FWH account register.

5. Type **4** to select the account, move the arrow cursor to ANB Business, and press (**ENTER**). You are now back in the ANB Business account register.

Memorized Monthly Paycheck and Withholding Deposit Entries

Since you will be paying your employees on a regular basis and making monthly withholding deposits, you will want to memorize these entries to simplify future recording of the transactions. Since the employees in this example are all salaried, the only changes needed each month will be new dates and check numbers on each transaction. All of the split transaction detail will be accurate. For hourly employees or employees making more than the FICA cap amount, some pay periods will require changes to the entries in the split transaction detail. While in the ANB Business account register complete the steps outlined below to memorize paycheck and withholding deposit transactions:

1. Highlight the John Smith paycheck transaction on January 31, 1991 and press ⌈F4⌉ to open the Quick Entry menu.

2. Type **2** to select Memorize Transaction.

3. Press ⌈ENTER⌉ to memorize the transaction.

4. Highlight the Mary McFaul paycheck transaction on January 31, 1991 and press ⌈F4⌉ to open the Quick Entry window.

5. Type **2** to select Memorize Transaction.

6. Press ⌈ENTER⌉ to memorize the transaction.

7. Highlight the Internal Revenue Service transaction and press ⌈F4⌉ to open the Quick Entry menu.

8. Type **2** to select Memorize Transactions.

9. Press ⌈ENTER⌉ to memorize the transaction.

10. Press ⌈CTRL⌉-⌈T⌉ to display the Memorized Transactions List. Your list should contain entries for Internal Revenue Service, John Smith, and Mary McFaul.

11. Press ⌈ESC⌉ to return to the account register.

COMPLETING THE PAYROLL ENTRIES

In this section you will expand your payroll transactions by adding some entries to the ANB Business account register. These transactions are added so the examples will contain enough pay periods to generate realistic reports later in this chapter. Notice that you will not record check numbers for the remaining example transactions in this chapter. This will not affect the reports prepared in this chapter.

Establishing Transaction Groups

In Chapter 11 you established a transaction group for the utilities payments. The object of transaction grouping is to batch together similar transactions that occur around the same time each month so Quicken can automatically record them for you the next time they need to be made. Remember, only memorized transactions can be batched into transaction groups. From the ANB Business account register perform the following steps to establish a transaction group for the payroll:

1. Press (F4) to open the Quick Entry menu.
2. Type **5** to select Set Up Transaction Group. The Set Up Transaction Group to Set Up/Change window opens.
3. Move the arrow cursor to 2. <unused> and press (ENTER). The Describe Group 2 window appears.
4. Type **Payroll** and press (ENTER) twice.
5. Type **6** and press (ENTER).
6. Type **2/28/91** and press (ENTER).
7. Select John Smith and press (SPACEBAR) to mark the transaction. Note the 2 in the group column, indicating that the transaction is now part of Group 2.
8. Move the arrow cursor to Mary McFaul and press (SPACEBAR). This transaction also becomes a part of Group 2.
9. Press (ENTER) to indicate that you are finished selecting transactions.
10. Press (ESC).

You are returned to the account register to record further transactions.

Recording February Transactions

In this section you will add the remaining transactions to the account register to complete the payroll entries for the month of February. You should be in the ANB Business account register to record the following transactions:

1. Press (CTRL)-(END) to highlight the next blank transaction form.

2. Press ⌐F4⌐ and type **5** to select Execute Transaction Group.

Quicken will display a list of account groups.

3. Select the Payroll Group and press ⌐ENTER⌐.

Quicken will display the date of the next scheduled entry of the group, 2/28/91.

4. Press ⌐ENTER⌐ to confirm that this date is valid and to enter and record the group of payroll transactions in the account register.

Quicken will display a message indicating that the transactions have been recorded. You can then make any required changes.

5. Press ⌐ENTER⌐ to close the message box.

If the date was not the last date of the month for payroll purposes you could have typed in the correct date in the Transaction Group Date window and then pressed ⌐ENTER⌐. In this example the payroll entries will not be modified since they are the same from month to month. If you have employees who work on an hourly basis you would need to select each new transaction, open the Split Transaction window, and make the necessary modifications to the dollar amounts recorded.

The payroll entries are the only February transactions that are being added to the account register at this time. Figure 12-6 shows a printout of the account register including the two payroll entries recorded on 2/28/91 as well as the remaining transactions that will be entered in this chapter.

Recording March Transactions

The March entries can be divided into three groups. The first records a deposit for federal Social Security and income tax withholding in February. The second and third entries record income earned during the month from consulting and royalties. The last two entries record the payroll transactions for March.

```
                              Check Register
      ANB Business                                              Page 1
      8/ 4/91

      Date  Num          Transaction        Payment  C Deposit    Balance
      ----- -----  ------------------------------  ----------  - ----------  ----------

      2/28         John Smith                1,538.00              5,257.25
      1991 SPLIT 000-00-0001
                       Payroll:Gross/B       2,000.00
                       Gross Earnings
                       [Payroll-FICA]/B                 153.00
                       FICA Withholding
                       [Payroll-FWH]/B                  257.00
                       Federal Withholding
                       [Payroll-SWH]/B                   52.00
                       State Withholding
                       Payroll:Co/B            153.00
                       Payroll Taxes
                       [Payroll-FICA-Co]/B              153.00
                       FICA Matching

      2/28         Mary McFaul               2,329.50              2,927.75
      1991 SPLIT 000-00-0002
                       Payroll:Gross/B       3,000.00
                       Gross Earnings
                       [Payroll-FICA]/B                 229.50
                       FICA Withholding
                       [Payroll-FWH]/B                  342.00
                       Federal Withholding
                       [Payroll-SWH]/B                   99.00
                       State Withholding
                       Payroll:Co/B            229.50
                       Payroll Taxes
                       [Payroll-FICA-Co]/B              229.50
                       FICA Matching

      3/ 1         Internal Revenue Service  1,364.00              1,563.75
      1991 SPLIT Form 941 Withholding Payment
                       [Payroll-FICA]/B        382.50
                       FICA Withholding
                       [Payroll-FICA-Co]/B     382.50
                       FICA Matching
                       [Payroll-FWH]/B         599.00
                       Federal Withholding

      3/ 1         Tyler Corp.                        25,000.00  26,563.75
      1991 memo: Seminars conducted Jan. 91
           cat: Inc Cons/B

      3/31         Big Books                          10,000.00  36,563.75
      1991 memo: Royalties
           cat: Inc Roy/B

      3/31         John Smith                1,538.00             35,025.75
      1991 SPLIT 000-00-0001
                       Payroll:Gross/B       2,000.00
```

FIGURE 12-6. Account register showing additional transactions

```
                                Check Register
ANB Business                                                    Page 2
8/ 4/91

  Date  Num          Transaction         Payment  C  Deposit    Balance
  ----- -----  ------------------------- ---------- - ---------- ----------
               Gross Earnings
               [Payroll-FICA]/B                       153.00
                 FICA Withholding
               [Payroll-FWH]/B                        257.00
                 Federal Withholding
               [Payroll-SWH]/B                          52.00
                 State Withholding
               Payroll:Co/B               153.00
                 Payroll Taxes
               [Payroll-FICA-Co]/B                    153.00
                 FICA Matching

  3/31       Mary McFaul                2,329.50               32,696.25
  1991 SPLIT 000-00-0002
               Payroll:Gross/B          3,000.00
                 Gross Earnings
               [Payroll-FICA]/B                       229.50
                 FICA Withholding
               [Payroll-FWH]/B                        342.00
                 Federal Withholding
               [Payroll-SWH]/B                          99.00
                 State Withholding
               Payroll:Co/B               229.50
                 Payroll Taxes
               [Payroll-FICA-Co]/B                    229.50
                 FICA Matching

  4/ 1       Internal Revenue Service   1,364.00               31,332.25
  1991 SPLIT Form 941 Withholding Payment
               [Payroll-FICA]/B           382.50
                 FICA Withholding
               [Payroll-FICA-Co]/B        382.50
                 FICA Matching
               [Payroll-FWH]/B            599.00
                 Federal Withholding

  4/15       Internal Revenue Service     104.00               31,228.25
  1991 memo: FUTA
        cat: Payroll:Co/B

  4/15       Bureau of Employment Services 520.00              30,708.25
  1991 memo: SUTA
        cat: Payroll:Co/B
```

FIGURE 12-6. Account register showing additional transactions
                        (*continued*)

THE ENTRY TO RECORD FEBRUARY WITHHOLDING The entry to record the deposit for taxes withheld during February involves the use of a memorized transaction. From the highlighted blank transaction form in the ANB Business account register perform the following steps:

1. Press ⌈CTRL⌋-⌈T⌋ to recall the Memorized Transaction List window.

2. Use ⌈DOWN ARROW⌋ to select the Internal Revenue Service transaction and press ⌈ENTER⌋.

3. Move the cursor to the Date field, type **3/1/91**, and press ⌈CTRL⌋-⌈ENTER⌋.

CONSULTING AND ROYALTY INCOME ENTRIES In the ANB Business account register enter the following information for the two deposit entries shown in Figure 12-6:

1. Type **3/1/91** and press ⌈ENTER⌋ twice.

2. Type **Tyler Corp.** and press ⌈ENTER⌋ three times.

3. Type **25000** and press ⌈ENTER⌋.

4. Type **Seminars conducted Jan. 91** and press ⌈ENTER⌋.

5. Type **Inc Cons/B** and press ⌈CTRL⌋-⌈ENTER⌋. This records the Tyler Corp. revenue transaction.

6. Type **3/31/91** and press ⌈ENTER⌋ twice.

7. Type **Big Books** and press ⌈ENTER⌋ three times.

8. Type **10000** and press ⌈ENTER⌋.

9. Type **Royalties** and press ⌈ENTER⌋.

10. Type **Inc Roy/B** and press ⌈CTRL⌋-⌈ENTER⌋.

After completing these steps you have recorded both income transactions for March.

MARCH PAYROLL ENTRIES In this section you will add the remaining transactions to the account register to complete the payroll entries for the month of March:

1. Press ⌈F4⌋ and type **5** to select Execute Transaction Group. Quicken will display a list of account groups.

2. Select the Payroll Group and press (ENTER). Quicken will display the date of the next scheduled entry of the group, 3/28/91.

3. Type **3/31/91** and press (ENTER).

This changes the date to the end of March and enters the group of payroll transactions in the account register. Quicken will indicate that the transactions have been recorded.

4. Press (ENTER) in response to the Transaction Group Entered window.

Recording April Transactions

The only transactions you will record for April are the Internal Revenue Service deposit for the March payroll and the Federal Unemployment Tax Act (FUTA) and State Unemployment Tax Act (SUTA) payments.

Complete the following steps to record the IRS transaction in the ANB Business account register, after first pressing (CTRL)-(END) to highlight the next blank transaction form. (This transaction will help you prepare several reports for the Internal Revenue Service later in this chapter.)

1. Press (CTRL)-(T) to recall the Memorized Transaction List window.

2. Use (DOWN ARROW) to select the Internal Revenue Service transaction and press (ENTER).

3. Move the cursor to the Date field, type **4/1/91**, and press (CTRL)-(ENTER).

In addition to your withholding tax liabilities, employers must pay unemployment taxes. This program is mandated by the federal government but administered by the individual state governments. Due to this method of administration you must make payments to both the state and federal government. At the time of this writing you must contribute .008 percent to the federal government to cover their administrative costs and up to .054 percent to the state agency that administers the program. These percentages apply to the first $7,000.00 of earnings for each employee. In some states the salary cap on earnings may be higher; however, the example in this chapter uses a $7,000.00 limit for both federal and state employer payroll tax contributions.

You must make deposits to the federal government whenever your contribution liability reaches $100.00. These deposits are made in the same manner as the FICA and federal income tax withholding payments earlier in this chapter.

Your actual contributions to the state agency will be based on historical rates for your business and industry classification. You may qualify for a percentage rate lower than the maximum rate allowed by law. The contribution rate for the business in this example is assumed to be .04 percent.

Generally, payments to the state agency that administers the program are made quarterly. Each quarter you are required to complete an Employer's Report of Wages form, summarizing your employees' total earnings during the quarter and the amount of your FUTA and SUTA liabilities.

From the ANB Business account register make the following payments for federal and state unemployment payroll taxes during the month of April. Follow the steps outlined below to record the FUTA and SUTA payments:

1. Press (CTRL)-(END) to make certain you are at the next available form for recording a transaction.

2. Type **4/15/91** and press (ENTER) twice.

3. Type **Internal Revenue Service** and press (ENTER).

4. Type **104** and press (ENTER) three times.

In the "Payroll Reports" section of this chapter you will see that Smith received $6,000.00 and McFaul received $9,000.00 in gross pay. McFaul has reached the salary limit for employer unemployment contributions for the year. The amount entered here was determined by multiplying the first $7,000.00 of McFaul's salary and all $6,000.00 of Smith's by the FUTA rate of .008.

5. Type **FUTA** and press (ENTER).

This is important because you will want to use the Memo field as a filter for your year-end Payroll report to determine the total deposits you made throughout the year for FUTA taxes.

6. Type **Payroll:Co/B** and press (CTRL)-(ENTER).

You have now completed the recording of the FUTA payroll tax deposit.

7. Press (ENTER) twice.

This accepts the 4/15/91 date for the transaction entry and moves the cursor to the Payee field.

8. Type **Bureau of Employment Services** and press ⟨ENTER⟩.

9. Type **520** and press ⟨ENTER⟩ three times.

10. Type **SUTA** and press ⟨ENTER⟩.

Once again this is an important part of the entry since you will filter some reports on this field at the end of the year. The payment amount of 520 was determined by multiplying 13,000.00 ($7,000.00 + $6,000.00) by .04.

11. Type **Payroll:Co/B** and press ⟨CTRL⟩-⟨ENTER⟩.

With the recording of these entries you have completed all the transactions that will be added to the account register in this chapter. These new transactions are shown in Figure 12-6.

WORKERS' COMPENSATION PAYMENTS As an employer you will make workers' compensation payments for your employees. These payments should be recorded in the Payroll:Co category, using the Memo field to note WCOMP as the type of payment. The entries would be recorded in the way just illustrated for unemployment insurance payments.

PAYROLL REPORTS

Through the use of filters and customization features you can obtain a substantial amount of the payroll-related information you need to prepare the various federal, state, and local payroll tax and withholding forms. However, as you will see in the following sections, there are some functions you must perform manually, such as totaling amounts from several Quicken reports to determine the numbers to place in some lines of tax forms.

The objective of this section is to prepare some of the reports you may find useful for your business filing requirements. Although it is impossible to provide illustrations of all the variations, preparing the reports that follow will help you become familiar with the possibilities. You can then begin to explore modifications that best suit your payroll and withholding reporting needs.

From the transactions you entered for January through April you can gather information that will assist you in preparing your quarterly reports: the FUTA form, SUTA form, workers' compensation report, and federal, state, and local withholding tax reports. Although you have not entered a full year's worth of transactions, you will see that Quicken can also help in the preparation of year-end W-2s, W-3s, 1099s, annual forms for federal, state, and local tax withholding, and other annual tax forms required for unemployment and workers' compensation purposes.

Payroll Report Overview

Quicken's Payroll report summarizes all your payroll activities in any period for which you need information—that is, you can prepare the report for weekly, monthly, quarterly, or yearly payroll summary information. You can gather information for all employees in one report, or you can limit the report to information concerning one employee at a time.

An important point to remember is that Quicken's Payroll report is preset to interface only with the Payroll category. If you recall, it was mentioned early in the chapter that all payroll-related charges would be charged against the main Payroll category. You also established subcategories for Payroll: Gross and Payroll:Co to keep track of specific types of payroll charges. If you don't use this format you will need to select Summary Report from the Reports menu and customize your reports to gather the information necessary for tax-reporting purposes. All the reports prepared in this section are based on the Payroll Report option in the Business Reports menu.

Employer's Quarterly Federal Tax Return

In the previous sections of this chapter you prepared entries that accumulated FICA withholding, the matching employer's contribution, and the federal income tax withheld from each of the employees' paychecks. You also recorded the required payments to the IRS made to a local bank authorized to receive these funds.

T
I
P

DATES FOR FILING FEDERAL PAYROLL TAX RETURNS

Form 941, Employer's Quarterly Federal Tax Return

First quarter (Jan - Mar)
If deposit required with filing   April 30
If deposit not required with filing   May 10

Second quarter (Apr - June)
If deposit required with filing   July 31
If deposit not required with filing   August 10

Third quarter (July - Sept)
If deposit required with filing   Oct 31
If deposit not required with filing   November 10

Fourth quarter (Oct - Dec)
If deposit required with filing   January 31
If deposit not required with filing   February 10

Form 943, Employer's Annual Tax Return for Agricultural Employees

Calendar year filing
If deposit required with filing   January 31
If deposit not required with filing   February 10

Let us now examine how you can use Quicken to assist you in preparing Form 941 (shown in Figure 12-7) to meet your quarterly filing requirements. Consult the special Dates for Filing Federal Payroll Tax Returns section for the deadlines for filing quarterly Form 941 and annual Form 943. Starting

Form **941**
(Rev. April 1990)
Department of the Treasury
Internal Revenue Service

4242

Employer's Quarterly Federal Tax Return

▶ See Circular E for more information concerning Employment Tax Returns.

Please type or print.

OMB No. 1545-0029
Expires: 5-31-91

Your name, address, employer identification number, and calendar quarter of return. (If not correct, please change.)

Name (as distinguished from trade name)

Trade name, if any

Address and ZIP code

Date quarter ended

Employer identification number

T
FF
FD
FP
I
T

If address is different from prior return, check here ▶ ☐

IRS Use

1 1 1 1 1 1 1 1 1 1 1   2   3 3 3 3 3   4 4 4

5 5 5   6   7   8 8 8 8 8 8   9 9 9   10 10 10 10 10 10 10 10 10

If you do not have to file returns in the future, check here . . . ▶ ☐   Date final wages paid . . . . ▶
If you are a seasonal employer, see **Seasonal employer** on page 2 and check here . . . . ▶ ☐

1a Number of employees (except household) employed in the pay period that includes March 12th ▶	**1a**	
b If you are a subsidiary corporation AND your parent corporation files a consolidated Form 1120, enter parent corporation employer identification number (EIN) . . ▷	**1b**	─
2 Total wages and tips subject to withholding, plus other compensation . . . . ▶	**2**	15,000 00
3 Total income tax withheld from wages, tips, pensions, annuities, sick pay, gambling, etc.	**3**	1,797 00
4 Adjustment of withheld income tax for preceding quarters of calendar year (see instructions) . . ▶	**4**	
5 Adjusted total of income tax withheld (line 3 as adjusted by line 4—see instructions)	**5**	1,797 00
6 Taxable social security wages paid . . . . . $ _15,000 00_ × 15.3% (.153) . .	**6**	2,295 00
7a Taxable tips reported . . . . $ _____ × 15.3% (.153) . .	**7a**	
b Taxable hospital insurance wages paid . . $ _____ × 2.9% (.029) . .	**7b**	
8 Total social security taxes (add lines 6, 7a, and 7b)	**8**	2,295 00
9 Adjustment of social security taxes (see instructions for required explanation)	**9**	
10 Adjusted total of social security taxes (line 8 as adjusted by line 9—see instructions) . . . ▶	**10**	2,295 00
11 Backup withholding (see instructions) . . . . ▶	**11**	
12 Adjustment of backup withholding tax for preceding quarters of calendar year	**12**	
13 Adjusted total of backup withholding (line 11 as adjusted by line 12)	**13**	
14 Total taxes (add lines 5, 10, and 13) . . . . ▶	**14**	4,092 00
15 Advance earned income credit (EIC) payments, if any . . . . ▶	**15**	
16 Net taxes (subtract line 15 from line 14). **This must equal line IV below** (plus line IV of Schedule A (Form 941) if you have treated backup withholding as a separate liability).	**16**	4,092 00
17 Total deposits for quarter, including overpayment applied from a prior quarter, from your records . ▶	**17**	4,092 00
18 Balance due (subtract line 17 from line 16). This should be less than $500. Pay to IRS . . . . ▶	**18**	─ 0 ─

19 If line 17 is more than line 16, enter overpayment here ▶ $ _____ and check if to be:
☐ Applied to next return   **OR**   ☐ Refunded.

Record of Federal Tax Liability (Complete if line 16 is $500 or more.) See the instructions on page 4 for details before checking these boxes.
Check only if you made eighth-monthly deposits using the 95% rule · ☐   Check only if you are a first time 3-banking-day depositor ☐

Show tax liability here, **not deposits.** IRS gets deposit data from FTD coupons.

Date wages paid		First month of quarter		Second month of quarter		Third month of quarter
1st through 3rd	A		I		Q	
4th through 7th	B		J		R	
8th through 11th	C		K		S	
12th through 15th	D		L		T	
16th through 19th	E		M		U	
20th through 22nd	F		N		V	
23rd through 25th	G		O		W	
26th through the last	H		P		X	
Total liability for month	I		II		III	

Do NOT Show Federal Tax Deposits Here

IV Total for quarter (add lines *I*, *II*, and *III*). **This must equal line 16 above** . . . .

Sign Here
Under penalties of perjury, I declare that I have examined this return, including accompanying schedules and statements, and to the best of my knowledge and belief, it is true, correct, and complete.

Signature ▶   Title   Date

For Paperwork Reduction Act Notice, see page 2.

FIGURE 12-7. IRS Form 941

from the Main Menu of your ANB Business account register, complete the following steps:

1. Type **3** to select Reports.

2. Type **2** to select the Business Reports item.

3. Type **6** and the Payroll Report window appears.

4. Press (ENTER) to accept the default report title of "Payroll Report."

5. Type **1/91** and press (ENTER).

6. Type **4/91** and press (F8). The Create Summary Report window appears.

Although the report is for the quarter ending 3/31/91, you need to include the March FICA and income tax withholding payment entered in the register on 4/1/91. Making April the last month of the report allows you to set the exact date in April to use as the cutoff date for the report

7. Press (ENTER) twice.

8. Type **4/1/91** and press (ENTER).

You have now set the final date of the reporting period to include the payment date of the last IRS deposit for withholding amounts.

9. Press (CTRL)-(ENTER) and the Payroll report appears on your screen.

This is a wide-screen report; it will be printed on several pages.

10. Press (F8) to print the report. The Print Report window appears.

11. Select the appropriate printer and press (ENTER) to print the report.

This is a case where selection of the compressed print option or the landscape option will help you capture more of the report on each page.

REPORT DISCUSSION The report prepared is shown in Figure 12-8. (Figure 12-8 is all one report—unless you use a wide-carriage printer the Payroll report will print on three pages.) Let's take a look at the information gathered and discuss how you can use it to complete the appropriate lines of the Employer's Quarterly Federal Tax Return form, shown in Figure 12-7.

```
                          Payroll Report
                       1/ 1/91 Through 4/ 1/91
                                                          Page 1
BUSINESS-All Accounts
8/ 4/91
                       INC/EXP        INC/EXP        INC/EXP        INC/EXP
                       EXPENSES       EXPENSES       EXPENSES       EXPENSES
                    Payroll Expens Payroll Expens Payroll Expens    TOTAL
       Payee        Gross Earnings  Payroll Taxes     TOTAL
------------------- -------------- -------------- -------------- --------------
Internal Revenue Service     0.00           0.00           0.00           0.00
John Smith               6,000.00         459.00       6,459.00       6,459.00
Mary McFaul              9,000.00         688.50       9,688.50       9,688.50
Opening Balance             0.00           0.00           0.00           0.00
                    -------------- -------------- -------------- --------------
OVERALL TOTAL           15,000.00       1,147.50      16,147.50      16,147.50
                    ============== ============== ============== ==============
```

```
                          Payroll Report
                       1/ 1/91 Through 4/ 1/91
                                                          Page 2
BUSINESS-All Accounts
8/ 4/91
       INC/EXP     TRANSFERS      TRANSFERS      TRANSFERS      TRANSFERS      TRANSFERS
        TOTAL         TO             TO             TO            FROM           FROM
                  Payroll-FWH Payroll-FICA-C  Payroll-FICA   Payroll-FWH Payroll-FICA-C

     -------------- -------------- -------------- -------------- -------------- --------------
          0.00       -1,797.00      -1,147.50      -1,147.50           0.00           0.00
      -6,459.00           0.00           0.00           0.00         771.00         459.00
      -9,688.50           0.00           0.00           0.00       1,026.00         688.50
          0.00           0.00           0.00           0.00           0.00           0.00
     -------------- -------------- -------------- -------------- -------------- --------------
     -16,147.50       -1,797.00      -1,147.50      -1,147.50       1,797.00       1,147.50
     ============== ============== ============== ============== ============== ==============
```

```
                          Payroll Report
                       1/ 1/91 Through 4/ 1/91
                                                          Page 3
BUSINESS-All Accounts
8/ 4/91
     TRANSFERS      TRANSFERS      TRANSFERS       BAL FWD        BAL FWD        BAL FWD
       FROM           FROM          TOTAL       Payroll-FWH Payroll-FICA-C  Payroll-FICA
    Payroll-FICA  Payroll-SWH

    -------------- -------------- -------------- -------------- -------------- --------------
          0.00           0.00       -4,092.00           0.00           0.00           0.00
        459.00         156.00       1,845.00           0.00           0.00           0.00
        688.50         297.00       2,700.00           0.00           0.00           0.00
          0.00           0.00           0.00           0.00           0.00           0.00
    -------------- -------------- -------------- -------------- -------------- --------------
      1,147.50         453.00         453.00           0.00           0.00           0.00
    ============== ============== ============== ============== ============== ==============
```

FIGURE 12-8. Payroll report (in four sections)

```
                              Payroll Report
                          1/  1/91 Through 4/  1/91
              BUSINESS-All Accounts
              8/ 4/91                                          Page  4
                  BAL FWD              BAL FWD             OVERALL
                Payroll-SWH             TOTAL               TOTAL

              ---------------      ---------------      ---------------
                       0.00                 0.00           -4,092.00
                       0.00                 0.00           -4,614.00
                       0.00                 0.00           -6,988.50
                       0.00                 0.00                0.00
              ---------------      ---------------      ---------------
                       0.00                 0.00          -15,694.50
              ===============      ===============      ===============
```

FIGURE 12-8. Payroll report (in four sections) (*continued*)

Line 2 This line shows the total wages subject to federal withholding. The first column of the Payroll report (Payroll Expense: Gross Earnings) shows that a total of $15,000.00 was earned by Smith and McFaul during the quarter.

Line 3 This line shows the amount of total income tax withheld from employee wages. The column titled Transfers From Payroll-FWH (on page 2 of the report) shows that the total federal income tax withheld from employees was $1,797.00. Note that $771.00 was paid by Smith and $1,026.00 was paid by McFaul.

Line 6 The amount of Social Security taxes accumulated during the quarter totals $2,295.00. You obtain the total of the FICA taxes owed from two columns on the Payroll report. The Transfers From Payroll-FICA-C ($1,147.50) and Transfers From Payroll-FICA ($1,147.50) columns (on pages 2 and 3) summarize the amounts of the employer FICA matching contribution and the employee FICA withholding for the quarter.

To verify this, the gross earnings for the quarter are subject to FICA withholding and matching contributions. This means the total in the first column of the report, $15,000.00, is multiplied by .153 to get the amount on line 6. This should equal the total calculated in the preceding paragraph— $2,295.00—which it does.

Although the $50,400.00 earnings limit for FICA withholding does not affect this example, this is a demonstration of how to determine whether any employee has gone over the earnings limit in the next section.

Line 17 This line shows the total deposits made to the IRS during the quarter. This amount can be obtained from the last column in the Payroll report. The Overall Total column shows that $4,092.00 was the amount deposited with the Internal Revenue Service during the quarter. Note that this amount includes the 4/1/91 payment. When you complete your IRS deposit slip you designate the quarter for which the payment applies. In this case the payment was made for the first quarter and would thus be included in this report.

Notice that the bottom portion of Form 941 requires the calculation of tax liabilities at specified time intervals during the deposit periods. Since you made your payments in a timely fashion during the quarter, you would not need to complete this portion. If you did need to complete this portion of the form for the example in this chapter, you would only need to complete Line H since you pay your employees monthly. Figure 12-9 shows the Federal Tax Liability report, which would capture the information for the first quarter to help you to complete Lines H, P, and X. If you pay your employees weekly you could produce this same report for weekly periods during the quarter. If you wanted to reproduce Figure 12-9 with your account register you could complete the following steps from the ANB Business account register:

1. Press (F5) to open the Reports window.

2. Type 2 to select Business Reports.

3. Type 6 and the Payroll Report window appears.

4. Type **Federal Tax Liability By Month** and press (ENTER).

5. Type **1/91** and press (ENTER).

6. Type **3/91** and press (F8). The Create Summary Report window appears on the screen.

```
                Federal Tax Liability By Month
                     1/ 1/91 Through 3/31/91
   BUSINESS-ANB Business                              Page 1
   8/ 4/91
                                                     OVERALL
                                                      TOTAL
      Payee          1/91        2/91       3/91
   -----------    ---------   ---------   ---------  ---------
   John Smith       563.00      563.00      563.00   1,689.00
   Mary McFaul      801.00      801.00      801.00   2,403.00
                  ---------   ---------   ---------  ---------
   OVERALL TOTAL  1,364.00    1,364.00    1,364.00   4,092.00
                  =========   =========   =========  =========
```

FIGURE 12-9. Tax report for employee federal tax withholding

7. Press ⌈TAB⌉ to move to Column headings:, type **5**, and press ⌈F9⌉.

The Filter Report Transactions window appears. A tilde (~) is used in the Payee matches row to tell Quicken to exclude transactions with this payee from the report.

8. Type ~**Internal Revenue Service** and press ⌈ENTER⌉ twice.
9. Type **Payroll-F . .** and press ⌈CTRL⌉-⌈ENTER⌉.

This command tells Quicken to include all Payroll category entries with *F* after the hyphen (FICA, FICA-Co, and FWH) in the report. This way Quicken will capture all payroll check entries in the report for the quarter.

10. Press ⌈ENTER⌉, type **C**, and press ⌈ENTER⌉.
11. Press ⌈F8⌉ and the Print Report window appears.
12. Select your printer and press ⌈ENTER⌉ to print the Federal Tax Liability report shown in Figure 12-9. Press ⌈ESC⌉ until the Main Menu appears.

Before leaving this discussion, notice that there are several columns on your Payroll report (Figure 12-8) with zero balances, the Balance Forward (BAL FWD) columns. These columns represent any unpaid balances in these accounts at the end of the year. In this example there were no balances in these accounts because the business just hired employees on January 1st. In future years there would be balances carried forward and shown in this report. However, you still record your first deposit of the year the same way.

Other Quarterly Reports

In addition to the federal quarterly return, you will need to complete several other quarterly tax returns and reports, depending on the state where your business is located. These additional reports and tax forms may include state (SWH) and local (LWH) withholding tax reports, state unemployment tax reports (SUTA), and a report for workers' compensation (WCOMP) payments. Figure 12-8 provides the information needed to prepare some of these reports. For example, the column titled Transfers From Payroll-SWH shows that $453.00 was withheld from employee wages for state withholding. You have not recorded this entry in your register; however, it would be handled in the same manner as the payments to the IRS when the check is sent to the state taxing unit. You will also need to monitor individual employees' gross earnings when completing several of the other forms, just as you did when you completed Form 941. Determining the total earnings for an employee for a given time period and determining your FUTA and SUTA contributions will be discussed in the section "Other Annual Tax Forms and Reports" later in this chapter.

Preparing W-2 Forms

At the end of the year you must give each employee who worked for you during the year a W-2 form. In the example developed here, assume that John Smith left your business at the end of March and received no further paychecks. The Payroll report prepared in this case is customized for John Smith and only uses the ANB Business account register. You will tell Quicken to limit the report preparation to the business account register since this is the account from which you write your payroll checks. Thus, all the information concerning John Smith's earnings are included in this account.

Starting from the Main Menu of the ANB Business account register, complete the following steps to gather information to complete John Smith's W-2 form:

1. Type **3** to select Reports.

2. Type **2** to select the Business Reports item.

3. Type **6** and the Payroll Report window appears.

4. Type **Payroll Report-John Smith**. Press ⌜DEL⌟ three times and press ⌜ENTER⌟.

5. Type **1/91** and press ⌜ENTER⌟.

6. Type **12/91** and press ⌜F9⌟. The Filter Report Transactions window appears.

Notice that Quicken automatically limits all Payroll reports to Payroll category transactions, as shown by the line "Category matches: PAYROLL.." Earlier in the chapter it was noted that this feature of Quicken required you to record all payroll activity in the Payroll category. Otherwise, Quicken's Payroll report will not gather your payroll transactions in this report. In that case you would need to prepare your reports from the Summary Report option.

7. Type **John Smith** and press (CTRL)-(ENTER). You are returned to the Payroll Report window.

You have filtered the Quicken report so that it will only include the payroll information for John Smith.

8. Press (F8) and the Create Summary Report window appears.

9. Press (ENTER) five times, type **C**, and press (ENTER). The Payroll report appears on your screen.

This restricts the report preparation to the ANB Business account, on which all payroll checks were written.

10. Press (F8) and the Print Report window appears.

11. Select the appropriate setting for your printer and press (ENTER).

The Payroll report shown in Figure 12-10 provides the payroll history for John Smith in 1991. (Again, this report must be printed in two sections unless you have a wide-carriage printer.) Although you have not entered the entire year's payroll transactions for Mary McFaul, the same steps would generate her W-2 information as well.

REPORT DISCUSSION   The Payroll report can be used to complete the following lines of the W-2 Wage and Tax Statement:
Line 9   The Transfers From Payroll-FWH column shows that $771.00 was the amount of federal income tax withheld during the year.
Line 10   The first column, Gross Earnings, shows that John Smith earned $6,000.00 during the year.
Line 11   The Transfers From Payroll-FICA column shows that $459.00 was withheld for FICA contributions.
Line 12   The first column, Gross Earnings, can be used to complete this line. Remember, FICA contributions are limited to the first $50,400.00 of earnings. For this reason you need to monitor the earnings of any employee likely to make more than that to determine when they exceed the earnings limit.
This may seem difficult. However, you can use the steps previously described to bring an employee's payroll summary (year-to-date) to the screen before preparing the paycheck. This will indicate whether FICA should be withheld for the paycheck you are writing. This procedure also should be

```
                        Payroll Report - John Smith
                          1/ 1/91 Through 12/31/91
       BUSINESS-ANB Business                                        Page 1
       8/ 4/91
                        INC/EXP         INC/EXP         INC/EXP       INC/EXP
                        EXPENSES        EXPENSES        EXPENSES      EXPENSES
                        Payroll Expens Payroll Expens Payroll Expens   TOTAL
             Payee      Gross Earnings Payroll Taxes      TOTAL
       -------------  --------------- --------------- --------------- ---------------
       John Smith          6,000.00          459.00        6,459.00      6,459.00
                     =============== =============== =============== ===============


                        Payroll Report - John Smith
                          1/ 1/91 Through 12/31/91
       BUSINESS-ANB Business                                        Page 2
       8/ 4/91
                        INC/EXP        TRANSFERS       TRANSFERS       TRANSFERS
                         TOTAL           FROM            FROM            FROM
                                     Payroll-FWH Payroll-FICA-C Payroll-FICA
             Payee
       -------------  --------------- --------------- --------------- ---------------
       John Smith         -6,459.00          771.00          459.00        459.00
                     =============== =============== =============== ===============


                        Payroll Report - John Smith
                          1/ 1/91 Through 12/31/91
       BUSINESS-ANB Business                                        Page 3
       8/ 4/91
                        TRANSFERS       TRANSFERS        OVERALL
                          FROM           TOTAL            TOTAL
                        Payroll-SWH
             Payee
       -------------  --------------- --------------- ---------------
       John Smith            156.00        1,845.00       -4,614.00
                     =============== =============== ===============
```

FIGURE 12-10. Annual Payroll report for John Smith (in three sections)

used to determine when the earnings limit of $7,000.00 has been reached for each employee for purposes of preparing your FUTA and SUTA reports, discussed in the previous sections.

Line 24 The Transfers From Payroll-SWH column shows that $156.00 was withheld for state income taxes during the year.

Line 25 The first column, Gross Earnings, can be used to complete this line.

Lines 27 and 28 In this example there were no local taxes due. If you do business in an area where local income taxes are withheld you can easily modify this example to record the appropriate amounts.

Other Annual Tax Forms and Reports

The information provided in the preceding reports can also be used to prepare other year-end tax reports. For example, Payroll reports for the full year, similar to those shown in Figures 12-8 and 12-10, can be used to complete sections of the following reports:

- Form W-3, Transmittal on Income and Tax Statements

- Form 940, Employer's Annual Federal Unemployment (FUTA) Tax Return

- Various state and local withholding and state unemployment tax (SUTA) reports

FUTA AND SUTA CONTRIBUTIONS In the "Recording April Transactions" section you recorded entries on 4/15/91 for your FUTA and SUTA contributions. When completing your quarterly and annual reports you can use Quicken's Filter option to prepare a report showing the total FUTA and SUTA contributions paid during the quarter or year. This would be accomplished by preparing a Payroll report and using Quicken's Filter Report Transaction window to complete the Memo matches: field with FUTA. Then prepare a second report and complete the Memo matches: field with SUTA. Figures 12-11 and 12-12 show filtered reports prepared from your account register using the Memo filter to show FUTA payments of $104.00 and SUTA payments of $520.00.

```
                        FUTA Payments
                  1/ 1/91 Through 4/30/91
          BUSINESS-ANB Business              Page 1
          8/ 4/91
                                          INC/EXP
                                          EXPENSES
                                    Payroll Expens
                       Payee        Payroll Taxes
          ------------------------- --------------
          Internal Revenue Service        104.00
                                    ==============
```

FIGURE 12-11. Report showing FUTA payments

```
                       SUTA Payments
                  1/ 1/91 Through 4/30/91
        BUSINESS-All Accounts                    Page 1
        8/ 4/91
                                                INC/EXP
                                                EXPENSES
                                          Payroll Expens
                    Payee                 Payroll Taxes
        ------------------------------  ---------------
        Bureau of Employment Services            520.00
                                        ===============
```

FIGURE 12-12.   Report showing SUTA payments

Reports filtered in this manner can be prepared to determine the total federal and state payments for unemployment withholding during the entire year. That information could then be used in completing Part II, Line 4 of federal Form 940 and the appropriate line of your state's SUTA form.

FORM 1099   The last payroll-related statement discussed here is Form 1099. You must provide a Form 1099 to all individuals who are not regular employees and to whom you have paid more than $600.00 during the tax year. The easiest way to record transactions for payments of this nature is to type **1099** in the Memo field when you record the transactions in your business account register during the year. You can then prepare a Transaction report for the year filtered by Payee and Memo field matches to gather the information needed to prepare 1099s for each payee. If you are not certain of all the payees to whom you have paid miscellaneous income, you may want to filter the Memo field for 1099 first and print all these transactions. You can then use that information to group your 1099 information by Payee matches.

chapter 13

PREPARING BUDGET REPORTS AND CASH FLOW STATEMENTS

Developing a Financial Management Program
Quicken's Budgeting Process
Modifying the Budget Report
Budget Report Extension
Preparing a Cash Flow Report

Operating a successful business involves more than just having a good product or service to sell to customers or clients; you also need to develop a financial management program that will allow your business to grow and develop. Financial management is more than just being able to prepare the basic reports your banker or other creditors request; it includes a plan of action that will show your creditors you are prepared to manage your business in a changing environment. This means you need to start considering developing a program to manage the finances of your business. Your program would consist of the following:

- A business plan
- The development of strong business relations with your banker or other creditors
- The use of budgets and cash flow statements to help in managing your financial resources

In order to develop a financial management program you need a sound accounting system that will provide the financial information you need to make better management decisions. Quicken can help you generate this type of information for your business.

DEVELOPING A FINANCIAL MANAGEMENT PROGRAM

If you look closely at the parts of the financial management program just listed, you will notice that two of the three parts do not directly involve the accounting system. Let's take a more in-depth look at the program components.

A business plan is a well-developed concept of where your business has been and where it is going. The special section entitled Preparing a Business Plan highlights the key points that should be covered in a business plan. You can see that nonfinancial considerations play a major role in your business plan—that is, you need to know your product and potential market before you can begin to budget sales and cost for your business. The budget process you follow in this chapter will demonstrate how budgeting and cash flow statements are prepared. More importantly, you will see that the decisions you make in estimating budget income and expenses come from nonfinancial considerations. In short, developing a business plan will force you to think through your business, both financially and operationally, which, in the long run, will make it easier for you to estimate the expected sales and related costs.

The importance of developing strong relations with your banker and creditors cannot be underestimated. However, a word of caution is needed here. Don't expect a bank to finance a new business for you. A good banker is going to expect you to provide a significant part of the capital needed. You might think that you wouldn't need the banker if you had the money to finance your ideas. But from the banker's perspective, it isn't good business to risk the bank's money if you aren't willing to invest your own capital.

PREPARING A BUSINESS PLAN

T I P

If you have never prepared a business plan before, it can be difficult to determine what to include. Your goal should be to create a concise document that presents a realistic picture of your company, its needs, assets, and products. Outside lenders will be especially interested in the financial history and resources of the firm and your sales projections. Be sure to include the following as you prepare your plan:

- A brief overview of your firm, its products, and its financing requirements. It is important to keep this short and simple.

- A brief history of the firm, including product successes and copyrights or patents held. Include a resume of the firm's owners or partners.

- A short description of your product(s). Include information on the competition, production plans, and prices.

- A description of the market for the product(s) and your distribution plans.

- Sales and cost projections showing current capital and financing requirements.

The special section entitled Sources of Funding shows some alternate ways of obtaining financing for your business if a bank is not a realistic source of cash. An important point to remember is that you need to maintain a strong relationship with your banker over the long term. Although you may not need a loan now, you could in the future. One way of doing this is to obtain a modest bank loan when your business is prospering. This would help strengthen the relationship you have with your bank, and then when you really need a loan, your banker will already be familiar with you and your business activities. This might make the difference between loan approval or rejection.

The final part of the financial management program is the use of budgets and the regular monitoring of your cash flow. A budget is a plan in which you estimate the income and expenses of your business for a period of time: week, month, quarter, year, or longer. Creating a budget report requires some advance work since you enter projected amounts for each category in the budget. Quicken guides you through the budget development process to minimize the work required. Then, you can enter your income and expenses

SOURCES OF FUNDING

T

I

P

It can be difficult to secure financing for a new business even if you have a good product. Banks are often wary of lending money for a new venture unless you are willing to take the high-risk position of offering your home or other assets as collateral. Some other financing options you might consider are

- A commercial bank loan under the Small Business Administration Loan Guarantee Program

- Borrowing against your life insurance policy

- Short-term borrowing through supplier credit extensions

- Finance companies

- Venture capitalists; you must normally give up a part of the ownership of your business with this option

- Small Business Investment Enterprises

- Economically disadvantaged groups or minority businesses may have other options for public or private funding

and check the status of your actual and budgeted amounts whenever you wish. You can also use your budget figures to project your business's future cash flow. This type of information is valuable in forecasting loans you may need and demonstrates to your banker that you are anticipating your financial needs. This is a sign of sound business and financial planning.

A cash flow report is related to your budget and allows you to look at the inflow and outflow of cash for your business. This report is valuable since it can enable you to identify problems stemming from a lack of available cash, even though your business may be highly profitable at the current time.

In this chapter you will learn how to use Quicken in the preparation of a business budget. Remember the concepts discussed here as you go through the example; you are learning more than just the procedures involved. Budgeting and cash flow statement analysis can give you and your creditors important information. Quicken provides the necessary ingredients to help you prepare a financial management program that will make you a better business manager.

In the chapter example you will prepare budget entries for several months. Transaction groups from Chapters 11 and 12 will be used to expedite the entry process while providing enough transactions to get a sense of what Quicken can do. After making your entries you will see how Quicken's standard Budget and Cash Flow reports can help you keep expenses in line with your budget.

QUICKEN'S BUDGETING PROCESS

Quicken allows you to enter projected income and expense levels for any category. You can enter the same projection for each month of the year or choose to change the amount allocated by month. For the business in this example, it is essential to be able to enter different budget amounts each month, especially for the projected income figures. Royalties are received at the end of each quarter, which causes some months to show a zero income in this category. Also, some other income generating activities are seasonal and vary widely between months.

Once you have entered the budget amounts, Quicken matches your planned expenses with the actual expense entries and displays the results in a Budget report. Although there is only one entry point for budget information, Quicken will collect the actual entries from all of your bank, cash, and credit card accounts in the current account group. Therefore, if you have not paid any business expenses from your personal checking account you may want to exclude this account from the Budget report. You can do this by selecting the accounts to use with the report. However, since in this example you have paid both personal and business expenses from the ANB Personal account you cannot exclude it here. Instead, you will use the class code of B to select all business transactions when preparing reports in this chapter.

Although Quicken can take much of the work out of entering and managing your budget, it cannot prepare a budget without your projections. Once you have put together a plan, it is time to record your decisions in Quicken. You can enter Quicken's budgeting process through the Main Menu (selecting the Reports option) or through the Reports menu from the account register or Write/Print Checks options. The process described in the next section assumes that you are at the Main Menu. Quicken's budgeting process will be presented in four stages: entering the monthly budget report menu, specifying budget amounts, entering the monthly detail, if required, and entering expense projections and printing the report.

The Budget Report Menu

The budget report is the starting place for the entry of budget amounts. It may seem a little strange to request a report when you have not yet specified your plan, but you must make this selection to enter Quicken's budgeting program. In fact, it will not allow you to create a budget report until you have made your budget entries.

1. From the Main Menu type **3**. The Reports menu will appear on your screen.

2. Type **7** and the Creat Budget Report window will appear on your screen.

3. Type **Johnson & Associates - Budget Report** and press (ENTER).

This is an optional entry since you can press (ENTER) to accept the default title, BUDGET REPORT. When you choose to customize the title you are limited to 39 characters.

4. Type **1/1/91** and press (ENTER).

You must identify the dates you want to use for a budget beginning and ending on your reports. The 1/1/91 entry matches the first month of income and expense entries you completed in Chapter 11.

5. Type **3/31/91** and press (ENTER). Your screen will look like that shown in Figure 13-1.

Again, the 3/31/91 entry is appropriate for the data from Chapters 11 and 12. All transactions with dates between these beginning and ending dates would eventually be included in the budget report—provided budget entries had been made for all the categories transactions had been assigned to.

6. Press (CTRL)-(ENTER) and an error message stating that you must supply budgeted amounts before the report can be produced will display.

7. Press (ESC) and Quicken will return you to the Create Budget Report window.

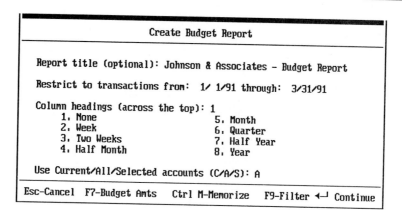

```
                          Create Budget Report

    Report title (optional): Johnson & Associates - Budget Report

    Restrict to transactions from:  1/ 1/91 through:  3/31/91

    Column headings (across the top): 1
          1. None                     5. Month
          2. Week                     6. Quarter
          3. Two Weeks                7. Half Year
          4. Half Month               8. Year

    Use Current/All/Selected accounts (C/A/S): A

  Esc-Cancel  F7-Budget Amts   Ctrl M-Memorize   F9-Filter ↵ Continue
```

BUSINESS-ANB Business

=== **FIGURE 13-1.**   Create Budget Report window with title and date
fields completed

The next section will describe the procedure for entering budget amounts
in Quicken categories.

Specifying Budget Amounts

You will be entering budget amounts for the categories you entered in the
ANB Business account register in Chapters 11 and 12. Later, when you
create your own budget, you will need to expand the budget entries to
include all the categories of income and expense you wish to monitor.

There are four points (as discussed in Chapter 7) to consider before you
complete the budget entries. First, you must enter a budget amount for each
category you want included in your budget report.

Second, all the categories in your category list are accessible in the
Quicken Specify Budget Amounts window, shown in Figure 13-2. This includes Quicken's predefined categories selected in Chapter 11, as well as any

```
                        Specify Budget Amounts
┌──────────────────────────────────────────────────────────────────────┐
│                                                    Budget    Monthly   │
│   Category         Type        Description         Amount    Detail    │
├──────────────────────────────────────────────────────────────────────┤
│ ▶ Bonus           │Inc │Bonus Income        │              │           │
│   Canada Pen      │Inc │Canadian Pension    │              │           │
│   Div Income      │Inc │Dividend Income     │              │           │
│   Family Allow    │Inc │Family Allowance    │              │           │
│   Gift Received   │Inc │Gift Received       │              │           │
│   Gr Sales        │Inc │Gross Sales         │              │           │
│   Inc Art         │Inc │Article Income      │              │           │
│   Inc Cons        │Inc │Consulting Income   │              │           │
│   Inc Roy         │Inc │Royalty Income      │              │           │
│   Int Inc         │Inc │Interest Income     │              │           │
│   Invest Inc      │Inc │Investment Income   │              │           │
│   Old Age Pension │Inc │Old Age Pension     │              │           │
├──────────────────────────────────────────────────────────────────────┤
│                          ↑,↓ Select                                    │
│  Esc-Cancel        F1-Help    Ctrl-E Edit Monthly Detail   Ctrl◄─┘ Done│
└──────────────────────────────────────────────────────────────────────┘
BUSINESS-ANB Business
```

FIGURE 13-2. Specify Budget Amounts window before budget amounts are entered

new categories added in the account register. If you leave the budget amount blank for any category when completing this window, the category will not be shown on the Budget report. This means that if you want a budget category to be included because you will be using it later in the year or in future years, you must type zero for the category to be included in the current report.

Third, you only set monthly budget amounts once. Quicken will then assume that the amount established should be used as the budget amount for all future months, unless you modify it.

Fourth, you can only assign budget amounts to income and expense categories. You cannot assign budget amounts to subcategories.

To set the budget amounts follow these steps:

1. Press **F7** to select Edit the Budget Amounts.

Since the Create Budget Report window is still on the screen, Quicken will interpret this command as a desire to enter budget figures and open the Specify Budget Amounts window. Normally, you would enter realistic amounts from your budget plan. In this exercise you will enter the budget amounts provided.

2. Press (**DOWN ARROW**) until the Quicken arrow cursor is next to the Inc Art category, as shown in Figure 13-3.

3. The cursor should be blinking in the Budget Amount column. Type **2000** and press (**ENTER**).

4. Type **10000** and press (**ENTER**) to create an entry for Inc Cons.

5. Type **3500** and press (**ENTER**) to create an entry for Inc Roy.

Quicken has now created monthly budget amounts for all three income categories for the amounts that you entered. Since income is not generated at the same level each month, you will need to make some revisions in the monthly detail.

Entering Monthly Detail for Budget Categories

Although Quicken generates the same entry for each month in the budget year, you can edit any entry to change the amount. With the arrow cursor on the category you want to edit, press (**CTRL**)-(**E**) and make the change. Follow these steps to edit the detail entries for each of the income categories previously entered:

1. Move the arrow cursor to Inc Art and press (**CTRL**)-(**E**).

2. Press (**HOME**) to move the cursor to Jan.

3. Type **50.00** and press (**ENTER**).

4. Repeat step 3 two more times to replace the entries for February and March.

5. Type **3575.00** for the April amount and press (**ENTER**).

6. Repeat step 5 to enter the same amount for the next month.

7. Move the cursor to Jul and type **3575.00**. Your screen will look like Figure 13-3.

8. Press (**CTRL**)-(**ENTER**) to return to the Specify Budget Amounts window. The arrow cursor should be pointing at the next category, Inc Cons.

9. Press (**CTRL**)-(**E**) to open the Monthly Budget For Category window.

10. Move the cursor to Jul.

```
                    Specify Budget Amounts
    ┌──────────────────────────────────────────────┬──────────┐
    │           Monthly Budget For Category: Inc Art│ Monthly  │
    │ Category                                      │ Detail   │
    ├──────────┬  Jan:50.00                         │          │
    │ Bonus       Feb:50.00                         │          │
    │ Canada Pen  Mar:50.00                         │          │
    │ Div Income  Apr:3,575.00                      │          │
    │ Family Allow May:3,575.00                     │          │
    │ Gift Receive Jun:2,000.00                     │          │
    │ Gr Sales    Jul:3,575.00                      │          │
    │▶ Inc Art    Aug:2,000.00                      │  .00     │
    │ Inc Cons    Sep:2,000.00                      │  .00     │
    │ Inc Roy     Oct:2,000.00                      │  .00     │
    │ Int Inc     Nov:2,000.00                      │          │
    │ Invest Inc  Dec:2,000.00                      │          │
    │ Old Age Pens                                  │          │
    │            Esc-Cancel   F9-Fill w/Amt  ↵ Continue        │
    └──────────────────────────────────────────────┴──────────┘
```

BUSINESS-ANB Business

FIGURE 13-3. Monthly budget detail for Inc Art

11. Type **12000.00**.
12. Press **F9** to fill the remaining months with this new entry.
13. Press **CTRL**-**ENTER** to return to the Specify Budget Amounts window.
14. Press **CTRL**-**E**.
15. Press **HOME** to move the cursor to Jan.
16. Type **0.00** and press **F9**.

This deletes the amount for each month and leaves a blank for every month. The result you want to finally achieve is shown in Figure 13-4. Since royalty income is received quarterly, only four months will have an amount entered; the other eight will be blank. As you can see, changing all the entries to blanks is faster than editing the entries for 12 months individually. Now you can enter the amounts for the months in which quarterly payments will be received.

17. Move the cursor to Mar, type **10000.00** and press **ENTER**.
18. Move the cursor to Jun, type **10000.00**, again, and press **ENTER**.
19. Move the cursor to Sep, type **10000.00**, and press **ENTER**.

```
┌──────────────────────────────────────────────────────────────┐
│                    Specify Budget Amounts                       │
│              ┌───────────────────────────────────┐   Monthly    │
│              │ Monthly Budget For Category: Inc Roy│   Detail    │
│   Category   ├───────────────────────────────────┤             │
│              │ Jan:                              │             │
│  Bonus       │ Feb:                              │             │
│  Canada Pen  │ Mar:10,000.00                     │             │
│  Div Income  │ Apr:                              │             │
│  Family Allow│ May:                              │             │
│  Gift Receive│ Jun:10,000.00                     │             │
│  Gr Sales    │ Jul:                              │             │
│  Inc Art     │ Aug:                              │  .00   Yes  │
│  Inc Cons    │ Sep:10,000.00                     │  .00   Yes  │
│ ▶ Inc Roy    │ Oct:                              │  .00   Yes  │
│  Int Inc     │ Nov:                              │             │
│  Invest Inc  │ Dec:10,000.00                     │             │
│  Old Age Pens├───────────────────────────────────┤             │
│              │ Esc-Cancel   F9-Fill w/Amt  ←┘ Continue│         │
└──────────────────────────────────────────────────────────────┘
```

BUSINESS-ANB Business

FIGURE 13-4. Monthly budget detail for Inc Roy

20. Finally, move the cursor to Dec, type **10000.00** (your screen should now look like Figure 13-4). Next press CTRL-ENTER.

You have now created detailed entries by month for three Quicken categories. Your screen should look similar to Figure 13-5. It may not match exactly since Quicken selects the monthly amount to display for each category based on the month of your current system date. This screen was prepared in August. Since the figures vary by month you may have a different number displayed in this screen, but your detail and end results should match exactly.

If you were to create a budget report at this time Quicken would produce the report showing actual and budgeted income for the first three months of the year. You can enter detail for all of your categories in subsequent sessions, but the remaining entries in this chapter will be added at the summary level.

Entering Expense Projections and Printing the Report

To complete your budget picture you need to enter projections for your expense categories or they will not appear on your budget report. Using the

```
╔══════════════════════════════════════════════════════════════╗
║                    Specify Budget Amounts                      ║
╟──────────────────────────────────────────────────────────────╢
║                                                Budget  Monthly ║
║     Category      Type      Description        Amount   Detail ║
╟──────────────────────────────────────────────────────────────╢
║  Bonus            Inc  Bonus Income                            ║
║  Canada Pen       Inc  Canadian Pension                        ║
║  Div Income       Inc  Dividend Income                         ║
║  Family Allow     Inc  Family Allowance                        ║
║  Gift Received    Inc  Gift Received                           ║
║  Gr Sales         Inc  Gross Sales                             ║
║  Inc Art          Inc  Article Income      2,000.00     Yes    ║
║  Inc Cons         Inc  Consulting Income  12,000.00     Yes    ║
║  Inc Roy          Inc  Royalty Income          0.00     Yes    ║
║ ► Int Inc         Inc  Interest Income                         ║
║  Invest Inc       Inc  Investment Income                       ║
║  Old Age Pension  Inc  Old Age Pension                         ║
╟──────────────────────────────────────────────────────────────╢
║                         ↑,↓ Select                             ║
║  Esc-Cancel      F1-Help    Ctrl-E Edit Monthly Detail  Ctrl↵ Done ║
╚══════════════════════════════════════════════════════════════╝
BUSINESS-ANB Business
```

FIGURE 13-5. Specify Budget Amounts window after entering monthly detail

information provided, complete the Budget Amount column for the categories. Remember the process involves using UP ARROW or DOWN ARROW to move the arrow cursor to a category, typing the budget amount shown in the list, and pressing ENTER. Follow these steps to complete the entries and produce the report.

1. Enter the following amounts for the categories shown:

Description	Category	Budget Amount
Computer Supplies	SuppComp	210
Dues	Dues	25
Equipment	Equipment	500
Equipment Maintenance	EquipMnt	100
Freight	Freight	20
Insurance	Insurance	50

Description	Category	Budget Amount
Miscellaneous	Misc	25
Office Expenses	Office	80
Overnight Delivery	Del Overngt	200
Payroll Expense	Payroll	5,500
Postage Expense	Postage	10
Social Security Tax	Tax FICA	150
Supplies	Supplies	50
Telephone Expense	Telephone	120
Travel Expenses	Travel	300
Water, Gas, Electric	Utilities	60

2. Press (CTRL)-(ENTER) after completing the last entry.

3. Press (F9). The Filter Report Transactions window appears on your screen.

4. Press (ENTER) three times and type **B** in the Class matches field, as shown in Figure 13-6.

5. Press (CTRL)-(ENTER).

6. Press (CTRL)-(ENTER) and the Budget report appears on your screen.

7. Press (F8) and the Print Report window will open. Select your printer and press (CTRL)-(ENTER). The report shown in Figure 13-7 will print.

If you need to change printer settings, refer to Chapter 3. If your printer has compressed print capabilities you may want to use that setting when printing reports to capture more of your report on each page. For example, your monthly report will be printed across two pages unless you use the compressed print feature.

REPORT DISCUSSION Let's take a look at the report shown in Figure 13-7. The report compares the actual expenditures made during the quarter with those you budgeted. An analysis of the income section shows you received more income than you budgeted during the period. This was due to receiving more in consulting income than anticipated, although you received

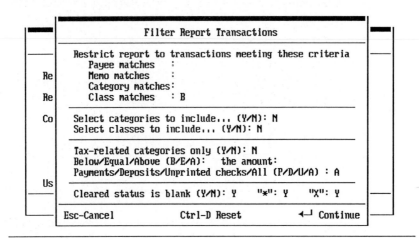

```
                    Filter Report Transactions

        Restrict report to transactions meeting these criteria
              Payee matches    :
   Re         Memo matches     :
              Category matches:
   Re         Class matches    : B

   Co   Select categories to include... (Y/N): N
        Select classes to include... (Y/N): N

        Tax-related categories only (Y/N): N
        Below/Equal/Above (B/E/A):    the amount:
        Payments/Deposits/Unprinted checks/All (P/D/U/A) : A
   Us
        Cleared status is blank (Y/N): Y    "*": Y    "X": Y

        Esc-Cancel          Ctrl-D Reset         ↵ Continue
```

BUSINESS-ANB Business

FIGURE 13-6.   Use of a filter to select only business transactions

no income from articles. You would want to examine whether these differences were caused by failing to project all the consulting activities you were involved in during the quarter, or perhaps the difference was caused by a client paying you earlier than you had anticipated.

The expense portion of the report shows the actual and budgeted expenses for the period. An analysis of individual categories is not worthwhile since the data you entered did not include expense entries for all the months in the report. However, you can see that the report compares budgeted with actual expenses during the period and shows the differences in the Diff column. In general, you are concerned with all the differences shown in this report, but you will probably only want to spend your time investigating the large dollar differences between budgeted and actual amounts. For example, you might decide to investigate in detail only those budget differences that exceed $300.00. For these categories you might want to examine the underlying transactions in more depth.

The essence of budgeting is to determine where potential problems exist in your business and detect them early. Quicken's budget reporting capabilities can help you in making these business decisions.

```
                    Johnson & Associates - Budget Report
                        1/ 1/91 Through 3/31/91
      BUSINESS-All Accounts
      8/ 4/91                                                        Page 1

                                    1/ 1/91      -      3/31/91
                Category Description    Actual     Budget    Diff
                --------------------  ------------------------------------

      INCOME/EXPENSE
       INCOME
          Article Income                0.00      150.00     -150.00
          Consulting Income        37,500.00   30,000.00    7,500.00
          Royalty Income           10,000.00   10,000.00        0.00
                                   ----------  ----------  ----------
       TOTAL INCOME                47,500.00   40,150.00    7,350.00

       EXPENSES
          Computer Supplies           375.76      630.00     -254.24
          Dues                          0.00       75.00      -75.00
          Equipment Maintenance     1,100.00      300.00      800.00
          Freight                       0.00       60.00      -60.00
          Insurance                     0.00      150.00     -150.00
          Miscellaneous                 0.00       75.00      -75.00
          Office Expenses               0.00      240.00     -240.00
          Overnight Delivery          270.00      600.00     -330.00
          Payroll Expense          16,147.50   16,500.00     -352.50
          Postage Expense              28.00       30.00       -2.00
          Social Security Tax           0.00      450.00     -450.00
          Supplies                     65.00      150.00      -85.00
          Telephone Expense           305.00      360.00      -55.00
          Travel Expenses             905.00      900.00        5.00
          Water, Gas, Electric         47.40      180.00     -132.60
                                   ----------  ----------  ----------
       TOTAL EXPENSES              19,243.66   20,700.00   -1,456.34


                                   ----------  ----------  ----------
       TOTAL INCOME/EXPENSE        28,256.34   19,450.00    8,806.34

      TRANSFERS
        TO Equipment               -1,500.00   -1,500.00        0.00
                                   ----------  ----------  ----------
      TOTAL TRANSFERS              -1,500.00   -1,500.00        0.00


                                   ----------  ----------  ----------
      OVERALL TOTAL                26,756.34   17,950.00    8,806.34
                                   ==========  ==========  ==========
```

FIGURE 13-7. Budget report for the first quarter of 1991

MODIFYING THE BUDGET REPORT

In the early stages of budgeting, it will generally take several months to develop sound estimates for all your expense categories. You can change your projections at any time by selecting Budget item from the Reports menu and using ⟨F7⟩ to edit the budget amounts before printing the report. You can also modify the report you just created to show different time periods or a selected group of accounts. Follow these steps to look at a monthly budget report for the same time period:

1. From the Main Menu type **3** and then **7**.

2. Press ⟨ENTER⟩ three times to accept Johnson & Associates - Budget Report as the title and 1/1/91 through 3/31/91 as the time period.

3. Type **5**, and press ⟨ENTER⟩ again. This tells Quicken you want a monthly report prepared.

4. Press ⟨F9⟩ (Filter).

5. Press ⟨ENTER⟩ three times.

6. Type **B** in the Class matches field and press ⟨CTRL⟩-⟨ENTER⟩.

7. Type **A** to choose all accounts and press ⟨ENTER⟩. The modified report will appear on your screen.

8. Press ⟨F8⟩ and the Print Report window will open. Select your printer, press ⟨CTRL⟩-⟨ENTER⟩, and the report will be printed. Since this report is too wide for one page, Figure 13-8 is split across two pages.

BUDGET REPORT EXTENSION

The reports prepared so far in this chapter give you an overview of the budget report preparation process by comparing budget to actual expenditures for the first quarter of 1991. For your own situation you need to extend the budget over a longer period. It is impractical to enter transactions for all of the included categories at this time, but you can still look at a report for a year, with budget and actual amounts shown monthly. To try working with a larger report, follow these steps from the Main Menu:

1. Type **3** and then **5** and the Create Budget Report window will open.

Johnson & Associates - Budget Report
1/ 1/91 Through 3/31/91

BUSINESS-All Accounts
8/ 4/91
Page 1

Category Description	1/ 1/91 Actual	- Budget	1/31/91 Diff	2/ 1/91 Actual	- Budget	2/28/91 Diff	3/ 1/91 Actual	- Budget
INCOME/EXPENSE								
INCOME								
Article Income	0.00	50.00	-50.00	0.00	50.00	-50.00	0.00	50.00
Consulting Income	12,500.00	10,000.00	2,500.00	0.00	10,000.00	-10,000.00	25,000.00	10,000.00
Royalty Income	0.00	0.00	0.00	0.00	0.00	0.00	10,000.00	10,000.00
TOTAL INCOME	12,500.00	10,050.00	2,450.00	0.00	10,050.00	-10,050.00	35,000.00	20,050.00
EXPENSES								
Computer Supplies	375.76	210.00	165.76	0.00	210.00	-210.00	0.00	210.00
Dues	0.00	25.00	-25.00	0.00	25.00	-25.00	0.00	25.00
Equipment Maintenance	1,100.00	100.00	1,000.00	0.00	100.00	-100.00	0.00	100.00
Freight	0.00	20.00	-20.00	0.00	20.00	-20.00	0.00	20.00
Insurance	0.00	50.00	-50.00	0.00	50.00	-50.00	0.00	50.00
Miscellaneous	0.00	25.00	-25.00	0.00	25.00	-25.00	0.00	25.00
Office Expenses	0.00	80.00	-80.00	0.00	80.00	-80.00	0.00	80.00
Overnight Delivery	270.00	200.00	70.00	0.00	200.00	-200.00	0.00	200.00
Payroll Expense	5,382.50	5,500.00	-117.50	5,382.00	5,500.00	-117.50	5,382.50	5,500.00
Postage Expense	28.00	10.00	18.00	0.00	10.00	-10.00	0.00	10.00
Social Security Tax	0.00	150.00	-150.00	0.00	150.00	-150.00	0.00	150.00
Supplies	65.00	50.00	15.00	0.00	50.00	-50.00	0.00	50.00
Telephone Expense	305.00	120.00	185.00	0.00	120.00	-120.00	0.00	120.00
Travel Expenses	905.00	300.00	605.00	0.00	300.00	-300.00	0.00	300.00
Water, Gas, Electric	24.00	60.00	-36.00	23.40	60.00	-36.60	0.00	60.00
TOTAL EXPENSES	8,455.26	6,900.00	1,555.26	5,405.90	6,900.00	-1,494.10	5,382.50	6,900.00
TOTAL INCOME/EXPENSE	4,044.74	3,150.00	894.74	-5,405.90	3,150.00	-8,555.90	29,617.50	13,150.00
TRANSFERS								
TO Equipment	-1,500.00	-500.00	-1,000.00	0.00	-500.00	500.00	0.00	-500.00
TOTAL TRANSFERS	-1,500.00	-500.00	-1,000.00	0.00	-500.00	500.00	0.00	-500.00
OVERALL TOTAL	2,544.74	2,650.00	-105.26	-5,405.90	2,650.00	-8,055.90	29,617.50	12,650.00

FIGURE 13-8. Budget Report by Month for the first quarter of 1991

```
                    Johnson & Associates - Budget Report
                         1/ 1/91 Through 3/31/91
                                                                    Page  2
BUSINESS-All Accounts
8/ 4/91
                            3/31/91         1/ 1/91                 3/31/91
    Category Description       Diff          Actual      Budget      Diff
    -------------------      --------       ---------    -------     -------
INCOME/EXPENSE
  INCOME
    Article Income            -50.00           0.00       150.00     -150.00
    Consulting Income      15,000.00      37,500.00    30,000.00    7,500.00
    Royalty Income              0.00      10,000.00    10,000.00        0.00
                            --------       ---------    -------     -------
  TOTAL INCOME            14,950.00      47,500.00    40,150.00    7,350.00

  EXPENSES
    Computer Supplies        -210.00         375.76       630.00     -254.24
    Dues                      -25.00           0.00        75.00      -75.00
    Equipment Maintenance    -100.00       1,100.00       300.00      800.00
    Freight                   -20.00           0.00        60.00      -60.00
    Insurance                 -50.00           0.00       150.00     -150.00
    Miscellaneous             -25.00           0.00        75.00      -75.00
    Office Expenses           -80.00           0.00       240.00     -240.00
    Overnight Delivery       -200.00         270.00       600.00     -330.00
    Payroll Expense          -117.50      16,147.50    16,500.00     -352.50
    Postage Expense           -10.00          28.00        30.00       -2.00
    Social Security Tax      -150.00           0.00       450.00     -450.00
    Supplies                  -50.00          65.00       150.00      -85.00
    Telephone Expense        -120.00         305.00       360.00      -55.00
    Travel Expenses          -300.00         905.00       900.00        5.00
    Water, Gas, Electric      -60.00          47.40       180.00     -132.60
                            --------       ---------    -------     -------
  TOTAL EXPENSES          -1,517.50      19,243.66    20,700.00   -1,456.34
                            --------       ---------    -------     -------
TOTAL INCOME/EXPENSE     16,467.50      28,256.34    19,450.00    8,806.34
                            --------       ---------    -------     -------
TRANSFERS
  TO Equipment              500.00      -1,500.00    -1,500.00        0.00
                            --------       ---------    -------     -------
TOTAL TRANSFERS            500.00      -1,500.00    -1,500.00        0.00
                            ========       =========    =======     =======
OVERALL TOTAL           16,967.50      26,756.34    17,950.00    8,806.34
                            ========       =========    =======     =======
```

FIGURE 13-8. Budget Report by Month for the first quarter of 1991 (*continued*)

2. Press ⌈ENTER⌉ to accept the current report title.

3. Type **1/1/91** and press ⌈ENTER⌉.

4. Type **12/31/91** and press ⌈ENTER⌉.

5. Type **5** to select Month for column headings and press ⌈ENTER⌉.

6. Press ⌈F9⌉ (Filter).

7. Press ⌈ENTER⌉ three times.

8. Type **B** in the Class matches field and press ⌈CTRL⌉-⌈ENTER⌉ to have Quicken select only business transactions.

9. Type **A** and press ⌈ENTER⌉.

The Budget Report by Month appears. Although there are no actual figures beyond the first few months you can follow the instructions in the next section to learn how you would look at a wide report like this on screen.

Wide-Screen Reports

The Monthly Budget report just generated spreads across more than one Quicken screen since it is wider than the screen width of 80 columns. It may be difficult to comprehend until you realize how it is structured. In this section you will explore the wide-screen report and become more familiar with Quicken results. The following discussion will help you become familiar with the Monthly Budget report generated from the additional data you entered.

Use ⌈TAB⌉, ⌈SHIFT⌉-⌈TAB⌉, ⌈PGUP⌉, ⌈PGDN⌉, ⌈HOME⌉, and ⌈END⌉ to navigate through the report and become familiar with the appearance of the wide screen for the budget report. Notice how easy it is to move around the report. ⌈HOME⌉ always returns you to the upper-left side of the wide-screen report; ⌈END⌉ takes you to the lower-right side of the report. ⌈TAB⌉ moves you right one screen and ⌈SHIFT⌉-⌈TAB⌉ moves you left one screen. ⌈PGUP⌉ moves you up, and ⌈PGDN⌉ down, one screen. Note that to open the Print Report window you only have to press ⌈F8⌉, as indicated at the lower-right corner of the screen.

If you have the compressed print option, it is recommended you use that setting to print wide reports. This printer option significantly increases the amount of material you can print on a page. When you print wide-screen reports, Quicken numbers the pages of the report so you can more easily follow on hard copy.

PREPARING A CASH FLOW REPORT

Quicken's Cash Flow report organizes your account information by cash inflow and outflow. In this example the results presented will be the same as the amounts in the budget. In Chapter 14 you will be introduced to depreciation expense, which would be shown on the budget report, but not on the Cash Flow report. This is because this expense does not require a cash outlay in the current year. Prepare a Cash Flow report for the first quarter by following these steps:

1. From the Main Menu, type **3** to select Reports.
2. Type **2** for Business.
3. Type **2** for Cash Flow.
4. Press (ENTER) to accept the default report title.
5. Type **1/91** and press (ENTER).
6. Type **3/91**.
7. Press (F8) to open the Create Summary Report window.
8. Press (F8) to open the Report Options window.

Notice that the Report Organization, option 2, is selected for Cash Flow Basis and that Transfers, option 3, is selected to include only transfers to accounts outside this report. Quicken selected these options by default when you selected the Cash Flow report. Notice that you can also select whether you want to display cents or subcategories and subclasses in your report.

9. Press (CTRL)-(ENTER) to accept the current settings.
10. Press (F9) to open the Filter Report Transactions window.
11. Press (ENTER) three times.
12. Type **B** in the Class matches field to restrict the report to business transactions.

This step is essential since you will need to include both ANB Personal and ANB Business in this report because business expenses were paid from both accounts. Without restricting the class to business, all of the personal expenses included in ANB Personal would appear on the report as well.

13. Press CTRL-ENTER.

14. Press ENTER five times to move to the Use Current/All/Selected Accounts field.

15. Type S and press ENTER. The Select Accounts to Include window appears.

16. Move the arrow cursor to Payroll-FICA and press SPACEBAR until Include appears in the Include in Report field.

17. Repeat step 16 until your screen appears the same as Figure 13-9. Payroll-FICA-CO, Payroll-FWH, and Payroll-SWH will be marked as include.

Equipment is excluded because Quicken does not show transfers between accounts included in the Cash Flow report. However, since the purchase of equipment involved the use of cash funds, that amount should be shown as a cash outflow. Quicken will show this as an outflow to the Equipment account on this report.

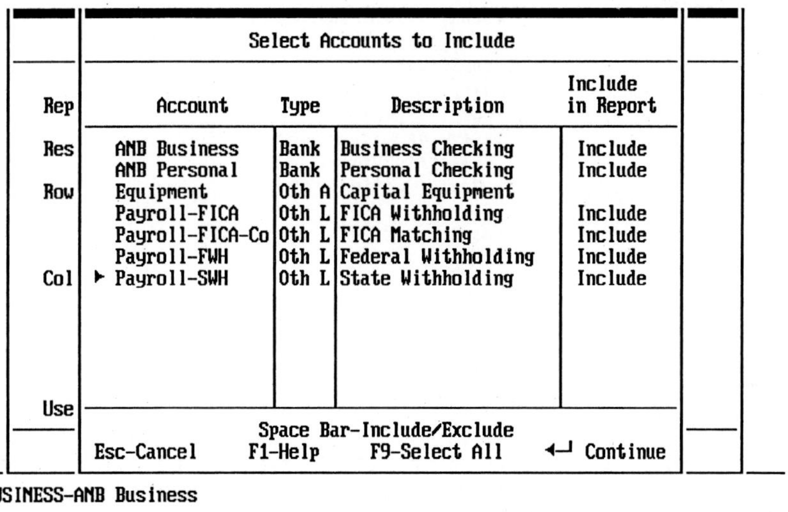

Rep					
				Include	
	Account	Type	Description	in Report	
Res	ANB Business	Bank	Business Checking	Include	
	ANB Personal	Bank	Personal Checking	Include	
Row	Equipment	Oth A	Capital Equipment		
	Payroll-FICA	Oth L	FICA Withholding	Include	
	Payroll-FICA-Co	Oth L	FICA Matching	Include	
	Payroll-FWH	Oth L	Federal Withholding	Include	
Col	▸ Payroll-SWH	Oth L	State Withholding	Include	

Select Accounts to Include

Space Bar-Include/Exclude
Esc-Cancel　　　F1-Help　　　F9-Select All　　↵ Continue

BUSINESS-ANB Business

FIGURE 13-9.　The Select Accounts to Include window

18. Press [ENTER] to create the Cash Flow report. Quicken will display the report shown in Figure 13-10.

Notice that this report shows the entire amount of payroll ($15,000.00) as a cash outflow, even though you have not paid the entire amount of federal

```
                                Cash Flow Report
                            1/ 1/91 Through 3/31/91
        BUSINESS-Selected Accounts                                    Page  1
        8/ 4/91
                                                    1/ 1/91-
              Category Description                   3/31/91
        ------------------------------  ----------------------
              INFLOWS
                 Consulting Income                   37,500.00
                 Royalty Income                      10,000.00
                                                    -----------
              TOTAL INFLOWS                          47,500.00

              OUTFLOWS
                 Computer Supplies                      375.76
                 Equipment Maintenance               1,100.00
                 Overnight Delivery                     270.00
                 Payroll Expense:
                    Gross Earnings       15,000.00
                    Payroll Taxes         1,147.50
                                        -----------
                 Total Payroll Expense               16,147.50
                 Postage Expense                         28.00
                 Supplies                               65.00
                 Telephone Expense                     305.00
                 Travel Expenses                       905.00
                 Water, Gas, Electric:
                    Electric Utilities       30.40
                    Gas Utilities            17.00
                                        -----------
                 Total Water, Gas, Electric            47.40
                 TO Equipment                        1,500.00
                                                    -----------
              TOTAL OUTFLOWS                          20,743.66

                                                    -----------
              OVERALL TOTAL                           26,756.34
                                                    ===========
```

═══════ **FIGURE 13-10.**   Cash Flow report for the first quarter of 1991

and state withholding to the governmental agencies at the end of the period. This is caused by Quicken's assumption that transfers between accounts included in the report are cash outflows. If you want to eliminate these amounts from the report you can re-create the report with only the ANB Personal and ANB Business accounts included. However, since the liability exists for the withheld amounts, the Cash Flow report shown in Figure 13-10 is a conservative approach to presenting the cash flow.

chapter 14

ORGANIZING TAX INFORMATION AND OTHER YEAR-END NEEDS

Depreciation
Customized Equipment Report
Depreciation and the IRS
Schedule C, Profit or Loss from Business
Year-End Activities

For the small-business owner it seems as though tax time is always just around the corner. If it is not time to file one of the payroll tax forms, it is time to file quarterly tax estimates or year-end tax returns. Just as Quicken lent assistance with payroll tax forms in Chapter 12, it can save a significant amount of time and effort when you are preparing income tax returns.

In this chapter you will see how Quicken can be used to gather information to complete the tax forms for your business-related activities. You will be introduced to the concept of depreciation and how it affects business profits. You will learn how to use Quicken to prepare your Schedule C, Profit or Loss From Business statements (see Figure 14-1). You can also use

| SCHEDULE C
(Form 1040)

Department of the Treasury
Internal Revenue Service ⁽⁰⁾ | **Profit or Loss From Business**
(Sole Proprietorship)
Partnerships, Joint Ventures, Etc., Must File Form 1065.
▶ Attach to Form 1040 or Form 1041. ▶ See Instructions for Schedule C (Form 1040). | OMB No. 1545-0074

19**89**
Attachment
Sequence No. **09** |

Name of proprietor | Social security number (SSN)

A Principal business or profession, including product or service (see Instructions) | **B** Principal business code
(from page 2) ▶

C Business name and address ▶ .... | **D** Employer ID number (Not SSN)

E Method(s) used to value closing inventory: (1) ☐ Cost (2) ☐ Lower of cost or market (3) ☐ Other (attach explanation) (4) ☐ Does not apply (if checked, skip line G)

F Accounting method: (1) ☐ Cash (2) ☐ Accrual (3) ☐ Other (specify) ▶ ....

	Yes	No
G Was there any change in determining quantities, costs, or valuations between opening and closing inventory? (If "Yes," attach explanation.)		
H Are you deducting expenses for business use of your home? (If "Yes," see Instructions for limitations.)		
I Did you "materially participate" in the operation of this business during 1989? (If "No," see Instructions for limitations on losses.) .		

J If this schedule includes a loss, credit, deduction, income, or other tax benefit relating to a tax shelter required to be registered, check here . ▶ ☐
If you checked this box, you MUST attach **Form 8271**.

Part I Income

1 Gross receipts or sales	1	47,500 00	
2 Returns and allowances	2		
3 Subtract line 2 from line 1. Enter the result here	3	47,500	00
4 Cost of goods sold and/or operations (from line 39 on page 2)	4		
5 Subtract line 4 from line 3 and enter the **gross profit** here	5		
6 Other income, including Federal and state gasoline or fuel tax credit or refund (see Instructions)	6		
7 Add lines 5 and 6. This is your **gross income** . . . . ▶	7	47,500	00

Part II Expenses

8 Advertising	8		22 Repairs	22	1,100 00
9 Bad debts from sales or services (see Instructions)	9		23 Supplies (not included in Part III) .	23	440 76
10 Car and truck expenses . . .	10		24 Taxes	24	1,147 50
11 Commissions	11		25 Travel, meals, and entertainment:		
12 Depletion	12		a Travel	25a	905 00
13 Depreciation and section 179 deduction from **Form 4562** (not included in Part III)	13	275 00	b Meals and entertainment .		
			c Enter 20% of line 25b subject to limitations (see Instructions) . .		
14 Employee benefit programs (other than on line 20)	14		d Subtract line 25c from line 25b .	25d	
15 Freight (not included in Part III) .	15		26 Utilities (see Instructions) . .	26	352 40
16 Insurance (other than health) .	16		27 Wages (less jobs credit) . . .	27	15,000 00
17 Interest:			28 Other expenses (list type and amount):		
a Mortgage (paid to banks, etc.) .	17a		Misc. Exp. 298.00		
b Other	17b		....		
18 Legal and professional services .	18		....		
19 Office expense	19		....		
20 Pension and profit-sharing plans .	20		....		
21 Rent or lease:			....		
a Machinery and equipment . .	21a		....		
b Other business property . . .	21b			28	298 00

29 Add amounts in columns for lines 8 through 28. These are your **total expenses** . . . . ▶	29	19,518 66
30 **Net profit or (loss).** Subtract line 29 from line 7. If a profit, enter here and on Form 1040, line 12, and on Schedule SE, line 2. If a loss, you MUST go on to line 31. (Fiduciaries, see Instructions.)	30	27,981 34

31 If you have a loss, you MUST check the box that describes your investment in this activity (see Instructions) . . . . . If you checked 31a, enter the loss on Form 1040, line 12, and Schedule SE, line 2. If you checked 31b, you MUST attach **Form 6198**.	31a ☐ All investment is at risk. 31b ☐ Some investment is not at-risk.

For Paperwork Reduction Act Notice, see Form 1040 Instructions. | Schedule C (Form 1040) 1989

FIGURE 14-1. Schedule C

Quicken features to help you prepare for recording the following year's transactions.

DEPRECIATION

Depreciation is an expense recorded at the end of the tax year (or any accounting period). The concept of depreciation can be confusing since it does not follow the same rules as other expenses. Depreciation does not require a cash expenditure in the current year; you are recognizing a part of a cash outflow that occurred in a prior year when you record depreciation expense. Tax rules do not allow you to recognize the full cost as an expense in the earlier tax year because the resource is used in business for many tax years. For example, resources such as a truck or piece of machinery are not expensed in the year purchased since they benefit the business over a number of years. Purchases such as paper, on the other hand, would be consumed in the year purchased and their entire cost would be recognized in that tax year.

A basic definition of depreciation is that it is a portion of the original cost of an asset charged as an expense to a tax period. For the example developed in this section, suppose you purchased computer hardware that is used in your business. This is an asset of your business that will help generate revenues in the current and future tax years. You may think the cost of the equipment you purchased should be charged to your business in the year you paid for it, just as other cash expenses apply to the year paid. This seems fair since the purchase involved a significant cash outflow for the year. Unfortunately, from an accounting or tax perspective, the purchase of a piece of equipment is an acquisition that will affect your business operations over a number of years and thus cannot be expensed or deducted from revenues only in the year of purchase. The cost of the asset must be expensed over the years that it is expected to generate business revenues. For this reason, accountants and the Internal Revenue Service require that you apply the concept of depreciation when you prepare your Schedule C, Profit or Loss from Business statements. However, you will see later that there is one important exception to the requirement that you depreciate your long-lived assets.

You can only depreciate assets that lose their productivity as you use them in your business activity. For example, you cannot record depreciation on the land where your building stands. Even though you may feel your land has lost value in recent years, you cannot recognize this decline until you sell the land. Thus, equipment is an example of a *depreciable asset* while land would not be. Throughout this chapter and on income tax forms you will see the term depreciable assets used. This means assets that have a life longer than one year and that will benefit business operations in several accounting periods.

Depreciation Terminology

There are several terms pertaining to depreciation that need to be discussed in more depth. You must always depreciate the *original cost* of an asset. Original cost is the total cost of the asset. For example, if you purchased a piece of machinery and paid shipping charges and sales tax, these additional costs are considered to be associated with getting the asset into an income-producing condition and are therefore part of the original cost. Figure 14-2 shows the Equipment account register after recording the transactions in Chapter 11. The first transaction recorded in the register shows the original cost of the High Tech Computer, $3,000.00. The printer purchase on 1/25/91 is recorded at its original cost of $1,500.00.

In Chapter 9, you learned to revalue personal assets to market value. You cannot do this with business assets. If your asset increases in value you cannot recognize this increase in your Quicken system. You must always *carry* (show on your business accounting records) your business assets at their original cost.

F1-Help	F2-Acct/Print	F3-Edit	F4-Quick Entry	F5-Reports	F6-Activities

DATE	REF	PAYEE · MEMO · CATEGORY	DECREASE	C	INCREASE	BALANCE
		BEGINNING				0|00
1/ 1 1991		Opening Balance [Equipment]				
1/ 1 1991		High Tech Computer Original cost o→[Equipment]/B			3,000|00	3,000|00
1/ 1 1991		High Tech Computer Depreciation Ex→[Equipment]/B	600|00			2,400|00
1/25 1991		Laser 1 Printer from Ha→[ANB Business]→			1,500|00	3,900|00

FIGURE 14-2. Equipment Account Register window

Another important term is *accumulated depreciation*. This is the amount of depreciation you have recorded for an asset in all previous years. Your assets will always be shown on the balance sheet at original cost minus accumulated depreciation. For example, for the $3,000.00 High Tech Computer asset you recorded depreciation expense of $600.00 in the previous year. You have an accumulated depreciation of $600.00 from the previous year, so your asset carrying value is $2,400.00 before recording this year's depreciation.

Establishing Accounts for Assets

You probably will establish an other asset account for each major type of depreciable asset used in your business. You would follow the same procedures used in Chapter 11 to set up the Equipment account. If you have equipment, office furniture, and buildings that you use in your business, including the portion of your home used exclusively for business purposes, you will depreciate the original cost of each of the assets. On the other hand, you may decide to establish a separate account for each asset if you have few depreciable assets. Quicken's default limit on the number of accounts in the system is 64, although you can increase this to up to 255 given sufficient memory and disk space. In the example, you will learn how to depreciate more than one asset in an account.

Depreciation Methods

The straight-line method of depreciation described in the next section is appropriate for income tax purposes. However, for the most part you will probably use the modified accelerated cost recovery system (MACRS) and the accelerated cost recovery system (ACRS) methods of determining your depreciation amounts. Generally speaking, MACRS covers tangible assets put into business use after December 31, 1986 and ACRS covers tangible assets put into place after December 31, 1980. Tangible assets are property that can be felt and touched. All the assets mentioned in our discussion (equipment, office furniture, and buildings) would fit this description.

The reason most taxpayers use MACRS is that the method builds in a higher level of depreciation deductions in the early years of an asset's life than would be calculated using the straight-line method of depreciation. Consult IRS Publication 534 before computing your depreciation on tangible assets.

Straight-Line Depreciation Method

In this example you will use the straight-line method to record depreciation on this asset. *Straight-line depreciation* expenses the cost of the asset evenly over the life of the asset. For example, the High Tech Computer has a useful life of five years, and you recorded depreciation expense at $600.00 in 1990. Since this method does not attempt to recognize more depreciation in the early years of an asset's life, it is always acceptable to the IRS. Many other depreciation methods can be used and may be more favorable since they recognize greater depreciation in the early years of the asset's life. IRS Publication 534 lists the many rules that apply to the selection of a depreciation method. One of the considerations that determines the depreciation method chosen is the year in which you placed the asset in service. A rule that applies to all types of depreciation is that once you select a method of depreciation for an asset you cannot change to another depreciation method. Table 14-1 lists some of the other depreciation methods. You will need to check with your accountant or check IRS Publication 534 for specific rulings on which methods you can use.

When using the straight-line method of depreciating an asset, use the following formula:

$$\frac{\text{original cost } - \text{ salvage value}}{\text{useful life of asset}}$$

The original cost of depreciable assets has already been discussed; however, *salvage value* is a new term. Salvage value is the amount of cash you expect to recover when you dispose of your depreciable asset. This is, obviously, always an estimate and in the case of a computer not easily estimated due to rapid changes in the computer field. For this reason, many accountants assign a salvage value of zero to this type of asset, stating in effect that it will have no value at the end of its estimated life. This is also the assumption made in the entries recorded here. When you record salvage values for your assets you can use the history of similar assets when estimating depreciation. If equipment that is five years old typically sells for 20 percent of its original cost, that would be a good estimate for the salvage value of a piece of equipment with an estimated life of five years bought today.

Depreciation Calculation

The amounts used in the depreciation entries in this chapter were determined by the calculations shown next.

High Tech Computer:

$$\frac{\$3,000.00 \text{ (original cost)} - 0 \text{ (salvage value)}}{5 \text{ years (useful life)}} = \$600.00 \text{ depreciation per year}$$

Laser printer:

$$\frac{\$1,500.00 \text{ (original cost)} - 0 \text{ (salvage value)}}{3 \text{ years (useful life)}} = \$500.00 \text{ depreciation per year}$$

Depreciation is generally recorded only once, at the end of the year, unless you need financial statements prepared for a bank or other third party during the year. The amounts calculated in this example are the annual depreciation expenses for the computer and printer—the amounts you would use to record depreciation for the year ending 12/31/91. (Note that even

Method	Description
ACRS	The Accelerated Cost Recovery System is an accelerated depreciation method that can be used for assets placed in service after December 31, 1980 and before December 31, 1986.
Declining-balance	This method allows the deduction of depreciation expense at a faster rate than straight-line. There are several different percentages used in computing this type of depreciation. One acceptable option is 150 percent of straight-line depreciation.
MACRS	The Modified Accelerated Cost Recovery System is an accelerated depreciation method used for assets placed in service after December 31, 1986.
Straight-line	This method is the easiest to compute since the cost of the asset is depreciated evenly over the life of the asset. It is also the least advantageous to the business owner since it does not accelerate depreciation expense in the early years of the asset's life.

TABLE 14-1.   Depreciation Methods

though the printer was acquired at the end of January, it would be acceptable to record a full year's depreciation on the asset since the difference between 11 and 12 months' worth of depreciation is so small that it would not be considered to have a material effect.)

In the examples developed in Chapters 11 and 13 the account register transactions have been limited to the first quarter of the year. (In Chapter 12 you completed several April 1991 entries in order to see the complete process of payroll accounting.) Since there is not a full year of expense entries, you can compute the depreciation on the computer and printer for just the first quarter of 1991. This is accomplished by dividing both annual amounts of depreciation by 4. Thus, the first quarter's depreciation charges that you will record are

High Tech Computer:

$$\frac{\$600.00 \text{ (annual depreciation)}}{4 \text{ (quarters)}} = \$150.00 \text{ depreciation for first quarter, } 1991$$

Laser printer:

$$\frac{\$500.00 \text{ (annual depreciation)}}{4 \text{ (quarters)}} = \$125.00 \text{ depreciation for first quarter, } 1991$$

Now that you are familiar with the method used to record depreciation in the example and how the amounts you will record were determined, you are ready to begin recording the depreciation entry in your account register.

Establishing Depreciation Categories

Before recording the depreciation entries in this chapter you will establish a depreciation category with computer and printer subcategories in your category list. Select the Equipment account from the BUSINESS account group, open the account register, and follow these steps:

1. Press CTRL-C to open the Category and Transfer List window.

2. Press HOME to move to <New Category>.

3. Press ENTER to open the Set Up Category window.

4. Type **Depreciation** and press ENTER.

5. Press (**ENTER**) to accept E.

6. Type **Depreciation Expense** and press (**ENTER**).

7. Type **Y** and press (**ENTER**).

8. Press (**ENTER**) to select <New Category>.

9. Type **Computer** and press (**ENTER**).

10. Type **S** and press (**ENTER**).

11. Type **Depreciation-Computer** and press (**ENTER**).

12. Type **Y** and press (**ENTER**) to complete the Set Up Category window.

13. Press (**ENTER**) to select <New Category>.

14. Type **Printer** and press (**ENTER**).

15. Type **S** and press (**ENTER**).

16. Type **Depreciation-Printer** and press (**ENTER**).

17. Type **Y** and press (**ENTER**) to complete the Set Up Category window.

18. Press (**ESC**) to return to the register.

You can now begin recording your depreciation expense transactions.

Depreciation Expense Transactions

Let's record the depreciation on the assets in your Quicken account. Starting from the next blank transaction form in the Equipment account register (Figure 14-2) in the BUSINESS account group, follow these steps:

1. Type **3/31/91** and press (**ENTER**) twice.

Notice that no check numbers are recorded in this register since all checks are written against the business checking account.

2. Type **High Tech Computer** and press (**ENTER**).

3. Type **150** and press (**ENTER**) three times.

4. Type **Depreciation-1991** and press (**ENTER**).

5. Type **Depreciation:Computer/B** and press (**CTRL**)-(**ENTER**).

You have just recorded the depreciation expense on the computer for the months January through March of 1991. The remaining steps will record depreciation on the laser printer you acquired in January.

6. Type **3/31/91** in the Date field and press ⌈ENTER⌋ twice.

7. Type **Laser 1** and press ⌈ENTER⌋.

8. Type **125** and press ⌈ENTER⌋ three times.

9. Type **Depreciation-1991** and press ⌈ENTER⌋.

10. Type **Depreciation:Printer/B** and press ⌈CTRL⌋-⌈ENTER⌋.

These register entries show how your depreciation transactions will appear after you record both of them:

3/31 1991	High Tech Computer Depreciation-19→Depreciation:C→	150 00		3,750 00
3/31 1991	Laser 1 Depreciation-19→Depreciation:P→	125 00		3,625 00

This completes the depreciation transaction entry for the first quarter of 1991. Remember, depreciation is normally recorded only at year end. However, for purposes of this example we have prepared the entries at the end of the first quarter.

CUSTOMIZED EQUIPMENT REPORT

After recording the depreciation transactions in the Equipment account you will want to look at a customized Equipment report. This report, which you will prepare shortly, summarizes all the activity in the account. Figure 14-3 shows the Equipment report for your business since 1/1/91. Notice that the report shows the depreciation expense taken during the first quarter for both the computer and the printer, as well as the total for the category. You can also see that there was a transfer of $1,500.00 from business checking for the purchase of the printer in January.

```
                              Equipment Report
                            1/ 1/91 Through 3/31/91
        BUSINESS-Equipment
        8/ 5/91                                                      Page 1

                                                     1/ 1/91 -
                          Category Description        3/31/91
        -----------------------------------------  --------------------
        INCOME/EXPENSE
          EXPENSES
            Depreciation Expense:
              Depreciation-Computer          150.00
              Depreciation-Printer           125.00
                                            ----------
              Total Depreciation Expense                 275.00
                                                        ----------
          TOTAL EXPENSES                                 275.00


          TOTAL INCOME/EXPENSE                          ----------
                                                        -275.00

          TRANSFERS
            FROM ANB Business                          1,500.00
                                                       ----------
          TOTAL TRANSFERS                              1,500.00

          BALANCE FORWARD
            Equipment                                  2,400.00
                                                       ----------
          TOTAL BALANCE FORWARD                        2,400.00


          OVERALL TOTAL                                ----------
                                                       3,625.00
                                                       ==========
```

FIGURE 14-3.   Equipment report

Finally, you can see that the balance forward amount of $2,400.00 is the $3,000.00 original cost of the asset minus the $600.00 accumulated depreciation taken in the prior year. Thus, when you prepare a balance sheet in Chapter 15, the equipment asset will total $3,625.00.

If you want to produce the Equipment report follow these steps starting from the Equipment account register:

1. Press (F5) and the Reports window appears.

2. Type **6** and the Create Summary Report window appears.

3. Type **Equipment Report** and press (ENTER).

4. Type **1/1/91** and press (ENTER).

5. Type **3/31/91** and press (ENTER).

6. Press (ENTER) to accept option 1 for the Row Headings field.

7. Type **1** and press (ENTER) to select Don't Subtotal for the column headings.

8. Type **C** and press (ENTER).

9. Press (F8) and the Print Report window appears.

10. Select the printer you are using and press (ENTER).

DEPRECIATION AND THE IRS

The transactions in this chapter record depreciation using the straight-line method to determine the amounts for the entries. This method was demonstrated in order to cover the recording process without going into too much detail about IRS rules for determining depreciation expense for tax purposes. However, we need to briefly discuss one additional aspect of deducting the cost of long-lived assets for IRS purposes, section 179 property. You should obtain IRS Publication 534 (free upon request) before making decisions concerning the amount of depreciation you will charge against income on your tax return.

Section 179 Property

Many small businesses will be interested in treating certain capital expenditures as deductions in the current year, rather than depreciating the cost of the asset over its life. This type of property is called "section 179" property. Buildings, air conditioning units, and structural components of a building do not qualify as section 179 property. For a complete list of qualified property and the specific rules that apply, consult IRS Publication 534.

Under section 179 of the Internal Revenue Service code you can deduct up to $10,000.00 of the cost of property in the current tax year. In this chapter you would have been able to deduct the entire cost of the laser printer this year against your business income and not depreciate the asset in future years.

SCHEDULE C, PROFIT OR LOSS FROM BUSINESS

Schedule C is the tax form sole proprietorships use when reporting business income and expenses during the year. Quicken can be used to provide the information you need to complete your form. If you examine Schedule C (Figure 14-1) you see that it is a business Profit and Loss statement. This statement can be prepared from the Quicken Reports menu.

Starting from the Main Menu for the ANB Business account register in the BUSINESS account group, complete the following steps:

1. Type **3** to select Reports.

2. Type **2** to select Business Reports.

3. Type **1** and the Profit and Loss Statement window appears.

4. Press (ENTER) to accept the default title.

5. Type **1/91** and press (ENTER).

6. Type **3/91** and press (F9).

7. Press (TAB) three times to move the cursor to the Class matches: row.

8. Type **B** and press (CTRL)-(ENTER). You are returned to the Profit and Loss Statement window.

9. Press (ENTER) and the Profit and Loss statement appears on your screen.

10. Press (F8) and the Print Report window appears.

11. Select the printer and press (ENTER).

The Profit and Loss statement is shown in Figure 14-4.

Completing Schedule C

With Quicken's Profit and Loss statement you can now complete the appropriate lines of the federal tax form Schedule C. Because Schedule C is basically just a Profit and Loss statement, many of the entries can be obtained directly from your Quicken report. Listed next is how you can complete the following lines in Schedule C.

```
                        PROFIT and LOSS STATEMENT
                          1/ 1/91 Through 3/31/91
        BUSINESS-All Accounts                              Page 1
        8/ 5/91

                                                    1/ 1/91 -
                          Category Description       3/31/91
        --------------------------------- ----------------------
        INCOME/EXPENSE
          INCOME
            Consulting Income                       37,500.00
            Royalty Income                          10,000.00
                                                    ----------
          TOTAL INCOME                              47,500.00


          EXPENSES
            Computer Supplies                          375.76
            Depreciation Expense:
              Depreciation-Computer      150.00
              Depreciation-Printer       125.00
                                        ----------
            Total Depreciation Expense                 275.00
            Equipment Maintenance                    1,100.00
            Overnight Delivery                         270.00
            Payroll Expense:
              Gross Earnings          15,000.00
              Payroll Taxes            1,147.50
                                        ----------
            Total Payroll Expense                   16,147.50
            Postage Expense                             28.00
            Supplies                                    65.00
            Telephone Expense                          305.00
            Travel Expenses                            905.00
            Water, Gas, Electric:
              Electric Utilities         30.40
              Gas Utilities              17.00
                                        ----------
            Total Water, Gas, Electric                  47.40
                                                    ----------
          TOTAL EXPENSES                            19,518.66


                                                    ----------
          TOTAL INCOME/EXPENSE                       27,981.34
                                                    ==========
```

════════ **FIGURE 14-4.**   Profit and Loss statement

Line 1   This line shows gross sales. The total income ($47,500.00) shown on your report would be placed on this line.

Line 13   This section shows depreciation and section 179 deduction from Form 4562, Depreciation and Amortization. The depreciation expense ($275.00) would be entered here.

Line 22   This line shows repairs. The amount you show for Equipment Maintenance ($1,100.00) would be entered here.

Line 23   This line shows the total of all your business supplies. You would add the amounts shown for Computer Supplies ($375.76) and Supplies ($65.00) using the calculator and enter the total ($440.76) here.

Line 24   This line shows taxes. The amount shown as Payroll Taxes ($1,147.50) would be entered here.

Line 25a   This shows the total amount of your business travel. The amount of Travel Expense ($905.00) would be entered here. This assumes that all these expenses are associated with travel and not meals or entertainment. You can establish separate categories for these items in your Quicken Category and Transfer List.

Line 26   The total for utilities and telephone is placed on this line. You would use the calculator to add the amounts shown for Telephone Expense ($305.00) and Water, Gas, and Electric ($47.40) and record the total expense as $352.40.

Line 27   This line shows the total wages paid. You would enter the amount shown as Gross Earnings ($15,000.00).

Line 28   This line shows your other business expenses. You would add the amounts shown for Postage Expense ($28.00) and Overnight Delivery ($270.00) and show the total ($298.00) as Misc Exp in this section.

Line 29   This line shows your total deductions. This is the amount of Total Expense ($19,518.66).

Line 30   This line shows your net profit (or loss). This is the amount of net profit ($27,981.34).

   You can round the cents to the nearest dollar when completing your tax forms.

After completing this exercise you can see there are many alternatives for establishing classes to help in gathering your tax information. Remember, one of the constraints faced in this example was that you were recording business expenses in both personal and business checking accounts. However, this example could be modified to use subclasses to designate lines on the different tax forms when recording your entries. This would allow you to capture the information by form and line number.

Other Business-Related Tax Forms

When you completed line 13, Depreciation, you used the Total Depreciation Expense amount from your Profit and Loss statement. This information must be included on Form 4562, Depreciation and Amortization. After reading through Publication 534 you would have entered the appropriate amounts for section 179 property and ACRS or MACRS depreciation. For the example this results in a total of $275.00 that would be shown on line 19 of Form 4562 and transferred to line 13 on Schedule C.

As a sole proprietor you also need to complete Schedule SE, Social Security Self-Employment Tax. The net profit from your Schedule C ($27,981.34) would be carried to line 2 of that form and the rest of the form can be easily completed. See the special Year-End Business Tax Forms section for a list of important tax forms for the small-business owner.

YEAR-END ACTIVITIES

You are not required to take any special actions at the end of the year to continue to use Quicken. The package allows you to select transactions by date if you want to purge some of the older transactions from your file. Unless you need the disk space or begin to notice sluggish response time from your system, you should plan on keeping at least three years of historical information in your file. You may find it convenient to be able to print historical reports for comparison with this year's results.

To copy accounts, categories, classes, and other information to a new account group, you will need to use the Change Settings option from the Main Menu. You can then decide how far back to go in copying transactions to the new file. You can also remove uncleared transactions from an earlier date from this file.

The following steps explain how to copy the BUSINESS account group you have been using since Chapter 11. Starting from the Main Menu in the ANB Business account register in the BUSINESS account group, complete these steps:

1. From the Main Menu, type **5** to select Change Settings.

2. Type **1** to choose Account Group Activities.

3. Type **1** and the Select/Set Up Account Group window appears.

4. Move the arrow cursor to BUSINESS and press ⟨**ENTER**⟩.

5. Move the arrow cursor to ANB Business and press ⟨**ENTER**⟩.

6. Press ⟨**ESC**⟩ and then type **5** for Change Settings.

7. Type **1** to select Account Group Activities.

T
I
P

YEAR-END BUSINESS TAX FORMS

Form	Title
Sole Proprietorship	
Schedule C (Form 1040)	Profit or Loss From Business
Form 4562	Depreciation and Amortization
Schedule SE (Form 1040)	Social Security Self-Employment Tax
Form 1040-ES	Estimated Tax for Individuals
Partnership	
Form 1065	U.S. Partnership Return of Income
Schedule D (Form 1065)	Capital Gains and Losses
Schedule K-1 (Form 1065)	Partner's Share of Income, Credits, Deduction, etc.
Corporations	
Form 1120-A	U.S. Corporation Short-Form Income Tax Return
Form 1120	U.S. Corporation Income Tax Return
Form 1120S	U.S. Income Tax Return for an S Corporation
Schedule K-1 (Form 1120S)	Shareholder's Share of Income, Credits, Deductions, etc.

8. Type **4** and the Copy Account Group window, shown in Figure 14-5, appears.

9. Press ⌈**F9**⌋ and the Set Maximum Accounts In Group window appears.

Quicken will automatically copy up to 64 accounts from the selected account group to a backup disk or another location on your hard disk. This number can be increased to up to 255 accounts if needed. In this example the predefined limit is more than enough to cover your needs. If you did need to increase the number of accounts to copy you would type the desired number and press ⌈**ENTER**⌋.

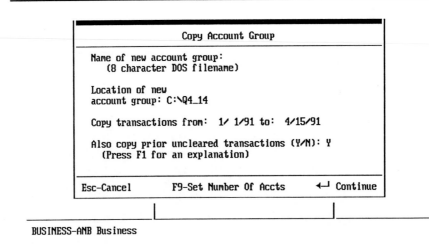

FIGURE 14-5. Copy Account Group window

10. Press (ESC) and Quicken returns you to the Copy Account Group window.

11. Type **Acct91** and press (ENTER). This is the name of the new account group.

12. Type a new directory location or press (ENTER) to accept the existing location.

13. Type **1/1/91** and press (ENTER).

14. Type **4/15/91** and press (ENTER).

You have now defined all the transactions between 1/1/91 and 4/15/91 as those you want to transfer to the new account group.

15. Type **Y** and press (ENTER).

This command tells Quicken to copy all uncleared transactions from the period prior to 1/1/91. This means that any checks that clear your bank after the year-end will be included in your account register for reconciliation purposes.

16. Press (ENTER). This acknowledges that the account group has been copied.

17. Type **1** and you are returned to the Select/Set-Up Account Group window.

You are now prepared to begin recording transactions in the next accounting period in the ACCT91 account group.

chapter 15

MONITORING FINANCIAL CONDITIONS

The Balance Sheet
Using Quicken to Track Accounts Receivable
Using Quicken to Track Accounts Payable
Quicken's Role in Your Business Record Keeping

Y ou have already seen that you can prepare financial statements with Quicken's report features. In previous chapters you created a Profit and Loss statement, a Cash Flow report, and an Equipment report. You can use these reports to monitor the financial condition of your firm and to see how your business has performed over a period of time. These reports not only help you assess the success you've had in managing the business, but they can also be used by outsiders for the same purpose. Bankers and other creditors review your financial statements to determine whether to make loans to your business. Quicken can prove a valuable tool in preparing loan applications or, as you saw in earlier chapters, in providing information to other users of financial statements, such as the Internal Revenue Service.

In this chapter a final major financial statement, the balance sheet, is presented. The balance sheet provides the reader with a snapshot of the financial resources and obligations of your business. Although the profit and loss statement, the cash flow report, and the balance sheet have been introduced separately, they are interrelated. Bankers and other readers will review these statements as a package when assessing the past and projecting the future success of your business.

In this chapter you will also learn to use Quicken to monitor your *billings* and *payables*. Billings are your business's accounts receivable—sales to customers on credit. They need to be closely monitored regardless of the accounting method you used for financial reporting (cash or accrual basis). Remember, when you sell to your customers on credit you are essentially extending them a loan. This means you need to closely monitor the customers to whom you are extending credit and determine their ability to pay within the time period you allow on credit sales.

Payables, on the other hand, are essentially credit that others have extended to your business. Quicken can help you monitor your payables so you obtain full use of your business's cash before making payment within the time period allowed.

THE BALANCE SHEET

The balance sheet shows your business assets, liabilities, and equity or investment at a specific date. Remember, assets are things of value that are used in your business to generate revenue. Cash, for example, is an asset that is used to acquire other assets, such as supplies and labor, which are then used to generate revenue.

Liabilities are the obligations incurred as part of your business operations. If you borrow from the bank this is a financial obligation. This obligation is shown as a liability on your balance sheet.

Owner's equity is the amount of personal resources you have invested in the business. In the example you've been working on in the preceding chapters, you opened your business checking with a $4,000.00 deposit and put $2,400.00 of equipment in the Equipment account ($3,000.00 original cost—$600.00 of accumulated depreciation). This $6,400.00 is the amount of your personal assets invested in the business and is your owner's equity at the beginning of the year. Bankers and other creditors are interested in your equity in the business. If you are asking for a loan, they will want to know how much of your own financial resources you are risking. This is measured by your equity in your business, as well as by any other personal assets you may be willing to commit.

Before preparing a balance sheet there are two concepts that need to be covered. First, the balance sheet is prepared at a specific date. Quicken will ask you to define the time period you want to use in preparing your balance sheet. For example, you will define the period 1/1/91 to 3/31/91 in this chapter's example; you are telling Quicken to prepare the balance sheet using transactions in that time period. The resulting printed balance sheet will show the balances in your business accounts on 3/31/91.

The second important concept is that the profit and loss statement and the balance sheet are related. While the balance sheet shows your assets, liabilities, and equity at a specific date, the profit and loss statement gives the detail of changes in your assets, liabilities, and equity between two balance sheets. Remember these two concepts as you prepare the balance sheets in this chapter: the balance sheet is prepared at a specific date and the profit and loss statement helps explain how assets, liabilities, and equity changed between two balance sheets. In the examples that follow you will see how the profit and loss statement demonstrates how changes in owner's equity occurred between 1/1/91 and 3/31/91.

Creating a Balance Sheet

In this section you will prepare a balance sheet as of 3/31/91 from the transactions you entered in the BUSINESS account group in previous chapters. This report will show the assets, liabilities, and owner's equity of the business at the end of the quarter. Starting from the Main Menu of the ANB Business account register in the BUSINESS account group, follow these steps:

1. Type **3** to select Reports.

2. Type **2** to select Business Reports.

3. Type **7** and the Balance Sheet window appears.

4. Press (**F8**) (Customize) to open the Create Account Balances Report window.

5. Press (**ENTER**) to accept the default report title.

6. Type **1/1/91** and press (**ENTER**).

7. Type **3/31/91** and press (**ENTER**).

8. Press (**ENTER**) to accept the default report interval, 1. None.

9. Press (F9) (Filter) and the Filter Report Transaction window will appear.

10. Press (ENTER) three times to move to the Class matches field.

11. Type **B** and press (CTRL)-(ENTER) to return to the Create Account Balances Report window.

12. Press (ENTER) to accept A for all in the Current/All/Selected accounts field. The balance sheet appears on your screen.

13. Press (F8) (Print) and the Print Report window appears.

14. Select the desired printer and press (ENTER). Your balance sheet will look like the one in Figure 15-1.

BALANCE SHEET DISCUSSION The total of the Cash and Bank Accounts is $32,580.34. This consists of the amount shown in your ANB Business checking account on 3/31/91 ($32,696.50) less $123.16. The deduction is the amount of cash used from your personal checking account to cover business expenses. (Remember that you wrote several personal checks and charged a portion of the cost to business by using the /B class entry.) These amounts were included in the Profit and Loss statement prepared in the previous chapter and the Cash Flow statement in Chapter 13. Thus, Quicken is adjusting your business cash by the amount of expenses paid from your personal accounts. The importance of this will be discussed shortly.

You can also see that the equipment is carried at a balance of $3,625.00. The carrying value of depreciable assets was discussed in Chapter 14. The Equipment report produced there shows the underlying transactions that explain the carrying value on this report.

The total assets are the resources available to your business on the date of the report. These resources are what is used to generate future income.

The liabilities shown are all related to the payroll prepared on 3/31/91. You owe the federal and state governments $1,817.00 for withholding and Social Security tax payments. On 4/1/91 you made a deposit with your bank for all the federal government payroll liabilities. However, this did not affect the balance sheet prepared on 3/31/91. The payroll taxes were liabilities on the date the statement was prepared, even though the deposit on 4/1/91 will reduce your total liabilities by $1,364.00. Likewise, the state withholding liability will remain on the balance sheet until you make a deposit to the state.

The difference between the total assets of the business and the total liabilities is the owner's equity in the business. In this case you have $34,381.34 of your equity invested in the business. Thus, the balance sheet presented shows that most of the assets used in the business were contributed by you, with only $1,817.00 outstanding to creditors.

```
                        Balance Sheet
                        As of 3/31/91
        BUSINESS-All Accounts                        Page 1
        8/ 6/91
                                              3/31/91
                          Acct                Balance
        -----------------------------------  -----------
        ASSETS

           Cash and Bank Accounts
              ANB Business-Business Checking     32,696.50
              ANB Personal-Personal Checking       -123.16
                                                -----------
           Total Cash and Bank Accounts          32,573.34

           Other Assets
              Equipment-Capital Equipment          3,625.00
                                                -----------
           Total Other Assets                      3,625.00


                                                -----------
        TOTAL ASSETS                             36,198.34
                                                ===========
        LIABILITIES & EQUITY

           LIABILITIES
              Other Liabilities
                 Payroll-FICA-Co-FICA Matching       382.50
                 Payroll-FICA-FICA Withholding       382.50
                 Payroll-FWH-Federal Withholding     599.00
                 Payroll-SWH-State Withholding       453.00
                                                -----------
              Total Other Liabilities            1,817.00


                                                -----------
           TOTAL LIABILITIES                     1,817.00

           EQUITY                               34,381.34
                                                -----------
        TOTAL LIABILITIES & EQUITY              36,198.34
                                                ===========
```

FIGURE 15-1. Balance Sheet as of 3/31/91

Creating Comparative Balance Sheets

In this section you will see how Quicken's Profit and Loss statement helps explain the changes that occur between two balance sheets. First, you will prepare a comparative Balance Sheet; then the relationship with the Profit and Loss statement will be discussed. Starting from the Main Menu of the ANB Business Account register in the BUSINESS account group, follow these steps:

1. Type **3** to select Reports.

2. Type **2** to select Business Reports.

3. Type **7** and the Balance Sheet window appears.

4. Press ⌐F8⌐ (Customize) to open the Create Account Balances Report window.

5. Press ⌐ENTER⌐ to accept the default report title.

6. Type **1/1/91** and press ⌐ENTER⌐.

7. Type **3/31/91** and press ⌐ENTER⌐.

8. Type **6** to select Quarter for the report interval and press ⌐ENTER⌐. This entry will cause Quicken to create a comparative balance sheet, with account balances shown at the beginning and the end of the quarter.

 Quicken will only prepare quarterly reports for periods beginning on the first of January, April, July, and October—that is, you cannot prepare a quarterly report for the three months beginning February 1.

9. Press ⌐F9⌐ (Filter); the Filter Report Transaction window appears.

10. Press ⌐ENTER⌐ three times to move to the Class matches field.

11. Type **B** and press ⌐CTRL⌐-⌐ENTER⌐ to return to the Create Account Balances Report window.

12. Press ⌐ENTER⌐ to accept A for All in the Current/All/Selected accounts field. The Balance Sheet appears on your screen.

13. Press ⌐F8⌐ (Print) and the Print Report window appears.

14. Select your printer and press (ENTER). Your report will look like that shown in Figure 15-2.

COMPARATIVE BALANCE SHEET DISCUSSION The comparative Balance Sheet prepared in this section shows the balances of the business on 1/1/91 and 3/31/91 side by side. You can see that the assets of the business on 1/1/91 consisted of the $4,000.00 initial deposit made to the business checking account and the $2,400.00 carrying value ($3,000.00 − $600.00) of the High Tech computer recorded in the Equipment account on 1/1/91. Thus, the total assets were $6,400.00. There were no liabilities at that time so the owner's equity is the $6,400.00 shown as the overall total.

The question you should be asking now is, "What is the cause of the changes in assets, liabilities, and equity between these two balance sheet dates?"

The change in assets is caused by the increase in cash, which is explained in the Cash Flow report. In Chapter 13 you prepared a Cash Flow report (see Figure 13-10) where you selected all accounts except Equipment in the preparation of the report. Remember that this was a conservative approach to the preparation of the report since federal and state withholding was included as a cash transfer, even though the deposit for these liabilities was not made until 4/1/91. In order for your Cash Flow report to accurately reflect cash transactions for the period 1/1/91 through 3/31/91 you would need to re-create the report using only the ANB Personal and ANB Business accounts. Figure 15-3 shows how the re-created report would appear. This is important since it shows the connection between the amounts in the Cash and Bank Accounts sections of the comparative Balance Sheets, as shown in Figure 15-2. There is a change of $28,573.34 in the total cash balance between 1/1/91 and 3/31/91, which equals the overall total or the amount of the net cash flow shown in Figure 15-3. If you were presenting financial reports to a banker you would want to use the Cash Flow report prepared in this chapter. If you were using the report for internal purposes the one prepared in Chapter 13 would be satisfactory and the more conservative of the two.

The increase in the Equipment account is explained by examining the Equipment report prepared in Chapter 14, and clearly the changes in the liabilities are related to the payroll withholdings you owe on 3/31/91.

The owner's equity (investment) in the business is the difference between the total assets and total liabilities of the business. As just noted, the owner's equity on 1/1/91 was $6,400.00, while the owner's equity on 3/31/91 is $34,381.34. Let's look at the $27,981.34 change in the owner's equity. This

```
                        Balance Sheet
                        As of 3/31/91
      BUSINESS-ALL Accounts                        Page 1
      8/ 6/91
                                           1/ 1/91      3/31/91
                    Acct                   Balance      Balance
      -------------------------------    -----------   ---------
      ASSETS

      Cash and Bank Accounts
        ANB Business-Business Checking   4,000.00    32,696.50
        ANB Personal-Personal Checking       0.00     -123.16
                                         ----------   ---------
      Total Cash and Bank Accounts       4,000.00    32,573.34

      Other Assets
        Equipment-Capital Equipment      2,400.00     3,625.00
                                         ----------   ---------
      Total Other Assets                 2,400.00     3,625.00


                                         ----------   ---------
      TOTAL ASSETS                       6,400.00    36,198.34
                                         ==========   =========

      LIABILITIES & EQUITY

      LIABILITIES

        Other Liabilities
          Payroll-FICA-Co-FICA Matching      0.00      382.50
          Payroll-FICA-FICA Withholding      0.00      382.50
          Payroll-FWH-Federal Withholding    0.00      599.00
          Payroll-SWH-State Withholding      0.00      453.00
                                         ----------   ---------
        Total Other Liabilities              0.00     1,817.00


                                         ----------   ---------
      TOTAL LIABILITIES                      0.00     1,817.00

      EQUITY                             6,400.00    34,381.34
                                         ----------   ---------
      TOTAL LIABILITIES & EQUITY         6,400.00    36,198.34
                                         ==========   =========
```

FIGURE 15-2. Comparative Balance Sheets at 3/31/91

```
                     Cash Flow Report
                 1/ 1/91 Through 3/31/91
    BUSINESS-Selected Accounts                     Page 1
    8/ 6/91
                                              1/ 1/91-
              Category Description             3/31/91
       ------------------------------------  --------------
       INFLOWS
          Consulting Income                       37,500.00
          Royalty Income                          10,000.00
          FROM Payroll-FWH                          1,797.00
          FROM Payroll-FICA-Co                      1,147.50
          FROM Payroll-FICA                         1,147.50
          FROM Payroll-SWH                            453.00
                                                 -----------
       TOTAL INFLOWS                              52,045.00
       OUTFLOWS
          Computer Supplies                          375.76
          Equipment Maintenance                    1,100.00
          Overnight Delivery                         270.00
          Payroll Expense:
           Gross Earnings          15,000.00
           Payroll Taxes            1,147.50
                                   -----------
          Total Payroll Expense                   16,147.50
          Postage Expense                             28.00
          Supplies                                    65.00
          Telephone Expense                          305.00
          Travel Expenses                            905.00
          Water, Gas, Electric:
             Electric Utilities       30.40
             Gas Utilities            17.00
                                   -----------
          Total Water, Gas, Electric                 47.40
          TO Equipment                             1,500.00
          TO Payroll-FWH                           1,198.00
          TO Payroll-FICA-Co                         765.00
          TO Payroll-FICA                            765.00
                                                 -----------
       TOTAL OUTFLOWS                             23,471.66
                                                 -----------
       OVERALL TOTAL                              28,573.34
                                                 ===========
```

FIGURE 15-3. Cash Flow report

change can be explained by examining the Profit and Loss statement prepared in Chapter 14, shown in Figure 15-4.

The Profit and Loss statement covers a period of time, in this example the first quarter of 1991. You can see that the net profit (total income − total expenses) is $27,981.34. This is equal to the change in the owner's equity between the two balance sheet dates. Thus, the net profit or loss of a business helps explain changes that occur between balance sheets from the beginning and end of the profit and loss period.

One final point to note is that the number −123.16 shown on the 3/31/91 Balance Sheet appears because you entered business expense transactions in your personal checking account. Although this is not recommended, it is not uncommon for small-business owners to encounter this situation. You must remember that the $123.16 is included in the Profit and Loss Statement as a business expense; thus, the reported net profit was reduced by that amount. Since cash was used for the payment, Quicken is telling you that the use of personal funds has reduced the total assets associated with your business activities.

 Although Quicken can handle the payment of business expenses out of both business and personal checking accounts, it is better to limit business expense payments to your business checking account. If the nature of your business necessitates the payment of expenses in cash, rather than from a checking account, you would probably find it useful to establish a Quicken cash account for your business and use it in combination with your business checking account to record payment of business expenses with personal cash.

Sole Proprietor Withdrawals from the Business

So far in the example you have not spent any of the cash generated from your business for personal use. In accounting it is called a *withdrawal,* or simply *draw,* when sole proprietors take cash or other assets out of the business for personal use. Obviously, these are not business expenses, so the profit and loss statement is not affected. On the other hand, you are reducing the assets of the business when you transfer cash from your business to your personal checking account.

In this section you will see how owner withdrawals affect the balance sheet of the business. Starting from the Main Menu in the ANB Business account register, follow these steps to record your withdrawal of cash from the business checking account:

1. Type **2** and press (CTRL)-(END) to move to the end of the account register.

2. Press (SHIFT)-(TAB) if you are not in the Date field.

```
                    PROFIT & LOSS STATEMENT
                    1/ 1/91 Through 3/31/91
        BUSINESS-All Accounts
        8/ 6/91                                       Page 1


                                              1/ 1/91-
                Category Description          3/31/91
        ------------------------------------ ---------------
        INCOME/EXPENSE
          INCOME
            Consulting Income                    37,500.00
            Royalty Income                       10,000.00
                                                -----------
          TOTAL INCOME                           47,500.00

          EXPENSES
            Computer Supplies                        375.76
            Depreciation Expense:
              Depreciation-Computer     150.00
              Depreciation-Printer      125.00
                                       -----------
            Total Depreciation Expense              275.00
            Equipment Maintenance                 1,100.00
            Overnight Delivery                       270.00
            Payroll Expense:
              Gross Earnings          15,000.00
              Payroll Taxes            1,147.50
                                       -----------
            Total Payroll Expense                 16,147.50
            Postage Expense                           28.00
            Supplies                                  65.00
            Telephone Expense                        305.00
            Travel Expenses                          905.00
            Water, Gas, Electric:
              Electric Utilities         30.40
              Gas Utilities              17.00
                                       -----------
            Total Water, Gas, Electric               47.40
                                                -----------
          TOTAL EXPENSES                          19,518.66


                                                -----------
          TOTAL INCOME/EXPENSE                    27,981.34
                                                ===========
```

FIGURE 15-4. Profit and Loss statement for the period ending 3/31/91

3. Type **3/31/91** and press ⟨ENTER⟩ twice.

The cash withdrawal is being handled as a transfer between your business and personal checking accounts. Just as it is not good practice to pay business expenses from a personal checking account, neither should you use business checks to pay for personal expenditures.

4. Type **Mr. Johnson** and press ⟨ENTER⟩.

The payee name matches the name of the business owner since it is a withdrawal.

5. Type **5000** and press ⟨ENTER⟩ three times.
6. Type **Transfer - Withdraw** and press ⟨ENTER⟩.
7. Press ⟨CTRL⟩-⟨C⟩ to open the Category and Transfer List window.
8. Press ⟨END⟩ to move to the end of the list.
9. Move the arrow cursor up to ANB Personal and press ⟨ENTER⟩.
10. Type **/B** after ANB Personal in the Category field and press ⟨CTRL⟩-⟨ENTER⟩.

The class designation tells Quicken that this transaction will affect the business checking account balance. This transaction appears in your ANB Business account register after recording the transaction as shown here:

```
3/31    Mr. Johnson                        5,000 00              27,696 25
1991  Memo: Transfer - Withdraw
      Cat: [ANB Personal]/B
```

11. Press ⟨CTRL⟩-⟨X⟩ to view the transaction in the ANB Personal register after highlighting the transaction you just entered.
12. Press ⟨ESC⟩ to return to the Main Menu.
13. Press ⟨TAB⟩ to move to the Memo field.
14. Type **Withdraw from business** and press ⟨CTRL⟩-⟨ENTER⟩.

This is an important step in the recording of the transaction. This memo is used to describe all withdrawals from the business, so it can later be used as a filter in preparing the Balance Sheet. Here is how this transaction appears in your ANB Personal account register after it is recorded:

15. With the withdraw transaction highlighted press (CTRL)-(X) to return to the ANB Business register.

16. Press (ESC) to return to the Main Menu.

Balance Sheet After an Owner's Withdrawal of Capital

Now that you have recorded your owner's withdrawal, let's take a look at the Balance Sheet of the business. Follow these steps from the Main Menu of the ANB Business account:

1. Type **3** to select Reports.

2. Type **2** to select Business Reports.

3. Type **7** and the Balance Sheet window appears.

4. Press (F8) (Customize) to open the Create Account Balances Report window.

5. Press (ENTER) to accept the default report title.

6. Type **1/1/91** and press (ENTER).

7. Type **3/31/91** and press (ENTER).

8. Type **6** to select Quarter for the report interval and press (ENTER). This entry will cause Quicken to create a comparative Balance Sheet with balances shown for the beginning and the end of the quarter.

9. Press (F9) (Filter) and the Filter Report Transaction window appears. Figure 15-5 shows how the window appears when completed.

10. Press (ENTER) to move to the Memo matches field.

11. Type ~**Withdraw..** and press (ENTER) twice.

12. Type **B** in the Class matches field and press (CTRL)-(ENTER) to return to the Create Account Balances Report window.

13. Press (ENTER) to accept A for all in the Current/All/Selected accounts field. The Balance Sheet appears on your screen.

14. Press (F8) (Print) and the Print Report window appears.

15. Select the printer you will be using and press (ENTER). Your Balance Sheet will look like the one in Figure 15-6.

EFFECTS OF OWNER'S WITHDRAWAL As you can see, the Balance Sheet after recording the withdrawal shows your total equity to be

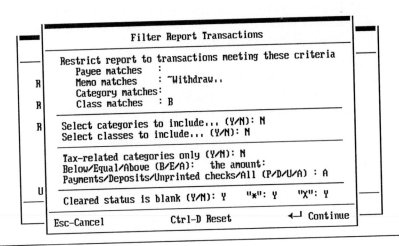

BUSINESS–ANB Business

FIGURE 15-5. Filter Report Transactions window for owner withdrawals

```
                          Balance Sheet
                          As of 3/31/91
      BUSINESS-All Accounts                              Page 1
      8/ 6/91
                                              1/ 1/91      3/31/91
                        Acct                  Balance      Balance
      ------------------------------------- --------    ---------
      ASSETS

        Cash and Bank Accounts
         ANB Business-Business Checking      4,000.00    27,696.50
         ANB Personal-Personal Checking          0.00      -123.16
                                            ----------   ----------
        Total Cash and Bank Accounts         4,000.00    27,573.34

        Other Assets
         Equipment-Capital Equipment         2,400.00     3,625.00
                                            ----------   ----------
        Total Other Assets                   2,400.00     3,625.00


                                            ----------   ----------
      TOTAL ASSETS                           6,400.00    31,198.34
                                            ==========   ==========
      LIABILITIES & EQUITY

        LIABILITIES
         Other Liabilities
          Payroll-FICA-Co-FICA Matching          0.00       382.50
          Payroll-FICA-FICA Withholding          0.00       382.50
          Payroll-FWH-Federal Withholding        0.00       599.00
          Payroll-SWH-State Withholding          0.00       453.00
                                            ----------   ----------
         Total Other Liabilities                 0.00     1,817.00


                                            ----------   ----------
        TOTAL LIABILITIES                        0.00     1,817.00

        EQUITY                               6,400.00    29,381.34
                                            ----------   ----------
      TOTAL LIABILITIES & EQUITY             6,400.00    31,198.34
                                            ==========   ==========
```

═══ **FIGURE 15-6.** Comparative Balance Sheet after recording owner's withdrawal

$29,381.34. This illustrates how the owner's equity in the business is affected not only by net profits and losses, but also by owner withdrawals of equity. You also know that an investment of additional cash or assets in the business increases the owner's equity. This occurred on 1/1/91 when you invested cash and equipment in setting up the business. Thus, the owner's equity change between the two Balance Sheets is accounted for by adding the net profits for the period to the beginning owner's equity and then reducing it by withdrawals ($6,400.00 + $27,981.34 − $5,000.00 = $29,381.34).

USING QUICKEN TO TRACK ACCOUNTS RECEIVABLE

In all the chapters in this section of the book you have been recording your revenues (income) and expenses on a cash basis. That means you have not been recognizing any income until cash is received or expensing any purchases until you paid for them. However, when you sell products to your customers they may not pay cash immediately. Instead, they may purchase the goods on credit and plan to pay you at a later date. For example, the computer consulting being done by the proprietor in the example was billed to customers and not collected until later in the month, or even in the following month.

Even though a cash basis accounting system does not recognize income until cash is received from the customer, you need to monitor your accounts receivable to know what cash you can expect to receive for goods that have been sold. You will also want to contact a customer when an account is not paid within a certain period after billing. When an account becomes late it is called a *delinquent account*. The importance of being able to monitor customer accounts cannot be overstated. You need to have the ability to know who owes you money and when you can expect to receive the funds.

Using the cash basis of reporting income and expense for tax returns, you can use Quicken to help keep track of the customer invoicing and to record the eventual collection of cash. At the time of collection you will recognize the income from the sales. The process described in the following sections shows how you can keep track of invoices through the use of an other asset account and recognize the income in your business checking account when you collect from the customer.

Establishing the Accounts Receivable System

You will keep track of customer billing through an other asset account called Acct Receivable. Starting from the Main Menu in the ANB Business account, follow these steps:

1. Type **4** to choose Select Account.
2. Move the arrow cursor to the < New Account > field in the Select Account to Use window and press (ENTER). The Set Up New Account window appears.
3. Type **4** and press (ENTER). You have defined this account as an other asset account type.
4. Type **Acct Receivable** and press (ENTER).
5. Type **0** and press (ENTER).
6. Type **1/1/91** and press (ENTER).
7. Type **Accounts Receivable** and press (ENTER).
8. Move the arrow cursor to Acct Receivable and press (ENTER). The account register appears on your screen.
9. Press (CTRL)-(C), move the arrow cursor to < New Category >, and press (ENTER). The Set Up Category window appears.
10. Type **Sales** and press (ENTER).
11. Type **I** and press (CTRL)-(ENTER). You are now back in the Category and Transfer List window.
12. Press (ESC) and you are returned to the Acct Receivable account register.

You are now prepared to monitor your customer billings in this account.

Recording Invoices

You will record a few customer invoices in this section. These will then be used to demonstrate how you can monitor your future cash receipts. Starting in the Acct Receivable account register, follow these steps to record the transactions, as shown in Figure 15-7:

1. Highlight the opening balance transaction in the register, move the cursor to the C (cleared) column, type *, and press CTRL-ENTER.

You have told Quicken to exclude the opening balance of zero from all reports you prepare using this account. This opening balance row would not have any meaning on the reports and could be misleading to readers.

2. Move to the Date field, type **2/1/91**, and press ENTER. This represents the date you expect the invoice to be paid by the customer.

3. Type **9801** for the first invoice number and press ENTER.

4. Type **Buy-A-Lot** in the Payee field and press ENTER three times. This records the customer name.

5. Type **125.99** in the Increase field and press ENTER.

The amount of the invoice is always recorded in the Increase field unless you are recording a credit invoice. A credit invoice is prepared when a business returns goods to you or when you agree to reduce the amount of your original invoice.

F1-Help	F2-Acct/Print	F3-Edit	F4-Quick Entry	F5-Reports	F6-Activities

DATE	REF	PAYEE · MEMO · CATEGORY	DECREASE	C	INCREASE	BALANCE
		═══ BEGINNING ═══				
1/ 1 1991		Opening Balance [Acct Receivab→]		*		0 00
2/ 1 1991	9801	Buy-A-Lot 1/1/91 Sales			125 99	125 99
2/ 1 1991	9802	Du-Wel 1/1/91 Sales			49 95	175 94

FIGURE 15-7. Account register transactions for accounts receivable

6. Type **1/1/91** in the Memo field and press (ENTER). This records the date you issued the invoice to the customer.

7. Type **Sales** and press (CTRL)-(ENTER).

8. Press (ENTER) to accept the date.

9. Press (+) to increase the invoice number by one and press (ENTER).

10. Type **Du-Wel** and press (ENTER) three times.

11. Type **49.95** and press (ENTER).

12. Type **1/1/91** and press (ENTER).

13. Type **Sales** and press (CTRL)-(ENTER).

You have now recorded the invoices that will be used to demonstrate how to account for the eventual collection of these receivables and recognize the income in your business checking account register.

Matching Payments with Specific Invoices

The steps outlined next show how to record the collection of cash from customers and how to recognize the income at the time of the collection. Starting in the Acct Receivable account register, follow these steps:

1. Highlight the transaction for invoice 9801 and press (CTRL)-(S). After completing the following steps, your Split Transaction window will appear as shown in Figure 15-8.

2. Move the cursor to the second Category field in the Split Transaction window.

3. Press (CTRL)-(C), move the arrow cursor to ANB Business by pressing (END) and (UP ARROW), press (ENTER), type **/B** after ANB Business, and press (ENTER) again.

The /B is used to follow the procedure of assigning all business transactions a class designation. When preparing the financial statements you would

```
┌──────────────────────────────────────────────────────────────────┐
│ F1-Help    Acct/Print     Edit     Quick Entry   Reports  Activities│
├────┬────┬───────────────────────────┬─────────┬─┬─────────┬────────┤
│DATE│ REF│ PAYEE · MEMO · CATEGORY   │DECREASE │C│INCREASE │BALANCE │
├────┼────┼───────────────────────────┼─────────┼─┼─────────┼────────┤
│2/ 1│9001│Buy-A-Lot                  │         │ │         │   0 00 │
│1991│SPLIT│1/1/91                    │         │ │         │        │
│    │Cat:│Sales                      │         │ │   49 95 │  49 95 │
│2/ 1│9002│Du-Wel                     │         │ │         │        │
```

```
                    Split Transaction
┌──────────────────────────────┬──────────────────┬──────────────┐
│         Category             │   Description    │   Amount     │
│  1:Sales                     │                  │    125.99    │
│  2:[ANB Business]/B          │  1/10/91         │   -125.99    │
│  3:                          │                  │              │
│  4:                          │                  │              │
│  5:                          │                  │              │
│  6:                          │                  │              │
├──────────────────────────────┴──────────────────┴──────────────┤
│        Enter categories, descriptions, and amounts              │
│  Esc-Cancel   Ctrl-D Delete   F9-Recalc Transaction Total  Ctrl↵ Done│
└─────────────────────────────────────────────────────────────────┘
```

Acct Receivable

Ending Balance: $49.95

═══════ **FIGURE 15-8.** Split Transaction window to record accounts receivable as sales and as payment when received

exclude Acct Receivable from the selection of accounts. This is appropriate since a cash basis taxpayer would only recognize the revenues from customers when paid.

4. Type **1/10/91** in the Description field and press **ENTER**.

5. Type **−125.99** and press **ENTER**.

6. Press **CTRL**-**D** to delete the amount from the third line in the Split Transaction window.

7. Press **F9** to recalculate the transaction total.

8. Press **CTRL**-**ENTER** to record the split transaction.

9. Move the cursor to the C column, type **∗**, and press **CTRL**-**ENTER**. This indicates that the invoice was paid in full, so it will be excluded from the accounts receivable aging report.

Quicken adjusts the balance in the accounts receivable register to reflect the collection of the cash and records the transaction in the ANB Business checking account at the same time.

Accounts Receivable Aging

In addition to monitoring the accounts receivable activity in your business, you are also interested in knowing whether your customers are paying their bills on time. You can use Quicken to assist in this monitoring by preparing an *aging* of your accounts receivable at the end of the year or at other times. When you age receivables you list all of the accounts not collected at a specific date by the length of time they have been outstanding. For example, you might decide to list all accounts not paid within 30 days of billing as one group, those between 31 and 60 days as a second group, and those over 61 days as a third group. Generally speaking, the longer the time that has elapsed since billing, the less likely you are to collect. Thus, the aging of accounts receivable is important in helping you monitor your customers' payments and detect any potential cash collection problems before they develop.

In the report that follows several accounts receivable transactions have been added. Since entering them would be very repetitious, you need not do so. You can still follow the steps needed to create the report; your report will simply have fewer entries.

The procedure required to create the report shown in Figure 15-9 follows. Start from the Acct Receivable account register and follow these steps to prepare an aging of your accounts receivable:

1. Press (F5) and the Reports menu appears.

2. Type **2** to select Business Reports.

3. Type **4** and the A/R by Customer window appears.

4. Press (F8).

5. Press (ENTER).

6. Type **1/1/91** and press (ENTER).

7. Type **3/31/91** and press (ENTER).

8. Press (ENTER) three times and the Select Accounts To Include window appears.

9. Move the arrow cursor to Equipment and press (SPACEBAR) so that only the Acct Receivable account is included; then press (ENTER). The A/R by Customer report appears.

The A/R (accounts receivable) by Customer report shows only those customers with an outstanding amount. Invoices that have been paid, such as 9801, have a balance of zero and are marked with an asterisk in the C field and thus are not included in the report.

```
                        A/R by Customer

                    1/ 1/91 Through 3/31/91
            BUSINESS-Acct Receivable
            8/ 6/91
                                                    OVERALL
                    Payee        1/91    2/91    3/91    TOTAL

            Big Builders        78.95    0.00    0.00    78.95
            Du-Wel               0.00   49.95    0.00    49.95
            Sims Construction    0.00    0.00  160.00   160.00

            OVERALL TOTAL       78.95   49.95  160.00   288.90
            ═════════════════   ══════  ══════  ══════   ══════
```

```
BUSINESS-Acct Receivable                                    (Filtered)
Esc-Create report              F1-Help      Ctrl M-Memorize  F8-Print
```

FIGURE 15-9. A/R (accounts receivable) by Customer report

10. Press F8 and the Print Report window appears.

11. Select the appropriate printer and press ENTER.

The method illustrated in this section to record accounts receivable transactions is ideal when each payment covers a single invoice. If most of your customers' payments cover multiple invoices you will need to assign subclasses to each customer (see Chapter 11 for a discussion of subclasses). You will also want to record a separate transaction for each payment.

USING QUICKEN TO TRACK ACCOUNTS PAYABLE

With cash basis accounting you need to monitor your accounts payable the same way you monitor accounts receivable. Quicken can help you keep track of payments owed and the due dates. Just as you don't recognize accounts receivable as revenue until payment is received, you will not recognize the cost of items purchased as an expense until you write your check to pay for the goods or services.

Recording Accounts Payable Transactions

Recording the accounts payable activity can take place directly in the ANB Business checking account. When you record an accounts payable transaction you are recording it before the actual check will be drawn. Thus, Quicken treats the recording as a postdated check. This means that the check is included in the account balance, but not for the current date. Quicken's current balance, shown in the lower-right corner of the register, will reflect the balance in the account before deducting the postdated checks. The ending balance reflects the balance after Quicken deducts the total of all postdated checks as well.

Starting from the ANB Business checking account, complete the following steps to record the accounts payable transaction shown here:

1. Type **5/30/91** in the Date field and press ⟨ENTER⟩.
2. Type * and press ⟨ENTER⟩. This enters asterisks in the Num field until you write the check; you record the number at that time.
3. Type **Pay-Less Books** and press ⟨ENTER⟩.
4. Type **125** and press ⟨ENTER⟩ three times.
5. Type **Invoice 564321** and press ⟨ENTER⟩.
6. Type **Supplies/B** and press ⟨CTRL⟩-⟨ENTER⟩.

These steps recorded the check in the account register. Remember, it will not affect the financial statements prepared for the first quarter of 1991. The transaction is excluded from reports for that quarter since the date, 5/30/91, falls outside the period defined for your reports.

When the payment comes due, you would just record the check number in the Num field and press ⟨CTRL⟩-⟨ENTER⟩ to record the transaction. If you paid the check before or after the due date you would record the new date as well as the check number and press ⟨CTRL⟩-⟨ENTER⟩.

Preparing an Accounts Payable by Week Report

In the previous section you entered an accounts payable transaction in the business checking account register. Figure 15-10 shows the transaction you

| F1-Help | F2-Acct/Print | F3-Edit | F4-Quick Entry | F5-Reports | F6-Activities |

DATE	NUM	PAYEE · MEMO · CATEGORY	PAYMENT	C	DEPOSIT	BALANCE
5/30 1991	*****	Pay-Less Books Invoice 564321 Supplies/B	125 00			25,709 24
6/ 1 1991	*****	Store-More Invoice 67543 Misc/B	50 00			25,659 24
6/ 3 1991	*****	Quick Charge Invoice 675111 Supplies/B	75 00			25,584 24
6/ 4 1991	*****	Rogers, Inc. Invoice 5643 Misc/B	89 79			25,494 45

FIGURE 15-10.   Account register transactions used to prepare accounts payable report

entered and several others that were added to prepare the Accounts Payable by Week report. From the ANB Business account register you would follow these steps to prepare the report:

1. Press **F5** and the Reports menu appears.

2. Type **5** and the Create Transaction Report window appears.

3. Type **Accounts Payable by Week** and press **ENTER**.

4. Type **5/30/91** and press **ENTER**.

5. Type **6/15/91** and press **ENTER**.

6. Type **2** and press **ENTER**.

7. Type **C** and press **ENTER** and the Accounts Payable by Week report will appear on the screen.

8. Press **F8** and the Print Report window appears.

9. Select the printer you will be using and press **ENTER**.

As you can see from Figure 15-11, the Accounts Payable by Week report prints a list of the accounts payable that will come due during the specified period, in this case 5/30/91 to 6/15/91.

```
                          Accounts Payable by Week
                          5/30/91 Through 6/15/91
BUSINESS-ANB Business                                        Page 1
8/ 6/91

Date    Num    Description        Memo          Category      Clr  Amount
-----  ------ ------------------ -------------- ------------------ - ----------

       BALANCE  5/29/91                                          25,834.24

5/30  ***** Pay-Less Books    Invoice 564321 Supplies/B          -125.00
6/ 1  ***** Store-More        Invoice 67543  Misc/B               -50.00
                                                               ----------
       TOTAL  5/30/91 -  6/ 1/91                                  -175.00

       BALANCE  6/ 1/91                                         25,659.24

6/ 3  ***** Quick Charge      Invoice 675111 Supplies/B           -75.00
6/ 4  ***** Rogers, Inc.      Invoice 5643   Misc/B               -89.79
                                                               ----------
       TOTAL  6/ 2/91 -  6/ 8/91                                  -164.79

       BALANCE  6/ 8/91                                         25,494.45


                                                               ----------
       TOTAL  6/ 9/91 -  6/15/91                                     0.00

       BALANCE  6/15/91                                         25,494.45


                                                               ----------
       OVERALL TOTAL                                              -339.79
                                                               ==========


       TOTAL INFLOWS                                                 0.00
       TOTAL OUTFLOWS                                             -339.79
                                                               ----------

       NET TOTAL                                                  -339.79
                                                               ==========
```

═════ **FIGURE 15-11.**   Accounts Payable by Week Report

QUICKEN'S ROLE IN YOUR BUSINESS RECORD KEEPING

Before leaving this chapter, let's take a final look at how Quicken has helped in the preparation of your business reports and financial statements. You have seen how you can use Quicken to record all your business transactions. You have prepared Profit and Loss statements, Cash Flow reports, Balance Sheets, and an Equipment report. In addition, you have used Quicken to assist in the preparation of tax forms and your payroll accounting throughout the year, as well as at year end. You have also seen how Quicken can be used to monitor the accounts receivable and accounts payable for your business, even though you use cash basis accounting.

You have also been exposed to some accounting terms and concepts. For example, you are now familiar with the use of the terms assets, liabilities, owner's equity, and depreciable assets. See Appendix B for a glossary of the accounting and Quicken terminology used in this book. Finally, and perhaps most importantly, you have been exposed to the financial statements you may be asked to prepare for your business. You have seen the technical aspects of using Quicken to prepare the statements and you have been introduced to the concepts that tie the financial statements together—that is, you now know that the Cash Flow report and Profit and Loss statement represent a period of time and that they help explain the changes that occur in the assets, liabilities, and owner's equity between comparative Balance Sheets for two different dates. With this knowledge you should be better prepared to manage the operating and financial activities of your business.

chapter 16

ADVANCED QUICKEN FEATURES

Maintaining Job Costs
Accrual Basis Accounting

I n Chapters 11 through 15 you used Quicken to assist in the recording and reporting of accounting information for both external and internal use. You recorded transactions in the account register, maintained employee records for payroll purposes, and used the information in the account registers to prepare financial statements and tax returns. In this chapter you will use Quicken to help monitor the costs associated with various jobs and to recognize income on an accrual accounting basis.

MAINTAINING JOB COSTS

The Profit and Loss statement (or income statement) prepared in Chapter 14 showed the income and expenses your business earned for an accounting period. Remember, this statement covered the period of time from January 1 to March 31, 1991. Although the Profit and Loss statement provides valuable information for both you and your creditors about the profitability of your business, you may find reports that are project-based provide better information for the day-to-day management of your business.

If your business is job- or project-based, you will find that Quicken's Class feature and a special Job/Project report can be combined to provide detailed information about the profitability of each job or project you work on during the year. An important feature of project monitoring is that you can choose the frequency with which you monitor costs: daily, weekly, monthly, quarterly, or yearly.

The approach described in the next section allows you, as the business manager, to have better information for decision-making purposes. You can monitor project cost and expected profits to better manage the assets of your business.

Adding a New Account Group

You added a new account group, BUSINESS, in Chapter 11 and recorded all your business transactions since then in that account group. Due to the advanced nature of the topics in this chapter, you should establish new account groups to record transactions and prepare Quicken reports. Although you could add the new examples to the existing group, separate accounts will allow you to focus on the new material. The first account group you will establish is called JOBS. You will then set up an account called Business Chk and record transactions in it. From the Main Menu follow these steps to set up the new account group and the new account:

1. Type **5** to select Change Settings.

2. Type **1** to select Account Group Activities.

3. Type **1** to choose Select/Set Up Account Group.

4. Move the arrow cursor to <Set Up New Grp> and press ⟨ENTER⟩.

5. Type **JOBS** as the name of the account group and press ⟨ENTER⟩.

6. Type **2** and press ⟨ENTER⟩ to select Business Categories.

7. Press ⟨ENTER⟩ to accept the data file location.

8. Move the arrow cursor to JOBS and press ⟨ENTER⟩.

You have now added the account group JOBS to your other account groups. The next step is to open the Business Chk account within the JOBS account group.

Adding the Business Chk Account

Starting from the Select Account to Use window, follow these steps:

1. Press (ENTER) to select < New Account >.

2. Press (ENTER) to accept 1, Bank Account, for account type.

3. Type **Business Chk** and press (ENTER).

4. Type **3000** and press (ENTER).

5. Type **1/1/91** and press (ENTER).

6. Type **Business Checking** and press (ENTER).

7. Move the arrow cursor to Business Chk and press (ENTER). You are now in the Business Chk account register.

Adding Transactions

Figure 16-1 shows the check register containing the details of each of the transactions entered in the Business Chk account for the period 1/1/91 to 1/15/91. The Acct/Print menu ((F2)) is used and Print Register selected to print Figure 16-1. Look closely at the figure and you can see that the Print Split Transaction Detail feature was used to provide a detailed printout of the split transactions recorded during the period. There are ten transactions included in this account register. Before you record the transactions in your account, let's discuss some Quicken features that will be encountered during the recording of transactions.

Remember, the objective of job or project management is to monitor the income and cost of the projects over the time the services are being performed. In the example developed in this chapter you are accumulating

```
                          Check Register
Business Chk                                          Page 1
8/15/91
Date   Num       Transaction       Payment  C Deposit    Balance
----   ----   --------------------  -------- - --------   -------
1/ 1           Opening Balance             X 3,000.00 3,000.00
1991 memo:
          cat:[Business Chk]
1/ 5 501    Lumber City             900.00              2,100.00
1991 SPLIT Plywood
              Const Mat/Ford        500.00
                Plywood for roof
              Const Mat/Rumney      400.00
                Plywood for
                sub-floor
1/ 9 502    97 Lumber             1,200.00                900.00
1991 SPLIT Shingles
              Const Mat/Ford        700.00
                Shingles for roof
              Const Mat/Shaffner    500.00
                Shingles for new
                garage
1/ 9        Shaffner              1,500.00              2,400.00
1991 memo: Draw on garage
                construction
          cat:Const Rev/Shaffner
1/11 503    Al's Building Supplies  750.00              1,650.00
1991 memo: Storm windows
          cat:Const Mat/Shaffner
1/12 504    Lumber City             45.00              1,605.00
1991 SPLIT Roofing cement
              Const Mat/Ford        20.00
                Cement for roof
                flashing
              Const Mat/Shaffner    25.00
                Cement for eaves
1/12 505    Jim Greene             300.00              1,305.00
```

FIGURE 16-1. Job/Project income and expense register

```
                            Check Register
Business Chk                                              Page 1
8/15/91

Date  Num      Transaction        Payment  C Deposit    Balance
----  ----   -------------------- -------- - --------   -------

1991 SPLIT Gross pay week of
              1/5/91
                 Wages/Ford          250.00
                 25 hours @ $10 hr
                 Wages/Shaffner       50.00
                 5 hours @ $10 hr
1/12 506   Ron Crothers             480.00                825.00
1991 SPLIT Gross pay week of
              1/5/91
                 Wages/Rumney        360.00
                 30 hours @ $12
                 Wages/Shaffner      120.00
                 10 hours @ $12

1/12       Ford                    3,000.00             3,825.00
1991 memo: Draw on roof work
           cat:Const Rev/Ford

1/15       Rumney                  2,200.00             6,025.00
1991 memo: Draw on kitchen work
           cat:Const Rev/Rumney

1/15 507   Lakeview Hardware        500.00              5,525.00
1991 memo: Plumbing materials
           cat:Const Mat/Rumney
```

══════ **FIGURE 16-1.** Job/Project income and expense register (*continued*)

information for a home repair and maintenance business. You will use split transactions to assign costs to more than one job and you will collect cash payments from your customers as you make progress on the projects.

As noted earlier you will also be using Quicken's Class feature. You used this feature in earlier chapters to mark business expenses by adding /B after the category designation. In this chapter you will use the same technique to assign cost and income to the three jobs in progress: Ford, Rumney, and Shaffner.

The first transaction added to your Business Chk register is dated 1/5/91 and uses Quicken's Split Transaction window to distribute the cost of plywood to a roofing project and a kitchen project. Figure 16-2 shows how your screen will appear after recording the transaction in your register. Notice that the plywood costs are charged to a category named Const Mat and that the Ford and Rumney classes are each charged with a portion of the plywood used on the jobs. When recording this transaction you will establish a new category named Const Mat and new classes for Ford and Rumney. Since these steps are not new to you, they are not shown in detail as they have been in previous chapters. This is a good opportunity for you to practice what you have learned.

Use your Quicken knowledge to record the transactions shown in Figure 16-1. If you need some assistance in adding categories or classes refer to Chapter 11 where the screens you will encounter are described in detail.

Preparing the Job/Project Report

After recording the transactions in the previous section, you are ready to prepare a report that summarizes income and expenses by job or project during the first half of January 1991. Starting from the Business Chk account register, follow these steps:

F1–Help	Acct/Print	Edit	Quick Entry	Reports	Activities

DATE	NUM	PAYEE · MEMO · CATEGORY	PAYMENT	C	DEPOSIT	BALANCE
1/ 5	501	Lumber City	900 00			2,100 00
1991	SPLIT	Plywood				
	Cat:	Const Mat/Ford				
1/ 9	502	97 Lumber	1,200 00			900 00

Split Transaction

	Category	Description	Amount
1:	Const Mat/Ford	Plywood for roof	500.00
2:	Const Mat/Rumney	Plywood for sub-floor	400.00
3:			
4:			
5:			
6:			

Enter categories, descriptions, and amounts
Esc-Cancel   Ctrl-D Delete   F9-Recalc Transaction Total   Ctrl↵ Done

FIGURE 16-2. Split Transaction window for Lumber City transaction

1. Press ⟨F5⟩ to open the Reports menu.

2. Type **2** to select Business Reports.

3. Type **5** and the Job/Project Report window appears.

4. Press ⟨ENTER⟩ to accept the default report title.

5. Type **1/91** and press ⟨ENTER⟩.

6. Type **1/91** and press ⟨F9⟩. The Filter Report Transactions window appears.

7. Type ~**Opening..** in the Payee matches field, and then press ⟨CTRL⟩-⟨ENTER⟩.

As you may recall from using this feature in earlier chapters, you have just told Quicken to exclude the opening balance from the Job/Project report. (Now the report will show only the desired job or project information.)

8. Press ⟨CTRL⟩-⟨ENTER⟩ again and the Job/Project report appears.

9. Press ⟨F8⟩ and the Print Report window appears.

10. Select the printer you will use and press ⟨ENTER⟩.

Figure 16-3 shows how your Job/Project report will look when printed. This report provides detailed information by job or project, which allows you to monitor the income and cost to date of the various jobs or projects in progress. Notice that the Overall Total column shows the complete income and expense picture for your business. This is similar to the information shown in the Profit and Loss statement prepared in Chapter 14, but you now have additional information that can help you make better decisions.

This report shows the income generated by each job for the first part of January and allows you to show the overall profit/loss ratio on each job or project as completed. This information can be used to plan costs on future projects and to decide if changes need to be made on the jobs in progress to increase profitability.

 In addition to this report, you could use the Filter Report Transactions window to customize other reports by job or project.

```
                              Job/Project Report
                            1/ 1/91 Through 1/31/91
        JOBS-Business Chk                                        Page 1
        8/15/91

                                                              OVERALL
        Category Description  Ford house  Rumney kitchen  Shaffner garage  TOTAL
        --------------------  ----------  --------------  --------------- ------
        INCOME/EXPENSE
          INCOME
            Construction Revenue  3,000.00      2,200.00      1,500.00  6,700.00
                                  ---------  --------------  ------------- --------
          TOTAL INCOME            3,000.00      2,200.00      1,500.00  6,700.00

          EXPENSES
            Construction Materials 1,220.00       900.00      1,275.00  3,395.00
            Wages & Job Credits     250.00        360.00        170.00    780.00
                                   ---------  --------------  ------------- --------
          TOTAL EXPENSES          1,470.00      1,260.00      1,445.00  4,175.00


          TOTAL INCOME/EXPENSE    1,530.00        940.00         55.00  2,525.00
                                  =========  ==============  ============= ========
```

FIGURE 16-3. Job/Project report

ACCRUAL BASIS ACCOUNTING

Throughout the last few chapters you have been recording transactions on a cash basis—that is, recording income when cash is received and expenses when checks are written. In Chapter 14 you modified the strict usage of the cash basis by recording depreciation on certain assets. Thus, you used what accountants refer to as the "modified cash" basis of accounting. This is the accounting basis most small-business Quicken users will follow.

If your business must use the accrual basis—that is, record income when services are performed and expenses when they are incurred—Quicken can help you there also. See the special section called Cash Versus Accrual Methods in Chapter 11, which discusses some of the major factors to consider when determining the method of accounting to use for tax accounting purposes in your business.

Accrual accounting requires advanced usage of Quicken, and thus detailed coverage of the method beyond the scope of this book. However, the example that follows shows a simple Quicken application that can be used to track your income on an accrual basis for financial reporting purposes. As you become familiar with Quicken you can experiment with other approaches to recording transactions on an accrual basis. For example, you might establish separate accounts receivable and payable accounts and charge the amounts to income and expense categories immediately. The cash receipts and payments would be recorded in the business checking account register when the actual collections and payments occur.

Adding a New Account Group and Establishing an Account

You will add another account group for this section of the chapter. This will allow you to experiment with the accrual method without mingling these transactions with the examples developed in previous chapters or the job costs material from this chapter.

By now the process should be familiar. However, you will probably want to follow the steps used in Maintaining Job Costs to establish the new account group. Use the following information:

Account group name:	ACCRUALS
Standard categories to use:	Business

Use this information in establishing your business checking account:

Account name:	1st City Chk
Account type:	Bank
Beginning balance:	6000
Beginning date:	1/1/91
Description:	Business Checking

With this information you have now added the ACCRUALS account group and the 1st City Chk account within that account group.

Adding Transactions

Figure 16-4 shows a check register completed with the transactions you will record in the 1st City Chk account for demonstration purposes. Notice that there are no split transactions. You will, however, establish some categories

```
                          Check Register
1st City Chk                                              Page 1
8/15/91


Date  Num      Transaction        Payment   C   Deposit    Balance
----  ----   ------------------    -------   --  -------    ---------


1/ 1         Opening Balance                 X  6,000.00   6,000.00
1991  memo:
             cat:[1st City Chk]


1/ 5 601   Stewart Construction 650.00                     5,350.00
1991  memo:Delivery of 400
              cu yd soil
           cat:Land Mat/DEC90


1/ 5         Kim Kaylor                         1,500.00   6,850.00
1991  memo:Landscape back lot
           cat:Land Inc/DEC90


1/ 8 602   Spena Tree Service    800.00                    6,050.00
1991  memo:Maple trees
           cat:Land Mat/JAN91


1/10         Oberle Farm                        1,200.00   7,250.00
1991  memo:Plant maples
              along drive
           cat:Land Inc/JAN91
```

FIGURE 16-4. Accrual basis transaction register

not found in the Quicken category list: Land Inc (landscaping income), and Land Mat (landscaping materials), and once again you will establish Quicken classes: 90 and 91. These classes will allow you to assign each income and expense transaction to an accounting period, either 1990 or 1991.

The accrual concept is apparent when you see that the 1/5/91 transactions are both assigned to the 1990 class. This means that Quicken will include these transactions in the 1990 financial statements prepared in the next section. Thus, income and expenses are assigned to the accounting period in which income was earned and expenses incurred, rather than the accounting period in which cash was received and paid. This demonstrates the essence of accrual basis accounting.

Starting in the 1st City Chk account register in the ACCRUAL account group, enter the transactions shown in Figure 16-4. When you have completed recording these transactions you can prepare the Profit and Loss statements for 1990 and 1991, as shown in the next section.

Preparing Accrual Basis Profit and Loss Statements

The steps outlined here show how you can prepare abbreviated Profit and Loss statements for 1990 and 1991 from the transactions recorded in the preceding section. Starting in the 1st City Chk account register, follow these steps:

1. Press (F5) to open the Reports menu.
2. Type 2 to select Business Reports.
3. Type 1 and the Profit and Loss Statement window appears.
4. Press (ENTER) to accept the default title.

Alternatively, you might want to use the title Accrual Basis P and L Statement on your report.

5. Type 1/90 and press (ENTER).
6. Type 1/91 and press (F9). The Filter Report Transaction window appears.
7. Press (ENTER) three times, type ..90, and press (CTRL)-(ENTER).

You are returned to the Profit and Loss Statement window. Notice that you defined the report period to include all of 1990 and the first month of 1991. This is necessary in order to include all transactions assigned to the 1990 class in the preparation of the Profit and Loss statement.

8. Press (CTRL)-(ENTER) and the Profit and Loss statement appears.
9. Press (F8) and the Print Report window appears.
10. Select the printer you will use and press (ENTER).

```
                    PROFIT AND LOSS STATEMENT
                     1/ 1/90 Through 1/31/91
        ACCRUAL-1st City Chk                          Page 1
        8/15/91
                                            1/ 1/90-
                    Category Description    1/31/91
                    ------------------------ ----------
                    INCOME/EXPENSE
                      INCOME
                        Landscaping Income   1,500.00
                                            ----------
                      TOTAL INCOME           1,500.00

                      EXPENSES
                        Landscape materials    650.00
                                            ----------
                      TOTAL EXPENSES           650.00


                                            ----------
                      TOTAL INCOME/EXPENSE     850.00
                                            ==========
```

FIGURE 16-5.   1990 Profit and Loss statement

The Profit and Loss statement shown in Figure 16-5 includes the cash receipts and disbursements recorded in January 1991 that were related to 1990 income and expenses. The 1991 accrual basis Profit and Loss statement can be prepared by completing the same steps. Why not print your 1991 statement now? Make the necessary modifications in the preceding steps and print your report. It should look like Figure 16-6.

```
                    PROFIT AND LOSS STATEMENT
                     1/ 1/91 Through 12/31/91
        ACCRUAL-1st City Chk                              Page 1
        8/15/91
                                              1/ 1/91-
                    Category Description      12/31/91
                    ----------------------- -----------
        INCOME/EXPENSE
          INCOME
            Landscaping Income          1,200.00
                                        -----------
          TOTAL INCOME                  1,200.00

          EXPENSES
            Landscape materials           800.00
                                        -----------
          TOTAL EXPENSES                  800.00


                                        -----------
          TOTAL INCOME/EXPENSE            400.00
                                        ===========
```

FIGURE 16-6. 1991 Profit and Loss statement

APPENDICES

Special Quicken Tasks
Glossary
Custom Settings
Standard Categories

The appendices that follow offer information supplementing the main Quicken features. You will find information on installation and a glossary of terms. You will also find information on customizing Quicken and a list of Quicken's standard category offerings.

SPECIAL QUICKEN TASKS

Formatting with a Hard Disk
Formatting with Floppy Disks
Installing Quicken
Starting Quicken
Upgrading from an Earlier Release

Quicken is easy to install with the right equipment. The package handles most of the installation work for you.

Since the package will run on so many different systems it is likely you have at least the minimum configuration. For the MS-DOS version of the software discussed in this book you will need an IBM PC, XT, AT, PS/2, or a compatible machine. You must have at least 320K of RAM in the machine and an 80-column monitor. You must have a hard disk or one or more floppy disk drives.

You will need MS-DOS version 2.0 or a later version as your operating system. You should also have available one 3 1/2-inch or two 5 1/4-inch formatted disks. If you have disks that have not yet been formatted, follow the steps in the one of the two following sections that corresponds to your system.

FORMATTING WITH A HARD DISK

Follow these steps to format a floppy disk with a hard drive system:

1. Make sure drive A is empty.
2. Turn the system on.
3. Respond to the date and time prompts if necessary. The C> prompt will appear.
4. Type **FORMAT A:** and press (ENTER).
5. Place a blank disk in drive A.
6. Press (ENTER) in response to the prompt. The system tells you when the formatting is complete and asks if you would like to format another disk.
7. Remove the formatted disk from the drive.
8. If you are working with 5 1/4-inch disks and need to format another disk, type **Y**; otherwise, type **N**.
9. Press (ENTER).

If you are formatting a second disk you will need to repeat steps 5 through 9.

FORMATTING WITH FLOPPY DISKS

If you do not have a hard disk, follow these steps to format floppy disks:

1. Place the DOS disk in drive A and close the door.
2. Turn the system on.
3. Respond to the date and time prompts if necessary. The A> prompt will appear.
4. Type **FORMAT A:** and press (ENTER).
5. Remove the DOS disk from drive A and replace it with a blank disk.
6. Press (ENTER) in response to the prompt message. The system tells you when the formatting is complete and asks if you would like to format another disk.

7. Remove the formatted disk from the drive.

8. If you are working with 5 1/4-inch disks and need to format another disk, type **Y**; otherwise, type **N**.

9. Press ⌈ENTER⌋.

If you are formatting a second disk, you will need to put another disk in drive A and repeat steps 6 through 9.

INSTALLING QUICKEN

Quicken is so easy to install that almost all you need to do is put the correct disks in the drive and type **INSTALL**. Quicken will display a few prompts during installation and expect you to respond with answers to questions such as which drive you want to use for installation. Quicken's installation program copies all the files to the hard disk or to a floppy. With a hard disk it will also perform some other tasks for you, such as checking your operating system configuration file and creating a file that makes it easy to start Quicken without changing to a different directory.

STARTING QUICKEN

To start the Quicken program, make the drive containing your Quicken program active. If you are using drive C, you will expect to see the DOS prompt C>. If the wrong drive is active, type the drive letter followed by a colon and press ⌈ENTER⌋. If you are using a hard disk, you will also need to make the correct directory active. You can change directories by typing **CD** followed by the drive name. To activate the QUICKEN4 directory you would type **CD\QUICKEN4** and press ⌈ENTER⌋.

Once you have activated the Quicken drive and directory, type **Q** to start Quicken. Quicken's Main Menu will appear. To start Quicken and open an account, follow the Q with the name of the account, as in **Q Investments**. If you enter **Q Investments Personal**, Quicken will open the Investments account in the Personal account group. If you want to open an account containing spaces, place the name of the account in quotes, as in **Q "ANB Business"**.

If you wish to bypass the Main Menu you can type a **2** to open the register window. Typing **Q 2** will start Quicken and display the register for the most recent account used. Typing **Q "ANB Business" 2** will start Quicken and display the register for ANB Business.

UPGRADING FROM AN EARLIER RELEASE

If you have been using Quicken 3.0, you don't need to do anything special to use Quicken 4. Since the file formats of the two releases are the same, all you need to do is install Quicken 4. You can use all the new features with your existing data immediately.

If you are upgrading from Quicken 1 or Quicken 2, you will need to contact Intuit, the developers of Quicken, for a conversion program. You will find a toll-free number at the back of your Quicken manual.

GLOSSARY

Accelerated Depreciation   A method of depreciation in which more expense is recognized in the early years of an asset's life.

Account   Quicken document where personal and/or business transactions are recorded that increase or decrease the amount of money in the account. Examples include bank, cash, credit card, other assets, and other liabilities accounts.

Account Balance   The amount of money in an account.

Account Group   A group of related accounts, such as a personal checking account, a savings account, and an asset account for your home.

Accounts Payable   Money owed to suppliers for goods or services.

Accounts Receivable   Money owed to you by customers or clients.

Accrual Basis   An accounting method in which income is recorded when services are provided rather than when cash is received. Expenses are treated similarly.

Accumulated Depreciation The total amount of depreciation expense taken on an asset since the time it was placed in service.

ASCII (American Standard Code for Information Interchange) A standard set of codes used for storing information. When you write information to disk with Quicken, the data is stored in ASCII format. This makes it easy to transfer the data to a word processing package or any other package that reads ASCII data.

Asset Any item of value that a business or individual owns.

Average Annual Total Return The average annual percent return on your investment. Interest, dividends, capital gains distributions, and unrealized gains/losses are used in computing this return on your investment.

Average Cost The total cost of all shares divided by the total number of shares.

Balance Sheet A financial statement that summarizes a business's assets, liabilities, and owner's equity at a specific time.

Book Value The cost of an asset less the amount of depreciation expensed to date.

Brokerage Account An account with a firm that buys and sells shares of stocks and other investments on your behalf.

Budget A plan indicating projected income and expenses. Budget also refers to a comparison between the projections and actual amounts for each income or expense category.

Cash Money or currency.

Cash Basis A method of accounting used for business or tax purposes. Income is recorded when cash is received, and expenses are charged when cash is paid.

Cash Flows The inflow and outflow of cash during a specific time period.

Category Identifies the exact nature of income and expenses, such as salary income, dividend income, interest income, or wage expense. Categories are distinct from classes.

Chart of Accounts A list of the categories used to charge income and expenses for a given account.

Class Allows you to define the time period, location, or type of activity for a transaction. Classes are distinct from categories.

Cleared Item An item that has been processed by the bank.

Control Codes Special codes that can request a specific feature or function from your printer, such as compressed printing. Each manufacturer has its own unique set of codes for each printer model manufactured.

Corporation A form of business organization that limits the liability of the shareholders.

Cost Basis Total cost of stock bought or sold plus commission.

Current Balance The present balance in an account. This does not include postdated items.

Deductions Amounts that reduce the gross pay to cover taxes and other commitments, such as health insurance premiums.

Deposit An amount of funds added to an account. A deposit is sometimes referred to as a "credit" to the account.

Depreciable Base The cost of an asset that will be expensed over its useful life.

Depreciation The portion of the cost of an asset that is expensed each year on a Profit and Loss statement.

Dividends Cash payments made to the shareholders of a corporation from current or past earnings.

Double Entry System An accounting method that requires two accounts be used when recording a transaction. For example, when supplies are purchased, both the cash and supplies accounts are affected.

Equity The amount of the owner's investment in the business. For individuals, this is the money invested in a property or other asset.

Expense   The cost associated with an item or service purchased or consumed.

FICA   Social Security tax paid by employers and employees.

Financial Obligations   Commitments to pay cash or other assets in return for receiving something of value—for example, a bank loan for equipment or an automobile.

Financial Resources   Objects or property of value owned by a person or business that are expected to increase future earnings.

Financial Statements   Periodic reports prepared by businesses to show the financial condition of the firm. Major financial statements include balance sheets, Profit and Loss statements (income statement), and cash flow reports.

FUTA   Federal unemployment tax.

FWH   Federal income tax withheld from employees' earnings.

Gross Earnings   Total earnings of an employee before deductions are subtracted.

Income   The money earned by an individual or business. On a cash basis it is the amount of cash received for goods or services provided. On an accrual basis it is the amount of income recognized and recorded during the year for services provided.

Income Statement   A summary of the income and expenses of a business.

IRA   Individual Retirement Account. Depending upon your income level, you may experience tax benefits from setting up an IRA.

Job/Project Report   A method of reporting revenues and expenses on a job or project basis.

Liability   The money you owe to a vendor, creditor, or any other party.

Life of an Asset   The number of years that the asset is expected to last.

Liquidity   A measure of how easy it is to convert an asset to cash.

Memorized Transaction   A transaction that you have asked Quicken to remember and recall at a later time.

Menu   A related list of commands, called "items," presented for selection. A menu is frequently used in software packages as a means of offering features to choose from.

Money Market Account   An account held with a bank or other institution used to preserve capital. Most provide limited checking account privileges.

Mutual Fund   An investment vehicle that allows you to purchase shares in the fund; the proceeds are used by the fund to buy shares in a variety of stocks or bonds.

Net Pay   The amount of pay received after deductions.

Net Worth   An amount determined by subtracting the value of financial obligations from financial resources.

P & L Statement   An abbreviation for Profit and Loss statement; it shows the profit or loss generated during a period.

Partnership   A form of business organization where two or more individuals share in the profits and losses of the business.

Payment   The amount paid to a vendor, creditor, or other party.

Payroll Taxes   The taxes a business pays on employee earnings—for example, matching FICA contributions, federal and state unemployment taxes, and workers' compensation payments.

Point in Time   A specific time where some activity is occurring.

Postdated Transaction   A check dated after the current date.

Reconciliation   The process of comparing a copy of the bank's records for your account with your own records. Any differences should be explained in this process.

Revenue   The money or income generated.

Salvage   The worth of an asset at the end of its useful life.

Security   An investment such as a stock, bond, or mutual fund.

Service Charge   A fee the bank adds for maintaining your account. This fee can be part of the difference in reconciling a bank statement.

Single Entry System   For any transaction to which only one entry is made, either to an income or expense category or to an account. An accounting method in which one account is used to record a transaction. When supplies are purchased, only the cash (or checking) account is affected.

Sole Proprietorship   The simplest form of small-business organization. There is no separation between the owner and the company.

Straight Line Depreciation   A method of expensing the cost of an asset evenly over its life.

SUTA   State unemployment tax.

SWH   State income taxes withheld from employee gross earnings.

Transaction Group   A group of memorized transactions that can be recalled together whenever you need them.

Transfer   A transaction that affects the balance in two accounts at the same time by moving funds between them.

Unrealized Gain/Loss   A gain or loss estimated on the basis of current market value.

Valuation   The current value of an asset.

CUSTOM SETTINGS

Making Changes to the Settings

Quicken allows you to change some settings to allow the package to work with more than one type of computer system. Changing the settings also provides a measure of control over some package features.

MAKING CHANGES TO THE SETTINGS

The majority of changes are made through the Change Settings item in the Main Menu. This is accessed by typing **5** when the Main Menu is on the screen. Changes relating to printed output are discussed in each chapter where output is created.

The important setting changes you may want to consider are summarized in this appendix.

Screen Colors

All color options are not available on every system since you are limited to the capabilities of the monitor attached to your system. Available options are listed on the next page.

- *Monochrome* One-color monitors that cannot display shades of gray.
- *Navy and Azure*
- *White and Navy*
- *Red and Gray*
- *Shades of Gray* One-color monitors that use shading to differentiate information displayed—similar to the way a color monitor uses different colors.

Monitor Speed

The best selection depends on the speed with which your monitor refreshes (or redraws) the screen. Available selections are

- *Slow* Slower refreshing of the screen to eliminate white marks called "snow."
- *Fast* Fast screen refreshing of information; it may cause snow if your monitor is not fast enough.

Printer Settings

Printer settings allow you to specify a check printer and two alternate report printers. The various printer settings are covered in the discussion of printer settings in Chapter 3.

Password

This allows you to establish a password for an account group or for transactions prior to a specified date. The options are

- *Main Password* Establishes a password for the current account group. Once you set a password for an account group, you will not be able to access the group unless you can supply the password.

- *Transaction*   Allows you to prevent changes to previous transactions up to a specified date. This is referred to as "closing an accounting period." When creating the password you must specify the password and a date; transactions on or before this date cannot be changed without entering the password.

Other Settings

A variety of setting items are grouped together in the Other Settings window. Any of them can be changed by pressing (ENTER) or (TAB) to move the cursor to the selected item and typing the desired option. You can change the following settings:

- *Beep when recording or memorizing*   A beeping sound normally occurs when you record or memorize a transaction. You can disable or reinstate it with this option.

- *Request confirmation*   When you press (ENTER) in recording the last field in a check or a register transaction, Quicken displays a prompt asking you to confirm whether it should record the transaction. If you turn off the confirmation with this option, the transaction will be automatically recorded without displaying the confirmation prompt.

- *Require category on transactions*   With the default setting of No, a category entry is optional. Typing Y, for Yes, prevents you from accidentally leaving a transaction without entering a category in the Category field.

- *Extra message line on check*   This allows you to print on your checks a message line that does not appear in the register.

- *Days in advance to remind*   This setting determines the number of days in advance that Quicken will remind you of transaction groups and postdated checks when you start the package. It is preset to three days in advance, but you can change it to any number from 0 to 30.

- *Change date of checks to today's date when printed*   If you set this to Y, all postdated checks will display the date on which they are printed. Otherwise, they will retain the original entry date.

- *MM/DD/YY or DD/MM/YY*   These allow you to select the date format.

- *Billminder active*   This setting enables hard disk users to activate and deactivate the Billminder feature.

- *Print categories on voucher checks*   Changing this setting to Y prints category information and split transaction detail on voucher checks.

- *Register settings*   This allows you to choose a 20-line or a 43-line register display depending on your monitor type.

- *Show Memo/Category/Both*   This option determines the information displayed beneath the Payee line of a nonactive transaction (a transaction other than the current transaction) in a register.

- *Use category Description/Name/Both*   This determines how much category and class information is included in a report.

- *Warn if Check Number is reused*   This gives you a warning to prevent using the same check number twice.

Electronic Payment

These settings allow you to configure Quicken to interface with CheckFree's electronic check service.

- *Modem Settings*   These options allow you to define how your modem is connected to your computer, the modem's speed, and whether your phone service uses tone or pulse dialing. You must also include the CheckFree phone number and turn on the electronic payment service with this option.

- *Account Settings*   This option allows you to select an account for electronic payments.

STANDARD CATEGORIES

Whenever you set up a new account group, you can select from three standard sets of categories. Selecting Home provides category options for personal use. Business is appropriate for business income and expenses. Selecting Both gives you categories for personal and business use. All three of these selections allow you to add new categories or delete existing categories. If you would prefer to use all custom categories, selecting Neither will let you build a category list from scratch for an account group.

Home Categories

Category	Description	Tax Related	Type
Bonus	Bonus Income	*	Inc
Canada Pen	Canadian Pension	*	Inc
Div Income	Dividend Income	*	Inc
Family Allow	Family Allowance	*	Inc
Gift Received	Gift Received	*	Inc
Int Inc	Interest Income	*	Inc
Invest Inc	Investment Income	*	Inc

Category	Description	Tax Related	Type
Old Age Pension	Old Age Pension	*	Inc
Other Inc	Other Income	*	Inc
Salary	Salary Income	*	Inc
Auto Fuel	Automobile Fuel		Expns
Auto Loan	Automobile Loan Payment		Expns
Auto Serv	Automobile Service		Expns
Bank Chrg	Bank Charge		Expns
Charity	Charitable Donations	*	Expns
Childcare	Childcare Expense		Expns
Christmas	Christmas Expenses		Expns
Clothing	Clothing		Expns
Dining	Dining Out		Expns
Dues	Dues		Expns
Education	Education		Expns
Entertain	Entertainment		Expns
Gifts	Gift Expenses		Expns
Groceries	Groceries		Expns
Home Rpair	Home Repair & Maint.		Expns
Household	Household Misc. Exp.		Expns
Housing	Housing		Expns
Insurance	Insurance		Expns
Int Exp	Interest Expense	*	Expns
Invest Exp	Investment Expense	*	Expns
Medical	Medical & Dental	*	Expns
Misc	Miscellaneous		Expns
Mort Int	Mortgage Interest Exp.	*	Expns
Mort Prin	Mortgage Principal		Expns
Other Exp	Other Expenses		Expns
Recreation	Recreation Expense		Expns
RRSP	Reg. Retirement Sav. Plan		Expns
Subscriptions	Subscriptions		Expns
Supplies	Supplies		Expns
Tax Fed	Federal Tax Withholding	*	Expns
Tax FICA	Social Security Tax	*	Expns
Tax Other	Misc. Taxes	*	Expns
Tax Prop	Property Tax	*	Expns
Tax State	State Tax Withholding	*	Expns
Telephone	Telephone Expense		Expns

Category	Description	Tax Related	Type
UIC	Unemployment Ins.	*	Expns
Utilities	Water, Gas, Electric		Expns

Business Categories

Category	Description	Tax Related	Type
Gr Sales	Gross Sales	*	Inc
Other Inc	Other Income	*	Inc
Rent Income	Rent Income	*	Inc
Ads	Advertising	*	Expns
Car	Car & Truck	*	Expns
Commission	Commissions	*	Expns
Freight	Freight	*	Expns
Int Paid	Interest Paid	*	Expns
L&P Fees	Legal & Prof. Fees	*	Expns
Late Fees	Late Payment Fees	*	Expns
Office	Office Expenses	*	Expns
Rent Paid	Rent Paid	*	Expns
Repairs	Repairs	*	Expns
Returns	Returns & Allowances	*	Expns
Taxes	Taxes	*	Expns
Travel	Travel Expenses	*	Expns
Wages	Wages & Job Credits	*	Expns

Both Categories

Category	Description	Tax Related	Type
Bonus	Bonus Income	*	Inc
Canada Pen	Canadian Pension	*	Inc
Div Income	Dividend Income	*	Inc
Family Allow	Family Allowance	*	Inc
Gift Received	Gift Received	*	Inc
Gr Sales	Gross Sales	*	Inc
Int Inc	Interest Income	*	Inc
Invest Inc	Investment Income	*	Inc
Old Age Pension	Old Age Pension	*	Inc
Other Inc	Other Income	*	Inc
Rent Income	Rent Income	*	Inc
Salary	Salary Income	*	Expns
Ads	Advertising	*	Expns
Auto Fuel	Automobile Fuel		Expns
Auto Loan	Auto Loan Payment		Expns

Category	Description	Tax Related	Type
Auto Service	Automobile Service		Expns
Bank Chrg	Bank Charge		Expns
Car	Car & Truck	*	Expns
Charity	Charitable Donations	*	Expns
Childcare	Childcare Expense		Expns
Christmas	Christmas Expenses		Expns
Clothing	Clothing		Expns
Commission	Commissions	*	Expns
Dining	Dining Out		Expns
Dues	Dues		Expns
Education	Education		Expns
Entertain	Entertainment		Expns
Freight	Freight	*	Expns
Gifts	Gift Expenses		Expns
Groceries	Groceries		Expns
Home Rpair	Home Repair & Maint.		Expns
Household	Household Misc. Exp.		Expns
Housing	Housing		Expns
Insurance	Insurance		Expns
Int Exp	Interest Expense	*	Expns
Int Paid	Interest Paid	*	Expns
Invest Exp	Investment Expense	*	Expns
L&P Fees	Legal & Prof. Fees	*	Expns
Late Fees	Late Payment Fees	*	Expns
Medical	Medical & Dental	*	Expns
Misc	Miscellaneous		Expns
Mort Int	Mortgage Interest Exp.	*	Expns
Mort Prin	Mortgage Principal		Expns
Office	Office Expenses	*	Expns
Other Exp	Other Expenses	*	Expns
Recreation	Recreation Expense		Expns
Rent Paid	Rent Paid	*	Expns
Repairs	Repairs	*	Expns
Returns	Returns & Allowances	*	Expns
RRSP	Reg. Retirement Sav. Plan		Expns
Subscriptions	Subscriptions		Expns
Supplies	Supplies	*	Expns

Category	Description	Tax Related	Type
Tax Fed	Federal Tax Withholding	*	Expns
Tax FICA	Social Security Tax	*	Expns
Tax Other	Misc. Taxes	*	Expns
Tax Prop	Property Tax	*	Expns
Tax State	State Tax Withholding	*	Expns
Taxes	Taxes	*	Expns
Telephone	Telephone Expense		Expns
Travel	Travel Expenses	*	Expns
UIC	Unemployment Ins.	*	Expns
Utilities	Water, Gas, Electric		Expns
Wages	Wages & Job Credits	*	Expns

INDEX

writing checks, 101-102

H

I

J

Q

The manuscript for this book was prepared and
submitted to Osborne/McGraw-Hill in electronic
form. The acquisitions editor for this project was
Roger Stewart, the technical reviewers were Campbell
Associates, the project editor was Laura Sackerman,
and Ann Krueger Spivack was the copy editor.

Text design by Marcela Hancik and Pamela Webster,
using Times Roman for text body
and Helvetica for display.

Cover art by Bay Graphics Design, Inc. Color
separation and cover supplier, Phoenix Color
Corporation. Screens produced with InSet, from InSet
Systems, Inc. Book printed and bound by R.R.
Donnelley & Sons Company, Crawfordsville, Indiana.

IMPORTANT QUICKEN COMMANDS AND SPECIAL KEYS

Working with Transactions

Press this:		To do this:
F3 1 or CTRL ENTER		Record transaction
F3 2 or CTRL D		Delete transaction
F3 3 or CTRL S		Split transaction
F3 4 or CTRL V		Void transaction
F3 5 or CTRL F		Find transaction
F3 6 or CTRL B		Find previous transaction
F3 7 or CTRL N		Find next transaction
F4 1 or CTRL T		Recall transaction
F4 2 or CTRL M		Memorize transaction
F4 5		Execute transaction group
F4 6		Set up transaction group
ENTER or TAB		Move cursor from one field to the next field
SHIFT TAB		Move cursor backward through fields
CTRL H		Display price history from the Update Prices window

Changing Data Organization

Press this:		To do this:
F2 1 or CTRL A		Select/Set up account
F4 3 or CTRL C		Display category/transfer list
F4 4 or CTRL L		Select/Set up class
F4 5 or CTRL J		Select/Set up transactions groups

Reports and Printing

Press this: **To do this:**

 Have Quicken memorize a report

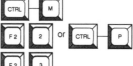 Print register

 Change printer settings

 Request Personal Report menu

 Request Business Report menu

Request Investment Report menu

Request memorized report list

Request transaction

Request summary

Request Budget report

 Request Account Balances report

Changing Location

Press this: **To do this:**

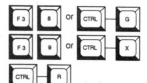 Go to date

 Go to transfer

Go to Register window

Go to Write Checks window

Return to previous screen

Other Activities

Press this: **To do this:**

 Back up all accounts

Write checks

Reconcile

Order supplies

 Calculator

IMPORTANT QUICKEN COMMANDS AND SPECIAL KEYS

Special Search Characters

Press this:

To do this:

Wild-card search for anything in location
of .. (if you search for "Pay.." Quicken
will locate all transactions in the
field you are searching that begin with "Pay")

Wild-card search for a single character

Means "not" when used with search text

Special Keys

Pressing this:

Does this:

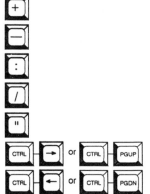

Increases date or check number in transactions

Decreases date or check number in transactions

Separates category from subcategory

Separates category from class

Copies payee name to check address field

Increases the date in the Update Prices screen

Decreases the date in the Update Prices screen

Moving or Editing on Screen

Press this: To do this:

| CTRL | HOME | Move to the first register transaction or check on screen |

| CTRL | END | Move to the last register transaction or check on screen |

| HOME | Move to the beginning of the field |

| PGDN | Move to next check or next register screen |

| PGUP | Move to previous check or previous register screen |

| ↓ | Move to next register transaction |

| ↑ | Move to previous register transaction |

| END | Move to the end of the field |

| INS | Turn insert mode on or off (toggle) |

| BACKSPACE | Delete character to left of cursor |

| DEL | Delete current character |

| CTRL | BACKSPACE | Delete contents of current field |

| TAB | Move to next field |

| ENTER | Move to next field (From the last field in the window, closes window) |

| CTRL | ENTER | Finalize entries in a window from any field |

| SHIFT | TAB | Move to previous field |

| CTRL | → | Move one word to the right |

| CTRL | ← | Move one word to the left |